Postcolonial Artists and Global

AKIN ADESOKAN

Postcolonial Artists and Global Aesthetics

INDIANA UNIVERSITY PRESS

Bloomington and Indianapolis

This book is a publication of

Indiana University Press
601 North Morton Street
Bloomington, Indiana 47404–3797 USA

iupress.indiana.edu

Telephone orders   800-842-6796
Fax orders   812-855-7931
Orders by e-mail   iuporder@indiana.edu

Library of Congress Cataloging-in-Publication Data

Adesokan, Akinwumi.
  Postcolonial artists and global aesthetics / Akin Adesokan.
    p. cm. — (African expressive cultures)
  Includes bibliographical references and index.
  Includes filmography.
  ISBN 978-0-253-35679-6 (cloth : alk. paper) — ISBN 978-0-253-22345-6 (pbk. : alk. paper) 1. Motion
pictures—Social aspects—Africa. 2. Motion pictures and globalization. 3. Africa—In motion pictures.
4. Intercultural communication in motion pictures. 5. Literature and globalization. 6. African diaspora in
literature. 7. Literature and society. I. Title.
  PN1993.5.A35A34 2011
  302.23′43096—dc22

                                                                        2011014035

1 2 3 4 5 16 15 14 13 12 11

To Nusiratu Asake and Tolani Arike, mother and daughter

In acknowledging that we are part of the Third World we are, to paraphrase José Martí, "affirming that our cheek feels the blow struck against any man, anywhere in the world."

Thomas Sankara, "Freedom Can Be Won Only
Through Struggle" (1984)

Finally, a word on the possible "sexism" of my language. This issue has dogged my steps for a while and I want to state my position on it once and for all. English is not my language. Though I have developed a taste for it, it was once forced upon me . . . Now that after thirty years of toil I have acquired reasonable competence in the language, I am told by the progeny of those who first imposed it on me that I have been taught the wrong English by their forefathers; that I must now relearn the language. Frankly, I am too old to do so.

Ashis Nandy, preface to *The Intimate Enemy* (1983)

Contents

Preface   xi

Acknowledgments   xvii

Introduction: Generic Transformations at the Crossroads
of Capital   1

1.   C. L. R. James Sees the World Steadily   30

2.   Fitful Decolonization: *Xala* and the Poetics of Double
Fetishism   57

3.   Tunde Kelani's Nollywood: Aesthetics of Exhortation   81

4.   Jean-Pierre Bekolo and the Challenges of Aesthetic
Populism   108

5.   Imaginary Citizenship: Caryl Phillips's Atlantic World   133

6.   Spirits of Bandung: A Sarcastic Subject Writes to Empire   156

Conclusion: Being African in the World   178

Notes   185
List of References   203
Filmography   219
Index   223

Preface

Living in Lagos, Nigeria, in the early 1980s, I was surrounded by art in all media: music, literature, cinema, television, radio, comic strips, photoplays, and theater, not to mention the unplanned spectacle of the expressive every day and night, the living art of the street itself. It was the heyday of Nigeria's profligate Second Republic, a democracy only in name, and these urban media were at once art, business, and life, catering to a network of relations across social classes. I was more interested in enjoying this expressive culture than in understanding how it came to be, but felt a sense of loss when much of it began to fizzle out, probably coincidentally, following the military overthrow of the government of Alhaji Shehu Shagari. By the end of that decade, the country was deeply enmeshed in the neoliberal economic dragnet of a structural adjustment program, from which it has yet to fully extricate itself. Where did all those manifestations of a vibrant artistic culture go? Why was sustenance so easily denied them? How does one think productively about subsequent or residual forms of this culture, which never totally disappeared, even deep in those years of structural adjustment?

This book is written in part with these questions in mind. It seeks to explore the aesthetic consequences of the decline of the nation-state prefigured in that disconcerting reality, turning toward works of art and the contexts of their emergence for possible leads. If all I cared for then was aesthetic pleasure, now I concern myself also with the complex socioeconomic and institutional questions of how art is constituted, focusing on the transformation of genre through the specific technological and social changes of the past several decades. These changes are mirrored in the move from the concept of *the Third World* to the concept of *postcoloniality,* and to get an accurate sense of what they represent requires even-handed attention to a number of structural formations that do not always appear to have much to do with one another. How could I have known that something called "the Washington Consensus" could be responsible for the poor quality of the movie being shown inside a theater in a Lagos neighborhood? What connections might exist between the publication of little pamphlets by a group of socialists in postwar Detroit and the best-seller status of a first novel by a young Indian woman in the final years of the twentieth century? Starting from the premise that genre, the aesthetic typology of kinds in textual production, is shaped by context, I focus on six authors and filmmakers who produce works within the historical span of both decolonization and globalization. The various aspects of both globalization and prior processes are marked by contradictions, but in representational terms, the works of these artist-intellectuals present a useful elaboration on the changes attending postcolonial cultural production. This is both because of the intellectual nature of postcolonialism—the fact that it is individuals, as artists, writers, and activists, who best articulate the problems of postcolonial society—and because of the usual tension between a pragmatic use of the apparatus of representation and a commitment to varieties of cultural or political assertion.

Focusing on the different contexts in which both decolonization and globalization thrive, I identify a complex social formation, the *crossroads of capital,* as resulting from the shuttle between the economic and the cultural spheres, using the West African marketplace as an example. Using this idea of the crossroads of capital, I place the increasingly popular notion of the "network society" (Castells 2000) in a historically specific setting, aligning Castell's term with earlier theorizations of the relationships between economic systems and diasporic and postmodern identities (A. Amin 1994; S. Amin 1990; Jameson 1991; Harvey 1990; Hall 1989). My primary objects are works of art, so I am interested in how these theoretical positions can be understood in relation to contexts of artistic production, and thus to a historical, materialist idea of genre. I approach this challenge by focusing on three manifestations of the peculiarity of postcolonial texts. The first is the fitful character of artistic representation within decolonization: the idea that some of what an earlier generation of artists engaged in anti-colonial critique considered the negative effects of the colonial encounter are among the principal barometers for understanding global identities today. The second is the aesthetic dimensions of uneven geographical development, that is, the imaginative ways in which globalization and its contents determine what is generically possible. The third is the way metropolitan location and the commodity form function to shape genres.

Postcolonial Artists and Global Aesthetics presents a perspective quite different from those of current discussions of the relationships between globalization and aesthetic changes. While disciplines with strong interests in African studies, such as anthropology, economic history, and political science, continue to develop cutting-edge analytical, quantitative, and ethnographic perspectives within their fields (Ferguson 2006; Comaroff and Comaroff 2006), such perspectives rarely, if ever, engage cultural forms in an aesthetic sense. This surprises me, because the aesthetic dimension of artistic forms seems to be a fertile ground for exploring questions of agency, which are always paramount to these disciplines and which, though manifesting themselves through very complex sociohistorical processes, are fundamentally about creativity, whether individual or collective. On the other hand, disciplines invested in textual forms, such as African cinema and diasporic and postcolonial literature, are still largely concerned with thematic issues in the broadest sense, paying relatively little attention to the analysis of system, beyond standard critiques of varieties of Eurocentrism or Afrocentrism (Harrow 2007b; Murphy and Williams 2007).

Kenneth Harrow's *Postcolonial African Cinema* is written with great charm and theoretical rigor, but it is also notably concerned with thematics, and I discuss its strengths and shortcomings at length in this book. Murphy and Williams's *Postcolonial African Cinema: Ten Directors* is exceptional for its interest in the figure of the postcolonial artist as an intellectual formation. But one could take the implications of such a formation farther, without being saddled with the burden of representativeness. Some fascinating comparative studies in post-colonial literature have displayed an acute interest in precisely these systemic questions, but they have been concerned only with literature, primarily the novel, with an occasional nod toward other genres (Slaughter 2007; Brouillette 2007; Huggan 2001).

The present book, written in part to fill this gap in scholarship on postcolo-nial textuality in literature, in cinema, and in other less visible genres, is thus different in both method and insight. In its method, the book attempts a rig-orous discussion of postcolonial texts by selecting eclectic texts—films with different technological formats (Ousmane Sembene, Tunde Kelani, and Jean-Pierre Bekolo), a travelogue-cum-social-history (Caryl Phillips), a political tract (Arundhati Roy), and an essayistic meditation on a sociopolitical movement (C. L. R. James)—and eschewing a simple thematic reading of them. By com-bining the thematic interests of the scholarly titles cited above with an analytical attention to systemic issues in the conception, production, and circulation of literary and cinematic works, I develop a way of reading these texts that is sel-dom attempted in the field of postcolonial studies. In each case I start with the text, but I see it as both product and producer of a vast range of political, social, economic, and aesthetic factors and meanings. I highlight what the text does and is unable to do, and what I think these capacities and incapacities imply. Al-though I arrive at the three specific aspects of postcolonial textual forms that I focus on through a dynamic movement between texts and the systemic contexts of their production, my premise avoids a simple equation between the two. For example, while James's and Sembene's works provide a sense of the fitful char-acter of artistic representation within decolonization, this fitfulness stands in a complex relationship to another of the aspects I attend to, that is, metropolitan location and the commodity form as shapers of genres, in ways that my read-ing of Roy's political writings makes clear.

In conceptual terms, I provide new insights by relating this idea of post-colonial textuality to four theoretical issues. First, I make a case for seeing the neoliberal capitalist system as decisive in the articulation between culture and economic change. In the introduction, I delineate the factors at work in this articulation as they occur both in the specific context of contemporary (West) Africa and in the world at large. I think it is important to set the idea of the crossroads, the localized, spatial imagery of the conjunction of economic and cultural spheres, side by side with the theoretical notion of uneven geographical development, in order to show that each influences the other. Second, I argue specifically that global relations between politics, economy, and culture catalyze genre formation. I thus extend the challenges that globalization poses for literary studies to other forms, like cinema and nonfiction. Studies of aesthetic changes under globalization are overwhelmingly biased toward literature, and particularly toward the novel. I have chosen to avoid the conventional "film-and-literature" approach, which highlights either thematic close-reading or adaptation, and of which there are some excellent critiques and compendia (Dovey 2009; Ray 2001; Naremore 2000).

The filmmakers featured here are connected with African cinema, but I place their work in a broader context by discussing generic changes in the context of institutional issues such as cultural mobility, expatriation, and commodification. I am not aware of debates on globalization in the field of film and cinema studies that compare with what is available in literary studies, although Chuck Tryon's *Reinventing Cinema* (2009) attempts a preliminary but fruitful exploration of how new media are changing the notion of cinema. Also, the "Changing Profession" section of the 2007 special issue of *PMLA* titled "Remapping Genre" focuses on the relationships between technology and generic changes by considering the database as the genre of the twenty-first century (Folsom 2007), including five responses to Ed Folsom's essay and his own final response. In order to address the central question of the status of artistic works in the context of expatriation and globalized media, I draw on the notion of exilic and diasporic filmmaking that the Iranian-born scholar Hamid Naficy develops in *The Accented Cinema* (2001). Third, I make artistic figures central to my analysis. I demonstrate that artists, cultural activists, cosmopolitan writers, and auteurs occupy positions in the social realm integral to the issues to which their work seeks to give expression. This means that the creator of a work of art lives in history, even if the work itself has an autonomy that is not reducible to history. Although the relationship between intellectuals and categories like the nation-state and the political establishment is fraught, I think that the active interest artists take in these phenomena suggests that they have an abiding faith in the possibility of building institutions in the postcolony, notwithstanding their skepticism about the concept of postcolonialism.

Finally, I use this book to make an unusual but necessary claim: that postcoloniality is meaningful only within the broad context of a political culture that puts the international dimension of Pan-Africanism in perspective by reestablishing the historical links between postwar tricontinentalism and current cosmopolitanism. Thus, though Pan-Africanism is often seen as a specifically African and black diasporic movement, I am convinced that its history is inseparably tied to questions of class and transnational social justice, both in the postwar period and now. Aimé Césaire's characterization of the situation of American blacks in the 1950s as possibly colonial ought to complement W. E. B. Du Bois's famous statement that the problem of the twentieth century was the problem of the color line. If they are to be any use in our time, the Pan-African movement and its myriad manifestations ought to speak equally and meaningfully to those on whose behalf the movement took shape and those who encounter it as a transnational idea. I hope that my proposition for rethinking Pan-Africanism, which supplements the critique of nation-state sovereignty, contributes to global conversations about citizenship that are aimed at addressing the ways in which bureaucratic systems disenfranchise their citizens, whether intentionally or accidentally. It is within the frame of this idea of Pan-Africanism that my inclusion of Arundhati Roy's work in this book is to be understood. While not jettisoning historical sovereignty as such, I am much more deeply invested in ideas as they transcend their national or geographical provenances. To put it in plain terms, the ethical basis of the claim is my conviction that the fate of the African continent and the fate of the rest of the world are inextricably linked.

Acknowledgments

While working on this book, I benefited from the kind support of many people and I would like to use this occasion to acknowledge the various forms of assistance they provided. My colleagues in the Department of Comparative Literature at Indiana University have been very supportive of my work, and I want to wholeheartedly thank Paul Losensky, Rosemarie McGerr, Angela Pao, Eyal Peretz, Oscar Kenshur, Vivian Halloran, and David Hertz for their warmth and genuine interest in all aspects of my work. Over the past several years, Eileen Julien has been more than a colleague; she is a loyal advisor and a trusted friend. I can never forget Eileen's unstinting support, her dependability, her sense of what is important, and her ease in following things through. Herb Marks and Perry Hodges patiently and enthusiastically listened to me after a supper at their home as I tried to explain the "aesthetic dimensions" of tricontinentalism. Early on, Bill Johnston and I started a two-man "reading club" which has shown a remarkable resilience and informed my understanding of contemporary writing; I thank Kasia Rydel-Johnston, Bill's wife, for her kind support of this idea. I am grateful also to Mariam Ehteshami, Howard Swyers, Connie Sue May, Denise Lynn, Meghan Rubinstein, Stephanie Fida, Meghan Keefer, and Aerin Sent-George for their help with various administrative matters.

Biodun Jeyifo and Natalie Melas, both former teachers of mine, read different drafts of the introduction to this book and offered very challenging suggestions. Because I cannot claim to have sufficiently risen to the challenges posed by their comments, I must absolve them of any responsibility for the quality of the work, but I thank them for agreeing to read for me. Tejumola Olaniyan has been a steady advisor and friend, always ready to avail me of his unique gifts of discernment on different issues. "Malam" Olufemi Taiwo advised me frequently during the process of writing this book and after; we go way back, as he likes to say, and still have a way to go. Ebenezer Obadare brought numerous references to my attention; his resourcefulness in this regard is outstanding. Jonathan Haynes was one of the readers chosen by the Press to read the manuscript, as I later found out, and he gave thoughtful attention to it, making explicit suggestions for improvement and supporting the work even while disagreeing with some of my arguments. I thank the other, anonymous, reader, too, whose comments were useful in a dialectical sense. I am grateful to Tunde Kelani (TK) for showing a genuine interest in my work, promptly responding to my questions, and bringing me up to date on his work. On the evidence of an email and without prior acquaintanceship, Anne Walmsley sent me personal copies of out-of-print books by C. L. R. James for free. I am grateful to her for this stunning generosity, and also to our ever-resourceful James Gibbs for making the contact possible. Purnima Bose graciously lent me her personal copy of a book by Aijaz Ahmad that was not available in the United States, ensuring that I received it the same day even though she was out of town! Adrien Pouille helped me with transcription and translation of the Wolof song in chapter 2.

I wrote this book without the aid of a grant or a fellowship; however, I received constant support for conference travel from Indiana University's Office of the Vice President for International Affairs and from the African Studies Program. For this I thank Vice President Patrick O'Meara, John Hanson, and Samuel Obeng, the latter two as directors of the ASP and whose tenures coincided with the writing. Maria Grosz-Ngaté, ASP's associate director, is indispensable in so many ways: she invited me several times to speak to her students in the Interdisciplinary Methodology seminars, and this gave me opportunities to test different aspects of this book. Michael Martin brought useful references to my notice and supported me in other ways as well. Dan Allen and Roger Crandall of IU's Center for Language Technology and Instructional Enrichment helped me with fine-tuning screen captures, and I thank them very much. Other IU colleagues—Carol Polsgrove (emerita professor), Marion Frank-Wilson, Beverly Stoeltje, Marissa Moorman, Patrick McNaughton, Audrey McCluskey, Osita Afoaku, Martha Wailes, Gracia Clark, A. B. Assensoh, and Abdou Yaro—were supportive in ways big and small, but always consequential. I thank Patti Anahory for the postcard from Assomada. I also thank Tim Murray, Olakunle George, Kunle and Bunmi Ajibade, Femi Osofisan, Odia Ofeimun, dele jegede, Hortense Spillers, Manthia Diawara, Grant Farred, Harry Garuba, Salah Hassan, Tade Ipadeola, Okwui Enwezor, Moradewun Adejunmobi, Muritala Sule, Molara Wood, Alexie Tcheuyap, Kevin Tsai, Susan Martin-Márquez, Sze Wei Ang, Jude Akudinobi, and Awam Amkpa, who either helped me with references or provided moral and intellectual support while I was writing this book.

I live in the midst of supportive friends who, though scattered all over the world, remain touchingly close and interested in what I do: Tunde Adegbola (TA), Gbemisola Adeoti, Pius Adesanmi, Sola Adeyemi, Waziri Adio, Omolade Adunbi, Kim Ady McDonald, Afam Akeh, Toyin Akinosho, Jahman Anikulapo, Ademola Aremu, Tunde Aremu, Olajide Bello, Amatoritsero Ede, Ntone Edjabe, Michael García, Esther Hu, Bode Ibironke, Ogaga Ifowodo, Dele Layiwola, Wasanthi Liyanage, Adewale Maja-Pearce, Sarah Ladipo Manyika, Obi Nwakanma, Maik Nwosu, Kole Ade Odutola, Sanya Ojikutu, Chika Okeke-Agulu, Niran Okewole, Ike Okonta, Dapo and Ladi Olorunyomi, Sola Olorunyomi, Kole Omotoso, Francis Onwochei, Sola Osofisan, E. C. Osondu, Remi Raji, Wumi and Romoke Raji, Nike Ransome-Kuti, and Kunle Tejuoso. (My friend and former teacher, the philosopher Olusegun Oladipo, died tragically in

December 2009, throwing those who knew him and his work into great mourning. Only hope . . .)

My editor, Dee Mortensen, has championed this book right from the moment when I tried to summarize it in a phrase, and she has been remarkably steadfast and supportive, seeing it through one stage, then another, with impressive thoroughness, faith, and humor. I thank Dee, Patrick McNaughton, editor of the Press's series on African Expressive Cultures, and June Silay, the project manager, for their efforts. Shoshanna Green, the copyeditor, worked on the manuscript in a very professional manner. I was constantly amazed at her great sense of form and her ability to induce clarity.

My immediate family was and remains a steady source of support. In many ways, my wife, Lucine Gordon, helped me to focus on this work and I remain grateful to her. My younger sister, Mrs. Tawa Ajanaku, deserves a lot of gratitude for the various ways she has helped me to maintain a sense of proportion in relation to Nigeria and West Africa. I also thank my other siblings, particularly my brothers, Alhaji Nurudeen Adesokan and Mr. Tajudeen Adesokan, for their unwavering support.

This book is dedicated to my mother, Nusiratu Asake, and my daughter, Tolani Arike. They belong to two different worlds; in my love for them, I am encouraged to engage the extremities of this world.

Grateful acknowledgments to California Newsreel for the permission to use the images in chapter 3.

An earlier, shorter version of chapter 5 is published as "The Ambiguous Adventures of Caryl Phillips" in *Africa in the World, the World in Africa*, edited by Biodun Jeyifo (Africa World Press, 2011).

Postcolonial Artists and Global Aesthetics

Introduction: Generic Transformations at the Crossroads of Capital

Kò sááyè àpàlà nilùú òyinbó;
Hárúnà tó re'be
Ogbón eré ló bá lo.
(There is no place for *apala* [music] in the white man's country;
Haruna [Isola] went there
On the pretext of his craft.)

—A Lagosian saying

Rather than ask, "What is the *attitude* of a work to the
relations of production of its time?" I should like to ask,
"What is its *position* in them?"

—Walter Benjamin, "The Author as Producer"

In 1973, while waiting to complete the film that would be released the following year as *Xala*, the filmmaker and novelist Ousmane Sembene[1] published a novel of the same title. As anyone familiar with the two works knows, there are significant differences between the novel and the film, and the distinct character of each is inseparable from the process of bringing them into circulation. The scenario for the film provided the basis for the novel, which in turn was used in developing the final film script. *Xala* the film is the subject of chapter 2 of the present book, so an extensive discussion of it lies ahead. In the meantime, however, I want to focus on Sembene's ambidexterity in working on the two texts, because the contexts of the choices he made in doing so are fundamental to the arguments at the core of this book. The film would become the more famous of the two works, but that is because "filmmaker" is the more frequently worn of Sembene's two hats. In shuttling between the scenario, the novel manuscript, and the film script, Sembene underlined the peculiar condition of making art in a postcolonial context, a condition he once captured evocatively in the neologism *mégotage* (calling filmmaking an act of "collecting cigarette butts"), and of which, in relation to this book, three issues are symptomatic.

The first is the socioeconomic and institutional context of a work and its contingency on the genre in which the work appears. By this, I mean that genre, the aesthetic typology of kinds in textual production, does not exist independent of context, and that for postcolonial texts in particular the context often determines the genre. The second is the challenge of representing decolonization, that is, the specific problems posed by speaking about or for societies existing under social systems which cannot survive if they must. In the film *Xala*, the economic arrangement in Senegal (or West Africa) is portrayed as neocolonial, but the work itself is made possible in part by this neocolonial system. Following directly from this, the third issue is the intellectual nature of postcoloniality, the fact that it is individuals, as artists, writers, activists, filmmakers, musicians, and so on, who have been able to clearly articulate the problems of postcolonial societies, but they do so in ways that reinforce the tensions between a pragmatic use of the apparatus of representation (whether technological, formal, or personal), and an intellectual commitment to varieties of cultural or political assertion.

The institutional and aesthetic challenges which these issues throw into relief are the focus of this book, and the purpose of this introduction is to describe its central arguments while laying a theoretical basis for the chapters that follow. If genre is contingent on context, as the first point indicates, what are the institutional contexts in which postcolonial texts are produced, and what is significant about them? I start from the premise that, in looking at postcolonial texts (works of art depicting contemporary manifestations of colonial modernity) of the last three decades, one sees fundamental changes in the ways those works are put together and in the socioeconomic institutions that sustain or fail to sustain them. These changes are reflected in the renaming of "the Third World" as "the postcolony." To get a coherent sense of what they entail, I think, requires a simultaneous attention to a number of structural processes that do not always appear to have much to do with one another. These changes are technological (compare the celluloid format of Sembene's *Xala* to the video format of Tunde Kelani's *Thunderbolt: Magun*); they are generic (the resolutely Aristotelian style of *Thunderbolt* stands in contrast to the reflexive questioning of mimesis in Jean-Pierre Bekolo's *Aristotle's Plot*); they are generational (the sense of belonging in the writings of C. L. R. James differs greatly from that in the work of Caryl Phillips); and they are political (Arundhati Roy's *An Ordinary Person's Guide to Empire* offers an unsettling riposte to neoliberalism in relation to both James's and Phillips's work).

None of these categories alone adequately captures what is significant in the relationships between the authors: technology affects genre, the relationships between James and Roy have generic dimensions as well, and generational questions are decisive in the different cinematic practices of Sembene and Bekolo. To understand the changes that have occurred in the field of postcolonial cultural production over the past thirty years or so, it is therefore necessary to pay vigilant attention to disparate and contradictory forces. There is nothing particularly abstruse or mysterious about these forces. Globalization, the socio-economic phenomenon of the present age, decisively affects everyone in the world, including those who, without being infants, may be unaware of its true dimensions. Indeed, such a lack of awareness makes the fact of globalization all the more important, ironically because it points to the residue of decolonization, another powerful aspect of an earlier era, and the ideological motor of the national struggle in colonized societies. Part of the reason that the changes appear complex is that the links between globalization and processes like decolonization are not always drawn, let alone drawn clearly, in critical attempts to understand them. The authors on whom I focus here span the history of both decolonization and globalization. By engaging directly with the various aspects of globalization and prior formations, their works elaborate usefully on the changes attending postcolonial cultural production. This is as it should be: one is clearer about how a thing has changed only in relation to what it used to be. Genre is the basis of these engagements, and its character is predicated on the complex, intangible shuttling between the cultural and the economic spheres. I will have more to say about this shuttling presently.

I am thinking of "genre" here as the formal, material, and institutional procedures through which art is created and does its work. These procedures are inseparable from context, and the relationship between them and the work is integral and constitutive. An example from the work of perhaps the two most dissimilar figures in this book—Ousmane Sembene and Caryl Phillips—is useful in elucidating this idea of genre. What is common to both Sembene and Phillips, to put it judiciously, is that their texts say things behind their backs; the works speak beyond their authors' declared or implied intentions. Most critics agree that Sembene's primary intention in the film version of *Xala* is to show the ideological impotence of the African elite who assumed political power after independence. However, he cannot depict Senegalese society of the early 1970s without representing issues of caste, class, and family honor, and doing so causes the solidarity that one might expect to see in the film between two marginalized groups, the poor and women, to break down or, more accurately, to not manifest itself. The film thus comes across simultaneously as a fable, a satire, a call to revolt, and a family drama, a multiplicity of generic identities inseparable from the negotiations hinted at in the opening paragraph of this introduction. The subjects Phillips takes on in *The Atlantic Sound* (slavery, racism, memory, contemporary relations of power) force him to engage with places about which he feels uneasy, talking mostly to people whose politics he does not necessarily endorse. The unease and the political differences are related to the subjects, of course, but Phillips seeks to displace them by resorting to narrative and formal techniques unevenly distributed between fiction, autobiography, reportage, and history, thus placing *The Atlantic Sound* in a generic no man's land. The artists set out to make a film about a corrupt elite, to write a book about the legacies of slavery and racism. However, the personal convictions driving their pursuits unfold within a welter of institutional, artistic, and other factors, each of which contributes to the unique shapes of the works.

The position of the artist-intellectual is indispensable to the functioning of these factors, and I think that the phrase *commissioned agent* represents a very appropriate way to capture that position. A commission agent is a mediator in certain kinds of commercial deals. On a metaphorical level, I mean, through this phrase, to suggest that the writers and filmmakers whose works I discuss engage representation through acts of commission. They do this both through their positions in the relations of production surrounding their works, as artists living in history and working with specific institutional modes of representation, and as individuals with convictions who voluntarily embrace a particular mode, even when, as is often the case in artistic matters, a certain degree of compulsion is always present. Thus, although they are commissioned by cultural institutions (in the so-called free marketplace of ideas), and their work emerges out of their personal and political commitments in struggle with and through those institutions, they are also artists, and postcolonial ones at that, and so they are agents, individuals who possess and exert agency.

As already indicated, not all the works I discuss here were produced under a neoliberal economic and sociocultural system. This difference, however, is less significant than the fact that there are links between the aesthetics of decolonization (James and Sembene) and the aesthetics of globalization (Phillips and Kelani). These links are structural, not causal, so making them manifest without falling into the traps of economic or technological determinism[2] requires carefully elaborating elements of postcoloniality and globalization, showing the links between larger systems such as politics and economy, "micro" formations such as expatriation, cultural mobility, and commodification, and institutional issues concerning the conception, production, and circulation of literary and cinematic works. I attempt such an elaboration in the rest of this introduction, beginning with the shuttle between the cultural and the economic spheres, the spatial formation I term the *crossroads of capital.*

The Crossroads of Capital

Discourses of globalization are notable for stressing the newness, the *phenomenality,* of their object of analysis, as the literary scholar Simon Gikandi argues in an essay titled "Globalization and the Claims of Postcoloniality" (2001). Gikandi is concerned that contemporary scholarship not lose sight of the historical relationship between old and new forms of globalization, especially the political and cultural importance of the once-powerful concept of the Third World that radically undermined a Eurocentric narrative of development and social change. As he claims, in their desire to secure the newness of theories of globalization . . . many critics and analysts of the phenomenon no longer seem interested in the "Third World" itself as a source of the cultural energies—and the tragedies—that have brought the new migrants to the West. (645)

Gikandi is not alone in emphasizing that the historical context of the consolidation of globalization is a powerful social and intellectual force. In *Spaces of Global Capitalism,* the Marxist geographer David Harvey has suggestively proposed a theory of "uneven geographical development" to refer to the process through which capitalism's need to manage its periodic crises causes uneven development around the world (Harvey 2006). To be sure, Harvey's theory is a reassessment, in the context of neoliberalism, of earlier accounts of the accumulation of capital to be found in the debates between Nikolai Bukharin and Rosa Luxemburg in the 1920s (Tarbuck 1972), and he summarizes the different ways in which the question has been approached (Harvey 2006, 71–74). But this notion of unevenness is germane because it is the operational basis of globalization, and the four approaches summarized by Harvey emphasize different political, environmental, and historical contexts. The different emphases result from the unevenness that sustains globalization, which prompts the anthropologist James Ferguson, writing in the same year as Harvey, to visualize the phenomenon of globalization as "globe-hopping" rather than as "globe-covering," connecting discrete points of the globe rather than blanketing it all (Ferguson 2006, 38, 40). Taking these different approaches into account, it is obvious that globalization, its structures, and its contents are not automatically democratic. Indeed, champions of decolonization may see some of globalization's most attractive aspects merely as palatable forms of what have been pejoratively called neocolonialism and cultural imperialism. Why celebrate the arsonist for rescuing people from the house he has set on fire?

Globalization is challenging from a postcolonial perspective in part because its resonant aspects, such as the notions of "network society" (Castells 2000), the "imperial age" (Guéhenno 1995), and "new ethnicities" (Hall 1997b), present an unusual opportunity for analyzing the objectives, methods, and results of national liberation projects that made decolonization such a powerful idea a generation ago. There is no discursive space here to do justice to the different aspects of decolonization, although I develop some of these in my discussion of the history of tricontinentalism in James's work in the next chapter. At any rate, other political projects also approached anti-colonialism as "nation-building," mostly taking bourgeois-liberal positions that eschewed the revolutionary radicalism often associated with decolonization. Twentieth-century anti-colonial nationalism was not a singular, unified process, least of all on the African continent, where the ideologies of nationalism ranged from the supposedly socialist Marxist-Leninist form in Nkrumah's Gold Coast to the bourgeois liberal-democratic form in Ivory Coast under Félix Houphouët-Boigny.[3] However, I want to focus on the sociocultural idea of the market, one of the formations within which different kinds of anti-colonial nationalism developed. This is because the unevenness which was characteristic of classical capitalism had an impact on how various forms of anti-colonial nationalism pursued their objectives. My aim is to use the idea of the market to flesh out the concept of the crossroads of capital, the shuttling between the economic and the cultural spheres. This shuttling, I think, encapsulates the generic issues in the complex relationship between the older generation of writers and intellectuals, who were shaped by decolonization (and its crises), and the current generation of figures who came to maturity in the context of fitful globalization.

Anthropologists, sociologists, and economic historians have all investigated the West African market, as both system and place. They see it mainly in relation to the practice of agriculture, which contributes a significant proportion of the resources and products (including labor) exchanged in markets (Bohannan and Dalton 1962; Bates 1981). According to some of these writers, the market as a system was "the diffuse interaction of suppliers and demanders whose activities determine[d] price" (Bohannan and Dalton 1962, 1), or the domain where rural farmers used labor and farm products to leverage their advantages in relation to unfavorable official policies (Bates 1981, 82). The first definition of the market was motivated by the need to distinguish between what Bohannan and Dalton termed "peripheral" or "primitive" economies and the "Western economy." The "peripheral" economy, they argued, was not "integrated with production decisions," because the dynamics of supply and demand that governed prices did not reflect on "resource allocation which [made] the interdependent formation of market prices—the market system—so crucially important in Western economic theory" (Bohannan and Dalton 1962, 8).[4]

More recently, however, the literature on markets has focused on empirical conditions arising out of global economic changes, which the rural-urban paradigm of Bates's study did not anticipate and which the earlier anthropological tradition, caught up in discourses of primitivism and peripherality, could not have foreseen.[5] The new focus on the market, exemplified in the special issue of the journal *Africa* guest-edited in 2001 by Jane Guyer and Karen Tranberg Hansen, does not neglect agricultural economies, but situates them within the neoliberal economic upheavals of the last two decades of the twentieth century. These later writers find both the center-periphery model of dependency theory and the rural-urban approach of classical economics favored by Bates to be inadequate because they tend to be determined exclusively by external considerations. From within, the picture is different, as analytical interest turns to

places where markets are pervasive but not classically capitalist, where the institutions of the formal financial and governmental sector offer few resources and impose even less coordination and discipline, and where there is a correspondingly high degree of local institutional inventiveness, using models from a variety of sources, including tradition and religion as well as experience of an earlier phase of formalized management. (Guyer and Hansen 2001, 198)

The authors Bohannan and Dalton also spoke of marketplaces, calling them "multifunctional institutions . . . utilized for purposes far beyond those purposes for which they were established" and "a meeting place where at least a certain minimum of security is assured and hence they can be used for political, religious, social and personal purposes" (Bohannan and Dalton 1962, 15, 18). Following this invocation of place and the new literature's focus on the market as the "bedrock of livelihood"(Guyer and Hansen 2001, 198) one arrives at a socialized and spatialized formation, the marketplace, an all-pervasive social relation where buying and selling, exchanging, is a way of life, the place where roads cross in an endless pursuit of both profit and other things. No one road leads to the market; this dictum justifies multiple occupations and improvisations.[6]

In an essay which develops a useful analysis of this notion of the marketplace, the writer and film historian Manthia Diawara writes of the West African market as a complex site of resistance, where "the collective unconscious" is shaped through traditional schemes of globalization that the bureaucratic state cannot effectively police (1998, 115).[7] Diawara claims that the nation-state, as the agent of the classical market, and the West African market have been antagonists in the contest for power from the outset. Because the modernizing influence of the state was opposed to the conservatism of the West African market and to sociocultural practices that the colonial state demonized, political power shifted to the state. He adds that a "more intelligent scenario of nation-building would have been to put the traditional market economy at the base of the political culture of the state, and to undertake at the same time to transform progressively the merchants into modern business bureaucrats and entrepreneurs" (118). It is obvious that this scenario favors disciplining the "traditional" economy in ways that the neoliberal structural adjustment programs have continued to attempt. By developing the market's mobilization of its resources in the service of a socialized practice of self-conception, however, Diawara effectively moves questions of economic formation into the broader terrain of sociocultural identity and history. This institutional redirection of the idea of the market (as marketplace) and its relationship to African poetic genres such as *oriki, yere don, makumbu,* and *izibongo* receives further elaboration in chapter 3.

Because of the inequality of demand and supply that sustains the market and the fact that capitalism thrives on uneven geographical development, the postcolonial African market, like globalization, is far from democratic, much less progressive. The gendered, hierarchical, corrupt, and socially oppressive practices through which the market reproduces itself and ensures its own survival certainly perpetuate the grimness of the postcolony. Consider, as an example, the Nigerian film *Ekun Oko Oke* (The Indomitable Tiger). This allegorical film about military dictatorship was produced in 2002, on a shoestring budget, by the famous actor Alhaji Kareem Adepoju. Adepoju dedicated the film to Chief Abraham Adesanya, a noted pro-democracy activist and leader of the anti-military National Democratic Coalition, in recognition of Adesanya's principled actions during the dictatorship. The film's documentary preface features footage of an assassination attempt on Adesanya in 1996. Adesanya's politics might not have changed for the worse, but in 2002 he was clearly close to the new civilian rulers, and Adepoju dedicated the film to him partly because he represented a credible patron under the new dispensation, although an artist might, as a matter of principle, want to keep such a figure at arm's length.

The difficulty of making practices such as this coexist with the transparent bureaucratic system that is characteristic of neoliberal capitalism is perhaps what underlies Diawara's contention that modern business bureaucrats are more progressive than merchants, and that the traditional market economy would have to be subordinated to the political culture of the state for the postcolonial African state to emerge from its impasse and be transformed into a rational, self-reproducing nation-state. In spite, and indeed because, of the small differences between the ideological orientations of the postcolonial market and free-market neoliberalism, the notion of the network, I think, is common to both. Adepoju's choice has to be seen within a particular social context, the patron-client dynamic that historians, anthropologists, and sociologists have described at considerable length. For example, Sandra Barnes notes that "patron-client relationships are *reciprocal*, but they are *unequal* in that the status of the patron is higher than that of the client and, further, the things exchanged are not of the same order" (Barnes 1986, 8). According to Barnes,

> the coming together of a series of patron- or middleman-client exchanges
> forms a network. An extensive network of people bound together by reciprocal
> obligations may stretch across large segments, or the whole, of a society so that
> it forms a system. (9)

Furthermore, as the British socialist historian Basil Davidson argues in *The Black Man's Burden,* the relationship is a normalization of the tension between the national struggle of the political and economic elites and the material struggle of the majority of the population in the postcolonial context. This tension, Davidson contends, is most clear in the conflict between the city and the village. Political power was city-based, grounded in bureaucracy and other state apparatuses that were far from democratic. "In these circumstances, authoritarian state power went together with expanding bureaucracies: that is, with hugely increasing quantities of persons who in one way or another looked to the state for patronage" (Davidson 1992, 209). The progressive chain of relations—from patron-client to network to system—shows that what is unfolding in these processes is more than simple disorder or a pathological "African" behavior, contrary to what a powerful scholarly tendency in African studies suggests.[8] Furthermore, the idea that practices such as these confirm "the failure of the state" requires serious reflection, and I attempt one such reflection in chapter 3. Indeed, as I argue below, these relations develop through and are sustained by the uneven geographical development mediated in the market, and this may explain why, for the most part, globalization and postcoloniality are mutually reinforcing although their relationship is also asymmetrical. The reality produced by this relationship is what I conceptualize as the *postcolonial asymmetry* in this book. The postcolonial asymmetry defines the tension between the idea of the *national struggle*, which characterized decolonization, and the *social struggle*, which is the material basis for the changes currently wrought by globalization. The linkage between globalization and postcoloniality can be visualized as a coiled spring, with effects eddying back and forth between the bureaucratic state and the deterritorialized economic machine: "African" and postcolonial social formations like clientelism, informalization, and the occult imaginary are reinforced by inchoate state policies restricted by neoliberal capitalism, and are thus rendered "African" by economic strictures which, working within these settings, themselves generate incommensurable social relations that are then concretized as informalization, clientelism, and the occult imaginary.[9] Putting this idea of a network of social relations side by side with the neoliberal idea of a "network society" helps me to highlight what is significant about the changes which globalization has set in motion in the last three decades. Moreover, doing so shows that while globalization, as well as the goods and images it transports, may be far from democratic, rational, progressive, and ultimately transformative social practices become possible when such changes manifest themselves through the kinds of representation that artists and writers are afforded.

One of the most eloquent arguments that the rise of network society rings the death-knell of the nation-state is to be found in *The End of the Nation-State*, by Jean-Marie Guéhenno, a former French diplomat and functionary of the United Nations.[10] Published in English translation in 1995, the book elegantly, and apparently effortlessly, argues that the rise of the network society has irrevocably undermined the legal and political basis of modern society. Guéhenno's ambitious thesis belongs in the ideological context of Francis Fukuyama's *The End of History and the Last Man*. He contends that elements of the network age (which he also calls "the imperial age")—religion, ideology, corruption, tribalism—pose a serious threat to the modern state system, "the institutional age" of politics (Guéhenno 1995, 19). With a stunning gift for the declarative, and a capacity for running vast historical or sociological realities through the mill of public-policy vocabulary, Guéhenno advances a critique of the politics of space shorn of the materialist concern with processes that marks similar undertakings, such as Harvey's.[11] Invested in the passage from the institutional age of the nation-state, with its pyramidal structure of power, to the diffuse age of "empire without an emperor," this obituary of modern sovereignty is unstinting:

The point is no longer to impose a common direction from above, but, more subtly, to manage identities and ensure the compatibility of these identities with other identities. The logic of the networks, which implies the multiplication and thus the decentralization of connections, suggests that the optimal size for managing these identities is much smaller than that of the great enterprises of the industrial age. (64)

One can glimpse in this description the world of instant communication, shrinking distances, and the primacy of rule, all mostly mediated by technology. Although Guéhenno recognizes "that the logic of the nation-state will coexist for a long time with the logic of the imperial age" (123), he stresses the logic of the network, for the book's central thesis is that the nation-state is no longer dominant. Pitched against the everyday conduct of the West African marketplace, this description of the network society shows that the world is both a network and a system. It is a system of rational calculations and fixed prices, of regulations passed down from Wall Street by way of the U.S. Treasury Department. But it is also a human network, like the Chinese *guanxi* that he cites: the relational practice of treating others as potential collaborators, people you will need in an ever-widening network of relations. Here is the basis of this book's central metaphor, the crossroads of capital.

The crossroads is an apt metaphor for this coexistence of the practices of the marketplace, uneven geographical development writ large, with the logic of neoliberal corporate capitalism. As an intersection or junction, the crossroads encapsulates the philosophical and practical dynamics of cultural pluralism. The crossroads is the point where journeys begin, but it is also the place to which the traveler may return, depending on where the chosen paths lead. It is also, practically, a meeting point, like the typical West African marketplace, the public space where the idea of economic transaction hardly exists alone, the place where roads cross in an endless pursuit of both profit and other things. The idea of the crossroads as a site of decisions and negotiations is highly developed in West Africa, as can be seen in the folkloric category of the "dilemma tale" (Brown 2002; Sekoni 1994; Bascom 1975). The crossroads is the mythical home of Esu (or Elegbara, Legba), the West African spirit of chance, contingency, and hermeneutics, whose domain includes the commercial fortunes of market women, border crossers, negotiators, and interpreters. It might also suggest Ananse or Anancy, the trickster spider, whose web anticipates the Internet! The pluralism that characterizes this space looks very much like the kind against which Abdul JanMohamed and David Lloyd once issued a warning, one in which "ethnic or cultural difference is merely an exoticism, an indulgence that can be relished without significantly modifying the individual who is securely embedded in the protective body of dominant ideology" (1990, 8). However, this warning may be balanced by the fact that the crossroads' pluralism exists in a more diverse and fragmented context of global flows than does the unified "national" setting of American multiculturalism.

Looking at globalization in these specific and general terms challenges us to confront a simultaneously human and rational network-system (Irele 2001, 78), bringing widely positioned, extremely differentiated and differentiating entities together under the sign of the world as one. This is what I endeavor to do in this book. These entities are the different works that I consider, works that are not only produced under dissimilar contexts but also appear in contradictory generic forms; the entities are also the conflicting impulses within a particular system, such as the uncanny relationship between neoliberalism and the commodity form that is highlighted in the phenomenon of Arundhati Roy. The idea of the crossroads clarifies the relation of this contradiction and incommensurability to capitalism. Given the profound unevenness of relations between and within different parts of the world, it is useful, I think, to approach ideas and processes shaped by globalization and decolonization within the antipodal frame suggested by the crossroads. If decolonization, the powerful ideological motor of the national liberation movements, lost steam for reasons that include the degeneracy of the ruling elite (Frantz Fanon's "pitfalls of the national consciousness" [1963, 148–205]) and capitalism's uneven geographical development, its deeper impulses remain alive, appearing in unexpected places and taking unexpected forms.

C. L. R. James wrote and worked with the aim of undermining, even destroying, capitalism, but who envisaged the maverick address proposed in the figure of Phillips? Sembene struggled to decolonize both Senegal and African cinema, but does Bekolo not conduct a different kind of struggle within the parameters of his generation, and are not the two struggles ultimately compatible? Could anyone have predicted that when the revolutionary idea of an African-centered cinematic culture really took off, it would be in the form of Nigerian videofilms, or that that supposedly apolitical form would produce an artist of Kelani's orientation? After the phenomenal success of Roy's *The God of Small Things,* did anyone seriously imagine that this "brand" would help further ideas with which Noam Chomsky would be well pleased? Ideas such as the importance of women's perspectives, mixed-race identities, and homosexual practices are supposed to indicate the exhaustion of the anti-colonial nationalism that had been quite powerful in the 1950s and 1960s, but these ideas often appear nowadays side-by-side with xenophobia, religious fundamentalism, ethnonationalism, and underground trade in illicit products.

"Antipodes" is a spatial term that denotes locations on exactly opposite ends of the globe. There is a basic difference in the trajectory of antipodal figures, objects, movements, formations, and textualities, but the diametrical opposition that is central to the conventional understanding of the term describes only physical geography, and originates in medieval conceptions of the world.[12] The classic antipodes are Western Europe and Australasia. Since the metaphorical antipodes are parts of the globe, interpenetrated by the instrumentality of communications, technology, and large-scale migrations of persons, goods, and images, it is important to recognize that their relationship is more complex than stark, immobile opposition. When we attend to the relational pattern of the crossroads, we become more aware of complicity, of all being in the same boat. Seeing the world as a crossroads of capital encourages us to be sensitive to the tagging of a bag of frozen fish fillets as "Produce of Chile and Namibia" in a North American supermarket; to the statement by a Cameroonian member of a Nigerian Pentecostal church in Lagos that the church did for him what his country could not; to the stocking of Togolese foodstuffs and Nigerian video-films in a store owned by a Guinean woman in Lisbon; to the growth in African cities of enthusiastic fan clubs for English Premier League football teams; and to the depiction, in a feature film, of an illiterate farmer, probably from Somalia, who cannot speak English but who "is now English" by virtue of having obtained a British passport at the cost of a kidney.[13] Welcome to the *polyforum,* "the public square where everyone has a right to be heard, but no one has the right to exclusive speech" (Fuentes 2006, 610). This idea of spatial relationship is comparable to the rhizome as both Deleuze and Guattari (1987, 6–9) have conceptualized it, and evinces sociocultural practices which crystallized as the marketplace. The *polyforum* is the fabric from which are fashioned communities such as MySpace, Facebook, YouTube, Flickr, Twitter, chat rooms, and the blogosphere, communities and subjectivities that are impossible to imagine without the mediation of technology and a new sense of being in the world.

This is not exactly the world as it is envisioned by the "modular" form of nation-state sovereignty, in which each nation exists in its sovereign space, entering into agreements with other nations, and minimizing the impact of such contacts as may exist through the territorially determined systems of taxation and national debt.[14] Commentaries on the crisis of the nation-state show that nations as sovereigns will still continue to do good in the world (Anderson 1998), that discourses of globalization can be strengthened by earlier discourses of modernization and Third World struggles (Gikandi 2001), and that "the logic of the nation-state will coexist for a long time with the logic of the imperial age" (Guéhenno 1995, 123). Yet there is ample evidence that the unprecedented movements of goods, services, and people in the last few decades, as well as the institutional factors motivating them, have transformed the model treasured by the newly independent nations of the mid-twentieth century. Globalization, the collective name of those institutional factors, implies that capital and images move in a way that affects communication, information, and other public transactions. The mobility of technologies and their contents, and the mobility of skilled people, present a point of entry into the following discussion of the relationships between globalization and the consolidation of genres in postcolonial studies.

Global Aesthetics

Recent studies of the impact of globalization on aesthetics have focused on changes within literary studies, especially the reconfiguration of the fields of English and comparative literature to accommodate the category of world literature (Beecroft 2008; Melas 2007; Casanova 2004; Damrosch 2003; Moretti 2005, 2000; Gunn 2001), although not all of these studies conform to the paradigm of English and world literature. The main premise goes like this: since globalization implies wide-ranging changes in the idea of the nation, and since these changes have been accompanied by accelerated migration and diffusion of peoples, the traditional focus on the analogy between nation, literary tradition, and language has to be shifted to transnationalism, the institutional framework for the mobility of capital, people, and images that defines globalization. Moreover, most of these studies favor thematic readings in their analytical approaches to transnationalism, and so even when their focus shifts from, say, anti-colonialism to cultural hybridity, they emphasize strategies for reading texts with hybridity as a thematic concern.[15] In these efforts at institutional reorientation, the field of postcolonial studies has featured prominently as an important branch of world literature. This is because works coming from outside of Western Europe and North America are seen to constitute the exception to literary history, the places to look for aesthetic innovations, especially when the rule is structured either by the field of English literary studies (often the British and American traditions) or by the genre of the novel.

In order to avoid the endless and impractical representativeness (along the lines of theme, region, gender, period, genre, and so on) which this reorientation entails, Franco Moretti, in a much-cited essay titled "Conjectures on World Literature," calls for a meta-thematic approach which he terms "distant reading," whereby the literary critic or historian substitutes "units that are much smaller or much larger than the text: devices, themes, tropes—genres and systems" for the established practice of closely reading a number of texts (Moretti 2000, 57).[16] He sees this approach as analogous to the synthesizing model of world-system theory in the work of Immanuel Wallerstein and the Braudel School in Binghamton, New York. The French critic Pascale Casanova works with a similar analogy in her book *The World Republic of Letters* (2004). She focuses on the structural relationship between the invisible formation of literary tradition and the linguistic, formal, and political rivalries among European nations which spread with the global expansion of capital. Casanova calls this structure the *world literary space,* a semi-autonomous terrain mapped in the metropolitan West (in Paris, to be specific). In this space, values are created around literary works in which the location of the writer, the system of evaluation, and aesthetic influences are so intertwined as to be understood largely as the effect of symbolic capital, a concept borrowed from Pierre Bourdieu, the principal inspiration for Casanova's sociological analysis.[17]

An exhaustive review of these and other interventions has been provided by Natalie Melas, who, in *All the Difference in the World,* makes a point of departing from the approaches they develop "without standing in antagonistic opposition to them," relying on Édouard Glissant's notion of Relation (standing in the world) as a model of worldliness that goes beyond the well-established practice in the field of comparative literature of conceiving of comparison as standing for the world (Melas 2007, 35–36). While acknowledging the far-reaching ways that these debates have reconfigured the field of literary study, I intend to focus my discussion here and in the rest of the book on areas that the debates have hitherto ignored, making generic transformation central to the issues and turning to forms other than fiction or the novel in addressing them. Far from seeking to displace the novel or the poem, I am interested in the institutional and aesthetic contexts in which artists—writers, filmmakers, essayists—work, and how those contexts shape and are shaped by their works in relation to questions of cultural mobility, expatriation, and commodification. Each of these issues has to be seen in relation to the political and economic formations described in the two last sections if the structural, though fractious, relationship between the earlier generation of writers and artists and those whose works are more visibly marked by globalization is to yield meaningful insights.

For example, it is obvious that during the career of James, the oldest figure in this book, capitalism took a form quite different from the form in which globalization now manifests itself. But it is also worth stressing that James's work is significant not only because it predates the others' but also because it is preoccupied with issues which the national struggle, running on decolonization, repressed in the process of highlighting but which have now returned, sometimes as a critical departure and sometimes as a deepened solidarity. Once this interest in the historical breadth of James's intellectual preoccupations is secured, the connections and discrepancies between the aesthetics of decolonization (typified in the satirical treatment of the elite in *Xala*) and the aesthetics of transnationalism (typified in the depiction of the urban gangsters and self-absorbed cinéaste in *Aristotle's Plot*) will be easier to identify.

The model of generic transformation which I adopt in this book comes partly from the materialist analysis of form in the epic and the novel inaugurated in Georg Lukacs's *The Theory of the Novel,* and partly from the formalist approach developed in Tveztan Todorov's *Genres in Discourse.* Making no pretensions to Lukacs's metaphysical stamina, and seeking for clues beyond the formal devices central to Todorov's analysis, I also draw on Moretti's earlier work, especially *Signs Taken for Wonders,* where he underlines the materiality of form as a function of the history of aesthetic values and "of the institutions designed to promote them" (Moretti 1983, 17). Equally important is Michael McKeon's magisterial *The Origins of the English Novel,* which brings a materialist dimension to Ian Watts's earlier study of the coincidence of the rise of the English middle class and of the rise of the novel. McKeon's point "that 'genre' is the principal category by which we acknowledge the inescapable historicity of form itself" (2002, 6), while leaning on Levi-Strauss's analysis of myth, is particularly germane to the kind of connections I am attempting to make between larger systems (politics, economics, culture) and the "micro" formations (expatriation, cultural mobility, and commodification) without which, in postcolonial studies at least, discrete analyses of texts cannot be very productive. Between these two poles lie the systemic issues concerning the conception, production, and circulation of literary and cinematic works. However, what I find most useful in these examples—the intellectual concern with genre as historical and material—has to be mediated on the one hand by the authors' primary focus on the novel, and on the other by the peculiar nature of postcolonial textuality, which they did not anticipate.[18]

Stuart Hall, the distinguished black British cultural theorist, provides a useful example of how to deal with the first limitation, that is, how to think about globalization and aesthetics in a generically broad way. In two related essays, "The Local and the Global: Globalization and Ethnicity" (1997a) and "Old and New Identities, Old and New Ethnicities" (1997b), both conceived as responses to a world no longer determined by the unitary conception of identity, Hall argues that identity shapes and is shaped by global mass culture. The dominant practice under capitalism, according to Hall, is "a homogenizing form of cultural representation, enormously absorptive of things . . . but the homogenization is never absolutely complete, and it does not work for completeness."[19] What there are, when this new world is perceived through the lenses of artistic representation and social practice, are "the aesthetics of the crossover, the aesthetics of diaspora, the aesthetics of creolization." These, according to Hall, are the new ethnicities, and ethnicity in this sense is "the space from which people speak," the space of self-representation enabled by the globalizing presence of capital (Hall 1997a, 28, 39, 36).

As an example of the process, Hall explains that the critiques of old social identities through Marxism, psychoanalysis, linguistics, feminism, and postcolonialism ("the five great de-centerings") are sustained through a conception of identity that derives from difference. In other words, just as the so-called global works through particulars, and capital maintains localities in order to exploit them for its own sustenance and reproduction, it also simultaneously produces their specific identity as culture, and it does this by making them both appear as, and actually be, different. This conception of identity is validated by the powerful influence of the five discursive systems, whose histories have in different ways been closely related to that of capital. Each is a critique of a different aspect of the traditional, which is to say European, notion of the subject, or as Hall prefers to put it, "the great collective social identities" (44).

The constant element in this process is capital, whose supposedly global power is exercised through what, in a fetching metaphor, Hall calls "local capitals" (28). The contradictory space in which capital exists is created and sustained through its need to negotiate its own crises by ensuring incommensurability even as it makes possible localized desires for parity with the cultural dominant. Hence the notion of uneven geographical development. The interesting thing about Hall's argument is that it is paradoxically presented as a questioning of the notion of Englishness:

> To be English is to know yourself in relation to the French, and the hot-blooded Mediterraneans, and the passionate, traumatized Russian soul. You go round the entire globe: when you know what everybody else is, then you are what they are not. Identity is always, in that sense, a structured representation which only achieves its positive through the narrow eye of the negative. It has to go through the eye of the needle before it can construct itself. (21)

In this regard England, or Englishness, epitomizes the contradiction in a most poignant manner, a fact captured in Hall's elegant reference to the country in one breath as both a privileged and unprivileged "corner of the global process" (19). England, the great imperial power which from the fifteenth century on controlled as much as two-thirds of the earth's surface as colonial possessions, is now perceived by most people as a colony of the United States, especially in light of the relationship between U.S. president George Bush and British prime minister Tony Blair at the beginning of the so-called war on terror in the early 2000s. But the long imperial period was a notable moment, Hall argues, when the "particular forms of English identity [felt] that they [could] command, within their own discourses, the discourses of almost everybody else . . . at a certain moment in history" (20). What can be deduced from Hall's use of England as the space and object of the critique of identity is his shuttling between the particularity of England and Englishness and the broader context in which that identity was fashioned as a universal model of national identities.

The interpenetration of the particular and the universal becomes more evident when one realizes that what Hall sets up in place of Englishness is not some abstract universalism but something equally particular: the United States. The difference between this new globalization and the old one is that whereas Englishness positioned itself as homogeneous and unitary, the American identity, driven by a new form of global mass culture (of which satellite television is the epitome [27]), is far from homogeneous. This analysis of capitalism's role in shaping mass culture is relevant to my discussion of genre because the tradition of cultural studies out of which Hall's work grew is distinguished for its blending of poststructuralist and Marxist critiques of system with an analysis of cultural identity associated with class. Indeed, his interest in the decisive role of global mass culture in the constitution of contemporary identities is also an elaboration of a tradition of twentieth-century expatriate Caribbean intellectuals, as I show in my discussion of James's work (see also Hall 1995, 1989).

The other limitation of extant scholarship on genre and history is that it takes no cognizance of specific postcolonial realities. Whether in the analysis of the historical transformations of form from the epic to the novel (Lukacs), of the relationship between tragedy and sovereignty (Moretti), or of the analogy between the middle classes and the English novel (McKeon), an emphasis on context inevitably leads to exclusions. Todorov is exceptional in focusing on the *kasala,* a poetic genre from Central Africa, but as Peter Hitchcock observes, this inclusion only serves to present the *kasala* as a secondary kind of poetic utterance, and Todorov as moving from an African genre of "comparative simplicity" to a European one of complexity (Hitchcock 2003, 323). The analyses are historical, they are materialist, they are formally adroit, but they are not enough. The specificity of postcolonial apparatuses of representation is a peculiar one, manifesting itself in a variety of ways, of which three are relevant to this discussion: the fitful character of the artistic representation of decolonization, typified in the differences in postcolonial subjectivity; the aesthetic dimensions of uneven geographical development; and metropolitan location and the commodity form as shapers of genres. I take up these points in turn.

Representing Decolonization

In the era of decolonization, attempts to represent (in the double sense of both making art about and speaking for) the constituents of the postcolony in many cases complemented or supplemented anti-colonial nationalism. Different writers and artists confronted the challenge differently, but their responses usually came down to anti-imperialist consciousness (Ngugi wa Thiong'o and the language question), political engagement (Wole Soyinka and Nawal el Saadawi battling political and clerical authorities in their countries), and literature as pedagogy (Chinua Achebe's novelist as teacher). These responses were efforts to revise colonial history or contest ongoing depredations of power, giving priority to a transformative, though fictional, interpretation of the past in relation to the present. Such was the intellectual atmosphere in the age of decolonization. Indeed, as the Marxist cultural theorist Biodun Jeyifo has argued through his notion of "genealogical fictions" in postcolonial reconstructions of the colonial experience, African writers have tended to downplay the influence of Africans who enthusiastically adapted to the "invented traditions" and values of European colonization (Jeyifo 1993, 102). In the writings of Achebe, Ngugi, and Ayi Kwei Armah, as Jeyifo points out, such figures are usually portrayed as negative icons, mimic men suffering from what the late Afrobeat musician Fela Anikulapo-Kuti, in his famous song, denounced as "kolo[nial] mentality." Jeyifo contends that the marginalization of these groups or figures in postcolonial genealogical fictions is not simply a distortion of historical fact, but exemplifies "the complexly determined cultural process that always attends the reconstruction of the past" (103).[20] In this process, it is safe to infer, the distinctions between bourgeois nationalism and revolutionary socialism in the process of decolonization are brought under a broad practice of cultural vanguardism. African and other postcolonial writers and artists could be critical of colonialism and its agents, but their criticisms were advanced from the standpoint of nationalism, and the artists took culture to be the most effective site for such criticisms. This is also borne out in Amílcar Cabral's famous statement that "national liberation is necessarily *an act of culture*" (Cabral 1979, 143, emphasis in original).

However, the setbacks of decolonization—the failures of the national liberation movements, the misadventures of bourgeois nationalism, the depredations of economic structural adjustments—have opened up new ways of looking at identities, not excluding the very categories of nation and culture. Much of the opportunity represented by the new perspectives on identity is implied in Hall's analysis, too. Not only the European notions of the subject, but also the traditions of colonized societies, have been shown to be elaborate constructions or colonial-era "inventions." The "opportunists, traitors, fools, or pathetic victims of a grand illusion in postcolonial fictions of genealogies" (Jeyifo 1993, 106) have acquired a different identity in the context of the complementary crisis of decolonization and the development of more open conceptions of marginalized identities. Such a reconception of African subjectivities now highlights the relationship between the repressions that made the attacks on the "traitorous" agents of colonialism possible, and the increasing visibility of different categories of cultural minority in the postcolony—women, children, the disabled, the poor, the homosexual—who were either misrepresented or not represented at all in fictions of genealogy. Probably because it has been closely identified with progressive political ideas and movements, the cultural aspects of this artistic process have not received the kind of critical analysis appropriate to them until recently.[21] As the literary critic Harry Garuba lucidly argues (n.d.), when viewed through the satirical lenses that Soyinka uses to frame the clownish Professor Oguazor in *The Interpreters,* the character Elvis Okeh in Chris Abani's *GraceLand* would be a mimic figure, not a self-inventing subscriber to the global mediascape.

However, in order to avoid starting from an inappropriate preoccupation with a monolithic Pan-Africanist or anti-colonial discourse, as did some earlier analysts, scholars need to theorize these new thematic concerns with postcolonial subjectivities in relation to intellectual formations like tricontinentalism and cosmopolitanism. For something fundamental is concealed under the argument that marginal or minority identities are being better aired in postcolonial studies today than are identities premised on anti-colonial nationalism, and this is the fact that postcolonial criticism, institutionally more established in North America and Western Europe, is disproportionately invested in the poetics of anti-colonialism, even if such an investment helps to emphasize the blind spots of that fictional genealogy. For example, West African authors and filmmakers who are removed from Achebe or Sembene by a generation face different challenges than did their predecessors in producing and sustaining their craft. Postcolonial criticism's investment in a set of authors whose works highlight anti-colonialism often overshadows the challenges faced by these new authors. What happens if the postcolonial critic turns from Achebe to the Nigerian-based intellectual Festus Iyayi, or the UK-based novelist Buchi Emecheta, as Adewale Maja-Pearce does in his provocative book *A Mask Dancing*?[22] Or, in the interest of comparative analysis, one could turn to Syl Cheney-Coker, the Sierra Leonean poet and novelist, who is stylistically different from both Achebe and Emecheta but whose career nonetheless makes clear the crisis of sustainability in literary culture that has resulted from both general postcolonial asymmetry and the brutal war of the late 1990s in Sierra Leone.

Exacting though the arguments may be, the lack of "great African novels" in the 1980s and the 1990s cannot be simply explained by the inability of African writers either to capture "the immense mutations of the world," as the Martinican novelist Patrick Chamoiseau argues (Taylor 1998, 142), or the failure to confront the dilemma of their time and place, as Maja-Pearce says of Nigerian novels of the 1980s (Maja-Pearce 1992, 33–34). A different but related fact must also be considered, the phenomenon of expatriation and metropolitan location and its impact on genre in a global context. As the Cameroonian scholar Ambroise Kom has argued in a lucid essay titled "African Absence, a Literature without a Voice" (1998), the successes of expatriated African writers such as Ben Okri and Calixthe Beyala in the mid-1990s have to be understood in relation to both the state of the critical enterprise on the African continent in the 1990s and the Euro-American context of their works' dissemination. While authors, literary magazines, and journals based on the continent were not guaranteed even a semblance of normalcy in terms of readership and institutional prestige, a handful of writers and artists living in Western Europe were relatively well promoted, and this foreign location had important effects on the dissemination and analysis of their works and on their careers. This metropolitan context makes questions of hybridity and commodification more germane than they would ordinarily be in an African context, where ideas and practices of cultural nationalism often led to claims of authenticity. Moreover, such questions pertain not only to literary works but also to their authors, who become foils for the examination of issues relating to nation and nationalism. This context, where I locate the works of Phillips and Roy, is selectively inclusive in ways that throw both the aesthetic dimension of uneven geographical development and the artistic exigencies of expatriation and metropolitan location into bold relief.

Aesthetics of Uneven Geographical Development

While literary culture suffered, and writers less visible than an Achebe or an Ngugi faced silence or exile, other forms of cultural production, like music, popular magazine publishing, and artisanal video, thrived in African settings. This is the second manifestation of the peculiarity of postcolonial texts, that is, the aesthetic dimensions of uneven geographical development. The institutionalization of structural adjustment programs (SAPs), which I discuss further in chapter 3, was the immediate economic reason for this downturn in literary publishing, but there is an additional cause to be sought in the relations of production in a postcolonial, or neocolonial, context, as Sembene's use of the word *mégotage* reminds us. In other words, while recent economic policies determine the formal or aesthetic choices that are available to artists, it is also important to keep institutional policies in mind. For instance, the French Ministry of Cooperation, until its absorption into the Foreign Affairs department in 1994, was responsible for much technical and financial assistance to filmmakers in former French colonies and thus for the lopsided development of cinematic practices in the West African subregion. The kind of institutional support provided by the Ministry of Cooperation cannot be discounted as an effect of the unseen hands of the market, because such a support comes with all sorts of strings attached. For example, as Manthia Diawara argues persuasively in his latest book, *African Film: New Forms of Aesthetics and Politics*, Robert Neslé, the French producer of *Mandabi*, one of Sembene's early films, needed the film "to advance his own career in the highly competitive French market" (Diawara 2010, 34). Given the contradictions of uneven geographical development, and the demands of artistic integrity that come into play under this kind of circumstance, it is not surprising that artists pursue different options in order to sustain their craft. From the point of view of the cultural analyst, what manifests itself is the coexistence of several generic modes and traditions.

In the market's contrapuntal spaces, older technologies survive and compete with the new: the long-playing vinyl record, the cassette tape, the compact disc, and the digital file all appear as means of packaging and delivering music. This is even more true in the postcolony, where "anachronistic" technologies survive not because of a lack of cultural sophistication but because of the difficulty of access. It may be too expensive, for instance, to make the leap from the video-cassette to the DVD. Yet it is not so much that digital technologies are less affordable as that the question of access is analogous to the question of uneven geographical development: in the farther reaches of the neoliberal "market," where technology cannot be treated simply as furniture, the uses to which such technologies are put are a function of sociocultural calculations that go beyond individual purchasing power. The fact that different technological formations overlap in a given social context, rather than appearing and being replaced sequentially, negates the idea of a simple delineation of spheres. As a result, in the West African annals of filmmaking, the modernist idea of the auteur (associated with cinema produced on chemical-based film stock) coexists with the more open and "democratic" tendencies of the digital format, even when the film stock itself is no longer affordable or practical in an institutional or technical sense. This is the socioeconomic and aesthetic context for the emergence of Nollywood, the phenomenal explosion of videofilms in Nigeria.

The commodified products of this cinematic practice are variously called video dramas, home videos, or videofilms because, in their earliest forms, they were shot with shoulder-borne or hand-held video cameras and distributed on mass-produced videocassettes for home viewing. This practice is different from the convention in most film industries, where films are distributed in video-cassette format after their theatrical release. Although the technology has become more refined with the profusion of digital cameras and studios, the word "video" remains crucial to the name. This naming has to do with the films' economic and cultural context, but it is also a function of the aesthetic consideration of conventional celluloid film, the apparatus of Hollywood and of African cinema as distributed, exhibited, and analyzed within but mostly outside the continent. The Nollywood films are considered videofilms because (with a few exceptions) they are not shot on raw or reversed film stock.[23] The questions of aesthetic value tied to these two considerations are important for our discussion of the impact of new technologies on filmmaking. Not only Nollywood but also a great variety of new filmmaking practices are dependent on digital technology; celluloid, the default technical apparatus for cinema, makes these practices difficult or impossible.

Video, the most recently developed format in the long history of the mechanical reproduction of sound and image, is appropriate to the postmodern age because of its technical flexibility. Scholars of video as a means of artistic representation have been at pains to underline its distinct identity in comparison to radio, television, and film, the other audiovisual media (Jameson 1991; Armes 1988; Hanhardt 1986). Armes has argued that video is the "key final link in a complex chain of developments in both image and sound reproduction" (1988, 9), and should be seen in the context of other technologies such as photography, the gramophone, cinema, radio, television, and the sound tape. Equally important to Armes's argument is the industrial context in which these technologies were developed—they were affected by issues of invention, patent, and commercial viability. Evidence of this is the role of the U.S. studios—Paramount, Fox, MGM, Warner Brothers, and so on—in the production, distribution, and exhibition of films. This is where Armes comes closest to John Hanhardt, editor of a rare, that is, particularly good, volume on video art, who is more interested in the use that artists make of video, separate from any conceptual connection to television or cinema (Hanhardt 1986). Hanhardt's interest in video as the technology of the genre of video art is closely linked to the rise of alternative filmmaking in the United States. In Hanhardt's reading, video formats which allow small-scale artists, whether filmmakers or video artists, to bypass the heavy capitalization characteristic of the film industry thus become useful for ideological purposes.

The technology of video has enabled the explosive and unprecedented development of a cinematic culture in Nigeria and other parts of the world. Such a development rests on the recognition that the technology can be adapted to many uses in the context of uneven geographical development. The aesthetic crises of Nigerian filmmaking in the 1980s (Haynes 1995; Adesanya 1997) were economic in the sense that filmmakers trained to use celluloid film stock could not afford the costs of postproduction as a result of the strictures of structural adjustment programs. Thus we face a paradox: information and digital technologies became available as a result of neoliberal economic structural adjustment programs that undermined the earlier practice of celluloid filmmaking, with its ties to the concepts of the auteur and the national cinema, whereas literary and other "high-cultural" forms were marginalized as publishers of African fiction and poetry drastically purged their lists. This is the broad context in which Nollywood emerged as a commodity form. It is also the context that nurtured a later generation of African filmmakers, of whom Jean-Pierre Bekolo is a good example. The challenges of making films in such circumstances are what prompted Sembene's coining of the word *mégotage,* a word suggesting "bricolage" and "montage", and alluding to the overwhelming contingency of making art in a postcolonial context.

The artists, like their audiences, are open to different formats, to using whatever works, given the socioeconomic structure I have already described. This does not mean that their works, in their variety of formats, lack conventions. To the extent that they are texts—objects of representation with a particular way of addressing an audience or displaying their languages—they are constituted through conventions. However, in the contrapuntal space of the market, those conventions are often the results of economic and sociocultural contexts. The critical question of open format, which enables such a synchrony between thematics and audience, can be considered a technological possibility in the sense that, as Bekolo ineffably puts it in the voice-over narration in *Aristotle's Plot,* the "container" (or form) is also potentially the material (content). (Fredric Jameson also develops this point, as I discuss below.) That this potential is not simply the result of digital technology is shown in the ways that the rhetoric of *mégotage* manifests itself in Sembene's work. The cameo appearances which have become a familiar motif in the films of this master of the modernist apparatus of celluloid film stock are largely the result of production contingencies. As Sembene said in a little-known interview, he took to playing parts in his films when some actors failed to show up. This comment points to the ways in which socioeconomic context (such as problems of professionalization) serves to shape form.[24]

In an essay titled "Globalization as a Philosophical Issue," Jameson advances a similar argument in relation to globalization, stressing that information technologies decisively underscore the incomplete character of modernity (Jameson 1998). He calls this impact communicational, in the sense that functional technologies like computers come prepackaged with cultural contents, and that the social transformation of the world, whether as "modernization" or "globalization," is in this case a cultural phenomenon. But there are also economic consequences, because "the ostensibly communicational concept has secretly been transformed into a vision of the world market and its newfound interdependence, a global division of labor on an extraordinary scale, new electronic trade routes tirelessly plied by commerce and finance alike" (56). This is the so-called mass-mediatization of the world, the dissemination of largely American cultural and economic products in different forms. In this process the "receiving societies," far from being passive consumers, necessarily engage in complex acts of negotiation and bricolage. Video is the quintessential mode of this dissemination because it is the visual template best suited to the fragmented, deterritorialized character of the financialized (corporate) phase of capitalism.

The crises that paradoxically spurred the economic and cultural reflexes constitutive of Nollywood were thus cushioned not just by the availability of video technology just as economies in the "developing world" were being deregulated. Their impact was decisive also because of a cultural attitude that enabled the social structure to adapt the flexible technology for cinematic purposes in the process of adapting to the strictures of structural adjustment. Jameson's argument in "Globalization as a Philosophical Issue" appears to be a revision of his view of video art in his influential book *Postmodernism,* where he is extremely skeptical about analytical attempts to collapse video and film aesthetics, stressing the distinctiveness of the experience of the screen image (Jameson 1991, 69–70). Since video, more than film, epitomizes the aesthetics of postmodernism, Jameson limits the modernist conception of textuality to the latter. This conception he evokes in terms of the difference between the televisual format and the "intermission of a play or an opera or . . . grand finale of a film, when the lights slowly come back and the memory begins its mysterious work" (70). Thus, Jameson contends that to treat a video as text, "to select—even as an 'example'—a single videotext and to discuss it in isolation, is fatally to regenerate the illusion of the masterpiece or the canonical text and to reify the experience of total flow from which it was momentarily extracted" (78).

There are at least three reasons for departing from this notion of textuality. First, reconstructing texts from memory or through print (for a play or a novel) is less arduous where there is a rewind button (a possibility allowed when film is reformatted as video), and still less when it is possible to select and unpack a sequence or "chapter" frame by frame, as digital formats allow. It is this capacity that makes the reading of a film possible; one could hardly write in detail about a film without having watched it at least twice, even if the objective were to de-canonize it. Secondly, the category of the experimental video (or "video art") (71) is formal because, before the art, video exists as a material apparatus.[25] Finally, as Brian Larkin has recently argued in *Signal and Noise* (2008), a fascinating study of the relationship between colonial modernity and the institution of cinema in Nigeria, the development of public infrastructures is a complex process embodying both the media (cinema and radio) and the immaterial forms they bring into being, like leisure. It is this ability of colonial or postcolonial "subjects" to turn technologies and other cultural importations to different but particular uses that constitutes their collective agency. Scholars have identified this ability in diverse ways (Fabian 1998; Appadurai 1996; Hannerz 1987; Ranger 1983).

Jameson's idea that the three dimensions of the material, the social, and the aesthetic are conjoined in the media (1991, 67) is sustained by the shuttle between the economic and the cultural domains. It is this conjunction that determines what I term the aesthetic dimension of uneven geographical development, the imaginative adaptation to economic strictures in ways that are generically new within the apparatus of representation. Nollywood videos are perhaps the most obvious technological example of this, but works by younger African filmmakers (Bekolo, Sissako, Saleh Mahamet-Haroun, Régina Fanta Nacro, and Moussa Sene Absa) also show this adaptation by their reflexivity, that is, the self-conscious ways in which they reflect on the complex relationships between technological and demographic changes and cinematic meanings. There is yet another compelling aspect to this conjunction, which one can grasp by thinking of the agency at work in this process in individual terms. This is crucial because my conception in this book of the postcolonial artist as an intellectual figure relies very much on this individuality, the idea that, although a work of art is autonomous, the fact that its creator (or creators) lives in history cannot be discounted. This leads me to the third manifestation of the peculiarity of postcolonial texts, that is, the impact of metropolitan location and the commodity form on genres.

Expatriation, Commodification, and Genre

Metropolitan location has ambivalent effects on the condition of postcolonial writers, and this ambivalence may be displayed in a number of ways. Depending on personal temperament and intellectual tradition, a writer or artist may self-consciously embody the ambivalence of being out of a specific national context, as does Caryl Phillips in relation to the Caribbean island of St. Kitts, so as to evince a critical attitude to that nation, and to nationalism. Such an attitude is evident early in Phillips's career, for example in his critical comments on the corrupt government of the late Guyanese president Forbes Burnham through an encounter with a young Guyanese in Moscow (Phillips 1999, 112). Or the artist may displace the ambivalence onto the work, until it bulks so large as to draw attention to the instability of genres, such as in Phillips's *The Atlantic Sound*. Indeed, the second possibility seems to follow logically from the first, especially if the work is nonfiction, or reflexive cinema, or performance art, genres in which the subjectivity of the artist is inseparable from the conceptual tenor of the work. It is important to add that metropolitan location or expatriation, as I think of it here, is a little more than a simple question of place, both because home and displacement under exile (the old way in which expatriation was thought of) are in intimate relationship, and because the artist is capable of transcending a simple conception of place.[26] I am thinking here of a figure like Arundhati Roy, who does not live abroad but whose work and activism exist within a context of celebrity and commodification that is principally a function of metropolitan cultural politics. I think that the differences between the figure of the artist and the artist's location in relation to positions on postcoloniality are crucial in Roy's case, and those differences resurface in Aijaz Ahmad's view of Edward Said's work (Ahmad 1992, 159–219). My simultaneous attention to decolonization and globalization, particularly in the work of the "younger generation" figures in this book, is intended to address the arbitrariness and occlusion that Ahmad thinks are characteristic of metropolitan intellectuals such as Said.

The critic James English has identified cultural mechanisms such as prizes, awards, and grants, which place value on works of art, as constituting a specific "economy of prestige" (English 2005). He shows these mechanisms to be connected to questions of value about the conception, production, and circulation of artistic works, and in his analysis of how such value comes to be conferred on these works one can glimpse the outlines of the relationship between metropolitan location and commodification of art that I am trying to address. There are strong, often unacknowledged, links between metropolitan location, the figure of the artist as an expatriate, the institutions of cultural capital, and the waning of nationalist sentiment that is often identified with cosmopolitanism. In *The World Republic of Letters*, Pascale Casanova argues that "literary space translates political and national issues into its own terms—aesthetic, narrative, poetic—and at once affirms and denies them," adding that the autonomy from specific national affiliations thus conferred on the world literary space is what made metropolitan Paris "the world capital of literature in the nineteenth century" (Casanova 2004, 86, 87). English pursues a similar argument by showing that the international success of Keri Hulme's novel *the bone people* was due to its being perceived as representing Maori literature more than New Zealand "national" literature (English 2005, 316). The global space in which the works and the authors circulate thus trumps claims of allegiance inherent in literary traditions tied to specific nations. For this reason, Ngugi wa Thiong'o's *Weep Not, Child,* a historically situated critique of colonial-era Kenya, would be less appealing than, say, M. G. Vassanji's *The In-Between Life of Vikram Lall,* which chronicles the lives of a man across several continents and periods.

These arguments about the status of literary works as globally circulating cultural goods are quite familiar by now, especially in postcolonial studies (Brouillette 2007; Huggan 2001). But I think that what critics consider as "exotic" in recent writings are not simply attempts to subvert prior codes of representation, as Huggan contends, but rather are more complex manifestations of difference based on race and culture, and underwritten by global economic inequalities. Indeed, Brouillette's work is notable for underscoring authorial self-consciousness and self-construction (2007, 68, 176), thus emphasizing the role of the artist, as a person living in history, in the formation of cultural value. However, she works only within the specific context of book history, thus limiting the scope of the contradictions between genres and institutions. Also, she reads self-consciousness in only one direction, to the point of downplaying situations in which matters are not so settled, as is the case in several of the figures in this book. The metropolitan context is a highly charged one for postcolonial intellectuals, whether pro-nationalist or not. European nations—Britain, France, Portugal, Belgium, and Holland—were responsible for most of the colonies in Africa, Asia, and the Caribbean. Anti-colonial nationalism and decolonization represented powerful ideological challenges to the governing values of the colonial project. While a generation of metropolitan "Third World" intellectuals set themselves against the ideals of imperialism represented through colonial power, as Edward Said (1990) observes with regard to the writings of C. L. R. James and George Antonius, the intervening period of decolonization showed the limits of "national consciousness" in ways that undermined the logic of anti-colonial nationalism.

The presence of intellectuals in metropolitan locations used to be discussed in terms of exile, but this category has been largely displaced by the more complex process of migration and expatriation, in which choice is implicit. As a result, the extent to which artists domiciled in a metropolitan culture are assumed to take an adversarial attitude toward that culture is also substantially curtailed. It is even more so if, as Casanova argues, this attitude takes on an aesthetic dimension or, as English submits, the translation of political issues into aesthetic ones is complemented (and complimented) by the kind of cultural prestige that prizes and awards confer on authors and their works. In this context, the figure of the artist is crucial. The subjective articulation of social issues in a former colony becomes the basis for a political critique that might warrant persecution if the writer were living in her own country (Nawal el Saadawi in Egypt), but garners celebration when the writer lives abroad. A good example is V. S. Naipaul's nonfiction about India, the Caribbean, and Africa.[27] Indeed, the figure of the writer has a role to play in the emergence of nonfiction as a genre of worldliness, and this emergence is hard to contemplate outside of the metropolitan culture of prestige described by Casanova and English, among others.

This institutional context is also central to Timothy Brennan's critique of "Third World" cosmopolitanism in his 1989 article "Cosmopolitans and Celebrities," prior to his more full-fledged analysis in At Home in the World (1997).[28] Brennan argues that writers feel the immediate impact of expatriation on the level of form, as the embrace of the cosmopolitan ethos "involves a flattening of influences, which assemble themselves . . . on the same plane of value" in which writers "consciously allude to the center-periphery conflicts raised by decolonization, and modify them by enhancing the role of the 'West' as, alternately, foil and lure" (1989, 4). This is very similar to Casanova's argument regarding the translation of politics into aesthetics. Of the writers Brennan discusses,

Salman Rushdie, in his fictions from the 1980s, perhaps shows this tendency most strongly. In those works, Rushdie goes beyond the modernist impulses in the novel and anticipates questions about genre that are significant because of his later dismissal of postcolonial nationalism. The emergence of these expatriated writers as citizens of former European colonies, and their relationship to the economy of prestige of multinational publishing, awards, and prizes, present an interesting standpoint from which to examine the questions of global cultural flows. Three issues are worth highlighting in this regard. First, the generic category of nonfiction is itself indispensable to focusing attention on an author's subjectivity and personal trajectory. Second, the very institutions that parlay the conception, circulation, and distribution of cultural works as factors in the economy of prestige are similarly indispensable. Third, artists also play a crucial role in the process.

A particular focus on these permutations quite plausibly reveals the links between different kinds of artistic endeavors. Within the general economy of prestige, a publishing company's awarding an advance to a writer for a travel book and a television network's commissioning an expatriate director to make a film both point to an interesting conjunction of issues around nationalism, representation, and metropolitan perception of "local" culture. Hamid Naficy touches upon this conjunction in his discussion of what he calls the "interstitial production mode" in the work of expatriate filmmakers. His "close-ups" on two of these filmmakers (Atom Egoyan and Michel Khleifi) show a dynamic of resistance to and cooptation by dominant cinema, and especially show the directors' constant dependence on national and transnational film funds and television channels for financial support (Naficy 2001, 56–59). It is noteworthy that although African directors like Jean-Pierre Bekolo and Abderrahmane Sissako have not had the professional success of Egoyan (whose *Exotica* was bought for distribution by Miramax [57]), as artists in expatriation they belong to the same metropolitan terrain where a combination of grants, awards, commissions, and entries at festivals go a long way toward conferring cultural value (see also Jost 2005). I have argued elsewhere (Adesokan 2010) that the situation of African filmmaking in expatriate discursive contexts is often partly determined by the requirements of Western European and North American funding, patronage, and exhibition or distribution.

Naturally this condition has an impact on genre, as we shall see in the discussion of Bekolo's work before and after *Aristotle's Plot*. As it is for cinema, so it is for literature, only less obviously. In effect, either category is a passenger lorry carrying goods as well, a vehicle for something else. Institutional dynamics are primary constitutors of meaning, and within them the artist struggles to assert artistic control, which can be used to critique those dynamics. That a director gets "free money" to make films, as Bekolo once quipped during a public event, does not make these institutional dynamics any less functions of the broader economic system—the unseen hands of the market. Sembene's recognition of these powerful dynamics, these apparatuses of representation, powerfully shaped his calculations as he shuttled between the scenario, the manuscript, and the final screenplay—the film and novel versions of *Xala.*

In conclusion, I want to draw out the implications of the processes I have been describing for the connections between the figures and works discussed in the rest of the book. Through its contacts with aesthetics, the phenomenon of uneven geographical development aids different postcolonial subjectivities by making images widely but unevenly available, thus presenting artists with different options of advancing genre and much else. But it also enables new critiques of unequal exchange, because uneven geographical development, like a reflective artist-intellectual's experience of metropolitan location, has a way of magnifying the relations between a given postcolonial context and the cultural dominant. This is apparent in the first epigraph to this introduction, a saying about the instrumental deployment of a local musical genre (*apala*) in the metropolitan experience of Haruna Isola, a musician whose audience was elsewhere. The remark is actually an interpretive commentary on the opening lines of the song he released after his trip.[29] The interdependence of incommensurable units—*apala* music on the one hand, and English grammar and British culture on the other—implicit in the remark is fundamental to the argument I am making about the relationships between genre, uneven geographical development, and the sociocultural negotiations that are characteristic of the crossroads of capital. The response to global inequality may not always be couched in the language of cultural imperialism, but it remains an ideological critique, as the second epigraph, from Walter Benjamin, shows, in part because a postcolonial site marked by socioeconomic dislocations is material. It elicits an ethical response, which in turn provides a basis for artistic representation.

C. L. R. James's 1976 essay "Toward the Seventh" is a retrospective analysis of the Pan-African movement, and in one sense, James's views on the movement's shortcomings receive a fuller, bitingly satiric treatment in Sembene's film *Xala,* released just two years before James's essay appeared in print. In another sense, his discussion of Pan-Africanism's historical links to a series of international movements committed to progressive politics implies that its importance is not limited to the African continent, and this stance is partly a result of James's status as an expatriate black intellectual. He thus approaches "Pan-Africanism" as the name given to the articulation of, or organizing around, complex issues for which either race or class sometimes stands. It is in this sense that his analysis finds a contemporary resonance in the political orientation of the nonfictional writings of Arundhati Roy, especially *An Ordinary Person's Guide to Empire,* a book which dusts off the mottled garb of tricontinental rhetoric for a thoroughgoing critique of globalization. While the careers of James and Sembene can be said to stand as exemplars of decolonization, Roy's is more intimately connected to neoliberalism. However, she deploys the prestige attached to that career to critique the system that benefits her.

The relationship between the three other authors and filmmakers is not as politically explicit; the basis for the comparison lies instead in the structural changes which attend the move from James's anti-colonialism to Roy's anti-globalization. Tunde Kelani's film *Thunderbolt: Magun* originates in the specific economic conditions of structural adjustment and video production in Nigeria that developed in the late 1980s. Although, like *Xala,* the film deals with a sex-related affliction, its status as a primarily commercial product connects it more closely to the postcolonial asymmetry and mutes the kind of radical critique of class politics seen in Sembene's work. Coming out of an institutional context similar to *Xala*'s but closer to *Thunderbolt: Magun* in aesthetic orientation, Jean-Pierre Bekolo's *Aristotle's Plot* stands on a conceptual middle ground, bridging the differences between Sembene's radical art and the populism of Nollywood films with an inclusive representation of generic possibilities in contemporary cinema. Caryl Phillips occupies a similar position in relation to both James, his precursor as an expatriated black intellectual and writer, and Roy, his more contemporary fellow postcolonial writer, who enjoys comparable access to institutions of prestige tied to neoliberalism. What he does with *The Atlantic Sound,* a genre-defying meditation on the legacies of slavery and racism, is as significant as what separates him from either writer.

1   C. L. R. James Sees the
World Steadily

Commenting on the writings of a cricket critic named Neville Cardus, C. L. R. James, the Trinidadian/black British writer, political activist, and theorist, makes a statement that is as true of James himself as it is of Cardus: "He says the same in more than one place" (James 1983, 195). This declaration that a piece of writing is only one instance of a vast and consistent reworking of themes and ideas also found elsewhere in his works is a succinct way of describing integration, the primary method in James's writings, which I have taken as a model in this book. In this chapter I use the occasion of "Toward the Seventh: The Pan-African Congress—Past, Present and Future," an essay James wrote in 1976, to elaborate on this method and to make three related claims. First, I claim that in spite of the diverse artistic, political, and cultural contexts of his literary output (in a career that spanned much of the twentieth century), James developed a style which he used to bring together ideas from different, often conflicting, political impulses and traditions. Second, given his personal and political choices, James's work represents a promising, though not entirely successful, integration of the two putatively antagonistic processes of socialist tricontinentalism and neoliberal cosmopolitanism. Third, although "Toward the Seventh" apparently concerns itself specifically with African realities, James's analysis and the topic's historical context indicate that Pan-Africanism goes beyond Africa, pertaining to questions of social justice across the world. In the spirit of this Jamesian method, I read the thematic, stylistic, and theoretical aspects of the 1976 essay in conjunction with a number of texts that say the same thing in other places.

Such a reading entails a constant shuttle between the essay "Toward the Seventh" and several other texts—both full-length books and shorter essays—in which the theoretical and stylistic patterns of integration are in view as James works toward the central questions of his political thought.[1] "Toward the Seventh" is a local example of integration, but that example is distilled from the other books and essays, which provide the occasion for the revision of "the theory" (of Marxist political analysis) that is presented in a condensed, integrated form in the essay. If this sounds rather like a dog chasing his own tail, the fact is that James himself describes how he arrived at this method. But I will come to that description shortly, and appropriately as a way of turning to the books.

The proposition that James works toward an integral idea of human culture implies that his oeuvre is the basis of this effort. Though he succinctly explores the idea of integration in *American Civilization* (1993), his study of cultural developments in the United States after the Second World War, the idea saturates his writings around the period of his break with Trotskyist politics in the early 1940s. I focus here, therefore, especially on the books whose conception and actual writing—if not publication—are tied to the political crisis surrounding that break, which he describes directly in his book on cricket:

> In 1940 came a crisis in my political life. I rejected the Trotskyist version of Marxism and set about to re-examine and reorganize my view of the world, which was (and remains) essentially a political one. It took more than ten years, but by 1952 I once more felt my feet on solid ground, and in consequence I planned a series of books. The first was published in 1953, a critical study of the writings of Herman Melville as a mirror of our age, and the second is this book on cricket. (1983, 19)

The remaining books in the plan are *American Civilization* (drafted in 1950 but published posthumously in 1993) and *Notes on Dialectics* (1980; originally published in 1948). The various essays collected in his selected writings (1980–1984) series, such as *At the Rendezvous of Victory* and *The Future in the Present*, *C. L. R. James on the "Negro Question"* (1996a), and *Nkrumah and the Ghana Revolution* (1977a) are also part of the plan, although this time in a dialectical sense.

Recent scholarly writings on James's life and work have focused on the cultural as well as the political conditions that defined him as a writer, and although much of this scholarship is invested in registering James's role in shaping contemporary cultural theory, there is hardly any agreement on the direct political objective of that role. There are three main currents in the scholarship. The first current sees James as an inspiration for a liberatory cultural praxis that is eminently useful for progressive and transformative multiculturalism (Brennan 1997; Farred 2003, 1996; Grimshaw 1996, 1991; McLemee 1996; Cudjoe and Cain 1995; Rosengarten 2008). Grimshaw, his former personal secretary, sees in James's work a dedicated effort to "explore and integrate all those elements essential to the complete understanding of a particular cultural activity" (1991, 34). Brennan specifically notes the stylistic "simplicity" of *American Civilization*, an approach "likely to be echoed by contemporary combative multiculturalism" (1997, 226). Rosengarten presents a very sympathetic account, perhaps the most comprehensive so far, of James's life and work in all their dimensions. The second current in the scholarship regards attempts to claim James for anti-imperialist politics as ideologically narrow and a disservice to the writer's capacious imagination and breadth of cultural affiliations (Dhondy 2001; Davies 1998; Said 1990). Said notes that, despite his affiliation with the anti-imperialism of Frantz Fanon, Amílcar Cabral, and Walter Rodney, James "stood stubbornly for the Western heritage" (1990, 36). Davies deploys this judgment to argue that James distrusted the discourse and practice of Pan-Africanism "because [he] knew where it would lead" (1998, 145n43). For Dhondy, who, like Grimshaw, was James's personal assistant, he championed "the Western intellectual tradition as the direction and salvation of modernity and the world, including Africa" (2001, 168). Dhondy's conclusion is closer to the third current in the scholarship, the least developed but the most useful for my purposes, which is epitomized by Paul Buhle's characterization of James's attitude toward Pan-Africanism as "paradoxical" (Buhle 1994).

Though Dhondy argues that Pan-Africanism for James was a culmination of a career of anti-imperialism rather than a starting point, I will make it a point from which to advance a complementary proposition. James was committed to Pan-Africanism not as an exclusive idea that can be grasped only within the frame of black nationalism, whether in Africa, the United States, the Caribbean, or Western Europe, but as one of several revolutions of the twentieth century, with ramifications beyond the continent. In other words, the internationalist trajectory of the Pan-Africanist political practice cannot be totally separated from the manner in which the cultures of neoliberalism have penetrated different parts of the globe. James's encounter with Africa, in the form of either conceptual Pan-Africanism or the earlier concerns with political agitation and organization in England and the United States, is mediated by Marxism. What is original about James's method is its creative synthesis of apparent disparities in the historical and political forces of an epoch. Empiricism is implicit in this approach, but for James amassing facts is not a goal in itself. On the contrary, the method is aimed at social transformation, and (this explains his fascination with so-called mass culture) is motivated by the philosophical conviction that political legitimacy resides in the will of the people.[2]

The two central conceptual impulses in James's writings, which constitute integration, are these: a steady and wholesome perspective on the world, and the alignment of the wishes of the one (the leader, the actor) with those of the many (the people or the audience). (There is a third, less central impulse, namely the use of the Aristotelian idea of drama to understand the flourishing of contemporary democracy.) They result as much from his Marxist method as from the aesthetic and cultural background of his colonial education. As he famously puts it, "Thackeray, not Marx, bears the heaviest responsibility for me" (James 1983, 39). They derive from the need to answer the question "What do men live by?" and its various reformulations. They are important to our understanding of what he is trying to achieve in "Toward the Seventh."

"Toward the Seventh" is the culmination of a long development of a political and theoretical perspective, written from the perspective of age and experience, and it encapsulates in substance and in style the approach that I have in mind. The essay's subject, the program of the much-anticipated Seventh Congress of the Pan-African movement, had equal relevance to the African continent, the Caribbean, and the United States. In fact, in 1976 James delivered it as an address in Dakar, Senegal, and in Washington, D.C., and also published it as part of a pamphlet in Jamaica.[3] In it, he argues that a socially relevant Pan-African movement depends on a set of prescient critiques: that the nation-state is no longer a useful basis for political solidarity in the form that the concerns of Pan-Africanism are to be posed; that bourgeois politics and cultural elitism are impediments to social transformation; and that women, the poor, and the young are to be the goal as well as the subject of the changes envisaged. Indeed, in true integrated fashion, the three critiques are related, in the same way that, he tells us right near the beginning, "to pose the Seventh Pan-African Congress . . . requires a steady view of the first six" (James 1984b, 238). This explains James's view of history as nonlinear, the idea of the future in the present: the prospectus calls for a retrospective, and this is evident in the essay's title.

It is important to note that James's critiques are motivated by activist politics. In the early 1970s, responding to political developments on the continent (in South Africa, Mozambique, Angola, and Guinea Bissau), James and a few others had authored a document titled "The Call" (244), arguing for the convening of the Sixth Pan-African Congress. "The Call" then served as the basis for the wide consultations on which he embarked, trying to garner support for the congress, which was held in Dar es Salaam, Tanzania, in 1974. He advances the prospective argument in "Toward the Seventh" to address the shortcomings of that congress. He begins on a historical note, reviewing a number of attempts that "those who were in charge of society" made to understand the social and moral crisis of capitalism as typified by the two world wars. The West "wanted to give people some ideas that the barbarism and degradation [in] which World War I had stuck Western civilization should not be considered inevitable" (James 1984b, 236). Books by H. G. Wells, Arnold Toynbee, and Kenneth Clark all reflected on the direction of human society; Clark also developed a television miniseries from his work. But each of these attempts fell short of expectations, the proof being in the constant return to the drawing board as yet another intellectual produced another book.

James does not spend time analyzing what these different historical accounts got wrong. He dismisses each out of hand: within twenty-five years of Wells's conclusion that "if we went along with good hearts and clear minds we would go some way" from the bestiality of the First World War there was an even more brutal second World War; Toynbee's thesis that history, like Christianity, would spring out of nowhere was not satisfying; Clark glibly submitted that "we have no idea where we are going," and quoted lines from W. B. Yeats's "Second Coming" into the bargain. There is a blithe, rather mocking, tone to James's dismissal of these writers ("Now, friends, I am not making jokes" [237]). Yet he is at pains to convey that "the people who rule the world" do not have solid ideas of its direction: "I have been thinking that for thirty or forty years, thinking that they don't know what they are doing, where they are going. But to hear them say it is a matter, I think, of importance. If any of you have different ideas, please remember that although you may think that things are going well enough, know that those who are in charge of the world don't think so, and that is very important" (237–238).

James prefaces his discussion of Pan-Africanism with a serial reading of a few of the authors' works for both thematic and stylistic reasons. In order to discuss his topic productively, he first has to place it in context, to establish what he calls "the kind of attitude we should have in thinking about such a subject [the Pan-African Congress] at this time." He follows the same approach in a talk about the life and times of his friend and late collaborator George Padmore, when he says, "I want to talk about George Padmore, and I am going to begin by talking about our early life in the Caribbean" (1984c, 251). Stylistically, it is typical of James to open with a preface, usually of quotations from an author or a set of seemingly dissimilar authors. We see examples of this in his deployment of Fyodor Dostoevsky and Aimé Césaire at the beginning of *Nkrumah and the Ghana Revolution* (1977a, 18–25) and of Alexis de Tocqueville and Walt Whitman in *American Civilization* (1993, 43–45, 58–66). And such quotation is not limited to beginnings; James almost always closes with similar quotations. The concluding chapters of *Nkrumah and the Ghana Revolution* feature extensive passages from the writings of Vladimir Lenin and Julius Nyerere, while "Toward the Seventh" ends with extracts from George Lamming's *Seasons of Adventure* and *Natives of My Person*. However, his quotation is condensed in "Toward the Seventh," and Timothy Brennan, in *At Home in the World*, described this Jamesian style as "simplicity," that is, an "extemporaneous discussion, matched up with extensive quotations from popular magazines and books, [an approach] likely to be echoed by contemporary combative multiculturalism" (Brennan 1997, 226).

The approach begins with a prolegomenon, an outline reviewing the context of the subject at hand, followed by a brief critique. Then the subject itself is presented, but only after James has offered a steady view of the historical paths taken to bring the subject about. This part is presented very differently from the prolegomenon. Then, as the subject proper is developed and discussed, into it are mixed aspects of the outline, in a process that can be described as dialectical. In the passage from *Beyond a Boundary* quoted earlier, in which he outlines his planned series of books, James describes the thematic dimension of his method; in *Notes on Dialectics* he outlines its stylistic dimension:

> You are sure of the end only when you can trace the thing stage by stage, the dialectical development accounting for all the major historical facts. Sometimes you can work backwards . . . Over and over again I have to look for an important missing link or links. If I cannot find them, I have to give up the theses and find another. If you read how Marx wrote *Capital* you will see he wrote it, a

draft, then reorganized that. He was searching for the logical movement which embraced all the facts. (1980, 204)

Contextualizing the Pan-African movement within a critique of the liberal historical imagination in the West turns out to be a dialectical procedure. Of course, James has already made a joke of Clark's broadside attack on Marxism ("that's why they don't know where they are going, because marxism [sic] has not told them" [James 1984b, 237]). But he also wishes to situate the 1900 convening of the first Pan-African Congress in London, by Sylvester Williams, in relation to similar events all over the world: "There were also many 'Pan' things beginning. There was Pan-Slavism and Pan-Arabism and so on . . . people were dissatisfied with the existing structure and the development of society, and they were searching for new roads and new ways" (238). In this context, the attempts at soul-searching that Wells and his successors embarked on after 1918 seem like complacent acts of navel-gazing which fail to take account of the world outside of Western Europe and North America.

James immediately presents his readers with a steady view of both an idea and its context. Williams's pioneering effort, and its three or four successor congresses convened by W. E. B. Du Bois between 1918 and 1929, have to be seen in relation to changes in the general social structure of the world, the age of high imperialism, and the emergent discourses of race, class, and nationalism.[4] This contextualization coincides with what one may term the Jamesian narrative of socialist internationalism, that is, the idea that there are coherent and active relationships among the twentieth-century revolutions (Russian, Indian, Chinese, Ghanaian) which undermined capitalist control of the world's productive forces. It also provides a broadly political complement to Stuart Hall's analysis of the five great decenterings that I discussed in the introduction, and to the Gandhi-King-Mandela complex developed in Arundhati Roy's work, to be discussed in chapter 6. The Fifth Pan-African Congress, held in 1945 in Manchester, remains the watershed of the Pan-African idea, when the different strands, generations, and tendencies of the black world met to confront the colonial situation on the continent in the immediate aftermath of the Second World War. It could not have succeeded without the earlier conferences organized by Du Bois. However, James writes,

> those conferences were not successful. For the most part they were conferences of people who were interested: intellectuals, people in the liberal spheres of society, and other people who were concerned with the development of civilization. There were some people from various parts, but only a few people from Africa. All were essentially people who were viewing the African question from an intellectual point of view . . . they were calling on well-meaning people, intellectual people in sympathy with the Blacks, to help form an organization of superior people who would lead the Black people out of the difficulties in which they were. (239–240)

Yet the 1945 conference was built on the foundation laid in the decade before the Great Depression, which "showed that the economic system by which [Western civilization] lived could not be controlled" (240). According to James, this was one of the two main reasons that Du Bois could not continue to organize the conferences. The other reason was the emergence of the great communist organizer Malcolm Nurse, better known as George Padmore. Although James is careful not to depict the young communist as superseding the then-liberal Du Bois, he comes close to doing so when he critiques the domination of the previous conferences by "people who were viewing the African question from an intellectual [and liberal political] point of view" (239). Padmore was not just a communist organizer, he had also established himself as a leader of the Communist International, heading the Negro department at the Kremlin. The significance of the 1945 Pan-African Congress, as James presents it, lies in the roles it played in two events: the consolidation of the struggles against European colonialism on the African continent and elsewhere, and James's rejection of Trotskyist Marxism. The two events are related, and I will get to the heart of both by discussing the second one first.

Up until his visit to the United States in October 1938, James was an avowed Trotskyite. His classic history of the Haitian revolution, *The Black Jacobins* (1963; originally published in 1938), was written in the true Trotskyite mode, internationalizing the proletarian revolution. Its theoretical premise was that the pre–Second World War revolutionary ferment in Europe would spur anti-colonial consciousness in Africa, Asia, and the Caribbean, in the same way that the revolution in France had served as a beacon for the one in San Domingo in the late eighteenth century. Despite this perspective, which differed sharply from the (Stalinist) focus on "socialism in one country," he was able to work within the nationalist paradigm dominant in the International African Service Bureau, founded by Padmore after the latter broke with the Kremlin over the colonial question. According to James's account in several places,[5] it was Padmore's departure from the Communist Party that jump-started activism in England on behalf of the African colonies, whether French, British, or Belgian. This unified activist front did not have to take into account the peculiarities of the national culture and economy of each colonizing power, the colonial phase of imperialism having been understood on a broadly conceptual level.

But his own departure for the United States led James to an intense involvement in the country's Socialist Workers Party, and also in both theoretical and practical work on the "Negro question." A West Indian intellectual with an English education, James was a black man in the United States, and this fact would greatly affect his work over the next fifteen years. Its personal effects were both positive and negative from the beginning (Grimshaw 1996). Traveling by road to the West Coast, James felt liberated by the physical expansiveness of the country. But returning from his historic meeting with Leon Trotsky in Mexico, he found the American color code a frustrating mystery in New Orleans (McLemee 1996, xv, xxi–xxii). It was James's involvements with Negro workers in the Midwest and in the South, his immersions in the media cultures of the magnificent mass society that was the United States, and the coalescence of these two engagements in the gradual elaboration of a Marxist tendency autonomous from orthodox Trotskyism (the famous Johnson-Forest tendency), that impelled him toward the resolution of his 1940 crisis. In fact, the "more than ten years" that it took him to get his "feet on solid ground" were precisely the years he spent on these projects: thinking and writing about the condition of black workers in the United States, organizing to improve it, working out a materialist perspective that eschewed the "democratic centralism" of Trotskyist Marxism, and reflecting on the political implications of Hollywood movies, comic strips, and radio dramas. The articles, essays, committee reports, and book-length manuscripts that resulted from his labor occupy the "shadow" that McLemee, in his introduction (1996) to the monograph on the Negro question, identifies as falling between the writing of the two classics *The Black Jacobins* and *Beyond a Boundary* (first published in 1938 and 1963 respectively).

The context of these revisions of traditional Marxism was the series of ideological battles between the Socialist Workers Party, the Workers Party that James and a few others subsequently founded, and the much smaller Johnson-Forest faction within that party. Both McLemee (1996, xxiv–xxix) and Bougues (1997, 49–75) provide thrilling accounts of the drama of James presenting his positions on party questions to members of various factions, some of whom accepted his interpretations and, hence, his leadership, becoming his apostles. The implications of this drama go beyond political infighting, as should be expected. Reassessing Marxist theory meant redirecting political power from Stalinist bureaucracy, which he identified as a feature of U.S. labor unions, and seeing the conditions of women, the youth, and "colonial" workers (black and proletarian) as fundamental to socialist politics in the aftermath of the war. These emphases manifest themselves strongly in his elaboration of a new Pan-Africanism in the 1976 essay.

Considering the intellectual atmosphere that preceded the 1945 conference in Manchester from this new perspective, James writes, "we were all waiting for the crisis of World War II which everybody saw coming, and we expected the revolution to break out during or at the end of the war, in the same way that it had broken out in Europe during World War I. But 1945 came and the revolution had not taken place" (1984b, 242). This failed expectation and the unexpected opportunity offered by the presence of African politicians at a conference in Paris crystallized in the 1945 congress. This congress is the watershed event in the history of Pan-Africanism, and it is against its achievements that subsequent congresses have been measured. However, what is more important here is how the conference influenced James's revision of his position on the

Marxist theory of revolution. Before I come to that revision, which he elaborated in *Nkrumah and the Ghana Revolution,* a few words are in order about the importance of the Fifth Congress of the Pan-African movement.

As I noted earlier, James's prospectus for the Seventh Pan-African Congress arises out of the need to shift the movement's concerns away from the purely governmental protocols and procedures which had marred the sixth congress, held in Tanzania in 1974. The fifth congress had been successful in the politically volatile atmosphere following the end of the Second World War, when decolonization was no longer merely an idea on the horizon. The presence at that congress of African politicians like Kwame Nkrumah, Nnamdi Azikiwe, and Jomo Kenyatta was historic, as was Padmore's decisive role in mentoring them or bringing them together. When he speaks of the revision of Marxist theory in relation to this congress, James indicates that he was involved with it. This seems implausible, since he is believed to have remained in the United States for fifteen years (1938–1953). According to Carol Polsgrove in her recent illuminating history of the circle around Padmore, "James had stepped out of the circle concerning itself with African independence when he moved to the United States. Although Padmore sent him documents from time to time, he had not been present at the pivotal Manchester Congress" (Polsgrove 2009, 156). It seems likely that James means that he was involved in a theoretical sense, that is, because he shared the general understanding of what Pan-African revolt entailed. Even so, Polsgrove argues that James's account in *Nkrumah and the Ghana Revolution* "reflects only a vague grasp of the organizational changes the England-based movement passed through in the early postwar years" (156). James claims that the "famous congress in 1945 did not have many people around it, not many people who knew what they were doing" (James 1984b, 245). The problem was no longer that sympathetic Western liberal intellectuals were trying to help Africans, as it had been in the series of conferences organized by Du Bois in the 1920s. At the fifth congress, there was "a body of people with advanced ideas," but still there was no "great mass of the population following us" (245). Nkrumah would return to the Gold Coast in two years; although the National Council of Nigeria and the Cameroons was established in 1944 by Nnamdi Azikiwe, until 1950 it functioned mainly as a body of agitators in active solidarity rather than as a political party. Jomo Kenyatta was similarly involved in political activities in Kenya.

This was the basis of "The Call," which James and others sent out in anticipation of the sixth congress. In it, they spoke of "not only the Sixth Pan-African Congress but all sorts of groups . . . all sorts of groups in every part of the world—in many parts of Africa, in the United States, right through the Caribbean . . . taking in hand and having in mind where we are going and what we are going to do" (245). Since this was more than a decade into the post-independence period, "The Call" was motivated by the recognition that the burgeoning gap between the vast populations and government leaders ought to be bridged. James was centrally involved in raising awareness of and organizing for the sixth congress, traveling to different parts of the continent, the Caribbean, and the United States. Driven in part perhaps by his enthusiasm for the progress that the conference's principal host, President Nyerere, had made in the socialist transformation of Tanzania, which he saw as the counterpoint to the degeneration of the revolution in Ghana, James took on the task of seeking participants.

> To prepare for the congress, I went around . . . I went to Nigeria, I went to
> Ghana, I went to somewhere else in Africa—I can't remember. I went to the
> Caribbean twice, I went to Guyana, I went to Trinidad, I went to Jamaica twice.
> I traveled all over the United States . . . I would have eight or ten meetings over
> the weekend between Sacramento, Los Angeles and San Francisco. (245)

When the congress was held, Nyerere strikingly, but paradoxically, shifted its focus toward global economic relations, and away from the racial concerns that seemed to limit the movement's appeal to black American nationalism. This move was striking because it deemphasized race in the constitution of Pan-Africanism and instead emphasized class, much like today's postcolonial trajectories of transnational social justice. The paradox lay in the fact that this gesture was already compromised by the congress's domination by politicians and national governments, which were more interested in maintaining political power than in promoting genuine social transformation either locally or in the world at large. Not all of these governments were as sanguine as Nyerere's about the ideological underpinnings of economic relations. When it emerged that some delegates from the Caribbean would not be allowed to attend unless they had the backing of their countries' government, James declined his own special invitation to attend (Hill-Rubin 1993).[6] His trenchant denial of a central role for the "national state" and for the bourgeoisie in "Toward the Seventh" has its roots in that missed opportunity, that is, in giving the Pan-African ideal over to politicians. Thus, the fifth still remained the most important landmark; there, specific ideas were advanced, "and advanced ideas they were" (245). What, then, does this event, the fifth congress, have to do with the revision of Marxist theory of revolution?

The development of "positive action" during the revolution in the Gold Coast provides James with an opportunity to analyze this revision. The Marxist (Trotskyist) theory of permanent revolution did not distinguish between the anticolonial struggle (such as was underway in African countries, Asia, the Middle East, and the West Indies) and the metropolitan struggle, the revolutionary ferment in European capitals. This was the theory on whose basis the Trotskyites expected revolutions to break out at the end of the war. It was the standpoint from which James had written *The Black Jacobins* at the end of the 1930s, hoping that the anti-colonial forces in the colonies would be inspired by the European anti-fascist movements, in much the same manner as the slogans of the French revolution had helped to urge the slaves in San Domingo into a successful revolution (James 1977a, 65–66). Classical formulations of this theory hold armed rebellion to be necessary to achieving political power, and political vanguards necessary to consolidating it. When James writes that "in time I was to learn that that trotskytes [*sic*] also saw revolutionary politics as the giving of leadership to masses who were otherwise helpless without it" (68), he is establishing a theoretical link between his in-depth critiques of Stalinist bureaucracy and championing of American Negroes on the one hand, and on the other hand, the attitude of the members of the International African Service Bureau (James included) toward the political developments in African colonies.

This is what the revision of Marxist theory entails—an unstinting critique of the bureaucratization of socialism in Stalinist Russia (a criticism already advanced in 1950's *State Capitalism and World Revolution*, which James co-authored with Raya Dunayevskaya and Grace Lee Boggs) amid abundant signs in the mid-1940s that other communist and Trotskyist parties, including those in the West, would follow that path. It also entails a realistic appraisal of the revolutionary potentials of the various African colonial populations, their capacities to plan and execute successful revolutions against the military and economic might of the colonial system. This is not to say that by 1945, James had abandoned the premise that the colonial and metropolitan struggles were intertwined. A good indication of his abiding conviction in this regard can be found in his essay on the significance of the British Labor Party's 1945 electoral victory (James 1977c, 106–118). Likewise, his analysis of Nkrumah's personalization of the party (James 1977a, 174) is, in effect, an elaboration of Trotsky's idea of "substitutionism."

The revision was not an event; it did not fall like a torrential rain once upon a war-weary night in 1945. It was, rather, a process that took "more than ten years" and produced several books on different subjects, yet thematically unified by their concern with human culture. James elaborated his ideas gradually, working them out in the context of the relationships among classical notions of dialectical materialism (from Hegel through Marx to Lenin), conditions in socialist circles in the United States and in the lives of black laborers, such social formations as mass culture, and the position and aspirations of women and the young. As a matter of fact, judging by the series of factions which he supported in the United States in the 1940s, James seems to have continued a pattern of political behavior he followed within British progressive circles in the mid-1930s.

Some of his books were written for party members and small groups who shared an ideological "tendency" (*Notes on Dialectics, C. L. R. James on "The Negro Question,"* and *State Capitalism and World Revolution*); they were written to be "read on a Sunday or on two evenings" (*American Civilization*, 38). Others patiently analyzed cultural and political types that emerged in the nineteenth century to influence the twentieth (*Beyond a Boundary* and *Mariners, Rene-*

gades, and Castaways). Still others plumbed the same subject over and over, long after its extraordinary impact had been felt (*Nkrumah and the Ghana Revolution* and *At the Rendezvous of Victory*). In these different writings we see James working out integration by actively perceiving people engaged in a particular kind of activity at a particular time, seeing them in relation to people in other places but doing similar things at the same historical time. The year 1945 was decisive because, on the occasion of the Fifth Pan-African Congress in Manchester, an unprecedented alliance emerged between nationalist revolutionaries from the African colonies and intellectuals of African descent with broad practical and theoretical experience of revolutionary politics. And it was the end of the war; much of Europe was in ruins. In his assessment of the process coalescing around the fifth congress in relation to the activism over which Padmore presided in London, James repeatedly notes that the impact of what happened in 1945 became clear only in retrospect: "It took the revolution in the Gold Coast to make possible a true evaluation of the policy elaborated in 1945 . . . What is written here does not embrace all that is involved and it is certain that it could not have been written at the time nor was there any need to do so" (1977a, 74).

Tricontinentalist, Cosmopolitan

A detour is in order here to situate James's critique of Pan-Africanism within a historical context that will establish its relationships to two ideas crucial to this book—cosmopolitanism and tricontinentalism. This book takes the position that to focus on a specific historical community (like the African continent) is not to engage in an act of exclusion or navel-gazing, although the continent is important enough to warrant any number of particular attentions and has continued to receive them. Rather, such a focus takes a full measure of the community in time, assessing its constitution in relation to economic and political developments that do not discriminate, or that do discriminate on the basis of indiscriminate positioning of spaces of profit, as the current structure of corporate globalization has shown. The Pan-African movement developed in the context of worldwide historical inequality, and though it is often seen in racial terms, it is more than a racial-cultural movement. Its contributions to twentieth-century progressive political discourse ought to be of as much use to those on whose behalf the movement was shaped as to those who encounter it as a transnational movement. Indeed, putting the international dimension of Pan-Africanism in perspective by developing in detail the relationships between tricontinentalism and cosmopolitanism also shows that the two processes are closer than they seem. James's simultaneous interest in activism and individual artistic consciousness suggests not only that the two formations are compatible, but that they may be working toward the same goals.

Although the idea of tricontinentalism became more pronounced in the cultural and political alliances forged in opposition to Western imperialism in the second half of the twentieth century, its origins, like those of Pan-Africanism, date back to the years between the two world wars.[7] It was in the aftermath of the Second World War, when the hold of European powers on their colonies began to slacken in complex ways, that new nations began to emerge and new political systems began to be clearly defined. One landmark event of decolonization was the Bandung Conference of April 1955, which brought African and Asian countries together in the Indonesian city of Bandung to signal the transformation of world political and cultural relations. But this conference existed in relation to the Non-Aligned Movement, which had originated almost a decade earlier, following Josip Boraz Tito's break with Josef Stalin in 1948.[8] While the Bandung meeting brought together political and governmental leaders primarily from Africa and Asia, the Non-Aligned Movement was tricontinental, because it occurred in the context of political tensions between the USSR and Yugoslavia and so was more than an occasion for cultural self-assertion.

The Non-Aligned Movement also included some of the socialist and communist countries of Latin America, following the emergence of Cuba under Fidel Castro, who came to power four years after Bandung and became a notable force in the struggle against imperialism. In *Postcolonialism: An Historical Introduction,* the critic Robert Young writes that the concept of tricontinentalism in postcolonial thought was inspired by the first conference of decolonized countries in Havana in 1966, eleven years after the Bandung conference (Young 2000, 6). Thus, while the Non-Aligned Movement was a governmental forum for countries opting out of the two camps (East and West) engaged in the Cold War, the Bandung Conference, no less governmental, was a decolonization-inspired effort to assert the historical and cultural dignity of colonial peoples of the world. The Non-Aligned Movement was meant to last as long as the Cold War, while the Bandung Conference was an ad hoc affair, but its principles would develop further in the context of global anti-imperialism. Common to both the Non-Aligned Movement and the Bandung Conference, however, was the notion of tricontinentalism, a more politically realistic way of thinking of the sociohistorical idea of the Third World. Tricontinentalism complicated the "positive neutrality" of nonalignment (Cuba was an ally of the Soviet Union and China) and broadened the anti-colonialism of Bandung (which, narrowly defined, excluded someone like Tito).

This concept, tricontinentalism, is one of the most important and profound social changes in the modern era. It enabled the emergence of the forms of cultural and political engagement identified in the works of the authors considered in this book. The different streams of twentieth-century postcolonial thought, seen in the work of figures as widely varied as W. E. B. Du Bois, Ho Chi Minh, Alice Walker, Mahasweta Devi, Pramoedya Ananta Toer, and Walter Rodney, constitute a rich and diverse intellectual history, at once political, cultural, and artistic.[9] Young writes further,

The "post" of postcolonialism, or postcolonial critique, marks the historical moment of the theorized introduction of new tricontinental forms and strategies
of critical analysis and practice. Unlike the words "colonialism," "imperialism"
and "neocolonialism," which adopt only a critical relation to the oppressive re-
gimes and practices that they delineate, postcolonialism is both contestatory
and committed towards political ideals of a transnational social justice. (2000,
57–58)

The idea of tricontinentalism which I outline here, and which is implicit in
Young's discussion, has to be clarified in one important respect. In "The African Crisis," a highly illuminating essay about Africa's socioeconomic and demographic relationship to East Asia, South Asia, and South America in the post–
structural adjustment years, Giovanni Arrighi has called the ideological premise
of the category of "Third World" into serious question (Arrighi 2002). Arrighi
argues that the economic doctrine of the early 1980s, the Washington Consensus, allowed some regions, including East Asia, to take advantage of greater
capital flow from North America than was available to others, such as Africa
and South America, leading to the "bifurcation in the fortunes of Third World
regions" (22–24). In this way, China and India, whose loyalties had, like those of
many African and Caribbean countries, lain with economic and political tricontinentalism, have, especially early in the twenty-first century, become economically formidable enough to constitute a different kind of imperial bloc in relation to the African continent. Although this must be borne in mind, the gains
of tricontinentalism can be recuperated by attending to two things. The first is
the intellectual capital that figures such as James sought to draw from their experiences as diasporic activists, claiming on the basis of class (and race) that
they could speak on behalf of the African peoples. This was the basis on which
Nyerere, convening the Sixth Pan-African Congress, argued for reorienting the
movement away from strictly racial concerns. The second is the fact that the bifurcation of the fortunes of the Third World manifests itself also as fragmentation,
a generalized inequality in the wake of globalization, as Arundhati Roy's political writing powerfully shows. India may receive more foreign capital than do
Nigeria and other sub-Saharan African countries, but this has not improved the
lives of all Indian citizens, whether rural or urban, Hindu, Muslim, or Adivasi.

The ideals of transnational social justice to which Young refers signify the
several developments in which James, as a writer and political activist, is crucial. Governmental structures and individuals associated with state power were
dominant in the different political groups which emerged to articulate the ideas
of tricontinentalism. As I have demonstrated in the introduction and earlier in
this chapter, the more progressive of these politicians, like Nkrumah, rose in
part through the political patronage of diasporic intellectuals—James, George
Padmore, and Horace Mann Bond in the United States (Bond 1956). But the
intellectuals contributed much more to decolonization than ways to capture

state power; indeed, they considered a desire for state power on the model of bourgeois liberal democracy a betrayal of anti-colonialism (see Ahmad 1992, 28). It is their principled opposition to this betrayal which pits most progressive intellectuals of the "Third World" against their respective governments, and which, in the context of postcolonial nationalism, is recast as suspicion of the nation. But there is a significant difference between the two impulses, which are exemplified by the figures of Achebe on the one hand and Rushdie on the other.[10] The significant point is that most expatriated postcolonial intellectuals are perceived to follow the second impulse—to distrust the nation—and the concept of cosmopolitanism is often articulated through such distrust.

The literature on cosmopolitanism is extensive and growing. From the Greek philosophical tradition of Stoicism, through the late-modern use of the term by Immanuel Kant, to its more contemporary deployments in scholarly writings, definitions of cosmopolitanism have tended to emphasize an abstract category ("the citizen of the world"), and to equate global citizenship with declining political obligations or loyalties, especially when these are tied to supposedly national or "ethnonational" currents.[11] These more dominant variants are usually identified, in Timothy Brennan's politically weighty phrase, with "GATT poetics" (Brennan 1997, 192) or with Bruce Robbins's "view from above" (Robbins 1999, 3), and in them the predominance of Euro-American, market-driven mobility normalizes the transnational image of global citizenship as the nemesis of "bad nationalism." It is these variants which Pheng Cheah, in his essay "Given Culture" (in the volume he coedited with Robbins), identifies in the approving stances of the critics James Clifford and Homi Bhabha, in whose work "globalization is reduced to cultural hybridization in transnational mobility and transnational migrant cultures are characterized as existing radical cosmopolitanisms that subvert national culture (Bhabha) or localism (Clifford)" (Cheah 1998b, 297).[12] Given the way discussions of these formations of cosmopolitanism are framed, they seem to have very little to do with the ideals of transnational social justice which provide the historical context for tricontinentalism. In fact, Robbins distinguishes between internationalism (the term he prefers, because of its political implications) and cosmopolitanism by arguing that the first is collective and stands for political engagement, while the second is individual and deeply invested in aesthetic spectatorship (Robbins 1999, 17). For Robbins, political action is the basis for distinguishing internationalism from cosmopolitanism. But as James's example shows, and as we shall see in greater detail in chapter 5 when I discuss political identification in the work of Caryl Phillips (of whom James is a forerunner), the idea that political action is the crucial marker of internationalism ignores the potential that aesthetics has when it is politically constitutive. The hybrid word "cosmopolitical," coined by Cheah and Robbins, is aimed at bridging this gap.

In his reading of *American Civilization,* Brennan argues, in his book on cosmopolitanism, that James wanted to become a popular (that is, commercially successful) author (Brennan 1997, 227). When James writes as a Marxist, says Brennan, he does so in a classical mode, and his thoughts on African independence and the role of slavery in the development of capitalism are all elaborations of his classical Marxism (230). James's involvement with the United States during those years thus points to the problems of cultural translation—he is aware that the country is a centralized power, and he is striving "to be professionally acceptable and honorably dissident at the same time" (234). The picture of James that emerges from Brennan's analysis is that of an ambitious writer, whose works before his arrival in the United States were a rehearsal for his hoped-for appearance on the best-seller list. Brennan depicts him as less interested in anti-colonial struggle, and as relating to U.S. blacks less on the basis of race than of class. Works such as *C. L. R. James on "The Negro Question"* (1996a) and *Nkrumah and the Ghana Revolution* (1977a) have certainly put to question Brennan's implicit suggestion that James is less anti-colonial than Frantz Fanon (Brennan 1997, 233) in relation to U.S. blacks. But there is validity to the argument that for James, race is secondary to class, and that it is through his integration of the question of class in the United States with anti-colonial struggle in Africa and latent nationalism in the Caribbean that his credentials as a cosmopolitan are most assured. Integration, for him, represents the meeting of artistic integrity and mass audience appeal, and he identifies this meeting in such forms as the comic strip, the radio drama, and the Hollywood film. He enthusiastically consumes these forms, seeing them as indicators of class politics in the wartime and postwar United States. He contemplates the revolutionary impulses in the frescoes of Michelangelo, the Olympian statues, and the etchings of Picasso in a single essay, insisting that they are all related aspects of human culture (James 1977b).

James's politically committed cosmopolitanism is visible as much in these intellectual and artistic interests as in his personal enjoyments—his frictionless friendships with the anti-communist Wright and the communist Padmore, his blithe remark that his aversion to certain books and authors is "a matter of taste," and his abiding interest in dialogues and "conversations," as evidenced in most of his essays. Grant Farred has conceptualized this aspect of James's intellectual interests as his "marginality," a distinct self-positioning outside both the hegemonic and the resistant cultures that ultimately aims to transform both (Farred 2003, 112). Derek Walcott elegantly sums James up as "proletarian in politics, patrician in taste" (1998, 118). Cosmopolitanism may have taken exile's place as the principal category under which the situations of expatriated intellectuals are discussed, just as globalization and postcoloniality have displaced the concept of the Third World, but the question of individual choice that is implicit in James's attitude toward his political or artistic contexts takes us right into the heart of what makes cosmopolitanism such a serviceable concept under neoliberal globalization. Familiarity with sociocultural nuances or gestures is said to be a defining feature of cosmopolitanism, which is the ability to move between cultures, apropos Kwame Appiah's characterization of Richard Burton (2006, 1–8), and James displays this ability by being committed to culture without denying the need to question the constitution of the category. This commitment is much in evidence in his discussion of Pan-Africanism, to which I now return.

"Toward the Seventh" is a succinct, extensively historicized account of the Pan-African movement. In it, James recalls what he said and did as the theoretician of the Sixth Pan-African Congress, responding to the limitations of the fifth. It is at once about the past, the present, and the future, but the relationship between the three is a necessary function of the dialectic that such a review necessitates. The gaze of the essay is trained on the prospects for the future: what the seventh should achieve. Just as James does not wish to dwell on the misadventures of the liberal intellectual culture (of H. G. Wells and others) prior to the Second World War, he also refrains from hashing over the shortcomings of the sixth congress. He is concerned with "definite programs and policies," which, he says, are not difficult to put across (James 1984b, 246). Executing these programs would require, as I enumerated above, going beyond the idea of the nation-state as the basis of political action on the continent, undermining the bourgeois and elitist tendencies that have become dominant in social and political relations, and developing the capacities of women, youth, and the poor.

To counter the national segmentation of political and economic relations, he proposes a type of regionalization, dividing the continent into four federated units. These units can then "integrate their economic development unimpeded by the old, outworn economic shibboleths, such as free enterprise" (247).[13] At this time (the mid-1970s), James takes an international and historical view of the nation-state. The idea of the "national state" that began with both the American and the French Revolution was, he says, a failure in the twentieth century. The process of disintegration was set in motion by the "bourgeoisie themselves" (246), and it can be seen as much in the break-up of Germany as in the division of Korea and Vietnam into north and south parts, each of which was then claimed by a bloc of the Cold War. Taking this historical view allows him to go beyond the particular context of each country's division. Thus he relates the break-up of countries like Germany and Korea to the brutal civil war in Nigeria, ignoring the immediate political causes of the war: "They would have divided Nigeria if they had the chance, but the people said not a bit of it and they finished up with Ojukwu" (246).[14] By relating the failure of the nation-state as a unit of political association to the prospects for the Pan-African movement, James is doing two related things: historicizing the movement as a phenomenon which shares time and space with other similar movements ("there were also many 'Pan' things beginning" [238]), and commending the rich heritage of that phenomenon as worthy of emulation not only by Africans, but by other people in other parts of the world.

James's words on this point are unambiguous: "In a new conference we must speak about the shape that the world is taking before our eyes, and we put forward for Africa and people of African descent the new ideas: the abolition of the national state as a political entity—that's number one" (247). James goes on to list and discuss two other ideas. His position on the status of the elite in this essay is closely related to this proposition for the abolition of the nation-state. Indeed, the question of leadership in the postcolony, and especially on the African continent, had long been debated. Frantz Fanon's famous critique of the misadventures of "national consciousness" addresses the same questions with the withering sarcasm appropriate for an object of contempt (Fanon 1963). Fanon's critique well suits the attitude currently dominant in postcolonial studies. James devotes a substantial amount of space to the subject in the second part of his study of the Ghana revolution. When James's view of the postcolonial bourgeoisies is placed in the context of his analysis of the aftermath of the Gold Coast revolutionary experiment, the position of the bourgeoisies is seen to be determined not by psychological factors (Nkrumah's failure was not due simply to his personal failings), but largely by the problems of socialist transformation in an age of multinational capital.

However, reviewing the Pan-African movement several years after the fall of Nkrumah, James adopts a less objective view of this class. He has come to regard the economic and political elite as fit only for destruction. The elite achieve their position at the expense of the majority of the poor, James argues. The extent of the gap between them is demonstrated by the vast disparity between the city and the countryside, a disparity which James sees in any number of African countries. He writes,

> You go to an African country, you go to the capital. There is a fine hospital, there is the church, there are two or three banks and so on. Take a motor car or walk five miles away from that center where Western civilization is flourishing and you will find people living as their ancestors lived five hundred years ago. (247)

The fault is not in the peasantry but in the postcolonial elite, which has adopted the ways and ideals of the West at the expense of the poor, and without a sound economic basis for that adoption. James draws on the experiences of countries like Cuba and Vietnam, which, he says, have undermined most theories of the evolutionary growth of peasant populations. Those theories held that it would take the poor of the nonindustrial countries one hundred years to advance to the level of their counterparts in modern societies. However, all available evidence of the revolutionary potential of the African poor (indeed the poor everywhere—James gives the example of Carolina Maria de Jesus, a barely literate author from Brazil) shows that all they need is the opportunity to develop (248). According to James's analysis, the elite systematically withhold such opportunities.

In case this begins to sound unduly romantic, it is necessary to reflect on the dimension that James brings to the analysis. He builds into the idea of the empowerment of the poor his earlier studies of the class dimension of the role of women, laborers, and youth. (This dimension characterized the Johnson-Forest tendency's critique of orthodox Trotskyism in the United States in the early 1940s.) He also poses the question of the destruction of the elite in a way that further confirms his integrative method. The destruction of the elite translates into the development of the masses. He does not say that you finish with one and then move on to the other. He says that to achieve the one is implicitly to achieve the other. But in order to show what is at stake in each case, he thinks of them first separately, since the elite have existed thus far at the expense of the masses. When critics such as Fanon speak of the parasitism of the bourgeoisie, their metaphor is based on the fact that the laboring populations are the source of wealth and social productivity. The relationship between the two groups means that the second and third objectives James envisions for progressive Pan-Africanism are closely linked.

In a remarkable conclusion, James cogently demonstrates these relationships of class and gender by analyzing passages from two novels by George Lamming, a rhetorical move that echoes his opening references to the works of Wells and Clark, resulting in a perfect closing arc. The novels are *Season of Adventure* and *Natives of My Person,* and in each case, James asks specifically what is required of the intellectual elite (248–249). In the first book, the intellectual elites, having risen at the cost of the abjection of those without their opportunities, must now assume responsibility for what happens to others. In the second, it is women, the stay-at-home wives of slavers, who, by their fastidiousness, impress upon their husbands what is missing from their moral make-ups. Thus, just as the elites of a developing country impede social progress by their parasitism on the poor, James argues, men such as those whom the women go to welcome in the final pages of Lamming's *Natives of My Person* constitute an elite in relation to the women (250). Reversing this relationship has to be seen as a political goal.

At the core of this discussion of the status of Pan-Africanism, then, is the condensation of the two main impulses in James's writing, as I argued earlier. These impulses are: taking a steady view of the whole world, and aligning the wishes of the one (the leader, the actor) and those of the many (the people or the audience). There is also a minor third, to conceive of social relationships and democracy through the Aristotelian idea of drama. What is central to all three is integration, a concept which, although aligning diverse energies might be expected to result in stasis, is, in fact, quite active. If "Toward the Seventh" exemplifies James's abiding interest in developing a postcolonial political program through the instrumentality of the Pan-African movement, it is in *American Civilization* that he tests its impact in the cultural realm. James analyzes the impact of mass forms on the American population in relation to the concretization of the ideals of freedom and individuality, contextualizing the notion of the pursuit of happiness in the writings of Alexis de Tocqueville, Whitman, and Melville. The popularity of Hollywood's thrillers and gangster films, as well as of comic strips and radio serials, he argues, was a response to the distance between how the masses were instructed to live and how they really did. During the Depression, the tension between these was reinforced by the structural imbalance in society engendered by the troubled economy. But these feelings were still represented relatively stably in popular forms, especially during the war, when blood was shed on a large scale:

> The Depression obviously marks a turning point. There was an interlude during the war, precisely during that period of actual shedding of seas of blood: violence, gangsterism of the type described disappeared. But with the end of the war, blood, violence and crime have achieved heights undreamt of in 1931. (James 1993, 130)

But James's aesthetic model, as well as his conception of the social role of the popular forms, is Aristotelian, which is interesting given that Bekolo's deployment of mimesis in *Aristotle's Plot* (discussed in chapter 4) already suggests the political stance of multifocality. His analysis of the means by which the popular forms generated the pursuit of freedom turns on the supposition that a story on film gave "to many millions a sense of active living, and in the bloodshed, the violence, the freedom from restraint to allow pent-up feelings free play, they have released the bitterness, hate, fear and sadism which simmer below the surface" (James 1993, 127). By seeing the mass forms as the bridge between the cultural tradition and popular audiences, James sees the audience of any art form as the whole population. In his view, the best model for this mass audience is classical Greek drama. Aeschylus, Sophocles, and Aristophanes played to the entire free population of Athens. This population saw the plays and awarded a prize to the best. The major difference between Athenian drama and the Hollywood products of the late 1940s was that the "Greek masses went to the theater as if they were going to the World Series, Independence Day and a film festival all combined" (149–150). This commensurability between the spiritual and intellectual life of the people and the means of artistic expression democratized free expression, in a way that the modern society of the postwar period had no choice but to embrace.

It is interesting that James, without rejecting the Aristotelian conception of tragedy, arrives at very much the same conclusions as the most influential anti-Aristotelians of the twentieth century, such as Bertolt Brecht and Augusto Boal. After all, he shares with them a materialist view of historical processes, as well as a conception (if differently formulated) of social forms as amenable to didacticism.[15] For James, an experience is understood, either as a political system or as a cultural activity, not so much by asserting difference as by exploring "the broader context [in] which social and historical forces become refracted through a particular creative personality" (Grimshaw 1991, 35). One such creative personality was Aeschylus, who "created practically single-handed the Athenian drama" (James 1993, 153); Herman Melville was another, as can be seen in *Moby Dick;* yet another was Charlie Chaplin. It must be stressed that James also conceives of this figure as a political personality.[16] The creative personality's ability to double as a political personality is crucial to James's understanding of the factors framing the relationship between a work of art and its audience, and it can clarify my discussion of genre in the context of tricontinentalism and cosmopolitanism.

The Aesthetics of Tricontinentalism

It is noteworthy that James develops these ideas during a long period of exile (or expatriation, for my present purposes), and that his objectives are political in nature. Toward the end of the introduction, I framed expatriation and commodified branding as the routes that postcolonial writers and artists take to either address or sidestep themes of national belonging. The scholar Ambroise Kom similarly argues that expatriation is decisive in the careers of writers such as Ben Okri and Calixthe Beyala, and that their location in Western capitals creates different audiences for them. Something fundamental happens to the writings of Okri once his primary audience is figured as domiciled in the West, even if he continues to be classified as a Nigerian-born British writer and to draw on themes identified with Nigeria. Within this new figuration, Okri, not Iyayi or Cheney-Coker, is thought of as espousing the ethos of hybridity. Phillips and Roy are considered similarly: they circulate in a metropolitan context, they are worldly, their works travel, they are in the world. They are cosmopolitan. But the literary works are not enough in themselves, because the figure of the expatriated postcolonial writer or artist is contentious: he or she distrusts the nation-state as the embodiment of oppressive practices such as patriarchy, the caste system, economic injustice, and political violence. It is not surprising, then, that a good number of expatriated postcolonial writers write essays as well as fictional or poetic works, in which they critique postcolonial practices.[17] Indeed, the breadth of the category of nonfiction attests to the instability of genre in postcoloniality, and the wide use to which it is put by the writers discussed here—James as much as Phillips and Roy—underlines the point. James's *American Civilization* epitomizes the author's cosmopolitan credentials because he does not consider either regional or racial categories to be the primary bases of his subject in the work, and as Brennan suggests, this is partly because he wants to be a commercially successful writer. Yet, in the opinion of many, he expresses regional and racial considerations even more concretely in *Beyond a Boundary* (1963), thus stressing their specificity.[18] From a literary point of view, what is immediately arresting about *Beyond a Boundary* is its generic openness, the fact that it resists easy categorization. This is important because it is precisely this openness that reveals James's fundamental cosmopolitan character—his generosity of spirit, his familiarity with a wide variety of cultures, which he extends to human relations.

The fact of expatriation does not change James's writing as it does that of Okri, or of any of the late twentieth-century postcolonial writers, unless one thinks of his work as a party activist and organizer as substantially displacing his literary vocation, in a manner one cannot observe in writers such as Naipaul, George Lamming, and, later, Phillips. Of the several factors to which this difference can be attributed, two are pertinent to the present discussion: the nature of neoliberal globalization and the ways it affects cultural forms, and the fact that fiction and nonfiction (essays) are not the only forms of writing at James's disposal; the political essays, party position papers, and meditations on *Moby Dick,* Stalinism, and American media culture count equally. The two factors are related, of course, and the connection between them is further evidence that the generic ethoses of cosmopolitanism and tricontinentalism must not be presumed to be mutually exclusive. If metropolitan location and intensified commodification of culture shape postcolonial genres so decisively as to make nonfiction, especially the essay, the default genre of cosmopolitanism, and if in the process they lead expatriated writers to be less directly invested in the political and social issues of their "original" locations, the question arises as to what happens to the aesthetic energies freed by the discourse of anti-colonialism. In what forms do the aspects of "genealogical fictions" (as argued by Jeyifo) or avant-garde poetics manifest themselves? In short, what are the aesthetic manifestations of tricontinentalism?

There is a long and distinguished line from the nineteenth-century conception of avant-garde art to the pre– and post–Second World War disquisitions on socialism-inspired emancipatory mass culture in the writings of Bertolt Brecht and Walter Benjamin (and Theodor Adorno, from a different perspective), which turn on the divisions between elite and mass cultures.[19] Within this conception, the masses, not the individuated consciousness embedded in the hero of the modernist novel, are the protagonist of social change. In relation to tricontinentalism, the ideological critique of culture finds an outlet in the Marxist distrust of the false consciousness built into bourgeois art, based on the political understanding that the spontaneity and naturalness of popular art are programmed to occlude true historical conditions.[20] This understanding is advanced in two principal ways: the Soviet Union–inspired practice of socialist realism and the post–Cuban revolution Third Cinema manifesto. Reflecting the Cold War divisions under which the category of the "Third World" has been constructed, Third Cinema is indeed the aesthetic handmaiden of tricontinentalism. The Third Cinema manifesto calls for documentary styles, for filmmakers to be the artistic equivalents of revolutionary cells, and for the production of films for which "the System" (imperialism) has no use (Solanas and Getino 1976), and these calls resonate with the broader goals of Third World artistic movements, such as the Fédération Panafricaine des Cinéastes (FEPACI), founded in the late 1960s. The idea that African cinema had revolutionary objectives was fundamental in the communiqués and charters that the federation issued in the mid-1980s (Diawara 1992; Bakari and Cham 1996). Recently, the degree to which Third Cinema actually affected filmmaking practices in the context of decolonization has been debated,[21] but there is historical evidence that filmmakers, writers, and artists from across the decolonizing and anti-imperial world saw themselves as sharing a common anti-imperialist cause. A few examples will do.

Firstly, in the wake of the Cuban missile crisis, the Russian director Mikhail Kalatozov traveled to Cuba to work on a major production, later released as *Soy Cuba* (I Am Cuba, 1964). It was a Soviet/Cuban coproduction noted for its skillful use of elements of socialist realism—pedagogical discussions, rhetorical sketches, agit-prop and documentary sequences, and realistic depictions of pre-revolutionary Havana and the Cuban countryside. Ironically, the film was dismissed, both in Cuba and in the Soviet Union, as not being sufficiently revolutionary; its use of tracking shots, photomontages, and unconventional *mise-en-scènes* which convey a sense of camera movement as if on an assembly line was unprecedented in cinema, and has rarely been seen since.[22] Secondly, while African filmmakers of Sembene and Souleymane Cissé's generation did not have the experience of training at the Cuban Film Institute (ICAIC), younger directors, including Flora Gomes of Guinea-Bissau, did, and this is evident in Gomes's first film, *Mortu Nega* (1988). So many innovative cinematic techniques have developed out of the ICAIC that they constitute a significant tradition in the history of cinema, especially in the works of well-known directors like Tomas Gutiérrez Alea and Julio García Espinosa.[23] These developments have to be seen in the context of the first tricontinental conference, convened in Havana in 1966, which gave the cultural rhetoric of the Bandung conference an aesthetic outlet that directors in many parts of the world were to find fruitful.

The point of identifying the aesthetic dimensions of tricontinentalism is to posit that the figure of the politically committed artist, as an activist or an author (auteur), is decisive in the constitution of postcolonial genre. As I will demonstrate in the next chapter, the differences between Sembene's novel and film versions of *Xala* become important because they illuminate the choices he has to make as he negotiates the postcolonial contours of *mégotage*. Moreover, in *God's Bits of Wood* (1970), his fictional account of the colonial-era railway workers' strike in Dakar-Bamako, Sembene employs a realistic mode closer to socialist realism in its objectives. The importance of this activist-artist figure can be placed in the context of James's career in a number of ways. First, the wariness with which socialist realism as an artistic method is currently treated (because of its association with Stalinist, Zhdanovian prescriptions, considered anathema in art) perhaps also reflects the prevalent attitude toward socialism as a political system. As I suggested above, the impact of neoliberal globalization on cultural forms cannot be separated from the fact that for writers of James's time and political orientation, writing goes beyond fiction and literary nonfiction to include the genres of the political essay and the pamphlet. Second, genre as such, in any of these forms, is not an end in itself, but is meant to promote the transformation of class relations. This is the all-important question of integration, in which a creative individual (a Melville or a Chaplin) is also a political personality. Third (a combination of the first two), the authors discussed in subsequent chapters validate these aspects of James's work in ways that underscore the continuing relevance of the Trinidadian political thinker. These relationships will also be discussed further in the conclusion.

The Limits of a Method

In order to rescue integration from the strictures of political fatalism that are endemic to mass forms, James also grounds it in what he calls *movement*,[24] an idea which can be clarified through his view of revolutionary politics. James believes that a definitive change has occurred in the global social structure—the old world (Europe, the nineteenth century) has passed and a new one (the postimperial world) has emerged. The world is progressively transformed by the four great revolutions (Russian, Indian, Chinese, and African) and their attendant social movements, and by the mass society of the twentieth century, for which the American culture of democracy provides the ideological axis. This investment in teleology is informed by James's training as a Marxist, and is often motivated by the practical question of how to promote a socialist transformation of the present order. It exists side by side with a passion for seeing the world steadily, the integrative approach which brings together the different elements of a particular time in a cultural form. In his writings from the period of the split with the (Trotskyist) Socialist Workers Party, especially *State Capitalism and World Revolution* (1986), James writes confidently and incessantly about the future. What McLemee calls the "forbidding" quality of this text and its theoretical twin, *Notes on Dialectics* (1980), is as much a result of their immediate ideological purposes as of the unattractiveness of a socialist society, especially in McLemee's context: an intellectual environment dominated by a neoliberal ideology. It sounds anachronistic these days to invoke the word "socialism" with such confidence, but this partly reflects the prevalence of a worldview that makes socialism impossible, even if a socialist society has to be differently thought of, given the absence of an industrial working class, the crucial basis on which the historical idea of a socialist society was developed.[25] Even in a later text, such as *Nkrumah and the Ghana Revolution,* James's assessment of the failure of the revolution rests on his conception of the decolonizing societies of Africa, Asia, and the Caribbean as "undeveloped" and "backward," and of contemporary Western capitalist democracies as "advanced." These are clearly Marxist, progressivist ways of talking about historical processes.

It would seem that, on the whole, there is asynchrony in James's method. Most critics have seen this asynchrony as manifesting a disjunction between Marxist class analysis and the cultural analysis that befits James as a theoretician of popular forms. According to this view, James is less threatening, more amenable to cultural critique, when the question of class is excluded from his writing.[26] The assumption is that once the stratified, goal-oriented idea of political class analysis is excluded, the messiness of culture can then be posited as an example of specificity. In this context, teleology, whether Marxist or Weberian, becomes an impediment to productive discussion. This mirrors the distinction current in cultural theory between "process" and "product" (or "becoming" and "being"), with the former being preferred. It is unnecessarily limiting to read James, or any text that attempts to integrate the practices of different academic disciplines, in this way. It is true that going through a process can provide incalculable joys, which may be satisfying in themselves. It is equally true that a process, conceived of as a journey, can be arrested, set back, or thrown off its course. Thus it must be borne in mind that the individual or group undertaking a process almost always has a goal in mind, however provisional or utopian, and the failure to attain it need not always be celebrated for being provisional.

The discussion of aesthetics and of the nature of art and representation (in *Beyond a Boundary* and *American Civilization*) is often arrived at through work, or more appropriately, *labor,* in the Hegelian usage of the term: political organization, immersion in cultural life and forms, mediated through theoretical reflections on all of them, with the world seen as a site of class antagonism. There is no doubt that a developmentalist conception of historical processes registers its presence strongly in James's writings. The asynchrony is between an evolutionary, progressivist approach to historical analysis and a revolutionary transformation of society that the analysis is meant to advance. The difference between this Jamesian notion of development and the classical evolutionism at work in Wells's *Outline of History* is James's awareness of agents who, in the context of the present book, are also important as writers, artists, filmmakers, and activists. This awareness manifested itself in the process leading to the revision of the Marxist theory of revolution around the time of the 1945 Pan-African Congress, through the activities of the International African Service Bureau in England. What partly rescues James's approach is its built-in ability to recognize the limitations, revise them, and posit a movement forward (for example, in the unsustainable idea of armed struggle in postwar Africa [James 1977a, 69]). In his hands, Marxism is "a guide to action in a specific system of social relations which takes into account the always changing relationship of forces in an always changing world situation" (74). But this self-critique is not entirely free of tension. In fact, as James's biographer Anna Grimshaw remarks, James fixates on certain events that constitute the core of his political life. Grimshaw suggests that the movement which is characteristic of the author's sense of history and of his own life is ironically marked by stasis; it is "a recursive movement" of the memory itself. "Instead of exploring the past in order to situate the present and imaginatively create a future, the past had become a timeless place linked to an immovable present; and his mind was able only to shuttle back and forth between fixed points in the past and present" (Grimshaw 1996, 16). This is a major critique of James's personal predilection, made by an insider, and Grimshaw concludes by relating the political theorist's search for "the single unifying thread" to his work in revolutionary organizations, which always necessitated a search for cogency, "the points of stability in an essentially fluid world" (17). Dhondy has similarly recorded the frustrating experience of taking dictation from James for a play about the life of Nkrumah (Dhondy 2001, 126–127). James's concept of integration is constantly mediated by movement, by negotiation. This sums up the dialectical relationship he depicts between a leader and followers in *Nkrumah and the Ghana Revolution,* between the hero and the crowd in *Beyond a Boundary,* and between the jazz musician and the audience in *American Civilization* (James 1977a, 100–107, 121; James 1963, 182–184; James 1993, 137). The relationship is implicitly both the one and the other—a critique of "categorization and specialization, that division of the human personality, which is the greatest curse of our time" (James 1963, 195). It is what makes James's break with orthodox Trotskyism so crucial for decolonization; it was not just a routine sectarian falling-out, but a culturally grounded inauguration of political possibilities beyond the framework of vanguardism.

In conclusion, I would like to relate James's political and intellectual choices to the cultural background he shares with many others of his generation. In an interview with James, Stuart Hall asked him,

> You've throughout your life developed and tried to make as clear as you could, often in magnificently simple ways . . . a view of life, vision of life. You often encounter people, writers, artists, ordinary people, people in opposite political camps from you, who don't agree with you. You never go principally to what divides you from them. You always find that which you can accommodate into your sense of historical development . . . Why is that? What is that? Where does that come from?"

James responds,

> I grew up in the Caribbean and I left there when I was thirty years of age. And I grew up in an atmosphere in which I knew everybody and everybody knew me . . . A microcosm of society on the whole. We, not me alone, Fanon had it, Césaire had it, Padmore had it, and Garvey had it in a way. (Hall 1996, 42–43)

This statement indicates the relevance of the cultural background of most Caribbean intellectuals, as it is mediated by the experiences of expatriation and political activism. It is an excellent background for political struggle in the twentieth century, in the sense that these individuals could put their ideas into practice only when they were in exile. One of the factors motivating the diasporic figures who championed the African cause (especially the Caribbean intellectuals in the West before World War II) was the need to rid themselves of the racist notion of cultural inferiority which colonialism attached to Africa. Thus in the 1930s George Padmore cast himself in the role of an African even without having visited the continent, and Aimé Césaire took on the identity of an African who compensated for psychic alienation through willful acts of cultural immersion. These are rhetorical stances made more valid by their intellectual quality and by the Western intellectual tradition, which frames questions of class and race in humanist terms. The self-making implicit in these gestures seems to me to apply to postcolonial subjectivities today, on the African continent and in the world at large. People of different cultural backgrounds are deploying all kinds of ideas to fashion identities for themselves: if it was psychically liberating for Césaire to become an African, why should the desire of an impoverished Ecuadorian to become an American, or a Norwegian to dye her hair green, be seen differently? In this connection, Hall's argument that the Caribbean sends "a tiny but important message to the world" in matters of identity becomes quite plausible (Hall 1995, 4). The bulk of James's intellectual career, like that of most of his contemporaries, unfolded in a condition of expatriation. In their books and their activism in the United States, Britain, Ghana, and the USSR, they achieved for others what they could not achieve in their own island homes. But they were always keenly aware of that background, and this is why today, as postcolonial intellectuals confront similar problems of making homes and careers in expatriation, the experiences of James and his contemporaries are relevant and useful.

2 Fitful Decolonization: *Xala* and the Poetics of Double Fetishism

Among the films of the late Ousmane Sembene, *Xala* (1974) has attracted probably the most extensive commentary. It is hard to imagine even a brief commentary or a notice, let alone a full-length essay about the filmmaker, which does
not make the film a point of reference, usually seeing it as a decisive instance
of his artistic politics, which a critic has recently termed "anti-neocolonialism."[1]
Produced after a decade in which many African countries had attained political
independence, this rich and mordantly uncompromising film is at once an unusual family drama and a satire, an allegorical fable of the emergent elite, the
much-vilified "comprador bourgeoisie" whom Frantz Fanon had famously critiqued in *The Wretched of the Earth* only a decade earlier. The film is an important moment in the history of decolonization in the twentieth century, especially its relationship to the politics of tricontinentalism.

Scholars of African cinema and postcolonial studies have often seen *Xala* as a
critique of the impotence of the ruling class that emerged at the end of colonialism. However, in this chapter I focus on the interplay in the film of aspects of
the postcolonial asymmetry, and I see the *xala* (temporary sexual impotence)[2]
as a form of discourse which commentaries on the film usually do not engage.
I argue that there is in *Xala* an unresolved tension between the filmmaker's attack on that elite and the use of the cultural idiom of *xala* as temporary impotence. Available studies of the film, mostly dedicated to Sembene's materialist critique of the double fetishism of imported commodities and marabout
or animist supernaturalism, have not paid sufficient attention to the paradox
of the power of the powerless, in this case women and the poor. Adding this
important dimension, I examine an unresolved and irresolvable tension in the
film between the filmmaker's attack on the postcolonial elite and his complex
use of the cultural idiom of *xala*. In order to problematize this tension, I discuss in detail the "marginal" stories in the film, especially the contradictions of
class which the more spectacular story of El Hadji Abdou Kader Beye's fall from
grace have tended to overshadow, in a manner analogous to the way different
kinds of identity and subjectivity are habitually neglected in the era of decolonization. In playing up these overshadowed narratives, I respond to James's injunction in his analysis of Pan-Africanism that to vanquish elitism is to focus

on the contradictions of class relations. These contradictions make it impossible for the beggars in the film to ally with the women in a polygamous marriage, and they are also embedded in the economic structure which makes the film possible. Sembene's figuration of the impotence of the elite and the curability of *xala* is thus a case of "double fetishism" (of European consumer goods and an African mode of sexual censure), and from this figuration we can deduce that decolonization did not fully succeed in part because the aesthetic, cultural, and economic forms of the critique of double fetishism were intertwined. The film-maker's choice to make two *Xala*s (film and novel) available is also a response to this inseparability of aesthetic and economic questions.

In the mid-1980s, the film was the subject of a dispute in the pages of the cinema journal *Screen* between the "cine-semioticians" and the "form-and-content critics" (these are the names they called each other), who disagreed about which theoretical mode was most appropriate for the analysis of African cinematic works. I discuss that debate below. But the controversy revealed that in spite of their different "film languages," the two sides were closer than they suspected. Subsequent criticisms of the films have not shied away from this question. So extensive is the psychoanalytic and semiotic commentary on the film that it is nearly impossible to appreciate the film outside of these proto-cols. While taking account of these commentaries, I go further in this chapter. On the basis of the proposition that Sembene's position as a committed artist is grounded in aesthetic populism (the need to make films that speak to the yearnings of a broad population in Senegal, and by extension in Africa), I look in detail at the "marginal" stories in the film: the domestic politics of El Hadji's polygamous home; the visual texture and the aural texts of the beggars' well-plotted ordeal and final revolt; the gossipy narratives enacted by minor char-acters in El Hadji's store; and the specific inscriptions of the aesthetics of social realism. I attend to the context—the historical, political, cultural, and economic milieus—not just of the film's conception but also of its reception by audiences and critics.

I also look at a number of ethnographic materials on the cultural practice that *xala* symbolizes, and relate Sembene's materialist decolonization of the practice to the discourse of *magun* in Kelani's film *Thunderbolt: Magun* (discussed in the next chapter). In that film, by contrast, the critique of sex-related affliction originates from a philosophical background that conceives of political engage-ment as an aspect of general social morality. The two modes of *Xala*'s rhetoric of power—the film's addresses to both gender and class politics—make sense in the context of post-independence Senegal and Sembene's status as the lead-ing figure of an African cinema whose history is contiguous with African in-dependence struggles. As we see in C. L. R. James's analysis of Pan-Africanism, questions of gender and class differences are central to social and political trans-formations, and part of *Xala*'s appeal lies in the way it focuses its attention on the issues of political control that were involved in the emergence of an African elite at the helm of the Chamber of Commerce and Industry. In 1974, the year of the film's release, President Leopold Senghor's government had encouraged the growth of Senegalese business, and Sembene took the opportunity to satirize the resulting bankruptcy scandals (Vieyra 1987, 37). Within that decade, two Senegalese writers also addressed the questions of beggars in the street and women's position in society, thus giving *Xala* a special resonance. In other words, *Xala* combines the two social problems that each text treats separately, and we can infer from the multiplicity of treatments that the problems are particularly pressing in Senegal.[3]

But the context of the film is not just Senegal. It was produced in the context of the neocolonial French Bureau of Cinema, whose paternalism it indirectly skewers in a joke about Jean-Luc Godard's *Weekend* (this additionally in the context of France's official linguistic policy), and also in the context of an international community of student activism and the Pan-African intellectual movement. The early 1970s also marked the dawn of dependency theory, which adopts the Marxist method of analysis to study economic relations between industrial and recently decolonized economies. These widely different currents are yoked in the film's complex articulation of marginality; it is this articulation that opens the film simultaneously to the interests of "cine-structuralism" and of psychoanalysis and postcoloniality (Harrow 2007a; Murphy 2000; Mulvey 1999; Mowitt 1993, 74; Gabriel 1986; Turvey 1985; Lyons 1984, 320). These interests bear reviewing.

Teshome Gabriel, a prominent African theorist of Third Cinema (d. 2010), debated film critic Julianne Burton, rejecting what he called "law and order criticism" of the cinema of the Third World by those he labeled "cine-semioticians" or "cine-structuralists."[4] In a review in *Screen*, Burton (1985) had sharply criticized Gabriel's *Third Cinema in the Third World: The Aesthetic of Liberation* because, among other things, it favored ideological discussion of Third Cinema films over their semiotic aspects, thereby effacing their ideological underpinnings. But Gabriel believes that films from Africa, Latin America, and parts of the United States and Europe should be seen first in their ideological contexts, and the layered readings favored by semioticians should follow. Both Burton and Mowitt (writing nine years later in *Camera Obscura*) suggested that understanding cinema apparatus requires semiotic readings, and that Gabriel's insistence on the ideological enthrones the form-and-content format (film as text) that merely stresses "marginal cinema'"s opposition to the mainstream, while overlooking the points where they are continuously engaged. Categorizing films from regions with disparate social formations and histories as Third Cinema, the critics argued, reflected a shared opposition to the mainstream rather than a coherent ideological affinity among the "Third World" regions.

In her extensive discussion of "oppositional film movements" and the Hollywood mainstream, Burton implicitly recognizes the geographical divide between the two realms, making it hard to know where, for instance, the British documentary tradition stands in relation to the mainstream of Euro-American cinema.[5] It is significant that in an essay purporting to undo the critical bias of Western critics toward non-Western artworks, Burton makes only a passing reference to Sembene's work, notably *Emitaï* (1971) and *Ceddo* (1977, released in Senegal in 1981), saying that they are "based on *tribal* African tradition" which represents collectivized action (Burton 1985, 17–18). Conversely, her plea for considering Third World films from the perspectives of psychoanalysis becomes an argument in support of critical theory. Instructively, Laura Mulvey, another critic relying on psychoanalytical theory, opens and closes her analysis of *Xala* with critical overtures to Gabriel's theory of *sem-enna-worq* ("wax-and-gold"), a poetic form which is Ethiopian in origin. This form was not developed in Senegal, but since it is rooted in uncommodified "folk culture," Gabriel adapts it to read the film language of *Xala*. This is a problematic theoretical move to make in studying a complex, allegorical, and satirical film, but Mulvey sidesteps this problem by doing the precise opposite: while not denying that the film is a specifically Senegalese and Wolof work, she uses its extensive critique of false French values for a psychoanalysis-informed discussion of it.[6] Mulvey's essay certainly moves away from Burton's concentration on the ideological underpinnings of the context. But her complete disavowal of "*intra*-national fissuring produced by colonialism" (Mowitt's phrase [1993, 89], referring to class and gender inequalities within Senegal), is curious in a reading that places Sembene between Freud and Marx.

"Folk culture" also forms the basis of the refreshing analysis of the film by Harriet Lyons. Drawing on the work of the folklorist Richard Dorson, who suggested that folklorists in contemporary Africa pay attention to practices and traditions that shared space with colonialism and its practices and technologies, Lyons looks at social practices among not just the Wolof but also the Bambara and the Dogon, and even peoples further east, toward Ghana and Nigeria, cultures on which Sembene has drawn for his own artistic purposes. Lyons's discussion is interesting in that it takes account of systems of discipline developed and applied outside of an ethnographic context, some of which are visible in the character of El Hadji and his various nemeses. In the works of African filmmakers like Souleymane Cissé (*Yeelen*, 1987) and the late Djibril Diop Mambèty (*Touki Bouki*, 1973), the reinvention of these social practices is evidenced both in characterization and in camera angles and the framing of shots against the wide expanse of Sahelian earth, often dismissed as "ethnographic."[7] In Férid Boughedir's documentary *Camera d'Afrique*, Sembene shows sympathy for this amalgamation of practices when he talks about the absence of nations in precolonial Africa and how this absence could be used to fashion a Pan-Africanist aesthetics. This aesthetics is signified in the borderless, nationless map of Africa in the final encounter between El Hadji and Rama, his daughter; the camera lingers on the map as Rama goes out after wishing that her mother may be happy. Focusing on the question of bilingualism in the film, Mowitt faults academic postcolonial studies for being preoccupied with cultural imperialism and over-looking the "enunciative strategies" (1993, 88) with which the film expresses its complex aims.

These readings of *Xala*, I think, presume wariness of "cine-theory" (semiotic, structuralist, and psychoanalytic) to be a kind of resistance to theory, and this presumption stops barely short of suggesting that non-European critics, especially Africans, do not sufficiently grasp "theory" to do justice to it in analysis. Thus the Western critic who is invested in psychoanalysis and semiotics and the African critic who eschews them are closer than they think: dependency theory and semiotics do not lack for political history, and when a third kind of critic (a Western postmodernist Africanist) chooses to transcend those origins another problem is uncovered, as we shall see later in Kenneth Harrow's critique of the "cinema of engagement," particularly the work of Sembene.

In the course of this discussion, we will see how the context of production allows Sembene to layer his film, so that it invites the different readings that have become its lot. It is not just that this what all art does: *Xala's* location in a space that leads its director to specify what scenes are or are "not necessary for a European public" (Ghali 1987, 47)[8] calls for more of the formal strategies that make it accessible but serious, simultaneously conceptual and narrative. As a film, *Xala* attends to the politics of filmmaking. The film historian Claire Andrade-Watkins, writing about the politics of financing film in Africa through the French Bureau of Cinema, observes that Sembene refused to produce his films through it (Andrade-Watkins 1996, 114). In 1992, while trying to finance his most ambitious (and never-completed) project, the story of Samory Touré, the nineteenth-century African nationalist who fought a war to resist French colonialism, Sembene was interviewed by a researcher studying the reception of his films within Senegal. In that interview Sembene confessed his frustration with the country's continuing dependence on outside assistance, and displayed a nationalistic attitude that nevertheless recognized the possibility that the countries of Africa might cooperate culturally (Ní Chréacháin and Ousmane 1992). In Boughedir's documentary, Sembene asks, "How can you be a sunflower and look up to the sun?" suggesting that the primary focus of his work is local.

Implicit in all this is the conviction that artistic independence is a political imperative, and when Sembene poses this question in the Senegalese socio-economic context, he is concerned with the necessity of artistic freedom. One of his films, *Ceddo,* remained unreleased until Senghor left power in 1981. Two others, including *Xala,* have been extensively censored. It is not difficult to see how these concerns affect the film *Xala*; ironically, it was the first film ever to be coproduced with the Senegalese National Cinema Society, which provided 60 percent of its funding (Vieyra 1987, 36). Ten scenes were cut out of the original film, a mutilation that Sembene describes as something akin to the cruelties of the Inquisition. Of these, two have been particularly controversial. The first is the scene of the removal of the bust of Marianne that symbolizes the ideals of the French Republic, and in the other the chief of police forcibly removes the beggars from the street. They both have to do with Senegal's relation to France or to white people.[9] Those scenes are restored in the version distributed abroad, so that although the Senegalese may not have access to them, their significance can be read back into their context. Sembene distributed fliers "to indicate which scenes got cut, so people can have a sense of what is missing" (Ghali 1987, 44).

Rhetorics of Power and Revolt

The plot of *Xala* requires a summary, considering the multiple levels of narration and the film's explicit critique of *rentier* elitism. A successful businessman, El Hadji Abdou Kader Beye, decides to take a third wife, N'Gone, on the same day that he becomes a member of the Chamber of Commerce. The entire business community is invited to the wedding, and a high-class ceremony gets underway. As El Hadji tries to consummate the marriage, however, his manhood fails him, and it is discovered that he is stricken with the *xala*, a curse of temporary impotence. Much of the film is taken up with his search for a cure. He is finally cured by the *marabout,* or Islamic healer, Serigne Mada (the word *serigne* is an Islamic term of address meaning "mister" or "sir" in Wolof), but his relief is shortlived after the check he gave to the *marabout* bounces. His business is in ruins, his Mercedes Benz (the last symbol of his prestige) is repossessed, and he is expelled from the Chamber. A blind beggar, Gorgui, offers to cure the affliction on the condition that El Hadji submit to a ritual of humiliation.

Sembene's basic narrative interest is with the double rhetoric of power: El Hadji Abdou Kader Beye represents the bourgeoisie's political control of gender and class relations. This control is immediately established through the capture of the Chamber of Commerce, an economic instrument neocolonially preserved in the character of the president's sidekick, Dupont-Durand, who provides cash-stuffed attachés for the Chamber members. El Hadji's announcement of his wedding reception thus intensifies political power by framing it as a reiteration of sexual prowess. The president of the Chamber claims in a speech that power has been wrested from the French in the name of the poor and ordinary people, but these are the people who are corralled by the police, and these arrests foreground the other rhetoric, that of class difference. Moments after his eviction from the Chamber, one of the white men comes round to lead a posse of policemen to clear the way for the big businessmen; the scene is later echoed and further imbued with rhetorical power when a *xala*-stricken El Hadji remonstrates with his president to clear the streets of "this human refuse." Sembene seeks to bring these two marginalized groups—women and the poor, the prone and the crippled—together cinematically in order to depict the conflict as largely one of class.

At his wedding, El Hadji scatters coins as a sign of elitist humanitarianism while the griots praise the noble lines from which the groom and the bride descend. However, the beggars' appearance questions these discourses as the camera quickly cuts to a shot of the arrival of El Hadji's first two wives. The nondiegetic sound that insinuates itself between the jarring noise of the ministerial entourage and that of the approaching wedding is in fact a song in Wolof which, Sembene explains (Ghali 1987, 47; Murphy 2000, 120), is a call to revolt:

> Borom jamono, borom jamono, borom jamono
> But am jikkooy kilifaay mbët ak baxoñ
> Bo toppe ci moom mu ne: bul dëgge samap geen
> Nga tollok moom mu ne: danga may def moroom
> Nga jitu mu ne: bul daàq samay gunóór.
> (Man to whom the world belongs [3x],
> Eschew the conduct of the leader of a herd of lizards
> If you follow him, he says, "Do not step on my tail!"
> If you walk alongside, he snaps, "You are treating me as an equal?"
> If you walk in front of him, he says, "Don't chase away my ants [i.e., food])."[10]

This song returns from time to time, notably whenever the beggars appear. That it is never rendered cinematically urgent by having a subtitle devoted to it is proof of its specific context: since the film already has almost an excess of argumentation, perhaps to make it concrete is to drift too far toward agit-prop. Significantly, this lack of emphasis also indicates the basic appeal of the film: Sembene does not seek to cause revolt in Paris with this song; he is content to discard the bust of Marianne, the emblem of the French Republic, since the French are not his business. Sembene once described himself as a modern griot, that is, a "man of learning and common sense who is the historian, the raconteur, the living news and conscience of his people" (Pfaff 1982, 31). By inserting this song into the cinematic moment when the traditional griots move into the new mood, reinventing the genealogies of their patrons, he critiques this oft-valorized figure of African intellectual heritage. His skepticism regarding the griot is frequently apparent, starting with the *gewel* who sponges off the cart-driver in his 1963 film *Borom Sarret,* and this skepticism seems to inform his ironic deployment of *xala* in the film under discussion. Even this temporary impotence comes to be associated with this same rejected humanity.

Meanwhile, the narrative unfolds on several levels in sequences that seem like digressions but are tightly controlled, tracing El Hadji's degeneration. The laying of the curse of impotence is not shown, for reasons of cinematic representation and because Sembene wanted to broaden the terrain of the ruse, not necessarily merely to increase narrative suspense. (This is comparable to the laying of the *magun* curse on Ngozi in Kelani's *Thunderbolt: Magun,* which I discuss in the next chapter.) Oumi, El Hadji's second wife, is the first person suspected of cursing him, and his reverie when she calls at his office to demand maintenance money points to this, merely to underscore the insinuation that the Bayden (the bride's aunt) makes after his manhood has failed him, and deepen the domestic politics outlined in the Bayden's second contact with the two older wives off the reception ground. It is sensible in a polygamous context to suspect the second wife, whose "custodianship" of the husband's phallus is challenged by the arrival of a third. During the reception scene, after the first wife, Hadja Awa, has departed in a gale of anger that sweeps from her headgear to rustle the hanging vines, the camera closes in on Oumi as she plucks the miniature effigy of the couple off the wedding cake, and then snaps off the effigy's head just as the camera cuts to the car key. It is easy for a West African audience to meaningfully connect these images in the context of domestic rivalry, a context that the dominant psychosexual and socioeconomic analyses of the film have thus far condemned to the margin. The point is that to read these images simply as indicating the sexual power that El Hadji wields is to miss the intriguing drama of social relations in a polygamous family. Indeed, to call them indicators of a domestic melodrama would be closer to the point. Even if that category does not do justice to Sembene's intentions, it gives the film a special charge as a localized discourse. In this sense, it is logical that beggars figure in the neutralization of the curse, but even more logical that El Hadji resorts to a dubious "local" cure for his affliction.

Sembene says that his film is an attack on a "double fetishism"—the traditional fetishism of the marabouts and the contemporary fetishism of the commodity (Lyons 1984, 325). Mulvey's reading of the figuration of fetish in the film as a halfway house between Freud and Marx is astute, at least to the extent that Sembene's materialist overtures are relieved against the false Frenchness of the elite, whose attitude obstructs change. But if, as Mulvey suggests, it is this relation to Frenchness that activates her extensive psychoanalytical reading of El Hadji's abject and crippled phallus, what is one to make of the fact that this relation to Frenchness is, at best, inconsistent and incomplete? When his colleagues offer him aphrodisiacs just before he attempts (unsuccessfully) to consummate his new marriage, El Hadji disparages the counsel and does not even touch the capsules. But he grudgingly accepts "native medicine" from Banjul (the Gambia). Yet when the Bayden asks him to sit on a mortar with a pestle between his legs he refuses, citing his modern outlook. There is more than sophisticated arrogance in these refusals; the image of the mortal and the pestle, especially the pestle, calls up associations with the phallus, and El Hadji's stubborn refusal to put it between his legs is a straightforward refusal to surrender his manhood to scrutiny.

Despite the suggestion of power and control, however, his hold on this manhood is unstable, and the Bayden poetically describes his condition as "neither fish nor fowl." At the house Oumi and Rama (who calls him a liar) both stand up to him, and this forces him to verbalize that power and thus leave it open to ridicule: a power requiring declaration loses much in potency. Sembene tries to underscore this contradiction by having a Muslim perform a "white" Christian wedding, and El Hadji's search for a cure only intensifies it. So it is not just the objects that acquire power by being invested with symbolic healing that are fetishized, although there is a good deal of meaning to be teased out of this particular reading. The source of El Hadji's power could also be fetishized, the one he flaunts to Rama when she stands up to him: "We drove the colonialists out of this country!" In *Xala* the novel, we are told that El Hadji went into small-time export-import trading after he had been sacked from his job as a schoolteacher for taking part in trade unionism during the colonial era. This backstory is missing from the film, but it is part of the fetish that he embodies, the one that grants him access to the more contemporary forms of fetishism. In certain societies, Senegal included, some fetishes acquire their potency through speech. The second marabout merely has to utter some verses from the Koran to restore El Hadji's virility, and does the same to take it away.

The marabouts' fetishes are false clues, though; they are medicine used to treat an ailment whose origins remain unknown. In making the first marabout so phoney as compared to Serigne Mada,[11] who actually cures the *xala,* is Sembene suggesting that the Islam-inspired marabout is more reliable than the one who uses a material fetish? Is he setting up a ranking of cures, disparaging the indigenous one? The spirited attack on "double fetishism" is anti-theological, a logical stance for an artist with obvious Marxist allegiances. The first marabout is a parody of the West African practice of divination, so here Sembene is consciously exposing the unprincipled attitude of the elite, whose psychological split is not an ambiguous case of double consciousness. To carry out the marabout's instructions, El Hadji has to subject himself to a form of debasement (crawling silently toward his young wife's bed with an amulet stuffed into his mouth) that is only ridiculous in light of the vehemence with which he earlier rejected the Bayden's injunction to put a pestle between his legs. Here is a case of an engaged artist employing the resources of a material culture to critique a segment of the population whose lack of principle mirrors the fraudulence of the socioeconomic context that sustains it. But it is also this materialist investment that leads Sembene to negate the idea of the fetish, in its embodiment as an actual object. We know El Hadji temporarily regains his manhood because he says so, but also because Oumi, whose *moomé* (the period that a polygamous husband spends with each of his wives) coincides with his resur(e)rection, takes him in after he has been told that the new wife is menstruating. Again, this detail, minor as it is in light of the larger critique of fetishism and neocolonialism, will not escape Senegalese or Nigerian spectators socially trained to observe the comic sexual intrigues inherent in dramatized polygamy.

The status of a fetish as an object establishes a parallel with the more pervasive culture of commodification in the context of the dependent Senegalese economy. Senegal is not dependent merely on the paternalism of France, otherwise the Chamber members would be more likely to ride in Peugeots than Mercedes-Benzes. Indeed, the critique of fetishism is here subsumed to a local discourse, that of the role and efficacy of the marabout, and in order to demonstrate the filmmaker's attitude to this discourse, Serigne Mada's utterances must hold the key to the recovery and subsequent loss of El Hadji's manhood, and Mada's asceticism must not prevent him from withdrawing his cure when the supplicant's check bounces. Nonetheless, traditional fetishism's mindless collusion with neocolonialism is mordantly critiqued in the camera's association of his temporary cure with the attaché case containing the first medicine man's fetish, which he clutches as he returns to the bride's place, pausing to stroke the wedding gift and then proceeding in a tracking shot that reverses the shot of his disgraceful exit. It is in scenes like this that Sembene suspends or interrupts the social realism he learned in Russian cinema to attend to the more semiotically urgent duty of cinematic representation.[12]

Xala becomes a significant rhetorical sign in the film when the Moorish merchant Ahmed Fall, on the one hand, and Rama, on the other, construct metanarratives around it, pointing to a reflexivity that implicates the eponymously titled film. But the degeneration of El Hadji, coupled with the two returns of the repressed, also constitutes a narrative plank for the story beyond this point. Sembene astutely deploys narrative strategies by having minor characters guess at the secret through gossip, since conventional characterization is underplayed and narrative crosscutting is enacted principally through social relations. The introduction of the vendor of the newspaper *Kaddu*, of a Serigne from the village, and of El Hadji's secretary, Madame (not Mademoiselle!) Diouf, adds another dimension to the bourgeois businessman's fall. Although she is loyal to her boss, Madame Diouf stands in rhetorical opposition to him. Her attention to the social decay symbolized by the women who come to empty dirty water down the damaged drains in front of the store (whose smell she promptly neutralizes with deodorant) and her willingness to patronize *Kaddu* suggest an independent spirit and an unaggressive sexuality that oppose El Hadji's excessive maleness and put her on a level with the merchant Fall. Here, a different kind of discourse takes shape.

The flirting between Fall and Madame Diouf represents a microcosm of the film's sexual politics, but Sembene does not wish to invest too much narrative time in it, as the relation is also complicated by the benign forms of double fetishism—Fall's nonbourgeois economic muscle and Madame Diouf's obvious Westernization. Fall entreats her to "have two husbands," since he already has two wives. This intramural discussion of the *xala* scandal is perhaps the only moment in the film when sexual desire is directly expressed. Fall's flirtatious bodily contacts with Madame Diouf and his projection of his economic power, in act if not in word, resonate with theatrical mannerisms much in evidence in popular performances all over West Africa. She remains calm and confident, second only to Rama in her facility with French and Wolof, stepping out of the store with ease when the bailiffs arrive to confiscate El Hadji's goods and property. Fall and Madame Diouf also serve to extend and rupture the metaphor of marginality: Madame Diouf is the only working woman in the film, and Fall

Fall flirts with Madame Diouf. *Xala,* directed by Ousmane Sembene, 1974.

is the only man with actual capital. Yet whereas Fall's latent agency as a creditor is resurrected when El Hadji solicits a down payment from him, Madame Diouf's expresses herself only in relation to El Hadji's business or in defense of her marital status.

The presence of the beggars in front of the store establishes a psychic link between the *xala* and El Hadji's past act of illicit accumulation. When the president of the Chamber asks, "Who could have done this to you?" El Hadji moves toward the window, through which the music from a beggar's *xalam* flows in. Mulvey's insights about this cinematic moment are very useful; the sound suggests the knowledge that El Hadji has chosen to efface as he moves up the social ladder, and his entreaty to the president to remove the beggars is an act of double repression. The need for the first repression is not known in advance (the second figures as an exercise of the power of physical control which the rich wield), and the spectator has to read this moment backward in light of what Gorgui, the blind cousin, discloses in the final scene.

A few scenes before, Sembene constructs an urban setting for what will seal the crooked businessman's fate. A minor street accident draws a crowd, including the villager Serigne. He has come to the city to buy provisions for his village's people after years of drought—a biting critique of President Senghor's failed agricultural policy, which resonates with El Hadji's act of expropriation— and while blundering around in the streets, he meets a journalist and newspaper vendor who offers to write about the drought to raise awareness of it. In the crowd around the accident, Serigne is pickpocketed by Thieli. Both Serigne and the journalist are rounded up and forced into the truck removing the beggars from the city, and in this way, a double act of suppression takes place: the story of the drought is abridged and the possibility of a newspaper report is destroyed.

The theatricality of this sequence merges with the nondiegetic song of revolt to ground a discourse of proletarianization which is the social root of the *xala*. The sequence from Serigne Mada's restoration of the *xala* to the gathering of the beggars in El Hadji's house is imbued with the poignancy of socialist realism. The nondiegetic song returns, accompanying the beggars (and perhaps foreshadowing their vengeance), and as they trek painfully and slowly back to the city, the spectator sees the ravages of the drought that Serigne (the robbed villager) had hoped to have reported in the newspaper. This song is actually more explicit than the earlier one, because the two sequences are ruptured by two short scenes: Modu's entreaties to Gorgui, and the return of the wedding gown and effigy to El Hadji's house. When Modu approaches the blind beggar for help with curing El Hadji's affliction, we hear the last of the first version of the song, a kind of appeal because the repossession of the Mercedes Benz has not entirely spelled El Hadji's doom. That comes with the return of the dud check; Modu's solicitation of Gorgui is a final admission of defeat, and it is in this sense that the song can be fully appreciated as a call to revolt.

It is often said that Sembene published some of his novels—especially *Xala* and *Guelwaar*—partly as a way of expressing himself while waiting to fund the film versions. (I mentioned this at the beginning of the introduction to this book.) This argument might suggest that the publishing climate was less unfavorable in Francophone Africa than in Anglophone, where, as I have shown in the introduction, the effervescence in audiovisual media coexisted with an intellectual despair informed by the downturn in literary publishing. Sembene's choice to publish novel versions of these films-in-progress was determined partly by economic necessity. Equally important, though, is the fact that Sembene made film his medium because he recognized that literature can be only a limited agent of social transformation in societies where the majority of the people are illiterate. In their very useful discussion of the film and novel versions of *Xala,* Josef Gugler and Oumar Cherif Diop look extensively at the economic as well as the aesthetic reasons for Sembene's choices (1998). The downturn in literary publishing might have been an opportunity to delegitimize the linguistic elitism supposedly built into literary culture (Sembene's premise might have taken account of other popular forms, such as newspapers), except that, as his own shuttles between cinema and novel show, vibrant literary and visual cultures are not mutually exclusive in a context of low literacy.

Yet the impact of this choice can still be felt on a generic level: the novel is a more discursively expansive text than the equally multivalent film. The film tells us very little about El Hadji's anti-colonial past; there is only the telescopic rhetoric

The lumpenproletariat at a tea stall. *Xala,* directed by Ousmane Sembene, 1974.

of the opening sequence in which the whites are ejected from the Chamber and his boast to Rama that "we drove the colonialists out of this country." But the novel tells us that El Hadji lost his job as a teacher because of his union activities. Needless to say, such information is guaranteed to undermine the critique of conspicuous consumption which the film relentlessly pursues. On the other hand, the concentration of image, diegesis, and nonvisual discourse such as the song results in a generically distinctive text. The song in particular has the stylistic quality of a commentary, an allegorical address from the point of view of the beggars, but one nonetheless structured by an omniscient twist.

The long shots in the sequence focusing on the trek of displaced persons back to the city attempt to bridge the conventional gap between the proletariat and the peasantry, such that, in his somewhat ragged work-cloth, the journalist–newspaper vendor blends easily with the beggars. In their gathering around the table of the tea-seller, each of the beggars is shot closely and individually, the camera highlighting their skin chapped by harmattan winds. The tactility of these shots simultaneously hints at affect and, for the first time, gives a voice to the travails of the masses. This sequence is of great significance to the film's finale because, whereas a ponderous silence frames the shots of El Hadji and Modu after the loss of the Mercedes, the vocalization of loss that rules the tea stall bespeaks boiling anger and frustration. Modu mourns the loss of the Mercedes by carrying along the wooden stool his boss had been sitting on. Mulvey writes, "The stool is like a shrunken, or wizened version of the proud object of display. It is a trace of, or memorial to, the Mercedes and its meaning for El Hadji. Because Modu has been so closely identified with the car and its welfare, his presence links the two objects ironically together" (Mulvey 1999, 413). By contrast, the beggars possessed little, as far as the film showed, so their fall is not a fall—they have been down for a long while.

Although it serves little purpose to apportion moral lessons between these two sequences, the forbidding appearance of the beggars is redressed later through the undressing of El Hadji. Reading the film as a "realist project" predicated on Raymond Williams's notion of realism, Gerry Turvey has suggested that Xala's refusal to invest El Hadji's fall and the return of his xala with personal significance opposes it to a fond stylistic preoccupation of European art cinema with individual loss. According to Turvey, Williams calls novels that thus segregate the personal and the social "fiction of special pleading" (Turvey 1985, 83). Perhaps Modu's mourning for the Mercedes, which Mulvey cites, inhabits this space: Modu's attitude toward the beggars is one of cagey solidarity, carefully concealed through a quasi-exploitative overture that admits one of the beggars as the cleaner of the car. The melancholia that results from the loss of the car does not degenerate into personal mourning, for the camera only shows the men's backs as they head down the street, and El Hadji's character at this point lacks the rhetorical power invested in the hero of modernist fiction.

Before the final confrontation between the beggars and El Hadji, a sequence of scenes details the final unraveling of the big man. Oumi's desertion reduces El Hadji's familial circle to a penumbra, the better to concentrate his disgrace. Rama returns with her politics of personal fetishes, which turns on the pivot of what Mowitt calls "bilingualism" (1993, 77), the articulation of her split as an educated African who seeks to egg her society on into an impossible precolonial future. While her first confrontation with her father centers on the question of sexual oppression, this meeting, less tense partly as a result of her father's fall from grace, moves their opposition to the more value-loaded domain of social interaction. When El Hadji offers her bottled water—his former car's leftovers—Rama retorts that she does not drink imported water. This identification with the lot of Senegalese who lack the means for conspicuous consumption is immediately grounded in her speech: she replies to his French inquiries in Wolof, and El Hadji questions this, seeing it as a sign of disrespect. As Rama departs, asking for nothing but her mother's happiness, the camera leads her out, pausing on a map of Africa that shows no national borders. Mulvey has echoed Gabriel's suggestion that the camera's resting on the map interpellates "Mother Africa" as the cinematic embodiment of Rama's progressive politics (Mulvey 1999, 419; Gabriel 1985, 340). But this optimism is ambivalent.

Indeed, ambivalence is central to Rama's personality. Apart from the split between the neocolonial reality and a decolonized possibility, she is created out of pure abstraction, much as is the character of Ibrahim Bakayoko in God's Bits of

Wood (Soyinka 1976, 117). This is why her most effective weapons are those of rhetoric, why she embodies much of what she stands for. Although she cannot be said to be a floating signifier, she does float through the space of the narrative, lacking a purpose except as the antithesis of her father's reactionary politics. Her "fetishes"—the scooter, her colorful costumes that mock the drab business suits of El Hadji, the posters of Samory Touré, Charlie Chaplin, and Amílcar Cabral in her room—strategically place her in that space toward which the film can at best gesture. There is a deeper emotional side to her in the novel, where she has a boyfriend. But the imperative of enunciation grounds this rhetoric quite persuasively, so that her most radical statement—calling her father a liar—is mediated by being uttered in Wolof. Whereas in the novel Rama challenges her father by declaring that "all polygamists are never frank," a statement that suggests the discursivity of Wolof in the context of Sembene's detailed, novelistic plotting of the conflict, in the film she declares that "polygamists are liars." This is another instance where Rama's gender politics coincide with the filmmaker's, and the latter utterance directly questions the traditional worldview that produces and sustains polygamy. The split that Mowitt identifies regarding Rama also marks Sembene's cinematic practice of deploying Wolof and Islamic practices (*xala* and maraboutism) while also questioning them. Rama is a loaded sign of what is realizable, Sembene's marker of the temporariness of El Hadji's impotence.

The father learns from the child, but how late! It is clear that the filmmaker expects the spectator to link the disagreement on language between father and daughter to El Hadji's appearance before the Chamber in session. He now occupies a dubious moral high ground compared to the colleagues who arraign him for corruption: Kebe, who accuses him of embezzling the tons of rice meant for the National Food Board, is the same fellow who collects a 15-percent bribe on an invisible tourism deal. When El Hadji asks to speak in Wolof, he is denounced as a "racist, a reactionary," and the bogus fetish he bought from the first medicine man is derided as a sign of backwardness. Here, in his retort that this fetish is more authentic than their own commodity fetishism, he is finally coming round to his preindependence radicalism, which he has not only destroyed through his subsequent conduct, but has also reduced to an impotent verb. The daughter has raised the father, but his downfall is complete, and he is expelled in a "democratic" gesture that is quickly ridiculed by his being replaced by Thieli, the pickpocket, who has sewn a business suit from the money he stole from Serigne the villager. Indeed, Thieli ultimately becomes a member of the Chamber of Commerce.

Gorgui, the blind beggar who retreats fearfully when a policeman steps on one of the coins El Hadji scatters among the beggars during the wedding reception, holds the key to El Hadji's curse of impotence. The arrival of the beggars in El Hadji's house—his only remaining possession, which he has with foresight registered in his first wife's name—marks the final rupture of the façade of primitive accumulation that shields the people from knowledge of their dispossession. These beggars know who caused their marginality, but their wounds and their crippled state keep them from concretely expressing this knowledge through action. Unwashed, unruly, they devastate the house; they take possession of it. Here Sembene suggests that the physical blemish that the elite find repellant has to be fully exhibited, as a prelude to the humiliation of El Hadji. It is bad enough to be spat on, but to be spat on by beggars ("this human refuse"), and in one's own house, is the height of humiliation, in spite of the aura of ritual which surrounds it. Mulvey writes, "The otherness of Africa that horrified the Europeans is perpetuated into a real horror for the ordinary people by colonialism, and grotesquely more so, by the irresponsible greed of the new ruling class" (Mulvey 1999, 418). She quotes Gabriel as suggesting that this act of spitting on El Hadji is a folk method of purgation. Lyons also calls it an "urban proletarian ritual," linking it with a griot's performance of an act of absolution on behalf of a patron (1984, 326). The belief that an offender can be purified by submitting to verbal abuse from the lowly, in many cases a griot, would explain El Hadji's humiliation in the hands of the beggars, except that these are not griots in the conventional sense of the word (although one of them plays the *xalam*) and their marginality, rather than being defined by a caste system, is produced, and barely twenty years old. Though not challenging the conventional reading of this scene, Sembene has argued that the ritual preceded by the nondiegetic song is an appeal to revolt. The beggars' ransacking of the refrigerator and attempt to rape the maid are gestures to this revolt, which they make in the only moment when they can act on their situation.

It is noteworthy that Lyons links this ritual to a balancing of gender politics, and I use this connection in my reading of the twin rhetoric of gender inequality and political oppression in *Xala*. Sembene prefers to address the question of gender oppression in terms of class because, as he says, the Western feminist model, by concentrating on the nuclear family as the domain of social control, leads to the deterioration of human beings. "Excessive maleness has to be curbed if real power over evil is to be achieved," writes Lyons, and "while the beggars spit on [El Hadji], he must wear the crown from his third wife's wedding veil" (1984, 326). There are interesting conjunctions here between the early suspicion that Oumi, the second wife, might be the source of the curse and her mysterious ritual before the camera during the reception, especially as these discrete images indicate the power of fetishism, and Sembene's strategy of critiquing it. The wedding crown is a European symbol, like the car key that the camera highlights when Oumi snaps the head off the miniature bride figure, and the key can be read as El Hadji's key to N'Gone's virginity and to the power of sexual domination. The fact that the *xala* is lifted without the intervention of a fetishized object, at a time when El Hadji has been stripped of all the appurtenances of power and pomp, completes the explosion of double fetishism.

Poststructuralist "Oversight": A New Fetish?

As I showed at the beginning of this chapter, earlier critics of African cinema, whether African, American, or European, whether adopting a semiotic and psychoanalytical or a Marxist theoretical approach, were not as different as their disagreements seemed to suggest. A critique of *Xala* on the basis of dependency theory might have more in common with a psychoanalytical reading drawing on the Marxist-Freudian notion of the fetish than with a reading concerned with either the context in which the film itself, considered as a text, was produced, or the professional context in which Sembene-the-filmmaker produced it. For instance, this is what Mulvey's approving citation of Gabriel's article indicates. The struggle was largely for control of the terms of discourse, and the two sides in the debate in *Screen* reflected this. If there was one significant way in which Burton and Gabriel differed, it was on the unspeakable presumption that the theoretically dense protocols of psychoanalysis and semiotics, which were affiliated with the linguistic turn of poststructuralism, operated on a very high level of abstraction and were, to put it crudely, above the heads of Africans! No one really dares to put it this way for fear of incurring accusations of racism, but the suggestion is nevertheless implicit in the perception of some Western, postcolonial, or metropolitan Africanist scholars that their African colleagues are "resistant to theory."[13] It is not often realized that the politically informed critical option which is favored by African critics and generally oriented toward Marxism, Pan-Africanism, and tricontinentalism is no less theoretical in the proper sense.

Indeed, to isolate the Marxist from the semiotic and the psychoanalytic in the ideological critique of representation is not only to decontextualize film in an oppositional context like the tricontinental socialist internationalism, but also to misrepresent the history of film theory. A seminal work of film theory, Stephen Heath's *Questions of Cinema,* is premised on this "trinity." Heath writes,

> Cinema brings historical materialism and psychoanalysis together in such a
> way that the consideration of film and ideology begins from and constantly re-
> turns us to their conjuncture, in such a way that from the analysis of cinema, of
> film, we may be able to engage with theoretical issues of a more general scope,
> issues crucial for a materialist analysis of ideological institutions and practices.
> (1981, 4)

But it is against the grain of precisely this kind of historicist approach that Harrow writes in his recent book, *Postcolonial African Cinema.* Harrow hopes to reorient criticism of African cinema away from the tradition of political engagement and that which favors a unified discourse of a cultural identity with which both the practice and theory of this filmmaking are identified. He contends that the presumption of a historical basis for African cinema as a mode of representation is one of several (five) shibboleths, because "there is no site where one can stand from which to evaluate the authentic" (Harrow 2007b, xii), and the concern with historical depth in criticism results from a misunderstanding of the nature of film, which he takes to be more about surface than about depth. Since Sembene's work remains primary to an understanding of the ideological and cultural background of this cinematic practice, Harrow singles Sembene out for special mention.[14] Sembene's films, according to Harrow, have a progressivist format, "the sense of a movement forward [which attests], in varying ways, to Sembène's embrace of the grand narrative of Marxism that shaped the generation of African intellectuals, creative artists, and thinkers after World War II" (9).

The real culprit in this approach is the principle of historicism, "the necessity to move forward, to measure one's progress in terms of distance from the past" (10), and Harrow's critique of this analytical principle is extrapolated from Robert Young's reading of Louis Althusser. In other words, Sembene's cinematic template is a validation of this notion of "historical temporality," and it is borne out in conventional continuity editing (the norm in commercial filmmaking) on the one hand, and in the social-realist mode of Russian cinema, on the other. Here we hear echoes of Jean-Pierre Bekolo's characterization of Sembene as too invested in the Western model (Ukadike 2002, 225). Harrow contends that this style is formally different from the reflexive styles of filmmakers such as Jean-Marie Teno, Bekolo, Mambèty, and Régina Fanta Nacro, who substitute the syncopated jump-cut for continuity editing. Although Harrow warns that, with "the spirit of ceddo still being very much with us" (2007b, xiii) he is not advocating a wholesale refutation of the past, the distinctions he makes between the two styles constitute nothing short of a definitive epistemological break with the anti-colonial history of African cinema.

There is no question about it: the tradition in the theory and criticism of African cinema that assumes a call-and-response relationship between the discourse of anti-colonialism (in the writings of Frantz Fanon and Aimé Césaire) and critical analyses of oppositional filmmaking (Gabriel's, for instance) is over-inflated and long overdue for reassessment. Furthermore, the cinematic practices of younger filmmakers, like Teno, Jo Ramaka, Sissako, Nacro, and Bekolo, are different in style and substance from those of Sembene and Med Hondo. However, what is going on is far more complex than a straightforward exchange of one style of editing for another. The younger filmmakers do not eschew explicitly political filmmaking, as evidenced by the recent films of Nacro and Sissako, and they are no less given to rhetorical and ideological self-positioning. They do it differently, to be sure, but the difference is conceptual; they do not always display their familiarity with aesthetic practices in the service of a discourse of cultural identity. Harrow's argument that the discourse of authenticity (*ceddo*) has been displaced and replaced by postmodernist youthfulness (*tsotsi*) rests on a paradox: the terms of the passage he proposes are no less progressivist, nor is the "new" guaranteed to lack its own versions of authenticity.

Thus, Harrow's critique of a historicist, culturally determined notion of African cinema—its practice and criticism—is wholly called for. And his prose is charming! The problem with the procedure seems to be a tendentious notion of what constitutes "historicism," a critique of cinematic ideology that sees historical materialism as the sole culprit, while resolutely revamping psychoanalytical and semiotic approaches in a deconstructive register more amenable to fashionable postmodernist criticism. This is the basis of the double meaning of "oversight" invoked in the title of this section; this poststructuralist approach oversees the decentering of unified discourses in African cinema but commits an oversight by underestimating the relationship between historical materialism and other forms of ideological critique of representation.

Harrow is able to sustain this oversight for four principal reasons. First, he thinks of anti-colonial nationalism as a unitary discourse grounded in an abstract "historicism." As I argued in the introduction by identifying the often conflicting projects of bourgeois nationalism and socialist struggle, the general "historicism" of the anti-colonial struggle will have to be unpacked with the goal of specifying the ideological differences between Casablanca and Monrovia groups of the old Organization of African Unity, or between an Amílcar Cabral and a Jonas Savimbi. Second, Harrow conflates cinematic practices and criticisms. While it is true that much of the early criticism of African cinema posited a logical connection with its practice and was largely biased toward the didactic form,[15] the films were themselves always more reflexive, open, and often contradictory, even Sembene's own. As my analysis above has shown, the figure of Rama in *Xala* and the use of the *xala* represent unresolved problems in dealing with the full implications of modernity in postcolonial Africa. Third, Harrow's extensive reliance on an aspect of Althusser's work to critique historicism neglects the connections between Marxism, psychoanalysis, and semiotics in film theory. Sembene's work as a filmmaker is cognizant of the two strains of Marxism as a social philosophy: historical materialism as the critique of political economy, and dialectical materialism as the critique of social alienation and commodity fetishism. In Harrow's hands, Sembene the Marxist becomes the basis for critiquing Sembene the anti-neocolonialist, and although the two are inseparable, Harrow's critique does not pinpoint where the unity lies. The intensification of neoliberalism in the aftermath of Soviet communism indicates the exhaustion of a certain kind of Marxist analysis, and the so-called wrong start of cinema of political engagement is a function of a different intellectual climate: an explicit identification with "Third World" political and cultural aspirations has relatively limited purchase in the present context of neoliberal globalization, and what is dismissed as the wrong start of cinema of political engagement seems wrong only in retrospect. Indeed, given David Murphy's argument regarding *Xala*'s commercial success (2000), this may be one instance where what is becoming conventional wisdom in African cinema scholarship—the idea that political engagement in a film is detrimental to its popular success—does not hold.

Fourth and finally, these three propositions are tenable only insofar as Harrow chooses to treat African cinema in virtual isolation. An approach that relates the history of decolonization to the global socialist revolutions in the 1960s and 1970s would establish not only political connections between events in southern Africa (Zimbabwe, Angola, and Mozambique) and in the Americas (Cuba and Chile) but cultural connections as well, as I demonstrated in the discussion of tricontinentalism and Third Cinema in chapter 1. By focusing solely on African instances of nationalism, historicism, and authenticity in cinema, Harrow has given an insufficient account of a complex, if problematic, tricontinental political and cultural solidarity.[16]

The ritual "cleansing" which dominates the final sequence of *Xala* is a rhetorical settling of scores between the bourgeoisie and the lumpenproletariat, the asymmetrical forces of the postcolony. But before their semi-public humiliation of El Hadji, the beggars embark on a series of acts of transgression whose significance must not be lost to the visual attractiveness of the ritual. The first thing they do upon entering the house is to physically attack the maid, perhaps with the intention of sexually violating her. (Contrary to Harrow's claim [2007b, 3], Rama is not victimized in this scene, unless he means in psychological terms, in that she must witness the disgrace of her father, which causes her to weep.) Then they raid the refrigerator; apparently the poor are no less susceptible to consumerism. Sembene once said that if those beggars had had guns they would have blown off El Hadji's head. The impotent anger simmering below the surface at the tea-seller's table finds an outlet in the attack on the maid. It is an expression of genuine frustration, but it points to something truly disturbing about "the power of the powerless": the tendency of the poor to prey on their own kind. This detail is often overlooked in analyses of the film because the rhetoric of Gorgui's trial and punishment of El Hadji is in line with the dominant ideology of the narrative—the dénouement that shows the *xala* to be a temporary affliction.

The scene is powerful for other reasons, of course, and one of these is the rhetoric of Sembene's dialectical camera. An irreducible conflict is the basis of the polarization between protagonist and antagonist, and in any number of Sembene's films the scene of confrontation recurs. Gorgui's judgment of El Hadji is only the climax of a steep loss of authority that is signaled by Rama's affronting her father's self-respect by stating that all polygamists are liars. There are similar confrontations between Sergeant Diatta and the infantrymen in *Camp de Thiaroye* (1988); between Djib (Kine's son) and his long-absent father, Boubacar Omar Payan, in *Faat Kine* (2000); between Ibrahim, fresh from France, and his reactionary father in *Moolaadé* (2004); and particularly between Barthélémy and the Commandant in *Guelwaar* (1993). Since the (usually male) elder loses out in the (often lengthy) war of words, Sembene may be suggesting that such a recurrent routing of the old order (in the persona of the "big man") is an inevitable consequence of decolonization. One of the striking things about this dialectic in Sembene's work is the way that *Moolade* and *Guelwaar* can be analytically juxtaposed through the characters of Barthélémy and Ibrahim. Both are returning from France, but while the one is disdainful of Thiès, his hometown, in what we are encouraged to read as a sign of alienation, the other returns with an opposition to female circumcision that is informed by his living in contemporary France. The recurrence of this dramatic turn marks Sembene's cinema, and is crucial to the structure that Harrow has set up as the target of his critique.

Yet it is this dialectical camera which introduces the paradox at the core of the film: Sembene's materialist attitude toward African cultural practices, as symbolized in the *xala*. As a progressive African of the contemporary world, Sembene occupied the paradoxical position of the intellectual doomed to simultaneously critique and defend the values undergirding those practices.[17] This position is visible, for instance, in his assigning to the dispossessed beggar Gorgui the power to inflict and remove the *xala,* and it permeates Sembene's work. The tension is between respect for the vitality of a culture resistant to colonial abuse (the power of the thunder-god in *Emitaï,* the group *ceddo* which resists religious impositions) and the condemnation of a highly hierarchical and oppressive past from which these practices have not been totally separated. Sembene's skepticism about African "magic" is obvious in the exaggerated way in which the first person El Hadji approaches for a cure displays his knowledge, and we are invited to view the shaman as a charlatan. But there is Serigne Mada, the marabout ("a man of his word," as Gorgui says), whose practice is derived from Islam, and whose feeling of betrayal at receiving a dud check from his client results in the restoration of the affliction. Moreover, the filmmaker uses the *xala* dialectically, as the basis of a cinematic ruse, and to underscore the alienation of El Hadji's social class from the genuine values of European and African cultures. It is this alienation that produces the double fetishism.

This ironic deployment of the *xala* effectively symbolizes the impotence of the *rentier* elite, but what does one make of the fact that Gorgui is the source of the curse? The film positions the viewer to recognize Sembene's progressive politics in his depiction of the lot of the beggars, and this identification is fully rewarded in the final scene. However, as I have just noted, in this scene the beggars not only eat yoghurt and quaff drinks but also attack the maid. This attack is an indication of the unpredictable morality of the poor, something that intellectuals must reflect on whenever they hear about mass protests complete with looting and arson. The point is that, in this film, Sembene's handling of the beggars and the *xala* represents a valiant attempt to rise above the Marxist notion of false consciousness while showing the contradictions of class consciousness. When El Hadji calls the invasion of his home a robbery, Gorgui retorts that it is vengeance. He accuses the fallen businessman in turn of dispossessing other members of the Beye family of their inheritance, with the consequence that he, Gorgui, has spent time in jail.

The irony of this is the transformation of a "national" (class-based) patrimony into a "family" (caste-based) one, as if the nationalization of the economy proclaimed by the president of the Chamber in the film's opening sequence had not deteriorated into the acquisition of private property. The house where the trial unfolds is held sacrosanct by the law enforcement agency. The questions of class which Gorgui's slippery discourse of familial inheritance obfuscates are further underscored when, after El Hadji has reluctantly accepted the beggars as his guests and the cop has departed, Hadja Awa (another victim of the socioeconomic arrangement) again defends family honor by threatening to call security. As I suggested in the introduction, the position of the engaged artist-activist, which is very much on display in this film and closely scripted into the final sequence, is often thought incompatible with popular yearnings. This is because such yearnings are usually understood in terms of the alienated consciousness of the masses—more in terms of the supernaturalism of a *xala* than of the contradictions of class which I have just analyzed. Sembene's rhetorical attempts to manage these contradictions are not matched by their complexity, and this is one blind spot of the film.

The other blind spot is due to the structure of the film, indeed to the structure of Senegalese (or West African) society in the early 1970s. As a modern African country in thrall to modernization and development policies, Senegal was an import economy, of which the commodity fetishism criticized in El Hadji and his class is a part. But commodity fetishism is only a conspicuous example of the dependent economy, and less dramatic but equally important examples are visible in the film. The formation of an elite class with professional ambitions requires the presence of a service sector, and it is worth noting that the actors playing Rama and Thieli also played the couple Anta and Mory in Mambèty's *Touki Bouki*. Also, it has been suggested that a party guest in the wedding scene, who later mocks El Hadji's sexual capacity, may be a transvestite (Murphy 2000, 106n27).[18] It is impossible to contemplate such a society without feeling that the neoliberal import economy has been galvanized, and a critique of commodity fetishism and sexual orientation (or sexual deviancy) does not exhaust the problem. In addition to luxury cars, designer bottled water, and expensive clothing, Senegal, like other modern economies, also imported television sets, and one of these is among the personal effects that Oumi, the second wife, piles into a truck when she deserts her husband.

The importance of the import economy in general and technology transfer in particular cannot be overestimated in a social structure in which the media are integral, especially because the critique of commodity fetishism only goes so far. It does not (although it ought to) attract attention to the contents of those commodities. These contents are present in diverse ways. The president's speech in the film's opening sequence is a proclamation of economic nationalization:

Oumi leaving El Hadji's house. *Xala,* directed by Ousmane Sembene, 1974.

Avant la face a notre de peuple, nous devoir montrer que nous sommes capable comme tous les peuples du monde. Nous sommes des hommes d'affaire. Nous devoir prendre tout le direction les bancs pays.

(Before our people we must show ourselves as capable, like other peoples of the world. We are businessmen. We must take over all the businesses, even the banks.)

Certainly Sembene expects this speech to be understood as self-serving, but it is interesting that *Xala* was one of the first films to be coproduced with the Senegalese National Cinema Society, an institution which, as Murphy has reported (2000, 98), developed as a result of the nationalization of the country's film distribution system. If Sembene acted like a fox, collaborating with this "neocolonial" institution to produce a film intended to attack it, the trickster-god of storytelling and hermeneutics, never negligent of his associations with the market and the crossroads, also succeeded in making the story say things behind the filmmaker's back, as the contradictions of class consciousness in the final sequence show. So we are confronted with the suggestive paradoxes of professional film and theater actors in a *rentier* economy; the making of an "anti-neocolonialist" film through the partial agency of a nationalized, neocolonial economic and cultural institution; the display of spectacular "cultural activities" in the film's opening sequence side by side with the genteel music of the wedding reception and the haunting song of revolt that saturates the entire film. These are the contexts of the film: the import economy exposed the parasitic qualities of the *rentier* elite, but one cannot fully appreciate this fact without accounting for the supplement, the powerful role that such an economic arrangement played in fashioning cultures of hybridity and bricolage in the postcolony. This need to specify the contours of double fetishism (cultural practice as "false consciousness" and the contradictions of the import economy) is what leads me to the next chapter.

3   Tunde Kelani's Nollywood: Aesthetics of Exhortation

Of the three directors whose works are the main focus of this book, the Nigerian Tunde Kelani is perhaps the least well known to an international audience, even one familiar with African films. However, having made sixteen full-length films in less than twenty years (1993–2010), he is perhaps the most prolific of African filmmakers, surpassing even the late Ousmane Sembene, who had completed fourteen films by his death in June 2007. Debates over who has produced more may not always count in artistic and intellectual matters, art being more about *what* than about *how much*. Nonetheless, Kelani's output is a function of a particular context, that of the cinematic phenomenon called Nollywood, and for this reason it matters a great deal. Nollywood is now widely acknowledged as the third largest film industry in the world, after the United States (Hollywood) and India (Bollywood). In fact, Nigeria produced 872 feature-length films in 2006, in comparison with 1,091 in India and 485 in the United States (UNESCO Institute for Statistics 2010). Kelani, a producer-director and the founder of Mainframe Productions, a film and television production company, is the most consistently active of the Nollywood directors, with an average of a film every year. He emerged as a filmmaker in the mid-1990s, alongside other talented figures like Amaka Igwe, Tade Ogidan, Zeb Ejiro, Opa Williams, Kenneth Nnebue, and Tunde Alabi-Hundeyin. Most of these directors are still active, but Kelani is now clearly in his own class. He is also among the most sought-after, appearing at conferences and film festivals both locally and internationally. What is it about him or his work that draws this kind of attention and enters him in the annals of global filmmaking, despite the relative youth of Nollywood as a cinematic phenomenon? This chapter sets out to address this question in all its ramifications through an extended discussion of *Thunderbolt: Magun* (2001), his first English-language film.

In a commercial filmmaking industry that thrives on films in popular genres that are produced in an average of three weeks, Kelani's deliberative, thoughtful, lush, and culturally sophisticated streams of images are something of a rarity. The sheer number and scope of Nollywood films, ranging from sublime tragedies drawn from mythology (such as Femi Lasode's *Sango*, 1999) to the lowliest slapstick imaginable, make the task of separating the wheat from the chaff an arduous one. By focusing on *Thunderbolt: Magun* and on the wider context in which this and thousands of other videofilms[1] are produced, I will demonstrate how Kelani approximates a bridge between the specificity of Nigerian cinematic practice and the aesthetics of contemporary cinemas driven by new technologies and decentralized economies. I shall be looking closely at the film to exemplify Kelani's work as an aggregation of the dominant trends in this cinema.[2]

Thunderbolt: Magun was produced in Nigeria in 2001, and released to the American art-film market the following year by the San Francisco–based company California Newsreel. It was the first of the Nigerian videofilms to be so distributed.[3] It dwells on greed, sexual jealousy, and ethnic suspicion, and it views "African cultural practices" as "scientific knowledge" in several didactic moves that are characteristic of Kelani's work as well as of the cinematic practice itself, and which I conceptualize here as the *aesthetics of exhortation*. By this term I refer to the West African tradition of aesthetic populism which understands politics as a subcategory of morality, and gauges the impact of a work of art according to how the audience responds to it, either by making it a commercial success or by drawing a useful example from it. Indeed, according to this logic, success in the market is a measure of quality: if it sells then it must be good, and vice versa. A dramatic or narrative text is thought to be fundamentally about notions of good and bad conduct and, in exhortatory and didactic registers, subsumes every aspect of human relations—social, political, economic, and so on—to this basic theme. On the other hand, it is this aesthetic orientation which, structuring *Thunderbolt: Magun* in a didactic form, jars with the reception of Nigerian films in the pluralist context of multicultural studies, and limits their capacity to travel outside their context of origin. This is also why the films continue to be loosely described as melodrama and social commentary, and why some critics still speak of them as apolitical, although this is now a minority position. However, what is really at stake in the aesthetic of exhortation, as I deploy it in this book, is the strong West African tradition of aesthetic populism that sees politics (or any thematics) as a subcategory of morality. It is easier to grasp the loose application of "melodrama" as a term of aesthetic description if one relates it to the philosophical question of communalism as Wiredu speaks of it (2000).

A Director and His Milieu

Thunderbolt: Magun presents its thematic interests within the context of the global discourse of the HIV/AIDS pandemic. The videofilm form's reliance on this kind of thematization of social issues encourages us to think of its strand of aesthetic populism as approaching opportunism, the tacking of topical issues onto a textual form for economic benefit. But this opportunism is strategic, as I will show. The film is Kelani's sixth, and his first in the English language. Having produced several subtitled films between 1993 and 1999, the cinematographer-turned-director found himself routinely dubbed a Yoruba filmmaker, a label which he claims does not bother him.[4] But then he learned of a novel in English by Adebayo Faleti (who stars in the film as the *babalawo,* master of secret preventive and curative knowledge), which the author had written in response to being routinely described as a Yoruba writer! This film exemplifies how Kelani has managed to build a bridge between specific Yoruba (and Nigerian) audiences and the "world."[5] Although Kelani argues that the dominant practices of Nollywood do not quite match his own, my contention here is that he uses *Thunderbolt: Magun* to meet Nollywood halfway, at what is approximately the halfway point of his career. Most of the Nollywood films that circulate globally are in English and rely on standard generic conventions, even though, as the UNESCO figures show, more than half (56%) of Nollywood releases are in Nigeria's three major local languages.

By foregrounding the image of *magun,* a system of libidinal regulation that draws on the occult, the film simultaneously deploys and questions the category of the "popular" to draw attention to the persistence of the symbolic order in the context of sexual subordination. In looking at this videofilm, I will highlight the coalescence and sublimation of certain recurring features of Kelani's cinematic practice. These include a complex address to Nigerian political society from the standpoint of Yoruba expressive culture, a predilection for allegorical and "popular" forms, subtle or (often) overt didacticism, the use of actors from both the English-language and Yoruba subgenres, the skillful use of light and exteriors in cinematography, and an astute sense of a transnational context. My discussion of this videofilm relies on the detailed inscription of the trope of enchantment, the figuration of occult imaginary, through which the film exemplifies what is significant about Nollywood as a cultural and economic phenomenon.

Although Kelani has often made light of attempts to categorize him as a Nollywood director, it was the phenomenon of Nollywood that enabled him to change from a cinematographer to a director. He began as a television cameraman in the 1970s, and soon emerged as a cinematographer on several of the films produced in the second half of the 1980s (including *Ireke Onibudo* and *Iwa*), that is, when celluloid productions were at their nadir. The change from the predominantly celluloid format to video in the late 1980s was occasioned by economic necessity, as various critics have pointed out (Adesokan 2004; Larkin 2004; Balogun 2004; Haynes and Okome 1997). In the mid-1980s the International Monetary Fund (IMF) foisted structural adjustment programs on many countries in developing regions of the world with the intention of regulating their economies on the logic of the neoliberal free market. Nigeria was one such country (Forrest 1994; Osaghae 1998; Hibou 1999). According to the sociologist Leslie Sklair (1991), structural adjustment programs were one of several attempts to protect the interests of transnational capital, maintained through the Washington Consensus procedure of payment or "servicing" of Third World debts. The hallmarks of these programs included devaluation of the local currency, control of interest rates, and removal of subsidies from public corporations. Life at the crossroads of capital being a series of improvisations and recycling of materials, everyday economic activities in the postcolony followed the pattern of large-scale reconstitution of standards and the undercapitalization of economic practices. The coexistence of different forms of economic activity—agricultural, commercial, and industrial—within the system of surplus extraction can be seen, in the context of structural adjustment, to have predisposed the social structure to a pervasive digital economy at a time when people are still trying to work out the "modern" intricacies of the analog. Small-scale enterprises mushroomed, rather than more heavily capitalized industrial undertakings.

To take three Nigerian examples: "pure water" is commonly sold in plastic sachets; motorcycle owners provide taxi services (called *okada*); and Nigerian-owned fast-food chains (such as Mr. Biggs, Tastee Chicken, Tantalizers, Chicken Republic, Mama Cass, and Sweet Sensation) have proliferated, ensuring that if America's McDonald's or Burger King arrive, there will be competitors waiting. As an economic form, the videofilm explosion is best seen in the context of these pervasive, informal, improvisatory social formations. It began with the owner of a video camera visiting a private party to record the event, with or without permission, and then producing videotapes for sale to attendees. It began as music videos featuring lip-syncing actors. It began as a script for a stage production that was shot as if for television. This informal approach to filmmaking developed in the context of economic adjustments, in which acclaimed directors in film and theater could neither sustain theatrical productions nor make celluloid films like their contemporaries in Francophone West Africa.[6] Shot with video cameras, the earliest films were not believed to measure up to the technical quality of celluloid films. This was the basis of Hubert Ogunde's dismissal (Adesokan 2008a) of the first videofilm produced in Nigeria, *Ekun* (Tiger; dir. and prod. Muyideen Aromire, 1989), while Ogunde was a member of the Censors' Board.

It was against this background that Kenneth Nnebue, a dealer in electronics at the famous Idumota market in downtown Lagos who had been producing films in Yoruba for some years, released an Igbo-language film, *Living in Bondage,* in 1992.[7] The film not only jump-started the Igbo-film subgenre, as audiences were relieved to find a visual form with whose culture and language they could identify, but also led to the explosion of English-language films. English-language Nollywood films resemble television soap operas in formal terms, and travel better among Africans (although they are not always completely translatable in other cultural contexts). *Living in Bondage* was the breakthrough work of this form,[8] but Kelani's Mainframe Productions was the first to move the form closer to conventional cinema. The main objection that well-established directors and producers had to the new phenomenon was the video format. Cinema, in the conventional sense, was shot on 35mm or 16mm celluloid film stock and processed in a postproduction laboratory using analog technology. This modernist mode originated in the Fordist era of mass production, but it has been surpassed, or at any rate disrupted, by today's digital technology.

In some of the Nigerian films in the late 1980s, before Nollywood really took shape, Kelani collaborated with the producer Wale Fanu (they both managed Cinekraft, a production company), combining fine cinematography with a sense of how to pace a story in the televisual format that was being concurrently deployed in thirteen-episode television serials like Jimoh Aliu's *Arelu* (1987) and *Yanponyanrin* (1989), Zeb Ejiro's *Ripples* (1988) and *Fortunes* (1992), Amaka Igwe's *Checkmate* (1991–1992), Laolu Ogunniyi's *Opa Aje* (1988), Yekeen Ajileye's *Koto Orun* (1992) and *Mama Mi l'Eko* (1994), and Mike Bamiloye's *Agbara-Nla* (1994). These two skills are evident in *Thunderbolt: Magun;* indeed, until making this film, Kelani had tended to understate the style of the television serials from which many other videofilms still draw their inspiration.

Two factors were crucial to Kelani's aesthetic choices in becoming a filmmaker. First, there was the economic factor. He told me, "By the time my partnership with Wale Fanu came to an end, I had come to the conclusion that we could never fund films originating from the traditional chemical-based celluloid and that it was time to start looking for alternative technologies."[9] The strictures of structural adjustment were difficult for filmmakers to escape. They were also aware of the ordeal of the legendary comedian Moses Olaiya Adejumo (Baba Sala), whose highly successful film *Orun Mooru* (1982) fell into the hands of pirates, an incident that may have contributed to the decline of his career. Besides, on the logic of the neocolonial extractive relationship, postproduction could be done only in the United States or England.[10] Kelani's call for alternative technologies is to be seen in the context of a decisive shift from the national mode of celluloid film stock, which is modernist and analog, to the digital mode, which is commensurate with the transnational economic process. Although some filmmakers, especially Ladi Ladebo, continued to produce 35mm films into the 1990s, this was increasingly difficult to afford, especially since Ladebo's films had limited distribution and exhibition facilities and were aesthetically different from what audiences usually embraced.[11]

The other factor was technical, and Kelani told me, "At [the beginning], the home videos already produced were disappointing and had [a] very bad reputation. I was sure that they could be better produced and was determined to select a story that drew on the same dramatic elements employed in the other attempts."[12] In Kelani's first film, *Ti Oluwa Nile* (The Earth Belongs to the Lord, 1993–1995), a three-part story about the moral irresponsibility of speculating in sacred land, his training as a cinematographer is particularly on display in the series of montages that underscore the haunting of the principal culprit, Otun Asiyanbi, as he vainly tries to escape the ghosts of his dead collaborators. Furthermore, Kelani's deployment of the Ifa verse ("Okanran-Owonrin") works as a form of narrative disclosure. The verse includes a parable about strangers engaging in land speculation, and this original parable becomes integrated into the plot in such a way that the narrative unfolds logically as the *babalawo* chanting the verse appears on screen or through diegetic voice-over. Although culturally specific, this deployment should also be seen in the wider context of the presence of occult images in Igbo- and English-language videofilms, as well as in the importance which supernatural effects had attained in Yoruba theater and television productions. This move has ideological as well as aesthetic consequences, and I will explore Kelani's exemplary place in Nigerian videofilm practice in the way they intersect. A full account of his career will reveal that Kelani approaches his Yoruba cultural template with more respect than irony. This respectful treatment of culture, which is reinforced by his use of cinema as a means of cultural redirection, is also the beginning of what one may call "neotraditional cinema," in which the apparatus of an expressive culture is put on display for didactic and educational purposes.

This is quite different from the earlier category of "folk cinema," which described the cinematic practice of the 1980s as a continuation of the "folk opera" idiom, which was itself loaded with class prejudices. The aesthetics of neotraditional cinema are exhortatory, viewing cultural and social institutions in a constructive manner, perhaps as the supplement or the logical outcome of this notably commercial form. *Ti Oluwa Nile* was the first film to consciously and extensively mix diegetic and nondiegetic music, crosscutting, and dream sequences, using a slower pace than was common in English-language films and television dramas, and in this way, it aspired to be cinematic. Ever since, Kelani's films have continued to draw attention to the pervasiveness of the artisanal approach in others' films, by making the viewer aware of the cinematic apparatus, especially the camera. Watching any of his films, one gets the sense that it is cinema, not television soap opera. In the majority of videofilms, the camera functions mostly as an item of photographic equipment, used to record the images of individuals interacting with one another. But in each of his sixteen films, Kelani consciously and meticulously creates cinematic styles that are still rare among Nigerian filmmakers. His second film, the two-part *Ayo Ni Mo Fe* (Ayo Is My Choice[13]), is both funny and serious without being unduly melodramatic, its sophisticated social commentaries are deftly counterbalanced with psychological insights, and it is exquisitely filmed.[14] This film was followed by *Koseegbe* (The Reformer's Dilemma) and *O Le Ku* (Fearful Incidents, parts 1 and 2), adaptations of dramatic and novelistic works by Akinwumi Isola, a leading Yoruba writer and scholar. These two are very faithful to the source texts. However, while Kelani's interest in maintaining the integrity of the Yoruba language suggests his possession of a cultural consciousness in the face of the general lowering of educational standards and the elite's neocolonial preference for English, the stylized acting in these films sometimes introduces a certain stiffness into the action. This kind of stylized acting, observable when an actor is speaking "proper" Yoruba (without linguistic code-switching), results largely from Kelani's collaboration with Isola, whose plays were once adapted for the stage and television by a traveling theater company.[15] It is one of the signs of the "neotraditional cinema," and it demonstrates the filmmaker's respectful allegiance to the Yoruba cultural tradition.[16]

The film *Thunderbolt: Magun,* the focus of this chapter, is both a thriller and a subtle meditation on human motives, unusually staged from the perspective of a female protagonist, in a series of flashbacks and crosscuttings that are both narrative and reflective. In *Saworoide* (Brass Bells), a 1999 political thriller that allegorizes corruption, a forty-two-second-long scene is made up of twenty shots, with different gradations and durations of framing. In addition to these films, exclusively produced by his television production company Mainframe Productions, Kelani has also directed or produced a number of feature films, including *Yellow Card* and *The White Handkerchief* for the South African cable network MNET's New Directions series and for Zimbabwe's Media for Development Trust.

His first film, *Ti Oluwa Nile,* is remarkable for its unprecedented mixing of actors from the traveling theater with theater arts graduates, and this is another reason for his influence on Yoruba filmmakers. The central character in that film, Otun Asiyanbi, is played by Alhaji Kareem Adepoju, the famous Baba Wande of Oyin Adejobi Theater, who subsequently produced *Ekun Oko Oke* (The Indomitable Tiger), which I alluded to in the introduction. We can argue that Kelani's cinema owes something to the practices of the traveling theater, since the skeleton of *Ti Oluwa Nile*'s plot was supplied by Adepoju. Besides, Kelani still relies on some proven actors from this tradition, especially those with ties to the late dramatist Ola Rotimi's Ori-Olokun Theater in the university town of Ile-Ife. In *Thunderbolt: Magun,* he draws on Igbo actors as well, and this affects the idioms in which his works relate directly to the Yoruba genre. Kelani's films play to the expectations of an audience already familiar with certain popular images, while also making concrete a constructive approach to the representation of such images. The aesthetics implicit in this move have offered fresh formal possibilities to the usually competitive Yoruba filmmakers, and I take up these issues in the conclusion, focusing on the implications of Kelani's work for the entirety of videofilm practice.

The primary image of *Thunderbolt: Magun* is the *magun* (literally "don't mount"), a means of enforcing chastity. In practice, it is a means of sexual subordination. "Magun" is a charmed lace (like a shoelace), which a man who suspects his wife of adultery puts in a place she is sure to pass through. When she unknowingly walks over it, she becomes afflicted. Ngozi, the film's protagonist, is living in Oleyo, where she is attached to the grammar school as a corper, a member of the National Youth Service Corps.[17] After she has a traumatic encounter with an apparition in the marketplace, she is taken by Mama Tutu, her landlady, to see a *babalawo* or Ifa priest. After preliminary divination, the priest discovers that the young mother is laced with *magun*. The following exchange ensues:

MAMA TUTU [FRANTIC]: Someone has put *magun* on you!
NGOZI: Magih?
MAMA TUTU: Magun! Heeh, how do I explain it to her?
BABA: *Magun kii s'arun.*
MAMA TUTU: Magun is not a disease.
NGOZI: *Hen-hen?*
BABA: *Sugbon, iku ni.*
MAMA TUTU: It is death.
BABA: *Eni ti nba nsesekuse, ti won ba fi le lara, eni to ba ba se isekuse yoo ku.*
MAMA TUTU: Put on you, so that anybody who commits adultery with you will die.
BABA: *Amo, ti oun naa ba je eni ti ara re mo, tii se onisekuse, to ba pe lara re naa, yoo ku ni.*
MAMA TUTU: But if you're innocent throughout the incubation period, you will die.
NGOZI: But why me?
MAMA TUTU: It can be anyone. Your enemy. Put on you so that anybody who has intercourse with you, even your husband, will die.

It needs to be said that Mama Tutu's translations are in fact interpretations, the density of the *babalawo*'s explanations being diluted by the extremely urgent and delicate duty of conveying the message to the afflicted woman. Additionally, the interpretations represent a management of the complicated linguistic terrain that is Nigeria. Yinka, Ngozi's husband, has heard stories about her infidelity; his friends tell him that she is enjoying the attention of a medical doctor, Dimeji Taiwo, a member of the board of the school which employs her. But Ngozi also has a sizable inheritance from her recently deceased grandmother (who is embodied in the apparition). Mama Tutu's mention of "your enemy" is significant because it draws attention to a key feature of the aesthetic world of the videofilms—the conception of social relations in terms of good and evil. However, *magun* is not yet fully developed either as a popular means of sexual subordination or as an allegory of parapolitical regulation and adjudication, and the issue is described in greater detail by the vice-principal of Oleyo Grammar School in the presence of Mama Tutu and Ngozi's father. His speech complements Mama Tutu's loaded interpretation of the *babalawo*'s discovery:

You know this AIDS they talk about? *Magun* is worse. They say one can carry AIDS for nine years. No one can carry *magun* for more than nine weeks. Whereas AIDS is sexually transmitted disease, *magun* is sexually assisted death. The carrier, usually a woman, is afflicted with the *magun*, and any man who contracts it, by having sexual intercourse with her, dies, either immediately, or very, very shortly afterwards. There are many types of *magun*, but three of them are most dangerous. One, the cockcrow. In this, the contractor crows like a cock, immediately after intercourse with the carrier: koo-koo-roo-koo! Then he dies, promptly. Two, the somersault. The contractor somersaults three times: fai, fai, fai! Immediately. The contractor may also bleed to death, either by vomiting or urinating blood continuously. Ah-ha-ha! The worst, but mercifully the least common: PJT, partners joined together . . . After sex, a man and a woman cannot be separated. They both die, one joined to the other. Women suspected to be unfaithful to their husbands are usually afflicted with *magun* . . . The incubation period lasts as long as she does not have sexual intercourse with anyone. But immediately this happens, the partner dies, even if he's the man who afflicted the carrier with it. If no intercourse occurs, the carrier still dies within a period of nine to twelve weeks. The poor thing won't even know, except [if] someone tells her. No headaches, no cold, no pains of any type. Just death, suddenly and finally. The whole process is beyond any medical comprehension. If I were a doctor, I'd name *magun* Instant Terminator AIDS. Better still, Thunderbolt AIDS.

The vice-principal's explication of *magun* is a commonplace instance of cinematic diegesis, but the fact that it is addressed to an audience that includes Ngozi's Igbo father indicates the diversity inherent within "national" spaces, in this case Nigerian political society. Many of the film's diegetic patterns depend on this shuttling between the discourse internal to a specific cultural system and the larger political discourse of exhortatory morality that applies to everyone who happens to see the film. *Thunderbolt: Magun* uses *magun* the affliction as an idiom that can be closely read. *Magun* is never iconized in the film, that is, it is never presented as a "fetish object." Nor is the spectator made aware of the moment when Ngozi is laced with the affliction. There is an echo here, undoubtedly unconscious, of El Hadji Beye's affliction with *xala* in Sembene's film. In fact, El Hadji's later brandishing of a fetish object in the meeting of the chamber of commerce rhetorically invokes an "authentic" African practice when all power has deserted him. Sembene is far from wishing to invest the gesture with any political or moral value. In Kelani's film, it is enough that both the word *magun* and the nondiegetic sparks of lightning that suggest libidinal force are imbued with a supernatural charge that can be imagined as part of a popular discourse of sexual surveillance. Moreover, their status as freely circulating words and icons is complemented by the sense of the cinematic image as a mobile object.

Imagining an African Cultural Practice

As a way of further clarifying the two filmmakers' different relationships to their cultural contexts, I would like to focus upon an important scene that presents the issues with deliberate didacticism, which is a key element of Kelani's cinematic practice. A notable, but notably unnamed, professor (played by the writer Akinwumi Isola) delivers the keynote address at an annual meeting of the Association of Obstetricians and Gynecologists. The medic Dimeji, Ngozi's importunate admirer, attends this conference and hears him speak:

> We are speaking here of a different culture, a different people who possess a different order of knowledge, scientific knowledge, which your so-called Western scientific precision tools have not been able to analyze. I have witnessed a demonstration of talismanic efficacy of some objects treated with herbs. And as a medical professional of long standing, trained in the West, I've had occasion to diagnose a psychosomatic pregnancy that resulted in the birth of a baby, despite the lack of fetal reading. Ladies and gentlemen, the existence of some yet unexplained forces, causes, and effects in African cultural practices can no longer be denied. And the purpose of my paper is to encourage a more humble, a more academic, a more research-oriented approach to the study of African medical practice, and the Western medical profession itself, if it can drop its toga of arrogant pride, still has a lot to learn from the so-called African herbalists.

This is overly didactic, and its antecedents can be identified in such films as Kelani's 1997 *O Le Ku* (where Isola plays a professor explaining, in the style of an instructional video, the etymology of Yoruba names as a corrective to the depredation of witty deconstructions), but its implications are not staged or resolved in simple ways. After the vice-principal's speech, Ngozi's father decides to pay the exorbitant fee of 60,000 naira (about $720 in 2001) charged by the *babalawo,* who now doubles as a medical herbalist. The trauma is now extensively individuated, as Ngozi, guided by Mama Tutu, takes a variety of medications to neutralize the affliction. In keeping with the "scientific" nature of orthodox medicine, the *babalawo* schedules and regulates her treatment at every stage. This regimentation can also be viewed as an attempt on Kelani's part to discipline the occult character of the affliction, in order to avoid conflict with the censors' board, ever eager to spot "fetish images" in Nollywood films. The affliction's deadliness thus reduced, it now remains for Ngozi to have intercourse with someone to complete the cure. There follows a series of pathetically bungled attempts, as Ngozi first tries to manipulate Dele Ibrahim (an old admirer who turns out to be Mama Tutu's nephew), then unsuccessfully begs her husband to sleep with her, finally settling on Dimeji, whose importunities are a partial cause of her present predicament.

Although he and his colleagues walk out on the keynote address and gather to argue about it, Dimeji is intrigued by the professor's claims that certain objects have a "talismanic efficacy." Coincident with this in the film is the popular discourse about AIDS and *magun,* the latter of which (as the vice-principal notes) is seen as far deadlier. Hoping to save the life of a woman he genuinely loves, and taking the professional risk of allowing herbalists to observe the testing of the *magun* cure in his hospital, Dimeji goes for broke and has sex with Ngozi. If *magun* is an example of African medical practice (as becomes evident in the film's climactic moment, when Dimeji displays symptoms of the second, somersault type of *magun*), the professor's high-minded exhortation of orthodox medical practitioners is an instance of what I refer to as *enchantment* in this chapter.

Enchantment is the explicit figuration in the videofilms of the occult imaginary. Focusing on the relationships between neoliberal capitalism, the global mediascape, and postcoloniality, several scholars have stressed the importance of this formation in the popular imagination (Larkin 2008; Meyer 2003; Comaroff and Comaroff 2001; Bastian 1993). They argue that those who are disadvantaged by global inequality respond to their situation by developing an imaginative understanding of the workings of a capitalism that, in the words of Jean and John Comaroff, "presents itself as a gospel of salvation [and] that, if rightly harnessed, is invested with the capacity wholly to transform the universe of the marginalized and disempowered" (292). The anthropologists Birgit Meyer and Brian Larkin see a reciprocal relationship between religion (Pentecostal churches and Islamic preachers) and the media in West Africa, in which the massive social dislocation characteristic of contemporary urban settings spurs people to invest faith in the unseen, which, in the case of Nigerian films, produces what Larkin calls "the aesthetics of outrage" (2008, 216). Obviously the kind of "African cultural practice" to which the professor of medicine in *Thunderbolt: Magun* is referring is specific and grounded; it is more than a simple response to technological or economic novelty. Indeed, the Comaroffs also stress that evidence of an "occult economy" exists globally, and they scrupulously avoid a culturally deterministic understanding of the phenomenon, either in their (South) African example or in its global manifestations. However, I argue that if one thinks of the occult imaginary in terms of "the unseen," these distinctions will stand without undermining the relevance of the aggregate deployment of enchantment in the videofilms.

What is crucial to the diegetic world of the films is the recognition of an order that is, strictly speaking, otherworldly and fantastic. Whatever differences there may be between "otherworldiness" and "fantasticness" are collapsed in the videofilms' referencing of a symbolic order that is resistant to actions and explanations that strive to maximize rationality. There are two basic strands of this occult imaginary as I use it here: Pentecostalism and sorcery. The latter includes the Ifa divination system (which is based on invisible evidence), although Kelani has brilliantly turned it into a quasi-secular idea in the film, the better to emphasize its value as a source of both medical cures and incalculable cultural power. Pentecostalism is the religious phenomenon which combines faith healing by charismatic pastors, who present themselves on prime-time television, and the yearning for material prosperity, which performers and audiences alike believe to be not just attainable but destined. But, as the Comaroffs argue, a telling parallel exists between occult economies and religious movements in the context of millennial capitalism, based on the idea of a "world, simultaneously, of possibility and impossibility" (314). What is salient to the videofilm form itself is the sense of a sociality where acting, as a form of spectacular self-presentation, is crucial, and reinforces the mutuality of the moral injunction and its embodiment in the personality of an admired actor.

The much-bemoaned inability of the bureaucratic state to generate social hope has had a remarkable impact on the growth of Pentecostalist churches, of which there are thousands (although there are no reliable statistics on their actual number) and which continue to proliferate. In Nigeria's major cities, especially in the southern parts of the country, there is hardly a major street, let alone a neighborhood of a few thousand inhabitants, where one will not find at least a score of them.[18] They vary in size; some meet in private sitting-rooms or store-fronts, some occupy a cluster of lean-tos, and some are vast and wealthy. The Redeemed Christian Church of God, arguably the largest of these churches, was founded in 1952 and occupies a multimillion-dollar complex called Redemption City along the busy Lagos–Ibadan Expressway. Presided over by Pastor Enoch Adeboye, the general overseer (fondly called Daddy GO), it has piped water, twenty-four-hour electricity, a bank, a gas station, and much else besides, and sits at the northern tip of Lagos, a dozen miles away from the city where most of these amenities are available only in fits and starts.[19] Pentecostal churches use exhortation, a feature of the videofilms, to promote their chiliastic doctrines, thus developing a whole subgenre that is related to any of the others only on the basis of the connection between enchantment and exhortation. I call the development of this subgenre the "Jesus Christ, Executive Producer" syndrome, a cheeky play on the credits on the packaging of *Majemu Ikoko* (Secret Covenant, dir. Debbie Animashaun), which unironically list Jesus Christ as executive producer, and on Tim Rice and Andrew Lloyd Weber's musical *Jesus Christ Superstar*.

The other feature of enchantment, sorcery, exists with or without a *babalawo*, as we see in *Thunderbolt: Magun*. In the absence of a *babalawo*, the work of sorcery is invested in a character with immense charisma (much like that possessed by Pentecostal preachers), who may or may not be a negative archetype and who has the power to hand down punishment as well as deliverance. Such a character can be found in films and television dramas prior to Nollywood, for example in the "juju battles" of Jimoh Aliu's serials (*Arelu, Yaponyanrin,* etc.). In *Living in Bondage,* for instance, Andy is tormented by an apparition of his wife until he enters a church for rehabilitation. The babalawo in *Thunderbolt: Magun* is capable of any of these acts, but it has to be remembered that Kelani deploys the figure as a master of curative medicine, and sets him against the practitioners of so-called orthodox medicine. Furthermore, whereas the film is ori-

The traditional healers are ready. *Thunderbolt: Magun,* directed by Tunde Kelani, 2001. Courtesy of California Newsreel.

ented away from even the Pentecostal practice of charismatic self-presentation, Mama Tutu's uncomplicated identification of Ngozi's "enemy" as perhaps the one responsible for her affliction indicates the insecurities reinforcing the occult imaginary.

For Kelani, there is another dimension to this question of enchantment. Because he believes that cinema can be a means of cultural redirection for the spectator who is besieged by global images shot through with imposed economic and cultural agendas, he conceives of the image in any of his films as an attempt to retrieve mutually shared symbols. His belief that the cinematic image becomes perceptible through the persistence of vision is perhaps old-fashioned, but it is also cleverly poeticized in the name of his production company.[20] As a filmmaker, Kelani is aware that the concentration of moving images in frames constitutes narrative in cinema, and he believes that some of what is lost to besieged societies in the profusion of external economic and educational policies may be regained if people see things with which they were once familiar. In *Thunderbolt: Magun,* the two aspects of enchantment discussed above are sublimated in the central discourse of *magun.* This sublimation ensures that the Pentecostal preacher or prayer-warrior makes no appearance, that there is no sorcery or magical appearance (although there is the benign apparition of

Ngozi's grandmother in the shape of a man), and that the power of the *babalawo* is medically curative, while his expertise is rhetorically customized in a mimetic competition with the protocols of orthodox medicine. The sublimation serves to bring up the social dimension of enchantment, that is, the issue of clientelism or recourse to the kinship structure in the absence of a civically responsible state. In much the same way that Kelani meets the dominant genres in Nollywood halfway by producing an English-language film about interethnic relationships, *Thunderbolt: Magun* plays with the aspects of enchantment through a professionalized Ifa priest.

To the extent that Ngozi's status as female and wealthy in this film is a key factor in the ordeal she goes through, we can measure how the sublimation of enchantment to the discourse of *magun* posits a complex relationship to the social dimensions of Nollywood. Remarkably, Ngozi's resort to the healer is not hurried. On the way to the *babalawo*'s house, she engages Mama Tutu in small talk about the efficacy of a certain category of Ifa priests. The viewer is made to understand that her fidelity, like her relationship to others, is a question of character; she is a fully aware self (she says, "I, Ngozi, an Igbo girl") and the film's protagonist. Character is, after all, the achievement of a moral position. Faced with a life-threatening malady tied to her sexual being, this exceedingly decent and good-natured woman stands up to the challenge, although with anxieties, to be sure. Even when her otherwise solicitous landlady proves all too human by divulging Ngozi's condition to her nephew, who promptly runs for dear life, Ngozi eventually forgives her, as she forgives Yinka for his initial distrust of her fidelity. *Magun*, the affliction, is also about power, and the film suggests this right from the opening frame. Before the encounter in the market that sets Ngozi looking for an explanation and then a cure, we are presented with what the actor-producer Bukky Wright described to me in an interview as a "man's world."

The vice-principal is a jolly, paternalistic figure, dishing out casually sexist remarks ("Hurry and marry") to the two female corpers, Ngozi and Janet, who only mildly challenge him. The first statement he makes in the opening sequence, "The incorrigible child is the lot of the mother," is addressed to high school students. But it ominously reflects the relationship between Yinka and his mother. Although the edges of the vice-principal's comments are blunted by the humor with which he delivers them, this is not true of Yinka's remarks, which are driven by insecurity and personal greed. The film's central preoccupation is first intimated when Ngozi is home for the weekend. "I hear stories," Yinka says laconically, in response to Ngozi's worried questions about his sudden coldness at the onset of foreplay in bed. Although this "misunderstanding" (his expression) is temporarily resolved after his wife has called on Mama Tutu and "God, your God" as witnesses to her fidelity, that is not the end of the matter. In his anxiety that Ngozi may become "swollen-headed" after "coming to

Yinka as the epitome of chivalry. *Thunderbolt: Magun,* directed by Tunde Kelani, 2001. Courtesy of California Newsreel.

sudden wealth" (through her grandmother's bequest), and in his unscheduled visit to Oleyo, which later becomes the subject of a domestic tongue-lashing ("I can visit my wife any time I wish!"), Yinka is presented as a deeply insecure man who is likely to subordinate his wife through *magun.*

Yinka's lack of sensitivity seems at first an artistic flaw. His presentation as either diffident or sly, able to relate to his wife only with aggressive suspicion although he was the perfect embodiment of chivalry while wooing her, seems gratuitous. Now we see a hustler, an opportunistic man who is more eager to inherit his wife's wealth than weigh the consequences her ill-understood affliction may have for her and their child Hero. This is a cultural context in which a man's extended family normally acts a counterweight to disruptive behavior, but Yinka's mother is all of his family. In the one scene when she visits Yinka in the house, their rancorous exchange is complicated by a resentment that is not fully explored. She describes the food offered to her as "poison." She and her son are Yoruba; is she opposed to Yinka's marriage to Ngozi, an Igbo woman? Are there intimations here of the stereotypical rivalry between a young wife and her mother-in-law? What can be deduced from this rancor is that Yinka lacks the kind of loose but sympathetic community of kinship that supports and sustains Ngozi. By loading power on the side of the moral degenerate, *Thunderbolt:*

Magun achieves a remarkable blend of aesthetic playfulness and the didacticism that I have identified as a principal feature of Kelani's work.

What I call the aesthetics of exhortation in this chapter is informed by didacticism, and it is one of the recurrent features of Nollywood films (Adesokan 2005, 2009b). There is a strong connection between exhortation and the figure of the actor, since it is in the actor's refusal, *in character*, to be broken out of accustomed personas by directorial control that genius and successful acting lie. There are no star actors in *Thunderbolt: Magun*, but that does not prevent the film from exhorting the viewer to the kind of morality which the figure of the actor is the conduit for expressing. The success of a moral injunction depends as much on its philosophical ring as on the personality of the actor who dramatizes it. In this film, Kelani emphasizes the first factor.

The sequence in which the culprit is established is important enough to merit a closer look. The gathering of eleven people—the *babalawo* and his two colleagues, Yinka and his mother, Ngozi and her father, Mike (an Igbo colleague of Yinka's), Ngozi's friend Janet, Mama Tutu, and the vice-principal—constitutes an example of a microcosmic political system, a meeting of an accidental extended family, ritually formalized in the vice-principal's courteous offering of a bowl of kola nuts. This parapolitical group can afford to arbitrate in place of a court of law, although its force is apparently moral.

Ngozi's affliction is expected to be neutralized by a cleansing act of sexual intercourse, and nobody is better placed to do this than her husband. In the event of a mishap, we are told, the presence of the three herbalists is more than enough insurance.[21] A terror-stricken Yinka wishes to know what Ngozi is afflicted with, and one of the herbalists (who now doubles as an elder) replies cryptically, "It is the power of our ancestors from time immemorial." Clearly, the entire group is ranged against Yinka, who is still presented as ignorant of the real problem, and the camera focuses on him extensively, tracking him and his wife as they head for an inner room to carry out the act. Yinka's refusal to cooperate is enough to convince the expectant crowd of his guilt. At this moment, the riddle of the *magun* unravels, the culprit is established for the first time, and the work of adjudication is at hand.

One after another, the elders take verbal aim at Yinka, whose shame is magnified in expressive close-ups that are characteristic of moments of emotional turmoil in Nollywood films. What happens here is not so much that good triumphs as that evil is exposed and discredited; in spite of hopes that Ngozi may be cured, the winner is not an individual, still less a community, but the moral universe in which the story unfolds. The dice are loaded against Yinka as a way of reinforcing the social prejudice against disruptive conduct. Yet all he receives for risking Ngozi's life is a scolding and subtle ostracism (administered by the *babalawo*'s colleagues, male and female; one may be the father he does not have, the other is a voice for his visible but silent mother). The affliction threatened Ngozi's life, but it is removed in a way that shows her tribulations as a brief setback, not a serious trauma. The guiding spirit of the grandmother (the apparition) is as vital as the *babalawo*'s medication.

The Videofilm in the World

The basis of this ordeal, to repeat, is the singularization of Ngozi's status as female and wealthy. When one of Yinka's colleagues first suggests to him that Ngozi is playing host to Dimeji at Oleyo, he reacts by saying, "Get thee behind me, Satan!" Yet the suggestion that he stands to lose nothing by her death, because "after all . . . she is a rich woman," must have finally convinced him. Even if his culpability is not established in advance for the viewer, because the laying of the *magun* is never dramatized, his subsequent refusal to make love to her lays him open to suspicion. I should like to historicize and contextualize this fascination with wealth and inheritance as part of a whole social practice of dedication to enrichment and the corruption and dehumanization that go with it. It is significant that Ngozi's wealth was inherited from a grandmother with traditional notions of chastity, and that Ngozi herself has an uncomplicated, good nature. Wealth in this case, as in several other instances of sublimation characteristic of the film, is not on vulgar display; rich as she is, Ngozi is far from willing to spend sixty thousand naira to cure her affliction. Indeed, when the *babalawo* first states the cost, Ngozi's visceral response is a sarcastic Igbo exclamation, "*Oso* sixty thousand?" ("Sixty thousand enough for you?"), in a loaded signifier of the prejudice against the Igbo as money-minded. It falls to her father to foot the bill, which he does quite willingly. So much for money-mindedness. If Ngozi's wealth remains under her control and does not go to her head as Yinka has feared, the same cannot be said of her sexuality. Having sought in vain to remove her affliction through sexual intercourse with Dele Ibrahim, and with Yinka having been shamed as the culprit, Ngozi is rendered more vulnerable as it becomes clear that Dimeji, although he has genuine affection for her, also has an opportunistic professional interest in disproving the efficacy of *magun*.

It is as the film approaches its climax that the individuality of the protagonist is sharply drawn, in a manner further suggesting the aesthetic distance between Kelani's work and the general fare. The framing of the scene of Ngozi and Janet, her long-suffering friend, sitting in a desolate market, each at an edge of the frame, suggests an ambiguous solidarity that is nonetheless stronger than either of the opportunistic exchanges in the two scenes of three men in the bar—first Yinka and his malicious friends, and later Dimeji and his professional colleagues. The lopsided relations of power in these scenes are balanced by a cinematic investment in the protagonist's ordeal; the camera concentrates on her accumulated experience of resistance and her search for wholeness, and scenes are replayed and layered with nondiegetic, atmospheric music at the critical moment of her sexual disempowerment, which is also the paradoxical moment of empowerment in a complex transaction in which she can only trade one man for another, placing her trust in the abstract goodness of human nature.

In the film's closing scene, Dimeji says to Ngozi, "I hope you don't think that all Yoruba people are bad." She replies, "There are only good people and bad people. These are the two tribes. You are a good man, and that's all I want in my life." Although it is tempting to compare this ending to the final sequence of Sembene's *Faat Kine* (2000), where Jean's car cruises into Kine's compound just as the women symbolically eject the three shamed men, I will instead concentrate on the political basis of inscriptions such as this in Nollywood films. Ngozi's statement is the clearest expression of the aesthetics of exhortation that I have repeatedly identified as being crucial to the form's conception of morality. It reiterates the vice-principal's earlier apologia at the moment when Yinka's culpability is established for the first time. After the husband has been subjected to a series of tongue-lashings, his father-in-law threatens to take Ngozi away, saying he had suspected Yinka all along. Turning to Ngozi's father with a solemnity that matches his avuncular joviality on previous occasions, the vice-principal, an eloquent but problematic interpreter, says, "Papa Ngozi, we are not a bad people. A bad man brings shame to his race. But a man is a man; a race, a race." The normativity embedded in the casual deployment of the word "race" in this statement is open to debate, but what is relevant is how it works. This essentialization of race implies that human behavior is contingent within the community, and that a social group is incommensurable with the idiosyncrasies of its individual members. It is definitely an opportunistic position; if an individual were to behave with exemplary goodness, his community would not hesitate to claim him as a symbol of a "racial" ethic. It is worthy of note that in this final statement by the vice-principal, we hear a resolution of the first of his gendered remarks in the film, that the badly behaved child is invariably influenced by the mother.

The aesthetics of exhortation in the videofilms create a particular notion of the self in a social setting, and embody a strategic, open attitude toward life, which can be related to populism as a flexible political ideology (Jeyifo 1984, 123; Laclau 1977, 147, 150–152). If this conception of social conduct operates on the level of moral injunction, rather than as a critique of a system—for example, the ostentatious materialism informing Yinka's greed—it is because of the form's sense of itself as a condensation of examples. An earlier form, traveling theater, assumed an addressee, and that assumption is transformed in the videofilms through the latter's positing of motion, in the multiple senses of moving images, of circulating icons and words, and of a portable commodity. Because of this mobility, the whole world is potentially accessible and addressable, thus signaling the emergence of a new genre. In this context, moral issues are presented as manifestations of the irreducible conflict of good and evil. This form of address speaks to a subtle kind of global consciousness. Posing social issues in ethical terms suggests a far from systemic understanding of the political under-

"You are a good man, and that's all I want." *Thunderbolt: Magun,* directed by Tunde Kelani, 2001. Courtesy of California Newsreel.

pinnings of phenomena like globalization.[22] This basic concern with ethics assumes a political morality that is situated in a particular place but which, being ethical, cannot be reduced to that place. It is universal, a conception of morality that can be generalized. The context, then, is of a practice of self-conception generated from African poetic genres, such as *oriki, yere don, makumbu,* and *izibongo,* and so pervasive that it has implications for the notion of the market in West Africa.

The institutional redirection of the idea of the market contained in Manthia Diawara's analysis of economic relation as social identity (the idea of the market as marketplace, which I discussed in chapter 1 and which he elaborates in *We Won't Budge* [2003]) is meaningful in terms of both its relationship to the African poetic genres of self-conception and its relationship to the multicultural impulse in current discussions of citizenship across national boundaries. The idea that the market is a space where identities take shape in far more complex ways than narrow economic calculations can elucidate is a social manifestation of practices embedded in different genres of African praise poetry. Although the genre extensively drawn upon here is the Nigerian *oriki,* there are similar or contiguous oral genres in other parts of the continent, like *yere don* in Sahelian regions, *makumbu* in central Africa, and *izibongo* in southern Africa.[23] The oral genre of *oriki* is crucial to understanding how people see themselves in society and how others see them. In *I Could Speak until Tomorrow,* Karin Barber's detailed and brilliant study of this subject, *oriki* figure as a mode of self-conception in society, a way of constituting and reconstituting a sense of the social structure and the role or place of an individual in it. *Oriki* are oral poems which, as appellations and epithets, are addressed to an individual to evoke the individual's state of being. Barber writes,

> [*Oriki*] evoke a subject's qualities, go to the heart of it and elicit its inner potency. They are a highly charged form of utterance. Composed to single out and arrest in concentrated language whatever is remarkable in current experience, their utterance energises and enlivens the hearer. They are "heavy" words, fused together into formulations that have an exceptional density and sensuous weight. An *oriki* can be a brief inscrutable phrase or an extended passage. Some *oriki* encapsulate in a laconic formula enormous public dramas, others commemorate little private incidents. All, however, are felt to evoke the essence of their subjects. (1991, 12–13)[24]

The addressee could be a human, an animal, an inanimate object, or a spiritual subject. It could be a city, a kind of meal, a famous warrior, or a group of people identified and addressed as related to a past which is not a historical past, but one "encapsulated in the present" (15), the current state of being, which is simultaneously defined and transcended. The *oriki* function as modes of social address and self-conception, but it is the latter that is more relevant in this context. Stressing this dimension of *oriki* thus requires less emphasis on ethnography than Barber gives; her interests range from theoretical issues of anthropological textuality and cultural feminism to agnatic lineage systems and the emergence and consolidation of political figures ("Big Men") in precolonial and colonial Nigeria.[25] In these different contexts. what is pertinent is the continuous, incremental way that social status is achieved. This incrementality is paralleled by the *oriki*'s own concern with potentiality, for "the qualities, actions and events that *oriki* refer to are to be interpreted as *symptoms* of a state of being" (33, Barber's emphasis). For example, "because the relationship between the big man and his supporters was not institutionalised it had to be continually recreated" (203).[26] The conception (and perception) of social status implicit in this process of recreation is comparable to how the griot (in the Sahelian context) sees and addresses the Mandinka or Soninke noble, whose self-knowledge (*yere don*) is often inseparable from the society's system of castes.[27] It is possible to see, in these practices, the features of the postcolonial asymmetry, especially when they are developed as instruments of survival in a situation of uneven economic or political forces.

Over a long period of time, the process of reiteration, the continual recreation of the relationship between the big man and his supporters (including his praise-singers, if he remains wealthy enough to pay them), legitimizes that relationship, depending on the scale of competition afforded by the numbers of big men. Again, it is not hard to see this legitimization as a concrete demonstration of the chain of relations structuring the patron-client exchange into a network that develops into a system. In other words, it becomes more feasible, economically and otherwise, to institutionalize the lack of a self-correcting system than to fully develop a rationalized system. In his discussion of the genre of proverbs in the Luba region of Zaire, Johannes Fabian emphasizes that the use of proverbs is a means of sociopolitical survival. The proverbs offer "ways to preserve some self-respect in the face of constant humiliation, and to set the wealth of artistic creativity against an environment of utter poverty" (1990, 19). These practices of socializing "cultural texts" reflect the market's principal identity as a social process in contemporary (West) Africa, the place where the vagaries of commercial transactions create the basis for interpersonal connections—or disconnections—that cannot be reduced to economic calculations. It is the elaborate codification of this socialized practice in the instrumental features of the postcolonial asymmetry which partially constitutes the "failure" of the state.

As cultural performances, these genres are all-pervasive and socially embedded, so it is not surprising that they undergo complex formal, rhetorical, and social changes. The changes occur in time and in space. Even in the 1970s, as Barber observes, the consolidation of a modern social structure around the civil service, the professions, and the educational system had begun to reshape the content and context of the *oriki* (1991, 245). In the late 1970s in Western Nigeria, there was an explosion of television programs conceived as public ombudsmen, an idea which coincided with growing urbanism and the straining of kinship and other ties, which necessitated the practice of clientelism. In such programs as *Agborandun* (NTA Ibadan, NTA Abeokuta) and *Gboro Mi Ro* (NTA Ikeja, Lagos), a host who was also an employee of the television station was joined by a number of elderly people with some sort of religious or juridical background, and they adjudicated civil cases involving individuals either unable to afford orthodox law courts or unsure they could get a fair hearing because their opponents were more influential. These programs reflected the coexistence of the influence of kinship, the bureaucratic state, and the religious imaginary as an aggregate parapolitical system.

The programs were often followed or preceded by dramas, all sharing the same audience as a manifestation of Raymond Williams's concept of total flow (2003). Also, as I argue above in the discussion of the juridical form of the gathering at the *babalawo*'s house in *Thunderbolt: Magun,* this parapolitical system has become the basis for an aesthetic choice in Nollywood films.[28] Furthermore, *yere don* as described by Diawara is qualitatively different from the praise a griot offers Douma Besso, one of the actors in Jean Rouch's *Jaguar,* who migrates to Ghana to work, but at the end of the film returns home to Niger. Diawara's account suggests a neotraditional hardening of difference among Malian immigrants in Paris, whereas Besso's individuality is celebrated at home, with little of the competitiveness observed among the Parisian crowd. Nevertheless, it needs to be emphasized that I am interested not in the textuality of these genres as oral narratives, but in their manifestation as instruments of social existence in different circumstances, best encapsulated in Fabian's idea of "survival." The aesthetic manifestation of *oriki* in Kelani's work has to be seen in his deployment of the practice of having elders settle quarrels. Presumably the bureaucratic option of the law court is either unavailable to Ngozi and Yinka or unsuited to the kind of tension that exists between them.

These genres are significant as sociocultural performances because of the ways they exhibit practices associated with the market, the confluence of different spheres where the basic rule is negotiation and compromise. Indeed, their presence across the Sahel and throughout equatorial Africa—the way, for example, that the trickster figure of the spider is replicated in different societies, while tales about him vary in their details—suggests the patterns of sociocultural exchange enabled by the market. When market women (and men) trade from Abidjan through Onitsha to Yaoundé and Bangui, as well as in places along the way, they trade in more than the obvious goods. They also make possible other forms of exchange—linguistic, sartorial, and sexual. Although driven largely by the kinds of circulation associated with globalization, the popularity of Nollywood films in other African countries (to the extent that stars become cultural icons in places like Zambia and Kenya) is not surprising when it is considered in light of the spatial structure of the West African market (Abodunrin 2009). A strand of this socialized practice, allegorized in the film as Ngozi's inherited wealth, is integrated with a dispersed transnational imaginary linking Nigerian businesses to trading in the Middle East, Hong Kong, the United States, central and southern Africa, and the United Kingdom. It follows the pattern of what Brian Larkin identifies as a "parallel, unofficial world economy" (2008, 293).

The form's extension of aspects of the social struggle suggests that those aspects operate in conjunction with the supposedly formal arrangements of the bureaucratic state more often than is usually thought. This is conviviality (Mbembe 2001), a term underscoring the ever-present, if inefficient, forms of rule definitive of the postcolony and their impact on everyday life. Much contemporary critique of modernization theory, fascinated with the liberating potential of oppositional politics and with the institutional pedigree of cultural studies, tends to overstate the limitations of modernization theory and other developmentalist paradigms. However, as I have demonstrated with respect to the sublimation of several discourses and tendencies in *Thunderbolt: Magun,* postcolonial cultural forms (like the videofilm), which are generically open to the vicissitudes of the market, show that there is more at stake than a wholesale rejection of "Western" standards, in spite of the high-minded rhetoric of the professor of medicine who addresses Dimeji and his colleagues. More importantly, they draw attention to the fact that those standards, as aspects of colonial modernity, were historically compromised within the context of uneven geographical development. In cultural terms, the immediate result of this compromise was the segmentation of publics that viewed the disparate elements of modernity as tokens of an as yet unrealized, but realizable, ideal (Barber 1997, 352), and conceived of social and cultural processes in terms of clientelism, improvisation, and other kinds of imaginative reconfiguration of social relations.[29] This has led cultural production to be simultaneously executed as economic.

When such an execution flexibly incorporates serviceable discourses like the AIDS pandemic, we see at work a strategic attitude toward a phenomenon like globalization. In *Thunderbolt: Magun,* this attitude is evident in different ways. Ngozi, hoping to pacify an increasingly jealous Yinka, takes Mama Tutu's advice to turn her husband's visit to her station into "an Oleyo night." This is a ritual pampering, consisting of serving the husband a delicious meal and a king-size bottle of Guinness stout (popularly known in Nigeria as *odeku* for its darkness and size, after a Lagosian man renowned for his impressive physical appearance). The subtext to this is the drink's supposed power as an aphrodisiac, and television and radio commercials advertising it rely heavily on this understanding. In practical, hard-nosed terms, however, the sequence was an attempt by the film's producer-director to enlist Guinness Nigeria Plc as a potential corporate sponsor. A cultural vanguardist proponent of popular art would call this a compromise of artistic integrity, but Kelani told me that the ploy did not achieve the hoped-for result in any case.[30]

With respect to AIDS, the strategy is far more nuanced and artistically daring, if also politically questionable. In its figuration of the politics of ethnic relations in Nigeria and its thematization of the AIDS pandemic within the matrix of the popular belief that *magun* offers a means of libidinal regulation, *Thunderbolt: Magun* exemplifies the contending pulls of audience expectations and artistic self-positioning within the discourse of contemporary global cinema. AIDS is a horrifying pandemic. Tying its fatality to sexual intercourse is certain to resonate with audiences who still tend to consider promiscuity taboo. More relevant is the fact that that the videofilms' preoccupation with social issues (women's [dis-]empowerment, social insecurity, child labor, oppressive sociocultural practices) has garnered them a complex form of patronage from nongovernmental organizations and development funders. This is one of the results of the videofilm's being simultaneously a cultural and an economic form, and it has far-reaching social effects. African films since the mid-1980s have tended to address similar social issues, such as Cheik Oumar Sissoko's tendentiously progressive *Finzan* (1987), whose focus on women's oppression vitiates any dramatic irony. However, Kelani's deployment of the discourse of AIDS stands out as a form of cultural self-insertion: before AIDS, African society had developed a much more effective system of self-regulation. And should *magun* seem to be an anachronistic supernatural device resistant to scientific demonstration, its potency can be brought home more urgently through the invocation of the more contemporary pandemic, especially given the exhortatory celebration of African cultural practices (*magun* and the *babalawo*'s curative expertise) by an orthodox medical practitioner.

But the focus of this address is particular. It is an aspect of social action long identified with the different forms of cultural production at the crossroads of capital, and which has been conceptualized in the example of the traveling theater (Barber 2000, 427–432 passim). That is, the producers of these forms share with their consumers an exhortatory attitude toward certain modes of social being, and see the plays or videofilms as worthy of being used as examples of social conduct. Therefore, the warning "Deadlier Than AIDS!" both uses *magun* to highlight the currency of AIDS and draws the audience's attention to the universality of the pandemic.[31] In the film *K.K.K.* (dir. Wemimo Olu Paul, 2002), the details of a lovemaking scene are replaced by intertitles about the deadliness of AIDS, which are splashed across the screen, and most non-Africans who have watched this film with me approve of the scene, calling it an innovative and result-oriented public service gesture. It could be said, of course, that most cultural forms targeted at mass audiences work in this way, as Theodor Adorno argues in "The Schema of Mass Culture" (2001, 93). The videofilm form goes further by being willing to collapse the distinction between the advertorial and the artistic gesture (as with *odeku* and the "Oleyo night") in an opportunistic move that is nonetheless also exhortatory. These different inscriptions of strategic opportunism and exhortation are ways of negotiating the uncertain terrains of censorship, patronage by nongovernmental organizations, and the social role of the form. They also function as signs of generic openness, of the reformatting of the genre of the dramatic video on the basis of whatever works. The practice of exhortation, in suggesting a parallel between AIDS and *magun,* is refracted from traditions of self-conception in these locales. In Kelani's first film, *Ti Oluwa Nile,* the family gathering, the law court, and the king's council simultaneously perform important adjudicatory roles. At the same time that the institutions of the state are perceived to be in disrepair, individuals reach for reconfigured forms of these institutions to fashion new communities and spaces of social engagement. It is within this context that Sandra Barnes's analysis of patron-client relationships in postindependence Lagos (1986) attains its impressive effect.

The generation of the videofilm as an economic, cultural, and artistic practice in West Africa results from, among other factors, a sense that the self in society is an active agent, creating its own image. As an aspect of social action, the videofilm represents a mode of self-conception and self-advancement through which people renegotiate the changing sense of selfhood in contemporary societies, without the large-scale differentiation of populations that was characteristic of an earlier phase of economic development, particularly in nineteenth- and early twentieth-century Europe. The most catalytic model of selfhood in this region in the twentieth century has been citizenship, membership in a geographically coherent nation-state. People are interpellated as Nigerians or Sierra Leoneans, and they assume these identities, even if only in name. But there is a simultaneous conception of the self in society that turns on the same axis as contemporary citizenship, and as a result of the shortcomings of the sovereign nation-state, this other conception has become both prevalent and crucial. The most far-reaching of these shortcomings is the postcolonial asymmetry, the tension that arises out of the inability of postcolonial sovereignties (in Africa and elsewhere) to integrate the national "political" struggle with the social "material" struggle. However, in cultural forms like the videofilm, the technologically savvy African cinema, and transgeneric postcolonial writings, elements of the social struggle are constantly being repositioned, sometimes as economic or populist strategies, sometimes as recuperation of ethical standards, and at other times as perplexing enchantments.[32]

Furthermore, as technologies are democratized, especially in the digital forms of mobile telephones and portable (and more affordable) cameras and computers, the effects are more immanent and unprecedented. The film *GSM Wahala* (dir. Afam Okereke, 2003) shows this in a spectacular way.[33] GSM (Groupe Spéciale Mobile, or Global System for Mobile Communication) is one of the standards for wireless telephony systems. Although developed for Europe, the system now operates in more than 212 countries and territories and is used by more than 1.5 billion people (GSMA 2011). The privatization of the Nigerian telecommunications sector at the urging of the International Monetary Fund introduced large-scale wireless telephony into the country. By 2002, three years after the end of military rule, mobile telephones, or "handsets," as they are mostly known, had proliferated on an unprecedented scale. The national Nigerian Telecommunications Limited had provided only half a million phone lines in nearly forty years since independence, while the deregulated telecommunications industry made a total of two million lines available between 1999 and 2003. And according to recent statistics released by the Nigerian Communications Commission, Nigeria's mobile services penetration increased from just 0.33% of the population in 2001 to 48.9% in 2009 (Pyramid Research 2010, 34).[34]

Existing systems have fragmented in other realms as well. Actors' caucuses and "cartels" have proliferated and supplanted the old theater and film production companies that had been headed by male actor-producers. An actress is now able to present her own film as an individual, working from the kind of self-conception that arises from her screen name. Like the *oriki*, this ownership of a film is a means to an end, a suggestion of potentiality, but it is also provisionally enacted as a state, a form of identity, and a social position. I call this development the "A Film by Moladun" syndrome, after the popular actress

Monsuratu Omidina (the wife of Baba Suwe), whose screen name is Moladun. She produced her first film, *Obakan,* after appearing in other people's films for many years. To this kind of orientation, Moladun's professional self-definition as an actress would defy closure, because she is also a producer and, because she originated the script, she can also serve as an "overseeing" director. The practice of self-aggrandizement which the "big men" of the nineteenth century constructed as *oriki* in a rivalrous context (Barber 1991, 195ff) is now potentially available to a vast number of people, but on both transnational and smaller, more fragmented scales. We are confronted with Carlos Fuentes's polyforum, the place where "everyone has a right to be heard, but no one has the right to exclusive speech" (2000, 610).

This is another sense in which *oriki* as a social genre has changed. The status of Oyin Adejobi, leader of the theater troupe that is the subject of Barber's richly expansive 2000 book *The Generation of Plays,* is different from that of a nineteenth-century big man in Okuku, in that he operates within the economic and social system of modernization. It is significant that the role of professional troupe leader is available to a greater number of people, to the point that it is no longer a specialization. Similarly, the kind of "homelessness" or "mobility" that was the lot of diasporic black intellectuals in the first half of the twentieth century (a Jamaican national was so by virtue of being from Jamaica; a black person in America did not have to be a U.S. national to be a black American) is now the condition of many people, within and outside the postcolony. The one difference is that whereas what was earlier called "deracination" or "homelessness" now carries the positive label of "cosmopolitanism," the condition of postcolonials is seen in terms of humanitarian emergency: refugees and immigrants.

In conclusion, I suggest that these changes are reflected in Kelani's work that I have focused on in this chapter. Many aesthetic standards common to the form are extensively sublimated in *Thunderbolt: Magun,* as a result of the filmmaker's positioning of the work as an English-language film. This in part explains why English-language films are considered the default Nollywood genre. But it is also clear that this particular film best aggregates his practice both as a Nigerian artist with specific political and social referents and as a player in contemporary global cinema, shuttling between the discourse internal to a specific cultural template (as an exemplum of "African cultural practices") and the larger, political discourse of exhortatory morality that represents a response to global phenomena. The suggestion of a moral order in the Ifa verse ("Okanran-Owonrin") that structures narrative disclosures in *Ti Oluwa Nile* continues to run through Kelani's work, most notably in the character of Opalaba, the palace wit in *Saworoide* and *Agogo Eewo.* This figure is now being reproduced as a new sociocultural type in most other films (notably in the Yoruba subgenre). But in *Thunderbolt: Magun,* the figure of the palace wit is diffusely presented, and mostly didactically. When the vice principal and the *babalawo*'s colleagues are not addressing weighty wisdoms to their internal audiences, the film deploys extra-diegetic music ("Omo Araye") that comments on envy and bad faith, and this music often complements the sustained attention to a cogent exhortation or message.

This responsible management of different demands, cinematic and otherwise, is coupled with an astute sense of a transnational context, which explains why Kelani's work travels faster than that of his Nigerian contemporaries, even though the majority of his films are not in English. More than any of his contemporaries, he has successfully problematized the tripartite distinction structuring the intermediate classes (Barber's formulation), for example in the multiplicity of publics that crowd the closing scene of his 2002 film, *Agogo Eewo*. That scene, bringing groups and individuals with conflicting and opposed ideologies together in a unified and rowdy dance of victory, stands as an important contribution to the theorization of this form (Adesokan 2009b). Moreover, he is one of the few practitioners whose work has a fairly stable, consistent, and formalized structure, an important factor in a socioeconomic context which almost makes a virtue of an infinite repetition of structures. Kelani's career as a producer-director has also shown that being committed to a local market and going to festivals as an auteur are not mutually exclusive, contrary to the argument against the dominant Francophone African cinema. However, the coincidence of Nigerian videofilm practice with a certain formation of transnational political and cultural practice aligned with development funders and nongovernmental organizations is profoundly catalytic. The Nollywood cinematic practice, which arose out of the inadequacies of the Nigerian state and which has successfully presented itself as a viable alternative to other "national" cinematic practices, is caught in its own contradictions. Through the kind of uncritical support and appropriation that the reversed opportunism of development funders suggests, it is also encouraged to "normalize" the social formations of improvisation and the parapolitical system within which it becomes possible.[35]

4   Jean-Pierre Bekolo and the Challenges of Aesthetic Populism

If Sembene's *Xala* highlights the preoccupations of the politically engaged film-maker, and Kelani's *Thunderbolt: Magun* reflects an awareness of film as a commercial product, Cameroonian-born Jean-Pierre Bekolo's work, especially *Le Complot d'Aristote* (*Aristotle's Plot*, 1996), stands between both, suggesting that the two concerns are not necessarily mutually exclusive. *Aristotle's Plot* is not a straightforward drama in the manner of either Sembene's *Xala* or Kelani's *Thunderbolt: Magun*, and perhaps this is what makes it such a conciliatory work when compared to both films. Taking a conceptual approach to the issues that preoccupy African filmmakers, *Aristotle's Plot* makes a germane point that is easily overlooked, namely that speaking to a society as heterogeneous as contemporary Africa means speaking to a diversity of audiences and thus requires a diversity of filmmaking practices. I argue in this chapter that the central impulse in Bekolo's work is to address the ideological fissures that have come to define African cinema: fissures between those who hold that a film, as an artwork, is justified by its singularity, those who argue for politically engaged cinema, and those who decry the unresponsiveness of African filmmakers to their audiences' desire for popular stories.

The divisions may look somewhat schematic but, in fact, three directors have taken these three positions. Djibril Diop Mambèty, the deceased but unforgettable Senegalese director, saw matters in stark terms, saying, "either one is very popular and talks to people in a simple and plain manner, or else one searches for an African film language that would exclude the chattering and focus more on how to make use of visuals and sound" (Pfaff 1988, 218). In a 2002 interview with the critic Michael Martin, the cinéaste Gaston Kaboré was asked to comment on the impact of new media on indigenous modes of expression, and he said, "while it is difficult for us today . . . we must continue to try to make people understand that Africans have contributed to world civilization and our universal patrimony" (Martin 2002, 166). Mweze Ngangura, who produced the popular musical comedy *La Vie Est Belle* (Life Is Rosy, 1987) is also on record (1996) as having attacked the so-called *cinema d'auteur* as didactic and militant in ways he judged to be unpalatable to mass audiences. Bekolo is foremost among those who attempt to integrate the different positions. He explicitly rejects an either/or solution to the problem of meeting these diverse needs, instead adopting a position which entails a complex artistic undertaking. Therefore it

is important, in discussing his work, to couple the last two of the three manifestations of the peculiarity of postcolonial texts I highlighted in the introduction, namely the aesthetic dimension of uneven geographical development and
the role of metropolitan location and commodification as shapers of genre.

In this chapter, I pursue the task by focusing on Bekolo as an example of the
generation of African (and diasporic) filmmakers whose careers coincide with
or are implicitly connected to the phenomenon of globalization. I look at this
phenomenon both specifically in the annals of African filmmaking and in the
general context of what the expatriate Iranian scholar Hamid Naficy calls the accented cinema (2001). Through the discussion of Bekolo's *Aristotle's Plot,* I argue
that the works of these filmmakers (such as Abderrahmane Sissako, Moussa
Sene Absa, Raoul Peck, Joseph Gaï Ramaka, Alan Gomis, Régina Fanta Nacro,
Mahamet Saleh-Haroun, and many others) represent a more fruitful articulation of the tensions between the poetics of decolonization and its aftermath—
the diverse subjectivities that are characteristic of postcoloniality—which are
mirrored in the three different positions on the proper preoccupations of African cinema. If, as I have argued in the introduction, artistic representations
of decolonization such as we see in *Xala* have to be set against new postcolonial
subjectivities which those representations did not always countenance, then
the paths taken by this generation of filmmakers can be seen to lead to more
complex understandings of African realities. One can no longer plausibly see
African identity as undifferentiated. Such a notion was perhaps useful in motivating the anti-colonial critiques of the artists who came to maturity as the
colonies were gaining independence. At the same time, the ways in which other
kinds of politicized representation persist in the works of younger artists cannot be ignored, either. The shortcomings of the poetics of decolonization are
of a generic order: artists engage with the public dimensions of the form of the
nation, what Fredric Jameson once controversially called the national allegory
(1986), while the private domains of sexuality, affect, and intracultural marginality remain largely unexplored. When they are explored at all, these subjectivities are pathologized either as cultural alienation, by "nativists," or as false
consciousness, by radical Marxists.

The three positions mentioned above can be roughly synthesized as two approaches, oppositional filmmaking and apolitical cinema, and I propose that
Bekolo's interest in questions of genre, as demonstrated especially in *Aristotle's
Plot,* represents a response to the two approaches. While the perspective of the
film's voice-over narration suggests the kind of subjectivity that motivates oppositional filmmaking, the interrogation of mimesis shows the imbrication of
style and substance, and the reflexive character of the film—as fiction spliced
with commentary—integrates the two. My discussion of the film will focus primarily on these issues. *Aristotle's Plot* has been discussed in diverse ways (Dovey
2009; Harrow 2007b; Haynes 2005; Murphy and Williams 2007), and in each
case, the writer stresses the film's conceptual nature, its character as a medita-

tion on the problems of African filmmaking, more than its status as a feature film. While acknowledging that *Aristotle's Plot* is generally understood as a conceptual work, I wish to go further by arguing that this particular aspect of the film is a function of the metropolitan context of its production. First, having to reflect on the travails of African cinema in relation to the larger history of cinema reinforces Bekolo's conceptual frame of mind, leading him to strike the rhetorical posture expected of an expatriated intellectual, seeing things in continental and institutional terms. Second, whatever the merits of the film's generic identity (as either a reflexive fiction film or an essay film), such merits have to be understood as the outcomes of severely limited aesthetic choices. Indeed, it is a mark of his imaginative attitude toward cinema that, in spite of those limitations (which I shall discuss later), Bekolo manages to turn out a film with this kind of conceptual orientation.

Bekolo arrived on the scene of African filmmaking at a very interesting moment. Writing in *The Specter of Comparisons,* Benedict Anderson describes a fascinating paradox of neoliberalism, the "enormous disintegration, which is also a process of liberation [in which the world has been] integrated into a single capitalist economy" (1998, 59). As we saw in chapter 3, the economic policies of structural adjustment programs introduced profound crises in many parts of the developing world. But they also introduced technological and demographic changes that prompted the replacement of chemical-based film stock by the generally more affordable and flexible digital format. The transnational movement of images, goods, and people (especially those with skills or talents) makes a conception of identity in simple oppositional terms less tenable, both practically and theoretically. The generation of filmmakers set to work by this decisive shift share a self-conscious, reflexive, ironic stance toward the explicitly anti-imperial character of the post-1960 cinema, especially as gleaned from the communiqués and deliberations around the establishment of the Fédération Panafricaine des Cinéastes (Federation of African Filmmakers) in 1969 (Diawara 1992; Bakari and Cham 1996). This does not imply that these directors and producers completely eschew political and didactic filmmaking. Their works could be said to be political in the broadest sense of the term, and some in the narrow sense, such as we see in Sissako's brilliant Brechtian critique, *Bamako* (2006). However, most of these filmmakers also depart substantially from the accents and registers in which the political traditions in African cinema are generally understood. Perhaps the most meaningful way to understand the political dimension of these filmmakers' styles is to say that they see film as a very unusual opportunity to take politics seriously.

Born in 1966 in Cameroon, Bekolo studied with Christian Metz in Paris, returning to Cameroon to work as a television producer and editor of music videos. This training and early work have had decisive effects on his style. One might be suspicious of segmentation along generational lines, but it is possible to stress his "generational" credentials because the youthfulness of his aesthetic choices has to do with his place in the annals of African filmmaking and the coincidence between this position and the global changes in the field of technology.

Although Bekolo attempts in *Aristotle's Plot,* as he does in the earlier *Quartier Mozart* (1992), to ask whether the category of African cinema is valid in theory and practice, he is interested in cinema for more than strictly cultural reasons: he envisages African cinema making a contribution to the form itself. If *Quartier Mozart* had not been his first film, it would seem as if he sets out an aesthetic thesis in *Aristotle's Plot* and then attempts to prove it in *Quartier Mozart.* The point of connection between the two films, however, is different: the critical success of the first brought him to the attention of the British Film Institute and made him a suitable figure from whom to commission a film to celebrate the centenary of cinema. However, that the challenges of aesthetic populism are an abiding concern for him is underlined by the thematic and aesthetic thrusts of his more recent film *Les Saignantes* (2005), a film which can be productively compared to the films coming out of Nigeria, especially Kelani's *Campus Queen* (2003).

Mimesis and Mimicry

A film commissioned by the British Film Institute, starring South African actors, and directed in Zimbabwe by a Cameroonian, *Aristotle's Plot* has an interesting status as an African film. Bekolo, its writer as well as director, received a commission to make one of a series of films to mark the centenary of cinema (1895–1995); other commissions were given to Jean-Luc Godard, Stephen Frears, Bernardo Bertolucci, George Miller, and Martin Scorsese, among others. Bekolo had made three short films prior to *Quartier Mozart,*[1] but it was that film, which was awarded the Prix Afrique du Creation at Cannes, that marked his emergence in the international arena, where he appeared as "a cagey and attitudinous guerrilla roaming the postmodern globalized mediascape" (Haynes 2005, 118). As I have suggested, the brilliance of *Quartier Mozart* in part led to his receiving the commission from the British Film Institute. And the fact that *Aristotle's Plot* is a commissioned work is in copious evidence throughout the narrative.

The film opens with a scene of a cop, a sergeant, dragging two men in handcuffs across a railroad track. A voice-over immediately establishes a partial context for the image:

> It started in the African bush, where I was with my grandfather chewing kola nut. I heard the drums telling me that I had a phone call from London. The British Film Institute wanted me to make a film to celebrate the centenary of cinema. One hundred years of cinema? My grandfather wanted to know who else was on the list. Martin Scorsese, Stephen Frears, Jean-Luc Godard, Bernardo Bertolucci, George Miller. Hmmm. Then I started to wonder: why

me? Was it Christian charity or political correctness? Was I accepting a challenge from someone already standing on the finish line? My grandfather spoke
to me . . .

This voice-over, identified with Bekolo himself, is present throughout the
film, ruminative and withering in its commentary. It offers a perspective like
that of a Greek chorus, in a film confessedly modeled on the template of "European storytelling—Aristotle's *Poetics*." Through its ironic invocation of the
African bush, chewing kola nuts, and listening to drums, the film quickly advertises its difference, its willingness and readiness to participate in a rhetoric
of alterity that is presumed in the gesture of listing Bekolo alongside the established Euro-American notables. Bekolo's distinct diction—his English is clearly that
of a Central African French speaker—further underscores this alterity, which
is of a piece with the coarse, urban texture of the film; and that texture is also
(and better) embodied by the gangsters, as well as by Donny Elwood's cheeky
soundtrack.

There are two narrative strands in *Aristotle's Plot*: the occasional disquisitions
on *The Poetics* conveyed in the sassy commentaries of the voice-over (the perspective of the "I," which Bekolo says is missing in African cinema [Eke et al.
2000, 25]), and the main plot, the drama involving the police sergeant, the cinéaste Essomba Tourneur (ET), and Cinema, the lead gangster at Cinema Afrique. The two strands rarely converge, but on the one occasion that they do,
Bekolo himself appears on camera, playing a bar attendant who serves the sergeant. Directors who appear in their own films, like Sembene and Sissako, often
put such appearances down to the contingencies of production (as discussed in
the introduction). While this might be the reason for Bekolo's appearance, the
viewer is invited to read it in relation to the subjective viewpoint of the narrative
voice-over. The juxtaposition of Bekolo's commentaries on Aristotle's opinions
on mimesis with the glorification of the precolonial subjectivity of his grandfather (who is presented as knowing better than Aristotle) is a contradiction
that the film will not resolve, and here the director seems to be paying a complex homage to the Senegalese filmmaker Mambèty, his kindred spirit in African filmmaking.[2]

Having resolved to pitch this narrative as a recuperation of "the root of European storytelling," Bekolo needs the format of an action film: a good guy and
a bad guy, and a mediator in the figure of the sergeant. The sergeant has been
instructed by his rather complacent boss to work out how a person who dies in
one film can reappear in another. As the sergeant starts working on this seemingly simple puzzle, an African filmmaker, Essomba Tourneur (ET), returns
from training in Paris. ET is both frustrated by the government of his country (which once put him in jail and has disrupted his personal life) and determined to rescue African cinema from foreign influence. (His name doubtless derives from the French verb *tourner*, to shoot film, and his nickname, of

course, signifies an extraterrestrial being, suggesting his "alienated consciousness" as well as a Hollywood type.) With the voice-over making ironic comments and the camera showing a close-up of the wall of a cinema with the legend "Action-Packed Movies," ET wanders the streets, pushing a trolley filled with his reels, searching for an exhibition hall. The streets of this African city are dusty and abandoned, and ET's dress and demeanor convey none of the self-assured worldliness often associated with the cultural brokers who supervise film festivals like the Festival Panafricain du Cinéma et de la Télévision de Ouagadougou (FESPACO). Indeed, texture is part of the aesthetic populism of Bekolo's work, and this is even more apparent in *Quartier Mozart,* where the plot unfolds against the background of broken-down vehicles and the lean-tos of the Yaoundé neighborhood. With the exception of the sergeant, the characters of *Aristotle's Plot* are not distinguished by costume or make-up, more evidence of Bekolo's desire to avoid the dominant form in commercial cinema without obviously doing so.

A local gang led by a character called Cinema has occupied a theater named Cinema Afrique. These gangsters are hooked on American action flicks and bear names derived from them: Schwarzenegger, Van Damme, Cobra, Bruce Lee, and Nikita. As the camera cuts between the suspicious cop questioning a bar attendant (Bekolo) about the veracity of mimesis and ET approaching Cinema Afrique, the voice-over, ever satiric and questioning, declares, "My grandfather told me, when I decided I wouldn't be a doctor, 'A filmmaker is an outlaw who doesn't have enough personality to be a gangster.'" What does this mean? One could think of it as Bekolo's own postmodernist bluff, glamorizing gangsters as self-making urbanites, more chic and action-oriented than the filmmaker who has an overwhelming sense of intellectual authenticity and a social conscience. Or one could take a different tack and think of the grandfather as evincing the kind of African subjectivity which has always been present, but which Africanist scholarship is only now acknowledging in all its social complexity.[3] The fact that this statement is reported second-hand, however, compromises its didactic force, for the sassy voice-over is framed as a different kind of mediator from the sergeant, endorsing neither the position of the serious cultural purifier (ET) nor that of the unreflective cultural consumer (Cinema and the other gangsters).

The youth are all the audience in the hall, and they offer running commentary on a film being screened. One says, "We want African movies that kick ass. Hey, we don't want any fucking Jean-Pierre Bekolo here, okay!"[4] Between Elwood's soundtrack, which puns on "cinéaste" as "silly-ass," and the gangsters, who have learned about American culture through the cinema, the charge of this sequence is conveyed through American slang and profanity like "what's up," "shit," and "fuck."[5] These words clash with the sound effects of Schwarzenegger and Bruce Lee action films, whose excitement the ideologically invested camera reflects only in the sheen of the youngsters' enraptured faces. We never

The gangsters pose in front of the New Africa cinema. *Aristotle's Plot,* directed by Jean-Pierre Bekolo, 1996.

see any of the films. Bekolo may have wanted to focus on the action in his own film and not give undue privilege to images from others. He may also have been concerned about the legal consequences of cannibalizing others' films, on which point I have more to say later when I discuss the generic character of the film.

ET finds a seat in the hall, despite the gangsters' attempts to intimidate him. But he, with his travels, his training, and his pride as an African intellectual, finds their Hollywood-derived fantasies offensive. His loud condemnations of the film being shown clash with the gangsters' own catcalls. It is hard to watch this scene and not be reminded of the global pervasiveness or dominance of American mass culture, and Bekolo's strategies in this scene require a closer examination. Just as the voice-over admits that the story is on track, and as soon as the sergeant embarks on his assignment, we are also informed that it is difficult to take *The Poetics* as an artistic model, because its second part, on comedy, is missing. Aristotle was interested in comedy as a supplementary form, but it is conceived of differently in African cinema, where the form (and allegory) is seen as corrective to explicit didacticism. But for Bekolo, who is somewhat aligned with the school of thought that values the imaginative potential of comedy, this moment provides an opportunity to venture into the realm of representational and political conundrums. He muses in the voice-over,

> As I went deeper, I had more and more questions. Why had the second chapter of Aristotle's *Poetics* disappeared? Why is the Sphinx's nose locked in the Brit-

ish Museum? . . . Why do they prefer the Cro-Magnon man to his colleague of Grimaldi? Why are we still talking about Thales or Pythagoras [i.e., rather than Aristotle]? Why did Bokassa proclaim himself emperor like Napoleon? Why are African filmmakers always asked political questions? . . . Why is an African filmmaker always a young, upcoming, promising filmmaker until he reaches eighty years old, and then he becomes the ancestor, the father, the wise man?

This stream of questions represents one of the devices Bekolo uses to foreground the tension between imagination and reality in art. Although he often leans toward the former, suggesting his opposition to the dominant trend of realism in African as well as contemporary global cinema, there are moments in this film when the question of aesthetic choice is far from soluble. Before concluding that cinema as a form is undermined by conventions of realism, he comments on those conventions:

> Because a plot is made of a series of events that have a beginning, I started suspecting that my invitation to be part of the British Film Institute celebrating one hundred years of cinema could only be a plot twenty-three centuries old. Aristotle's plot. Even if I was trying to avoid it, I was already trapped in the formula, the "how-to." Today, Aristotle's formula produces gangsters, magicians, corrupt governments, suffering artists, forgers . . .

Here is an interesting moment in the layers of irony and self-mocking that structure the commentaries. The sergeant's assignment may seem simple, but it is a profound interrogation of mimesis, and is one of the complicated (one might even say confounding) attempts in the film to sustain different simultaneous discourses. The discourses are diffusely stitched into the film, but they represent the two preoccupations that are central to African cinema as an institutional form—oppositional filmmaking and apolitical cinema. Bekolo's corrective, or supplement, to them is his conceptual interest in aesthetic typology, crucially addressed in the generic character of the film. These preoccupations manifest themselves in the definition of African filmmaking against its eternal Other, that is, the Hollywood systematized commercial form. In Bekolo's view, as conveyed in *Aristotle's Plot*, the formalized style of Hollywood is reducible to mimesis—Hollywood is the deterioration or simplification of Aristotle's formula (Adesokan 2008b, 8). Relating this interrogation of mimesis to the bureaucratic state's suspicion of art (which is expressed in censorship) would seem to conflict with the wisdom of the grandfather, which the voice-over says anticipated all the questions that dramatic or literary representation throws up. This explicit interrogation of mimesis is unsatisfactory in two major ways.

First, the selection of a story with a bad guy and a good guy, which is believed to be the core of the Hollywood action genre, is implicitly conflated with the Aristotelian conception of tragedy. This is a conflation of a specific genre, the action film, with the general rules of mimesis and poesis, and it is a misrepresentation of mimesis as such. What subsists as "European storytelling" or

"Hollywood formula" is a reduction of drama, which is itself a compression of ritual, a process that has taken centuries to evolve. Bekolo is aware of this process, which is why he speaks of "a plot twenty-three centuries old," but by rhetorically isolating the supposed effects of the "formula" (its production of "gangsters, magicians, corrupt governments, suffering artists, forgers . . ."), he severs the link between the process and the formula and loses sight of the contradictions within mimesis as such, which are manifested in the simplified Hollywood formula and in the modern antitheses of Aristotelianism (such as the Brechtian alienation effect).

The other way in which Bekolo's questioning of mimesis is unsatisfying follows from this. At several points in the commentary, Bekolo restates the Aristotelian preference for a story that inspires pity and fear, leading to the purging of harmful emotions. However, the classicism of Hollywood's format of good guy versus bad guy does not exactly tally with the Aristotelian model, in which tragedy results from the weaknesses inherent in character and thought (as embodied in action) and their conflict with divine law, not from the machinations of an evil antagonist.[6] It may be easy to pity Othello and detest Iago, but who is there to hate for the fate that befalls King Oedipus? The problem, it appears, is that Bekolo's approach to Aristotle's formula is marked by the ambivalence characteristic of the cultural broker who must negotiate several terrains. In their efforts to be accessible to a wider, possibly apolitical, audience, certain African filmmakers tend to confuse the issues that this pervasiveness of American mass culture stirs up. One common response to this dilemma is, as I have suggested, to resort to the comic form, seeing it as the antithesis of political engagement. Doing this collapses the distinctions between African audiences' fascination with American gangster films and their interest in intellectually challenging political drama. This applies to the Zairean filmmaker Mweze Ngangura, producer of the musical comedy *La Vie Est Belle*, who has been a consistent champion of "entertainment cinema."

In his polemical "African Cinema: Militancy or Entertainment?" Ngangura recalls an encounter at FESPACO with a thirteen-year-old member of the audience who would like to see an African Rambo film (1996, 61–62). He uses this story to buttress his argument that the works of African filmmakers enjoy only limited popularity on the continent. But the irony escapes him: Hollywood films like the Rambo series are rated in ways that stipulate what minors can see and in what circumstances, and the boy's desire questions the looseness of laws concerning the exhibition of foreign films in Africa, a situation that highlights the usefulness of the didacticism that Ngangura is attacking. How comedy is supposed to work in this context—whether as parody and caricature, or as a way of rechanneling the anxieties supposedly at work in tragedy and other "serious" modes—is not always clear, partly because of the polemical or rhetorical nature of such propositions.

A frustrated ET returns to the streets. He wishes to take a taxi to the city center. In a scene shot in a Harare market that parodically reverses the usual relations between Africans and Europeans, we watch as a hustling crowd of white cab drivers struggle over his luggage. But this scene could also be read as a parody of European cultural brokers' jostling for the attention of African directors. When ET eventually meets the investigating cop, this reversal acquires even greater poignancy: in the makeshift cell before the cop is a white suspect, whose plaintive French is drowned in the cop's vituperative English, the language of law enforcement. The encounter between ET and the sergeant cleverly conflates moral and narrative plausibility (the cinéaste is willing to rat on the gangsters who hold the clue to the sergeant's puzzle); perhaps this is an instance of the logic of mimesis which Bekolo calls "Aristotle's formula." The sergeant has despaired over the task set him by his boss, and here comes someone to complain about goings-on inside Cinema Afrique, occupied by Cinema and his gang. The encounter seems random but, in fact, it follows plausibly from the convivial relationship between ET and the state. We have been informed that the government has tried to silence this artist, but now he seeks to exploit the obvious contradiction in the state's concurrent desires for modernization and cultural self-preservation. In fact, before he stumbles upon the sergeant, ET has spent time waiting in an office, eventually using an official typewriter to draft the letter of complaint later handed to the law officer. The state and the engaged artist join in an opportunistic collaboration.

A comic misunderstanding ensues between the two men, as ET tries to convince the suspicious policeman. "Cinema" is not supposed to be someone's name, the sergeant says; it's a silly reflection of reality in which someone who has died is brought back to life. With his help, however, ET dislodges the gang in a commando-style attack that parodies an action film, as does much of what is to follow. The theater is renamed Heritage Cinema, and its interior is transformed; ET mounts African art on the wall, including an enigmatic mask whose outlines are earlier suggested in a shot of a bullet-pocked wall and superimposed light bulbs. The Heritage Cinema begins showing African films, but the only person who comes to watch them is an African American in search of his roots, who arrives wearing *kente*. The images in this sequence are multiple and complex, and apart from the voice-over, the only sound we hear is the *kora* music soaring through the shadows of the cinema hall, in ironic homage to the authentic tendency in African "calabash" cinema. But the transformation is also plausibly figured as a relegation of French authority on the linguistic level, even if the dislodging of English-language American films would seem to suggest the contrary; the only time French is spoken in this film is when the incarcerated Frenchman pleads with the sergeant.

The gangsters are exiled to a village, then return to the city to stage a counter-invasion during a screening. The African American protests, in a parody of back-

Action! *Aristotle's Plot,* directed by Jean-Pierre Bekolo, 1996.

to-Africa rhetoric: "If you don't know where you're coming from, how will you know where you're going?" One of the gangsters slits the throat of the projectionist (played by the South African director Lionel Nkagane); then they drag the lone spectator out, shooting him in yet another parody of Aristotelian off-stage killing, which floods the canvas of shadows with the vast redness of simulated blood. They also steal ET's films. Throughout this sequence, the soundtrack is alive with the nondiegetic sounds of the action film, suggesting suspense.

Back in the village, the gangsters establish a theater to show films to the populace. Here, Bekolo allows some moments of realism to underline the inventiveness of this group of supposed "cultural bastards." They build their cinema hall, which they name New Africa, using discarded tools and bits of wire and tack. This is a loaded instance of bricolage, as is suggested by Cinema's speech as the construction is underway: "We're building a new thing, a New Africa. We'll take what we can get. If it's old and it's good, fine. If it's new and it fits—phew—action!"

Given the economic and artistic contexts out of which the cinema has re-emerged in Nigeria, it is possible to appreciate the logic of this improvisation, this use of whatever works or is available, and to see how, on a formal level, the kind of self-invention at work here also constitutes the narrative template of *Quartier Mozart.* However, the gangsters' loot is made up of "boring" African films, as they discover when they settle down to screen them. Their disdain for the films is a reversal of ET's denunciation of action films before he is thrown out of the old Cinema Afrique, but it takes a different form. ET's reaction was to shout expletives at the screen in a manner that the gangsters found objectionable or distracting. But they themselves are exacting in their requirements, detailing what cinema does and ought to do:

> These movies, you go out, take a piss, have a meal, they're still doing the same thing when you come back. And they call that culture, African culture . . . chickens chasing dogs and goats chasing chickens with traditional music.

If we see the gangsters' inventiveness as reflecting the rise of new cinematic practices, we can also understand ET's intellectualist dismissal of Hollywood films as mirroring the attitude of older Nigerian filmmakers, trained in the celluloid format, toward the earliest video products.[7] Interestingly enough, just before some of the gangsters step out to complain about the unexciting film, the camera is trained on its audience. Yet there is more at stake, for ET soon appears, in a Schwarzenegger costume complete with sunglasses and a Harley-Davidson. In an extended parody of the action-film genre made up of tracking shots of gun battles, he engages the gang in a shootout to recover his films. The dead rise, and another parody ensues, this time of a Western-style face-off between the good guy and the bad guys, except that this one is a karate duel. This endless run of parodies of conventional genres is fitting in a film that casts itself as a parody of classical mimesis, but it also calls into doubt the sustainability of the conceptual grounds of Bekolo's film. What is one to make of the glorification of the grandfather's wisdom when the classical illusionism of Hollywood is the style that prevails? Is Bekolo suggesting that the integrity of that African subjectivity is only rhetorical, especially in the metropolitan context which glorifies versions of authenticity as part of an institutional discourse of difference? What does ET stand for—is he the purveyor of a disalienated African cinema sustained by its cultural needs or the populist broker of new media and subjectivities? If these identities are not mutually exclusive, it is reasonable to suggest their commonality, but why do this through the fight-to-the-finish format of the action flick? As far as one can see, these conceptual questions are never satisfactorily addressed in *Aristotle's Plot*; Bekolo waited almost a decade before returning to them in a more profound, self-questioning manner in *Les Saignantes*.

Even after ET has recovered his films, the gang members manage to pull themselves together, with some of them riding a donkey cart while Cinema, determined to show the others action, drives wildly in circles, raising dust and screeching his tires in the manner of an action film. ET returns to the city and sits listening to a radio announcer reporting from Hollywood: "Nobody is dying in Hollywood. There have been news of gunshots and accidents but no deaths reported in forty-eight hours." Here is the moment when the original conundrum that the sergeant was detailed to unravel is brought back. Listening to this report on the radio, ET rises and goes to lie down in the road. Meanwhile, the cop has been making merry, believing that, with the attack on Cinema Afrique, he has completed his task. Cinema is back with a car, and he runs over ET, for which the sergeant shoots him, only to be mobbed in turn by a crowd. The three men that we saw in the opening frame are together again, each bloodied but alive, and this reprise is telling: the cop's quest is a ploy to meddle in other people's creativity, and he is no more than a bumbling, ineffectual mediator between those who have little respect for him but alternately fear and resent him. It is only by the force of the handcuffs that he secures ET's and Cinema's attention while he delivers a lame homily about the interdependence of the head and the heart. And as if to prove him right, the film ends with ET and Cinema riding into the sunset. This is telling; it confirms the mutuality of authorial singularity and aesthetic populism, which Bekolo strongly believes in, as he has reiterated in a recent interview (Adesokan 2008b, 4).

The extensive parodies prior to this final sequence are just one aspect of this extremely layered and problematic film. By questioning Hollywood's systematization of mimesis, Bekolo is claiming that the two conceptual binaries—oppositional filmmaking and apolitical cinema—are not mutually exclusive. This claim is not only the conceptual ground of *Aristotle's Plot*, it is also at the center of my own juxtaposition of his work to that of Sembene and Kelani. Yet Bekolo's method departs substantially from the understanding of oppositional filmmaking which Michael Martin uses in discussing African and diasporic films in his 1995 anthology. In his introduction, Martin characterizes oppositional films "as a political orientation and oppositional cultural practice" within the hegemonic structure of postcolonialism (Martin 1995, 3). Bekolo's critique of the institutionalization of formula implicates many filmmaking styles in African cinema, including his own. The voice-over's insistence that cinema and realism are incompatible indicates Bekolo's belief that mimesis is not the only form of signification possible in cinema. This questioning of mimesis approaches a dénouement when the antagonisms between ET and Cinema are resolved in the final shot, both riding into the sunset in a gesture of negotiated difference framed in the language of a Western. As an auteur, a cinéaste ("silly-ass"), an "artist maudit," ET faces a different kind of reality and is brought to realize that the form is a container which can be filled with any kind of content. This suggests that Bekolo is equally, or even more, concerned about the diversity in the supposedly unitary discourse of African cinema. This tension arises out of the need to underscore the institutional instability undergirding the production and reception of African films—much of their infrastructural support is still of European provenance—rather than the distinctive quality of each film as an artistic or cultural product. Thus, when he relates to African cinema as a category in *Aristotle's Plot*, this relationship is subjective, a sort of lovers' quarrel.

Commissioned Agent

When ET questions Cinema's authority to speak about films, the lead gangster responds by saying that he has seen many films. None of these films is made by an African director, but that fact does not worry Cinema, who dismisses African films as "shit." Ironically, however, the visual evidence of his claim is constituted by his cinematic identity, a series of identity cards, each engraved with the image of an African filmmaker. We see images of African directors but none of their films; Hollywood icons are represented in the spectacular identities of the gangsters but no Hollywood films are visible. To build a film on ceaseless questioning of conventional narrative and dramatic storytelling is an interesting aesthetic choice, but we can get a sense of the fractious relationships between African filmmakers if we pay attention to the institutional context of that choice. The relationships between these filmmakers, especially those of different generations, are often masked by the blanket discourse of solidarity which constitutes African cinema. Bekolo himself speaks to this tension in two different and contradictory statements made within six months of each other. Asked by interviewers at Michigan State University about the generic form of the film, he responds, "I decided not to make documentaries for the simple reason that, in the case of Africa, they tend to focus more on reality, indeed ethnology, while ignoring the imaginative process" (Eke et al. 2000, 25). However, in an interview with Frank Ukadike, the director says, "While I was doing *Aristotle's Plot,* I wanted clips from Ousmane Sembene's films. He wrote to me to say that not one piece of his movie would ever be cut off . . . Souleymane Cissé also said he would never give me a clip of his film" (Ukadike 2002, 224). While it is plausible that Bekolo's first statement is about documentaries in general, it is also the case that the documentary option was available, indeed contemplated, in making the reflexive *Aristotle's Plot.* In a third, more recent interview, he puts the matter in a slightly different way: "[*Aristotle's Plot*] was a commissioned film, and in the commission they wanted us to introduce the work of certain filmmakers, and I also wanted to introduce Djibril Mambèty, Lionel Ngakane and so on . . . That was how it was set up. But we had to change that format because we couldn't get that cooperation" (Adesokan 2008b, 10).

These different statements are the basis of my claim, at the beginning of this chapter, that the film's generic identity has to be understood in part as the consequence of limitations on Bekolo's aesthetic choices. There is no knowing exactly how clips from other African films would have been used in the film, but we know how the other directors' head shots were used: in Cinema's ID cards. The absence of images from African films in a film in which the characters proudly identify as action-film heroes does not negate the fact that the conjunction of personal and institutional positioning significantly shapes cultural forms like African cinema. The wholesale corralling of different cinematic practices under the unifying rubric of "African," while defensible as a way of marking cultural practice, masks a deep division within the field of African filmmaking, not to mention its relationship to the cinema of diaspora that shares space with it at international film festivals. Still, in spite of aesthetic, professional, and personal differences, Bekolo and Sembene both address African audiences, and both harbor ultimately compatible artistic visions. The discourse of identity implicit in this cinematic practice is often extended, in criticisms of African cinema, to focus on its political origins, stressing the extent to which the structural adjustments and new technologies that came to prominence in the 1980s have supposedly compromised those origins.

These institutional dynamics are even more decisive when they manifest in the context of the metropolitan patronage of postcolonial arts, and especially in the kind of commission that made *Aristotle's Plot* possible. But the dynamics entrench unequal relations in such a complex way that genre is called upon as the rhetorical ground on which to thrash out the terms of their constitution. An example is instructive here. While the British Film Institute (BFI) sets Bekolo to work in the distinguished company of the Godards and the Scorseses, the institutional peer of the BFI on the African continent, FEPACI, the Fédération Panafricaine des Cinéastes, puts together a commemorative volume of writings also marking the centenary of cinema (1995). That volume, carrying a foreword by Sembene, is a bilingual compilation of the different communiqués, reports, and charters associated with the emergence of African cinema. How, one may ask, can this volume of writings and a film like *Aristotle's Plot* be compared? Certainly, the existence of both indicates the diversity of African cinema, and one may even go further to point out something else—the incommensurability of an industrialized, institutional system that counts an integral history of mechanical reproduction as part of its legacy (Hollywood) and a much more recent system of cultural difference (African cinema) that is often sustained by Euro-American television funds and grants, the same institutional forms it purports to undermine. Bekolo's decision to develop his film in the generic interface of the personal essay and free-flowing aggregation of documentary and fiction is thus an extravagance possible only in a commissioned or sponsored work, and this fact underscores the vexed question of the accessibility of African cinema. The self-conscious director who can do this is not so worried about the commercial viability of his undertaking, and the metropolitan provenance of the film's conception already determines its appeal.

Yet there is more to these institutional dynamics than a narrow focus on the ways they make films inaccessible can reveal. Those dynamics—of funding, commissions, and access to small or art film channels—represent important avenues through which these works are introduced to foreign multicultural audiences, either at the same time as or after they appear at festivals and museums. Two examples of the crucial role played by these modes of insertion in generating interest in expatriate films are worth specifying here. First, according to Hamid Naficy in *An Accented Cinema*, his remarkable study of exilic filmmaking, there is a strong link between "accented films" (marked by the displacement of their directors) and non-Hollywood modes of production. These modes of production are interstitial in that "they resonate against the prevailing cinematic production practices, at the same time as they benefit from them" (Naficy 2001, 4).

Borrowing the notion of interstitiality from the cultural critic Homi Bhabha, Naficy says that it is relevant to accented filmmaking because the directors operate "both within and astride the cracks of the system, benefiting from its contradictions, anomalies, and heterogeneity" (46). He argues further that filmmakers working through these modes are better understood as partial and multiple rather than as merely marginal.

A few qualifications are necessary in deploying Naficy's ideas in a discussion of *Aristotle's Plot*. Naficy does not address African filmmaking directly (although he discusses the works of a number of North African directors). Also, the concept of exilic filmmaking, associated with ideas of lost place, trauma, and return journey, is a little too specific to speak meaningfully to the complexities of metropolitan location at work in *Aristotle's Plot*. Bekolo is more of an expatriate than an exilic filmmaker, and his film comes out of contexts signally different from those Naficy identifies as interstitial or collective. With these qualifications, I still find Naficy's delineation of the impact of the global television system and the multiplicity of metropolitan programming sources quite useful for discussing the institutional dynamics giving rise to a work like *Aristotle's Plot*. In particular, Naficy's argument that noncommercial or independent television channels—such as Channel Four in England, Arte in France and Germany, Canal Plus in France, ZDF in Germany, and a host of others—represent alternative sources of funding and broadcasting for accented films suggests an important institutional context for the proliferation of multicultural works (44). Simply put, the opportunities created by these networks or avenues of production and exhibition are invaluable, because Hollywood is highly capitalized and gigantic, and these channels constitute a cultural alternative—or corrective—to the hegemony of the dominant mode (see also Diawara 2010, chapter 2).

The other example of the consequential role metropolitan institutions play in advancing the objectives of expatriate directors is provided in the reflections that Rod Stoneman, a former commissioning editor of film and video at Channel Four, offered in *Ecrans d'Afrique* in 1993. Titled "South/South Axis: For a Cinema Built by, with and for Africans," Stoneman's essay makes a number of practical arguments for external funding of the kind that enabled Bekolo to produce *Aristotle's Plot*. He begins by deploring a pattern common among African filmmakers, in which the "same people conceive, write, raise the finance for, direct and produce most African movies—and then they organize the festivals and run the magazines" (Stoneman 1996, 176). This situation of "ultra-auterism," he argues, binds the continent's cinematic practices to a system of dependency and overdetermines the character of films through specific production modes. "Filmmakers," Stoneman writes, "are now addressing the complex and pertinent issue of how money coming from the North affects or modifies the overall range of cinema in the South. Is there an unconscious predilection for certain kinds of product, a selective prioritization of certain types of films? What kinds of African films are more difficult, or even impossible, for European television?

Do specific interventions change particular films?" (177). To escape this bind Stoneman thinks that it is imperative that a "body of professional, entrepreneurial, cultural producers [emerge] to articulate potential funding sources . . . and strengthen individual production processes" (176). The range of funding sources envisaged by this obviously experienced and sympathetic insider reveals a genuine desire to render the cinematic tradition within which most African directors work self-sustaining: "a balanced combination of monies from several disparate directions (indigenous and Northern, television and cinema, commercial and state)" (177). Not only is a film drawing its funds from these different sources likely to be less beholden to any one of them, thus assuring its relative independence, the diversity of sources is also likely to ensure wider distribution, considering that each of the sources of funds is also a potential resource for dissemination.

Several things are worth remarking upon in Stoneman's argument. First is its assumption that external support for African filmmaking, however limited, is necessary. Although he is concerned that the director's artistic integrity not be sacrificed to the exigencies of the production budget, and he also quotes the Senegalese director Ramaka to the effect that dependence on such funding inhibits productivity (176), Stoneman's argument appears to be premised on the indispensability of support from Europe and North America. This is in spite of the suggestion in the essay's title of a South/South cooperative model. In a very telling moment, he writes that "it is essential for Northern funders to maintain a pluralistic, open attitude and develop their support for a wide range of forms and tendencies in film" (177). It is obvious that Stoneman is drawing from his experience as a commissioning editor of non-European films, and as I have argued, the overall tenor of his essay is indubitably sympathetic. Nonetheless, his inability to imagine a wholly African or truly South/South funding pattern shows how critically influential metropolitan institutional dynamics are in the development of postcolonial cultural forms.

Another remarkable point developing from Stoneman's argument is the manner in which foreign funding determines the types of film which get made. Three types—"village films," "modern social films," and "magic realist films"— illustrate the politics of production modes. Village films appear to be motivated primarily by the interest of foreign funders in the anthropological aspects of African life. Although Stoneman does not make the connection, this part of his argument is reminiscent of the debate among filmmakers and critics in the late 1980s and early 1990s about the typology of African films. In that game of spot-the-difference, filmmakers and critics saw a divide between the "didactic cinema" (epitomized by the likes of Sembene and Med Hondo) and the "cinéma de calebasse" ("calabash cinema" exhibiting a "natural" Africa, epitomized by Idrissa Ouedraogo's *Yaaba*), between "message films" and "entertainment films," and between the "Old School" and the "New School," as Akudinobi (1997) calls two of the trends. A simple delineation of this divide is the contention, on the one hand, that political cinema as a category is now dated, that Africans cannot afford to make films opposed to Europe because the relationship between them has changed to the point that Europe is not so much the Other as integral to the self. On the other hand, those who profess the "old school" of filmmaking dismiss films like Ouedraogo's as simplistic attempts to exoticize African realities through beautiful images and an obsequious neo-Negritude (Diawara 1994, 394; Ukadike 1994, 247–249).

Thus, not only is foreign support crucial to the very existence of many African films, according to this argument it also affects genre in ways that make certain kinds of film not just available but highly visible in some circles. Since Stoneman's essay was first published, apartheid has been formally ended in South Africa, so something like the South/South alliance he called for has appeared, although not quite as he envisaged it. Sembene's 1988 *Camp de Thiaroye* was funded by a consortium of producers and institutions in Senegal and Tunisia. Indeed, Bekolo does not see the commissioning of *Aristotle's Plot* as free of these tensions between institutional support and the aesthetic outcome. It is worth returning to the voice-over's suspicious questions about the BFI's motives in including Bekolo in the elite line-up for the centenary of cinema:

> The British Film Institute wanted me to make a film to celebrate the centenary of cinema . . . My grandfather wanted to know who else was on the list. Martin Scorsese, Stephen Frears, Jean-Luc Godard, Bernardo Bertolucci, George Miller. Hmmm. Then I started to wonder: why me? Was it Christian charity or political correctness? Was I accepting a challenge from someone already standing on the finish line?

A cultural institution like the British Film Institute might well view this sassiness with amusement, taking the deliberate pushing of the envelope as inherent in the artistic temperament, just part of the package. Or perhaps not. The problem is that the comment reflects much of what transpired in the process of making the film, a delicious kind of poetic justice in a film questioning the relationship between art and life. As Jonathan Haynes has pointed out, there is a contradiction at the core of this enterprise, which simultaneously suspects and exploits foreign support for African films (Haynes 2005, 126). A little incident developed from the commission. It happened that Bekolo did not fully cooperate with the BFI, in part because he took offense at being offered a small budget for the film, compared with what the other luminaries secured. In the end he obtained funds from a multiplicity of sources, including the French producer Jacques Bidou, the French Ministry of Cooperation and Development, the EEC, Framework International (of Zimbabwe), the Amsterdam-based Hubert Bals Fund, and Kola Case, Bekolo's own production company (126–127).[8] This diverse sourcing would seem to respond to Stoneman's injunction, except that the sources are almost exclusively Western and wholly noncommercial, and they came together haphazardly and only after the filmmaker had parted ways with the BFI, rather than in the kind of organic way Stoneman envisages. Nonetheless, Bekolo's sassy polemicism—biting the hand that feeds him—runs contrary to the desire for multicultural representation which might have motivated the BFI's inclusion of him in the lineup of stellar American and European directors. If, as I claimed at the beginning of this essay, Bekolo's remarkable success with *Quartier Mozart* was one of the reasons he caught the attention of this cultural institution, he actually performed contrary to expectations. In the unwritten rules of such institutional patronage, the commission is viewed as a stepping stone to even bigger things, and an artist-director favored in this way is not expected to rock the boat.[9]

Without underestimating the relevance of these institutional critiques, especially since they are so integral to the generic character of *Aristotle's Plot,* I want to return to the film by highlighting two aesthetic issues it does not so much dodge as suggest. The first has to do with the connections or disparities Bekolo wishes to imply between Aristotelian mimesis and African narrative resources, and the other concerns the importance of conceptual filmmaking in moving African cinema beyond the dichotomies that have continued to plague it. As I have argued, these issues are crucial to the argument of *Aristotle's Plot,* and the film is problematic to the extent that it suggests them within a polemical discourse that nonetheless leaves them generally latent. Quite regularly in the film, the voice-over mentions the grandfather as the embodiment of a precolonial subjectivity that is equal or superior to Aristotelian insights as they are couched in the overbearing products of Hollywood formula. Indeed, at a crucial moment in the film, when the struggle between ET and Cinema comes to a head, Bekolo's voice-over presents itself as the wisdom of this African grandfather:

> My grandfather's words started to fill my mind. What is an initiation ceremony? Crisis, confrontation, climax, and resolution. Sound, story, images, narration, rhythm. Is there anything in this cinema which is not African? Fantasy, myth, we got. Walt Disney, we got. Lion King, we got . . . Aristotle, catharsis, and kola nut, we got. What don't we got? Why don't we got an African Hollywood? Probably because we don't want to produce our cinema outside of life, because when it is out of life, it is dead.

These instructive meditations take the viewer back to earlier ones, in which the grandfather asks his grandson about the rationale for the BFI commission. The narrating grandson names other commissioned directors to his auditor, but does not sustain what appears to be an interesting and potentially productive intramural discourse between them. Now the voice-over goes deeper into this contentious terrain, and although what the grandfather tells him is not entirely clear, the associations between African initiation ceremonies and Hollywood dramatic procedures lead the audience to surmise that the narrator is making a specific ideological point: his cultural resources are a worthwhile basis for a viable cinematic culture. This point is important for the light it sheds on

Bekolo's own work—the creative uses he often makes of indigenous practices such as witchcraft (Mama Thecla in *Quartier Mozart* and the Mevoungou in *Les Saignantes*)—as well as for its suggestion of points of contact between supposedly opposed film cultures. If African initiation ceremonies, myths, and legends only require inventive formal strategies to be transformed into the equal of Hollywood, then there is no reason why African filmmakers should not be able to forge sustainable cinematic cultures. Hardly controvertible, except that the narrator's provisional identification of obstacles to this achievement confuses things even more. The argument about the relationships between cinema and life is less clear. When Bekolo says that an "African Hollywood" would exist if directors, scriptwriters, and producers looked outside of life for material, is he arguing that the psychological basis of practices like initiation ceremonies are "material" they can use? If he is understood to be making this point affirmatively—saying that African cinema will remain vibrant for as long as it is tied to the cultural resources from which it develops, perhaps in contrast to the aestheticism common to Western postmodern works—then it is even more difficult to accept his premise, because it seems to have abandoned the earlier critique of Aristotle's formula.

One way that scholars have tried to understand the impact of African cultural resources such as folktales, myths, and legends on contemporary arts is by looking at the opposition between the representational mode of Western dramatic forms and the presentational mode in certain African contexts (Barber 2000; Jeyifo 1984; Soyinka 1976). According to this argument, Western drama, which is structurally similar to Hollywood, proceeds through the mimetic standard of illusionism, in which the drama unfolding either on stage or on screen is but a reflection of reality, a sort of mirror of a larger issue, whether political, social, or historical. On the other hand, African drama, especially the genres discussed by these scholars, proceeds through an anti-illusionist standard, developing its material instead through the presentational mode, which does not presuppose a mimetic relationship between an experience and its enactment. As Soyinka trenchantly puts it in his famous essay "The Fourth Stage":

> In our journey to the heart of Yoruba tragic art which indeed belongs in the Mysteries of Ogun and the choric ecstasy of revelers, we do not find that the Yoruba, as the Greek did, "built for his chorus the scaffolding of a chthonic realm and placed thereon fictive nature spirits . . ." on which foundation, claims Nietzsche, Greek tragedy developed: in short, the principle of illusion. (1976, 142)

Although Soyinka is referring here to ritual enactment, his point is relevant because, as I have already suggested, drama is a contraction of ritual, whether in the West African or Levantine context. The distinctions reflect the ways in which context shapes form, the incorporation of elements like improvisation, music, and other narrative devices into a dramatic piece becoming so decisive as to create a different performance style, which can then be read in broad cultural and geographical terms. Bekolo shows his awareness of these arguments through the distinctions he draws between imagination and reality (or cinema and life), but it is hard to see how the different parts of his argument fit together. One is then left to read other contexts into his premise to get a broad sense of what, for him, constitutes imagination, and exactly how it is different from reality. An important such context is his highly provocative interview with Ukadike, which I briefly drew upon earlier.

A third of the way into the interview, which was conducted just two years after the release of *Aristotle's Plot,* Bekolo tells the interviewer, "All these questions you have asked me I have answered in *Aristotle's Plot*" (Ukadike 2002, 224). This is a telling statement because the interview, with its fixations on "imagination," is an unpremeditated recapitulation of the themes in *Aristotle's Plot.* It is as though the voice-over commentaries in the film are limited by running time, and the conversation provides the director with the opportunity to return to them. It is perhaps even more accurate to say that these were the issues preoccupying the director at the time, and the film needed to be discussed in such an extended manner. Quite often in the interview, Bekolo speaks of imagination in abstract terms, as if it is some sort of talisman that all cinema, not just African cinema, needs to manifest its true identity. He says, "To make a film, even in a black American community, it has to be true to reality. Why? Imagination is the essence; maybe that's the thing I could not define" (225). He had attempted to discuss this thing he "could not define" earlier in the interview:

> That thing is exactly what compels the rap singer to disrespect the rule of law when he puts his fingers on the gramophone machine and stops the record from playing normally as he manipulates it to create a different kind of rhythm . . . That may also be the same thing that makes people fight us. I feel like I am part of that thing; I can't define it very well, that essence, but that very thing is what I want to address. (221)

Such statements, together with reverberations from *Aristotle's Plot,* give a better idea of what he sees as constituting imagination, and Bekolo frequently links this "essence" to two other issues—Eurocentric paternalism as a form of political oppression, and its aesthetic manifestation in rules of composition, in short, in formula. The argument is thus that there is an essence in African artistic temperaments which manifests itself in black culture and which relies on imagination rather than logical or verifiable accounts, the stuff of reality. All of this ties in with another distinction which is fundamental to Bekolo's idea of filmmaking. This is the distinction between the container and the content. The container is the technological know-how, including the very idea of form, while the content is what a filmmaker, an artist with a vision, brings to the form. Bekolo argues that African directors such as he studied abroad "to take the container and we ended up getting the content" (219), implying that they have adopted

Western ideas of what constitutes a good storyline. One result of this, he thinks, is that African events are usually presented as tragedy in Western narratives and scripts by African artists which attempt to reinforce this perspective easily find funding and promotion. These are some of the conceptual issues with which *Aristotle's Plot* grapples, through the relentless outpouring of views, ironies, and dismissals on the voice-over. However, being constantly juxtaposed to the conflict between the good guy (ET) and the bad guy (Cinema), which is framed in the classical form of the action film, they lead the film down a blind alley.

Multifocality: The Head and the Heart

The other aesthetic issue that is of significance in the film is the idea of conceptual filmmaking. Bekolo presents it more clearly than he does Aristotelianism, and in fact *Aristotle's Plot* can be said to have advanced the kind of cinematic experience often associated with Mambèty. Characteristic of this experience is a preoccupation with the practice of auterism, that is, the identification of a particular style with a particular director. Equally significant, however, is the sense that a film is more than a conventional story (hence Bekolo's unease with formula), so that even when a drama is unfolding, it is juxtaposed to other narrative, descriptive, and conceptual issues, against which its larger significations are to be grasped. This aspect of *Aristotle's Plot* undergirds my claim, at the beginning of this chapter, that the film places Bekolo at the forefront of a generation of directors (such as Ramaka, Nacro, Sissako, Gomes, and Absa) whose careers are connected to the phenomenon of globalization. These directors do not always proceed on the basis of the kind of anti-imperialist critique that is characteristic of the work of Sembene, Hondo, or Haile Gerima, indicating the kind of ideological changes which the African continent, as part of the developing world, has gone through within the first two generations of African cinema. These changes are not difficult to understand in social terms; they are reflected in the differences between the poetics of decolonization and those that result from the impact of global flows on postcolonial subjectivities. What is significant is that these younger directors do not always represent the changes thematically, and so attempts to talk about the generational differences in simple thematic terms quickly break down. This is especially true when arguments are based on Sembene's late work, such as *Faat Kine* and *Mooladé*.

The differences between these poetics are largely conceptual. Critics assume that filmmakers are familiar with a variety of aesthetic practices, including some that do not originate in Africa; but this familiarity does not lead them in the direction of either a cultural-nationalist critique or an identity-based discourse of cultural solidarity. For a quick example of this difference, one might compare Sembene's *Camp de Thiaroye* (1988) and Ramaka's *Karmen Gei* (2002). Sembene's film is about the ill-treatment of demobilized African soldiers who fought on the side of the French in World War II. When cultural tension develops between an African sergeant and an African American soldier, they manage to reach an understanding partly through jazz music, specifically a track by Charlie Parker ("Honeysuckle Rose"). Ramaka's film is a reimagining of Prosper Mérimée's *Carmen,* a fact which in itself invites reflections about the place of contemporary Africa in the artistic heritage of the world. Although the director makes several political points, his concerns are substantially different from Sembene's, because he focuses on deep emotional conflicts within Karmen and in her relationships with others, female and male. Although the film extensively uses jazz, the music is not deployed to advance any thematic purpose, as it is in *Camp de Thiaroye.* Even in *Ceddo* (1977), where Sembene uses jazz music nondiegetically, the eruptive soundtrack is meant to link the branding of the slaves to the African American artistic heritage, of which the music is a significant aspect.

A conceptual approach to filmmaking is thus, for these younger directors, an ideological break with the earlier generation. Different directors create their *mise-en-scènes* according to their personal familiarity with, and deployment of, various aesthetic practices: Sissako uses texts from Aimé Césaire's *Notebooks of a Return to My Native Land* and *Discourse on Colonialism* in *La Vie sur Terre* (1999); Gomes famously pays homage to Federico Fellini in *Udju Azul di Yonta* (1992); Saleh-Haroun quotes from the speeches of the late Burkinabe president Thomas Sankara in *Bye-Bye Africa* (1999); Bekolo reflexively uses direct address (which is often identified with Spike Lee's *Do the Right Thing*), still montages, and thought bubbles in *Quartier Mozart,* and questions the relationship of cinematic genres to political power even more reflexively in *Les Saignantes.* This list of examples is not exhaustive, but Sissako's recent assemblage in *Bamako* (2006) provides a crowning moment. The Brechtian staging, in a Bamako courtyard, of a trial in which the World Bank is charged with responsibility for African poverty collapses the distinction between performers and spectators, while the juxtaposition of individual stories and images abstracted from the central drama of the protagonist's extended family is meant to underscore the alienation effect on which the film is based. Moreover, with the parodic insertion of "Death in Timbuktu," a spaghetti Western sequence, Sissako simultaneously critiques both the predatoriness of the World Bank and the IMF and the desires of mass audiences. The sequence is on a par with Bekolo's parodies.

These issues of conceptual filmmaking are decisive in *Aristotle's Plot,* and Bekolo uses ET, the cinéaste, to draw attention to African cinema's failure to articulate them. ET is the discontented artist who is serious enough about the integrity of African films to bring the full weight of state power to protect them. And when he has a chance to show the films, they turn out to be uniformly preoccupied with cultural identity (to the extent that the African American spectator would find "his roots" watching them) and ethnography ("chickens chasing goats"). He is the film's protagonist, yet Bekolo as filmmaker is no more partial to him than he is attentive to the fantasies of the gangsters. The mimetic truisms of good and evil are simultaneously set in motion and subverted, because Bekolo seems equally interested in the process of subversion and in the Aristotelian unity of action which constitutes the story. This is what his multifocality entails—the conception of cinematic address as consisting of multiple foci, which this film turns into an ideological and aesthetic argument. This multifocality involves the playfulness with which the film relates to cinema, stylistic tendencies, and Aristotelian rules, as well as the category of "African cinema." By extension, it also calls into question the homogeneity of political filmmaking, the main stream of "Third World" filmmaking to which African cinema is supposedly a tributary.

But these generational differences do not necessarily eventuate in a postengagement cinema, a cinema in which filmmakers turn away from political themes. If anything, political filmmaking has deepened, as recent works by Nacro (*The Night of Truth*), Ramaka (*And What If Latif Was Right?*), Peck (*Sometimes in April*) and others have shown. Certainly, the films depict desire differently from works in the age of decolonization, when the task of fashioning a cultural or political unity often overrode others. But such are the social contradictions characterizing neoliberalism that attempts to engage with any aspect of it cannot always evade political issues, even if the rhetorical register eschews the premise of an earlier age. While some critics see early African cinema as subverting the domination and objectification of Africans (for example, Akudinobi 1997, 100), it is now clear that in their preoccupation with the politics of representation involved in anti-colonial discourse, the early films—such as Med Hondo's *Soleil O* and Sembene's *Emitaï*—were paradoxically enabling the cinema's external condition of possibility.

The more the films focused on colonial domination and its aftermath, the larger the context of signification and referentiality they thus opened up by co-opting the Other, both as the cinematic apparatus and as the "Western subject." Whether through coproduction with European television channels, the institutionalization of African cinema in FESPACO, or commodification through VHS tape releases, the referencing of the Other beyond cinematic representation is also built into the process of circulation. In an age when the CFA franc is devalued and Youssou N'Dour's music is explosively popular, the market has stepped into the space of that signification and broadened it, and an African filmmaker planning the shots of a film thinks of how it will be received in a European or North American cinema. In this sphere of representation, Bekolo, an exemplar of African directors, seeks to confront the conflation by multifocally following two tracks, and we see him doing this in the negotiated relation of difference between Cinema and ET as they ride into the sunset. They are shown to be working toward the same (or at least similar) goals: the production of images and ideas through which those who use them can find the kind of fulfillment that suits their taste. This is an intellectual duty, which is why Bekolo's film has a conceptual character. As a postcolonial, expatriated intellectual himself,

Bekolo engages issues that go beyond the distinction between "entertainment" and "militancy."

In conclusion, I want to relate this discussion of conceptuality in African filmmaking to questions of agency, because it seems to me that such an engagement with the self in cinema represents a productive context for dealing with the tough questions that African filmmakers confront. There is a direct relationship between the voice-over and agency in a number of the recent films, in which the "I"-perspective introduces subjectivity in ways that are urgent and depart from earlier practices.[10] The problem with the voice-over in *Aristotle's Plot* is discursive. Bekolo seems to intend its commentaries to be like those of a Greek chorus, which are notionally narrative and comment on the unfolding dramatic conflict. At the same, he frames them as poetic antitheses of the conventional understanding of cinema, resorting to ironic non sequiturs ("Because when cinema becomes your life, you are dead. It is dead. We are all dead") and unsustainable comparisons. The supposed equivalence of the opposition between life and cinema and that between a mother and child seems to derive from the kind of anti-realism positions on African filmmaking usually identified with Mambèty, who once described himself as "a history of a dream" (1993). What is interesting about this kind of subjectivity is its status as an artistic extravagance: the posture is procedurally unsustainable if the director is keeping an eye on the bottom line. In other words, it is in experimental works that there is space for such distinctively poetic meditations, and Bekolo, like Mambèty, addresses the need to protect that space. Unlike Mambèty, however, he does not think of protecting it as incompatible with developing works that appeal to general popular audiences, such as we see in Nollywood films.

Nonetheless, his attitude in this regard is specifically intellectual in the sense that, with the exception of *Quartier Mozart,* Bekolo's work has tended to present the mutuality of cinematic practices as more discursive than practical. It is as though he thinks of this mutuality as an argument to be tested, such that, even in *Quartier Mozart,* which unfolds with less reflexivity than either *Aristotle's Plot* or *Les Saignantes,* the populist moments are refracted from aesthetic ideas of what topics appeal to a general audience. This intellectual understanding of aesthetic issues is very much at work even in discussions of world literature, as I have argued in the introduction, drawing on Pascale Casanova's work on metropolitan location as an important factor in the transference of political issues to the aesthetic terrain. Bekolo's location in Paris deepens his conceptual approach to issues, encouraging him to see representation—in the two primary senses of the word—in continental and institutional terms. The unease he feels about the BFI's cultural patronage becomes more poignant in the sarcastic posture of Arundhati Roy's political writings, as I show in detail in chapter 6. But he never quite translates his political concerns to the aesthetic domain. That is the forte of Caryl Phillips, to whose work I now turn.

5 Imaginary Citizenship: Caryl Phillips's Atlantic World

Born in the Caribbean, raised in England, and now mainly resident in the United States, the writer Caryl Phillips is an interesting figure through whom to examine the contradictions of belonging in this age of unsettled nationality. These contradictions manifest themselves not just in Phillips's life. His writings, fictional and nonfictional, explore what it means to be in, but not of, a society, to belong legally to a country but feel excluded from it because of its history of treating one and one's kind, whether racial, cultural, economic, or sexual, as outsiders. In this chapter, however, the focus of discussion will be on Phillips's nonfictional writings, primarily *The Atlantic Sound,* a hybrid account of the author's travels to three of the prime sites of the Atlantic slave trade, which was published in 2000. The book culminates an exploration of issues that Phillips had conducted in other works of nonfiction, particularly *The European Tribe,* his first published book (1999; originally published in 1987), and *A New World Order,* a collection of essays (2002; originally published in 2001). Focusing on these works, I think, will show that there is a structural connection between nonfiction as a literary form and the situation of artists who produce their works in the general institutional context of diasporicity, cosmopolitanism, and expatriation.

These three concepts have gained currency in cultural theory in recent times, although literary critics formerly discussed them under the rubrics of exile and alienation.[1] Moreover, they pertain to the condition of most people in the world today; indeed, in this chapter, I contend that the large-scale migration to the West from Africa, South Asia, and the rest of the postcolonial world that began in the mid-1980s is an intensification of the earlier experiences of displacement that framed exile as a historical concept. As I argued in the conclusion of chapter 1, it was in the context of their "homelessness" that twentieth-century Caribbean intellectuals were able to work for African political and cultural independence. However, given the institutional changes wrought by technology and migration in the past several decades, this homelessness has acquired a different kind of importance. The cultural deracination experienced by these exiled figures is now a global pattern.

This pattern, at once cultural and economic, is best captured in the idea of the *polyforum,* "the public square where everyone has a right to be heard, but no one has the right to exclusive speech," according to the Mexican novelist Carlos Fuentes (2006, 612), or, as Phillips himself puts it, "a new world order in which there will soon be one global conversation with limited participation open to all, and full participation available to none" (2001, 5). This premise is underscored by the striking encounters between Phillips and his interlocutors in *The Atlantic Sound,* both because and in spite of the author's self-consciousness as a writer with specific aims. In the three texts produced between 1989 and 2001, the period when Phillips's career as a novelist could be said to have crystallized, the author moves from the frustration of being in, but not of, Europe to the awareness of alternatives to Europe, which is not to say that he no longer experiences the frustration. The ethnically and socially marginalized populations of twentieth-century Europe were in that continent but not of it, enduring a cultural exclusion that was determined on the basis of race, class, gender, and sexuality, and Phillips first addresses this dilemma in *The European Tribe.* However, fourteen years after this work's first publication, global capitalism has become so corporatized and transnational as to render the idea of belonging, of well-defined cultural boundaries, complicated for a significant and increasing number of people in the world, irrespective of other, older forms of identity. Phillips's nonfictional works move between two poles—Europe's disconnection from the lived experiences of its minorities, and the changed notions of contemporary identity represented in the cultural pluralism of the United States.

My argument in this chapter relies on the tension implicit in this move. The conditions of ethnic minorities have improved not only in Europe but also in the rest of the world since the publication of *The European Tribe,* as Phillips himself acknowledges in the afterword to the 1999 edition of the book. Associated with this progress is the presence of what he calls "alternatives to Europe" (1999, 134), created by new forms of political identification. His repeated return to the field to rework the themes set out in the earlier text is an indication that this movement is not lateral. Perhaps it is best thought of as *shuttling*, a movement back and forth and back again. Shuttling is enabled by Phillips's mode of political identification, which straddles cosmopolitanism, transnationalism, diasporicity, and aestheticized genre-bending.

There are two strands to the argument I am advancing here. The first strand is my claim that, following an intellectual path charted two generations earlier by the Trinidadian writer, activist, and political theorist C. L. R. James, Phillips, in his nonfictional writings, is attracted to the pluralist culture of the United States, as opposed to the "old certainties" of Europe. James argues in *American Civilization* that the United States' conscious attempt to build a mass society out of the Industrial Revolution marks a decisive cultural break from Europe (1993, 43–45). The other strand is my contention that, having arrived at that space of pluralism, Phillips defines his own intellectual trajectory against the racial and national culture of black America which partially makes his arrival possible. As a young man, Phillips decided on a career in writing after an eye-opening encounter with the perniciousness of racial exclusion in Richard Wright's *Native Son,* an encounter for which his experiences as a black Briton had partly prepared him. A black British writer, he lives in the United States, but he retains his British passport and maintains a home in London. From this vantage point he negotiates what he calls the "high anxiety of belonging,"[2] declaring that it is difficult to base any idea of belonging on the concept of "race." This is the contradiction hinted at in the opening sentence of this chapter: race, the grounds on which Phillips identified with *Native Son's* protagonist Bigger Thomas, is no longer a valid ground for such an identification now that Phillips is fully inducted into the institutional domain that was enabled partly by the political sacrifice and bargaining of the black civil rights movement. Although belonging, the sense of a home, of fidelity to a discrete, specific space, is the nodal form in which identity is conceived, Phillips's sense of belonging in these texts is largely geographical, even territorial, a residue of the nationalist imaginary that equates "home" with land.

The essays in Phillips's *A New World Order* focus on a variety of writers who are grouped geographically, showing that a "national" or "regional" frame is at work. The regions are "the United States," "Africa," "the Caribbean" and "Britain," only complicated by an aesthetic consideration which necessitates the inclusion of two figures who are not writers: the filmmaker Steven Spielberg and the musician Marvin Gaye (once in exile in Europe) in the United States section. Although Phillips treats the different authors unevenly—V. S. Naipaul is discussed in thirty-two pages, and Jamaica Kincaid in three—this text is highly structured by the particularity of geography. Wole Soyinka belongs in the same section as J. M. Coetzee but not as Zadie Smith, and James Baldwin shares more with Spielberg than with George Lamming. This geographically informed conception of identity is striking because, although Phillips's strong determination to unburden his nonfictional writings of "race" may seem iconoclastic, it cannot be fully appreciated without an understanding of the political and institutional context of racial identity in the United States. This idea that race is underwritten by the institutional politics of the United States is also borne out in the scholar Paul Gilroy's use of quotation marks around the word "race," intended to indicate that such a usage of "race" is unselfconscious, and characterizing it as "race thinking" (Gilroy 2000). This point can be clarified further by looking at his description in *The European Tribe* of the months Phillips spent in the mid-1980s traveling across Europe to explore what it meant to be in, but not of, the continent. The narrative starts in Gibraltar, a British territory south of Spain, and takes him as far east as perestroika-era Russia. But it is when he zeroes in on England that his writing takes on a distinctly polemical tone. This section of the book is suggestively titled "The European Tribe," hinting at an interesting parallel between the book's central theme and England's marginalization of its nonwhite populations. Yet there is also a distinctly American flavor to this critique of racial exclusion in Thatcherite England, and it debunks the argument that class is to England what race is to the United States. In this closing chapter of the book, Phillips's rhetoric strives to name and exorcise the evil of racism, and in doing so he draws on the currency of racial relations in the United States. He does so both to indicate a generalized, transatlantic political solidarity and to demonstrate the social contours of American media culture in postwar Europe. In a sense, Phillips's critical attitude toward Europe in this part of the book reflects his awareness of American discourses of race. In later work, Phillips dates the waning of British imperial power to between "the handing over of India in 1947 and the Suez crisis in 1956" (2001, 242), but there is little in the polemical earlier writing to suggest the subordination of Britain by its former colony, the United States. This subordination is one consequence of America's global military and cultural dominance through capitalism, but the Atlantic Charter of 1941 (the political basis for the United States' entry into the Second World War) had so decisively reversed relations between Britain and the United States that the decolonizing events of 1947 and 1956 had become politically inevitable.

In *The Atlantic Sound,* Phillips approaches these issues in a manner that throws into relief complex questions of identity as they pertain to the borders of the nation and the literary genre. His approach may be due to the circumstances of his life. Born in the Caribbean island of St. Kitts, he was brought up in north England and now lives and works in the United States, while spending about two-thirds of his time in England and the Caribbean. His work is frequently described and categorized as "Caribbean literature"; yet he is also a postcolonial black British writer, although his own delineation of "a new world order" suggests a certain disdain for such a concept. For writers of Phillips's background, a disavowal of postcolonial identity is an implicit recognition of these multiple identities, and also a gesture to a condition that is simultaneously denied and affirmed. Phillips is on record as taking exception to the kind of identification associated with postcoloniality, and even with the concept of the Third World, its historical precursor. In a roundtable discussion with the writers Anita Desai and Ilan Stavans, he declares, "I would run a mile from being involved in anything that said Third World . . . I was born a British citizen in a British colony that didn't become independent until 1983, so the question of nationality was not a particularly pressing one for me" (Desai, Phillips, and Stavans 1994, 81–82).[3] The irony, which seemed to escape these writers, is that they are from different regions of the "tricontinent" and owed their encounter to American academia. Such is the nature of what Phillips calls his material (Phillips 1995) that he continually returns to those regions whose representational value reinforces a politics of otherness. This is the basis of *The Atlantic Sound.* In it he deals with people who gain or lose homes, people who deliberately give up certain citizenships and take on, or aspire to, others. Home, for Phillips's interlocutors, is not where you are taken in, but where you are likely to be challenged, even turned out. The lens through which Phillips explores these issues is the guardedness characteristic of the cosmopolitan, post-Edwardian travel writer.[4] Besides quotidian observations of the ports the author visits, the book also contains historical accounts of buildings and social practices, portraits or biographies of individuals, and stories of casual encounters, missed encounters, and the "negotiation of the third world" (2000, 133) in Accra, Liverpool, and Charleston. This complex mix of topics may be suited to the hybridity of the travel genre, but it is also a result of a certain kind of intellectual position within the structure of neoliberalism, and it calls for a political attitude.

African American writers like James Baldwin, Albert Murray, Ralph Ellison, Alice Walker, Toni Morrison, Ishmael Reed, and others had named the beast of racial prejudice and privilege in a manner that most of their black (and white) contemporaries in Europe had not or could not. The literary and intellectual environment created by their work made writing an option for Phillips. This one "alternative to Europe" has its own blind spots, but Phillips steps beyond them through aesthetic gestures impossible to appreciate without a sense of how he comes to occupy this position. This is a long way from his declaration in *The European Tribe* that unity through numerical strength was the only way of maintaining solidarity in the racist ambience of Europe.

The Crossroads of Genres

The Atlantic Sound recounts Phillips's visit to three major ports of the Atlantic slave trade—Liverpool in England, Cape Coast in Ghana, and Charleston, South Carolina, in the United States. These travel accounts are juxtaposed with biographical profiles of historical and contemporary figures struggling with the legacies of slavery and racism, as well as architectural histories of castles in Ghana, public buildings in Liverpool, and the absent monuments to slavery in Charleston. It also includes an epilogue symbolically titled "Exodus," an account of the author's trip to the Israeli city of Dimona in the Negev desert, rendered in short passages alternately poetic and descriptive. The list of personalities in the book is healthily eclectic: a nineteenth-century trader who visits Liverpool from what was then the Gold Coast; a young black Liverpudlian who has made a radio documentary about a "journey of return" to contemporary Ghana; another young Ghanaian immigrant who has just been deported from England; members of the Hebrew Israelite Community now living in a desert settlement at the edge of Israel, among them a Chicago-born African American woman; an eighteenth-century black minister stationed in the slave castle at Cape Coast; a white federal judge in South Carolina at the onset of the civil rights movement; a Brooklyn-born activist building a community of black returnees in Ghana; and a black woman in Charleston who bears witness to the era of segregation. The text is constructed in part out of newspaper reports, poetic eulogies, law reports, and epigrammatic quotations from canonical and noncanonical writers—W. E. B. Du Bois, Langston Hughes, Richard Wright, Robert Frost, and William Gilmore Sims. What brings these varied groups, individuals, and genres together in one book cannot be reduced to race in the historical sense of the term, but their grouping is hardly comprehensible without an idea of how human communities have been constituted and dissolved on the basis of racial and national sentiments. The idea of belonging through which Phillips tries to displace race as the basis of identity has a history, and that history influences how Phillips deploys mutually reinforcing human characters and narrative forms in making his argument.

Like most contemporary accounts of travel by black writers whose locations are influenced by the large-scale dispersal of populations that attended the Middle Passage, *The Atlantic Sound* does not overlook the question of racial identity. In its author's often-expressed desire for contact with black people in Liverpool, or in his unwillingness to accept an American's mocking dismissal of other Americans who have chosen to settle in Ghana, the book can be located in the generic company of Richard Wright's *Black Power,* Maya Angelou's *All God's Children Need Traveling Shoes,* Eddy Harris's *Native Strangers,* and other works dating back to the mid-eighteenth century.[5] Yet there is also in Phillips's book a particular, but ambivalent, attention to the status of citizenship at the crossroads of capital, which is unprecedented in the genre. In the twentieth-century variant of this tradition of travel writing, the traveler's crucial objective has been to combat the trauma of racial denigration in the United States by assuming a common ancestry with contemporary Africans (although this assumption is questioned in the course of travel). This is what I have elsewhere characterized as the "national-racial mode," the powerful representation of American exceptionalism as a site of limited entitlement for black people, and the African continent as a place where that limitation could be redressed (Adesokan 2009a). This does not exactly suggest the interwoven careers of nationalism and racism which some criticisms of racial identity have identified (see Balibar 1991). In this case, Ghana does not have the same psychological salience as, say, Israel, and that is because, for the traveling black writer, the global power of the United States remains the unuttered incantation behind the assumed transformation of the stranger into a native. Transcending the national-racial terms of previous explorations by incorporating enigmatic biographies and accounts of multiple sites, and in part as a result of its author's background, *The Atlantic Sound* establishes a different paradigm for an understanding of identity. This aesthetic desire for clarity in situations of thick complexity is a remarkable feature of Phillips's work, which demonstrates the cultural plurality of the African diaspora. Yet his book never fully surrenders its reluctance to recognize the productive transactions between the supposedly anti-essentialist politics of fulfillment and the emotive forms of identity politics against which some contemporary black writers and critics define themselves.

The Vintage paperback edition of *The Atlantic Sound* categorizes the book as history. Such a categorization of a work of nonfiction has several implications. Even in fictional works like *Crossing the River* and *The Nature of Blood,* Phillips's use of historical materials has established a unique style. These works deal, respectively, with an earlier phase of the Atlantic slave trade and with anti-Semitism in Renaissance Venice, temporalities that are hard to access imaginatively without relying on historical materials. Furthermore, these books' status as affective memories is best established through the weighted "objectivity" of their sources (especially the log of the ship captain John Newton for the former novel and R. Po-Chia Hsia's *Trent 1475* for the latter). In nonfictional writings, this formal preference for historical texts becomes constitutive of the genre in the sense that the materials are drawn from sources as varied as the author's peregrinations. The generic hybridity implicit in the mixing is most determinate in *The Atlantic Sound.*

When Phillips records his itinerary—from Connecticut through Puerto Rico to Guadeloupe, whence he sails for Liverpool by way of Costa Rica and Guatemala—he is being factual, recording actual events. And his itinerary was purposefully designed: by moving from the Caribbean to England he reenacts the journey of the *Windrush* generation of emigrants, transported to England in the 1950s to make up the postwar shortfall in the labor force. Among these emigrants were Phillips's parents, who took him on this journey when he was four months old. This section, the book's prologue, is titled "Atlantic Crossing," and here he records his movement from the Caribbean in the company of three Britons, an elderly American, and four Germans, with whom he was "initiated into the routine of life on board the ship" (2000, 6). The feel of this opening is that of a travel book, with prearranged meetings and hotel bookings, and it invites comparison with V. S. Naipaul's *The Middle Passage,* where the journey is reversed. The main text is divided into three chapters, each dealing with a somewhat antipodal trip to one of the three ports, but in no part of this book is there a hint as to which port was first visited, or when. At best, the reader may surmise that all the trips were made in the 1990s. The antipodal structure of the trips is striking: leaving home, being bound for home, and the reality of home. The anxiety about home and belonging that this structure addresses is displaced, with Phillips's characteristic nuance, on the different figures of a nineteenth-century businessman (John Narh Ocansey), a twentieth-century economic refugee (Mansour), and a civil-rights-era judge (Waties Waring). This conscious designing of the shape of his travels and therefore of the book is crucial to the author's project. The book's objectives remain unstated, as if it were thinly imagined and merely happened to include historical personalities as characters. But it is still possible to tease out a political posture which strives to transcend the messy combination of black essentialism and white racism through the particular critical insights of the author.

The first result of this design is to afford the author the advantage of measuring his credentials as a cosmopolitan, worldly figure against the anxiety that marked the migration to England of West Indians of his parents' generation. He observes, as the ship sets sail,

> For me this will be no Atlantic crossing into the unknown. I fully understand the world that will greet me at the end of the journey, but for West Indian emigrants of an earlier generation the Atlantic crossing was merely the prelude to a larger adventure—one which would change the nature of British society." (7)

The knowledge and self-assurance of which the author boasts are on display everywhere in his encounters in Liverpool. Ignoring the fact that St. George's Hall is open to tourists only a few days in a year, he decides to view the "enormous neo-classical edifice" (105). After he has walked around the building for a few moments, the friendly guide asks where he comes from. The guide seems more interested in making small talk than in the question itself, and without missing a beat, Phillips replies, "London," an answer that does not surprise the woman (107). This kind of ready confidence, as readers of such classics of the West Indian immigrant experience as Samuel Selvon's *The Lonely Londoners* and George Lamming's *The Emigrants* will recall, was not available to blacks of a previous generation. But both Liverpool and London have a specific historical resonance for Phillips. The chapter on Liverpool carries the title "Leaving Home," and here he reflects on the experience of a nineteenth-century businessman from the Gold Coast, John Narh Ocansey, who is visiting England for the first time to investigate his father's business transaction with an English commission agent, Robert Hickson. The elder Ocansey had paid Hickson for a steam launch, to be used in his palm oil business in colonial Addah, but after many months the launch had not been delivered. This story, which Phillips adapts from Ocansey's own account (*African Trading, or, the Trials of William Narh Ocansey*, published in 1881), serves as the background for Phillips's own visit to Liverpool. He explores Liverpool's economic history during the imperial era, discussing its economic status at different dates, in order to provide a cultural basis for John Ocansey's ordeal, and the text oscillates between history and fiction. Yet this is the part of the book where his skills as a novelist are most noticeable.

Phillips uses John Ocansey's first name for two reasons. First, it suggests that he is similar to the English people Phillips also identifies by first names—Lyle, Robert, George—by virtue of having a similar Christian name. Second, it is a device that indicates fiction, as are the structure and pace of the narration, of which more will be said presently. John is in Liverpool at the height of the maritime trade, but this is also the time when the discourse of race was being systematically established. Racial issues are muted here—John lodges with Mrs. Lyle, a woman of kindly disposition, and she and the Methodist George Quilliam and others of Liverpool's Methodist Free Church constitute his "family" in the city. They constantly assure John that Hickson's fraudulent acts are not typical of the English people, and when he shows his doubts about the ensuing legal tussle, they express mild indignation at his distrust of their legal system, which, they assure him again and again, is based entirely on principle. Indeed, Mrs. Lyle's unstinting devotion counterbalances Hickson's mercilessness and the impersonality of the judicial system.

While waiting for his case against Hickson to come up in court, John meets Christian Jacobson, an African from Quitta (Keta?), who has been similarly defrauded, this time by a Glasgow-based trading company, although for a considerably smaller amount. The two walk together around Liverpool until Christian decides to cut his losses and return home. Phillips details the wearying monotony of "come-today-come-tomorrow" to which John is subjected by the court, but eventually his case is heard, and although the judge finds Hickson guilty of the lesser charge of converting the Ocanseys' money to personal use, this is small comfort to John. He now has to return home empty-handed after months in this strange city. In the meantime, he has lavished emotion on his ordeal and on the eventual impact of the whole business on his father. Phillips conveys John's wanderings and frustrations in Liverpool in painstaking, almost mundane detail, which, together with the use of his first name, gives this section of the book the structure and texture of a novel. The critic who describes the entire book as composed of "serenely fictionalized narratives" (Mishra 2001, 51) is probably thinking of this section, but the description applies equally to other parts of the book. In the visually challenging monotony of everyday life in Liverpool, in the workmanlike assiduity of the legal proceedings, in the heartfelt solicitude of John's Methodist acquaintances, Phillips is suggesting that the alienation which the encounter with Europe's social system represents for the most venturesome foreigner is a deeply felt sign of alterity. He notes that "perhaps [John] would have seen this city in a different and more generous light had the troubles of his father's business not dominated his mind" (2000, 93).

The meticulous inscription of John's everyday experience in Liverpool is weighted in syntactical punctiliousness that has become a signature of Phillips's work. In such books as *Cambridge* and *Crossing the River* (especially in "The Pagan Coast," the section of *Crossing the River* presenting letters from the freed slave Nash Williams to Edward, his former master), this preference for well-worked sentences is so marked as to become a rhetorical ploy. In these works, as in the documentation of John Ocansey's ordeal, Phillips invokes the nineteenth-century prose form to represent black or African alterity, although with a deliberate attempt to question it. Three excerpts will serve as examples of this stylistic predilection:

From *Cambridge:*

> John Williams introduced me to the Christian religion while I dwelt on board the ship. Unfortunately, I was unable to make a coherent sense of either his words or his ideas, being more concerned with avoiding English jaws and my

possible fate as meat to match the drink. But after talking awhile with Anna, and marveling at her pure and godly thoughts, I begged my master for full and proper instruction in Christian knowledge so that I might be received into Church fellowship with both experience of the Bible and a conviction of belief. (1991, 107)

From *Crossing the River:*

Some emigrants, who style themselves as lay ministers of the Gospel, asked permission to enter my settlement and to preach the word of God. They gained admission with my blessing, and with that of the agents of the colony, as my present settlement lies beyond the furthest position in the interior to which we are generally encouraged to travel. (1993, 33)

From *The Atlantic Sound:*

On the following Sunday, 17 July, John and Christian were invited by Mr. Quilliam to attend an "open-air" service. While John knew that such services were not the common practice in England, he realized that Mr. Quilliam probably thought that this might be a good opportunity for the two Africans to see the "darker" side of English life where those of a lower station . . . found a place to worship. (2000, 77)

The linguistic register of these passages is meant to display the psychological dilemma of characters who can find neither home nor subjectivity, and who are therefore made to neutralize this lack by emotionally articulating the transcendental power of the religious lexicon. It is little wonder that the Bible—the holy scriptures—figures prominently in each case, since Christianity is the only refuge of these lonely characters, inhabitants of the twilight moment when black and white ceased to approach each other as potential equals.[6] Implicit in this also is the role of Christianity in the colonization of Africa, an enterprise whose wheels were lubricated with the greasy admixture of paternalism, racism, and cultural disruption. In passages reminiscent of Olaudah Equiano's association with vaguely named personages of Whitehall chapel, John, a Christian from the Gold Coast, makes an effort to befriend Liverpudlians by way of social encounters with the Methodists, which seem to be the only option open to self-conscious black travelers in the city at the time. For this reason, the Methodist Free Church on Russell Street becomes "his second home" (Phillips 2000, 67).

By regularly framing the chronicle with epigrammatic passages quoted from the preface and constantly shuttling between an omniscient narrative, reportage, and personal observation, Phillips strives to place John's tragic story in a generic no-man's-land appropriate to the book's contingency of subject matter, site, and personality. Phillips's attitude toward Liverpool during his visit is shaped by his memories of the racism he experienced while growing up in north England, and Liverpool's racism is reflected in its football team, Everton. In

Phillips's view, Liverpool also bears a striking architectural resemblance to the American south, and he is told by Stephen that a particular house was originally built for a financial agent of the Confederate government during the American Civil War (108). This section of the book is classic travel writing, with Phillips training an ethnographic and accusatory eye on the famous port city. And this is where the second result of the book's design begins to manifest itself, although less straightforwardly than does Phillips's exuberant self-confidence.

His two guides, Stephen (in Liverpool) and Mansour (in Accra), are young black men with aspirations. Stephen has produced a radio documentary for the BBC about his visit to Ghana as a diasporic black. "Stephen," writes Phillips, "is wound tight, like a metal coil" (100), and the reader immediately recalls Phillips's own attitude as a twenty-something black Briton setting out for Europe in the mid-1980s. In fact, Phillips and Stephen seem to greatly resent each other. This tension is most obvious when, in order to better understand the condition of blacks in Liverpool, Phillips inquires about local politicians, and the guide narrows things down to the question of whether Jews had been involved in the slave trade. Phillips challenges him to provide evidence.

> Predictably, he did not, and my evening in the bar with Stephen collapsed as
> he became increasingly frustrated with my inability to acknowledge Jewish cul-
> pability, and I grew increasingly worried that I had perhaps chosen the wrong
> person to act as a guide during my time in Liverpool. (102)

Of course, Stephen is far too useful to Phillips's quest to be easily dispensed with, and the next day the author is relieved that "there appears to be no hint of the acrimony of the previous evening" (107). Stephen is useful because, through him, Phillips discovers that "Liverpool-Born Blacks" consider themselves a special class of black Britons, since they were not part "of the 'recent' wave of post-war Caribbean migration which is generally known as the 'Windrush' generation" (110). Phillips thinks Stephen is proud of this status—the younger man traces his "roots" (Phillips's scare-quotes) to 1842—and his pride constitutes a form of nationalism which, in the context of "the fallacious argument that the Jews were largely responsible for the slave trade" (102), limits their collaboration. Although both later mischievously bait some bigots in a local bar, the only thing they agree on is the ignorance of Liverpudlians about "the true story of how and why [the] buildings came to be built" (108). Nonetheless, Phillips's early perception of this "erudite [fellow] clearly interested in literature" (98) as a demagogic, mildly anti-Semitic cultural nationalist prevents him from seriously engaging with Stephen's point of view. What comes forth, instead, is the studied detachment of the traveler-writer, who is not prepared to grapple with the inconveniences of ethnic positioning. Phillips's tendency to address such misgivings to himself, rather than in the context of a conversation within the book, merely underlines the generic instability of the text.

Antipodal Figures

The resentment between Phillips and Stephen is particularly poignant when compared to the sensitive respect, even care, which Phillips extends to Mansour, the Ghanaian guide, who, after all, is a sort of Stephen in reverse. Mansour is a young Ghanaian who has had cosmopolitan aspirations as an unsuccessful immigrant in Libya, Saudi Arabia, Nigeria, and England, from where he was deported some time before Phillips's visit. Mansour is determined to decamp again from Ghana, and divulges his plan to the man he now chauffeurs, asking for help in procuring an American visa. To his credit, Phillips struggles against a knee-jerk condescension toward this fellow black man down on his luck. After deliberating for a couple of days, the traveling writer sums up Mansour's prospects with the suggestion that he had better make his way up in Ghana, "a democratic country of eighteen million people with a diversified economy" (198).

Given that they both appear in this book, it is possible that Mansour's aspiration is qualitatively similar to that of Judge Waties Waring, a white federal judge and civil rights activist in South Carolina in the 1940s. Waring, whose story is reminiscent of that of Joanna Burden's family in William Faulkner's *Light in August*, lost his social status in this deeply segregated society as a result of two actions. As a defender of equal rights, he handed down the ruling that allowed black voters to participate in the state Democratic Party primary in 1948, and in 1951 he offered a dissenting judgment that paved the way for *Brown vs. Board of Education*. At the height of his career, he divorced his Southern wife for a "Yankee" woman. Phillips interviews his surviving associates to recuperate a memory damaged by racial suspicion and bigotry, and he portrays the judge and his courageous second wife, Elizabeth, with deep sympathy.

In a critical but sensitive review of the career of C. L. R. James in *A New World Order*, Phillips quotes the older man's statement that Hollywood mass forms have political value and editorializes thus: "In truth, a 'serious study' of Hollywood was likely to teach more about the cultural expressions of capitalism than about the 'deepest feeling of the American people'" (2002, 163). Although this comment actually minimizes the depth of James's argument in *American Civilization*, it is remarkable that Phillips, encountering a personal aspiration in the context of neoliberal corporate globalization, is unwilling to extend to a young African the same kind of understanding he thinks Waring deserves. He writes of Waring (who, as a judge, often administered the oath of citizenship to new immigrants), "He was painfully out of tune with his home, and he decided that he had no choice but to leave. It was simply too burdensome to be among those who openly hated you in a place you called 'home'" (2000, 255). Can't it be said of Mansour, too, that he is out of tune with his home? The bigotry that forces the judge from his community is the affective relation of the economic immiseration that has turned millions of Mansours into refugees in their places of birth. In this regard, Etienne Balibar's argument that immigration is "the main name given to race within the crisis-torn nations of the post-colonial era" (Balibar 1991, 52) implies that the two phenomena are closer than they appear.

By suggesting that Mansour stay and make his way up in Ghanaian society, Phillips reveals his insensitivity to the fact that although Waring had no choice but to leave Charleston, Mansour not only had no choice but to leave his home but also, unlike Waring, had nowhere to leave for. Hence his deportation from England. Ruby Cornwall, an African American associate of the Warings, pointed out, "We [blacks] didn't have the same choices that he had. He could go away, but this was our home. We had to stay here" (Phillips 2000, 253). In Liberia, Somalia, Sierra Leone, Rwanda, and Sudan, countries without Ghana's exemplary management of ethnic relations, economic and other tensions have resulted in ethnic and communal clashes and even civil wars, which are partly driven by the kind of bigotry that ran Waring out of South Carolina. Mansour's desire is to be anywhere he can be fulfilled, a profound, if opportunistic, identification with the pursuit of happiness, what is called the American Dream. In the aftermath of the crashing of hijacked planes into the World Trade Center on September 11, 2001, the spiritual success of this dream has paradoxically revealed patriotism to be a pragmatic aspiration.

It may be useful here to consider these questions of choice in the light of Craig Calhoun's argument (2002) that cosmopolitanism is linked to what he calls "constitutional patriotism," after Jürgen Habermas. This concept, like the cosmopolitanism with which Calhoun identifies it, suggests political loyalty in both the narrow legal sense of constitution-making and the broader, creative sense of culture-forming. The issue of nationalism was never totally absent from the German debates to which Habermas contributed the idea, but the full measure of the notion of constitutional patriotism was conceived out of the Kantian cosmopolitan ideal: "that people should see themselves as citizens of the world, not just of their countries." The ethnonationalist sense of being a people, argues Calhoun, is still different from nationalism, because in it "is an ethnic solidarity that triumphs over civility and liberal values and ultimately turns to horrific violence." Contemporary European history offers the examples of Nazi Germany and Serbia under Slobodan Milosevic. Postnational society need not supersede the nationalism that arose out of the Enlightenment because at work in nationalism is an active process of political and cultural participation, and to see "nationalism as a relic of an earlier order . . . is to fail to see both the continuing power of nationalism as a discursive formation and the work—sometime positive—that nationalist solidarities continue to do in the world" (150). Calhoun thinks that Habermas's notion of constitutional patriotism relies too heavily on forms of ethnic nationalism in which attempts to constitute society are seen as rationalistic systems of exclusion. "He works," Calhoun writes, "with an overly sharp dichotomy between inherited identity and rational discourse," which results in "a decidedly thin form of identity, to be produced by the rational discourse of the cosmopolitan public sphere" (155). Habermas's striving will thus remain Sisyphean, Calhoun submits, "so long as culture is treated as inheritance and placed in sharp opposition to reason, conceived in terms of voluntary action" (157). Relying on the idea that social solidarity is a choice rather than a necessity, or that culture is learned rather than inherited, Calhoun makes the useful point that culture-forming is creative. He adds that this process of culture-forming, however informed by rational or pragmatic choice, is never fully divorced from creativity or imagination.

This creative conception of membership in a community underpins the choices that the two antipodal figures in Phillips's book—Mansour and Waring—make. Although they are separated by more than economic and social circumstances—Mansour's desire is personal, while Waring is pursuing social equality in a hostile environment—what constitutes their shared "structure of feeling," a phrase which Calhoun borrows from Raymond Williams, is the fact of a social imaginary to which all who wish may aspire. For Mansour, this is a life of personal fulfillment in America, to which, his present circumstances notwithstanding, he considers himself entitled, although he has failed to realize a version of it in Saudi Arabia, Nigeria, or England. In other words, he aspires to escape the fate, as Pheng Cheah writes in another context, of "those postcolonials for whom postnationalism through mobility is not an alternative" (1998b, 302). In an earlier time, Waring and Mansour might have met as equals. A federal building somewhere in the United States would be an appropriate place for such a meeting between these antipodal figures, the one administering the oath of citizenship on the other. Imagining such a meeting allows them to be compared, much as James Clifford imagines comparing Alexander Von Humboldt and an indentured Asian laborer, and there is also a ground of equivalence between them, since we now have knowledge of them, in excess of their individual intellectual or discursive resources.[7] Perhaps Mansour's aspiration, like Waring's for a just society, would be easier to grasp if Calhoun's fine distinction between nationalism and ethnonationalism, the variety on display in racist Southern society, were to be briefly suspended. Does the one produce the other? To stress the negative aspects of nationalism, that is, to raise it to the level of a distinct formation ("bad nationalism"), is also to draw attention, on another level, to the immanence of cosmopolitanism as an institutional practice of political marginalization. The well-heeled cosmopolitanism of the traveling writer is purchased partly at the expense of the extremely marginalized, like Mansour. Furthermore, the fact that emigration, which was at least sometimes an option for members of Phillips's parents' generation, is much less possible for people of the late twentieth and early twenty-first centuries should raise concerns about the potential for democracy around the world.[8] That Mansour's ordeal is presented slightingly, as a singular yearning for opportunity, is itself the result of a flawed perception of world history, with insufficient attention to uneven geographical development: economic dislocation has been an integral part of African history as far back as the slave trade period (Ekeh 1990), and the experience of immigrants can be as traumatic as the ostracism experienced by the Warings. On the other hand, because the Warings are white, their story acquires a special force when chronicled as an aspect of black Atlantic history in the wider context of the civil rights movement. As Phillips's narration confirms, their ordeal was reported nationally and put them on the lecture circuit, a few years before the emergence of Martin Luther King, Jr. In their different ways, Mansour and Waring are victims of these subtle practices of exclusion that limit choice.

Phillips's attitude toward Mansour is made even more problematic by his own unresolved tension about what constitutes citizenship in the aftermath of the massive migration that relocated his family to north England. It is a tension because, in spite of his critical attitude toward positioning of all sorts in this text, Phillips is aware that his presence in these different places is a result of two kinds of self-knowledge, personal (derived from his history) and political-aesthetic (derived from his status as a writer). His personal self-knowledge determines his choice of subjects to interview and places to visit, but the other kind manifests itself in his constant alertness to signs of difference. These signs of difference are most noticeable in Ghana. Phillips observes,

> Third world travel imposes patterns upon one's life. There is a stubborn predictability to the encounter, which is enlivened by different languages, different sights and different smells. Otherwise the pattern remains much the same. (2000, 133)

This passage, a set-piece of travel writing, appears in the section on Accra, soon after his arrival. This is where newspapers and magazines in a waiting room fall apart in the humidity, where roadside hoardings list no product name or phone number. To be sure, these observations suggest the writer's admirable measurement of his material, and point to the workings of a remarkable, if largely subsumed, subjectivity. They are visible marks of the writerly posture, proudly struck. As moments in a literary text, they are also priceless, for this is no sociology textbook, after all. Indeed, when Phillips later visits Charleston, there is an interesting moment when he listens for a creak in the elevator and observes "the rhythm of the south" (260), implying that the most powerful country in the world also harbors elements of tropicality, the atavistic difference that sets the Third World apart. There is also a comic and self-deprecating moment when the author walks up to a building and knocks on the door, only to discover that it is a mausoleum. These anecdotes point to Phillips's concern for the aesthetic quality of his work, beyond the ordinary duty of chronicling his travels and reflecting on the consequences of his subjects' experiences.

His observations go beyond the merely aesthetic when they are presented as a measure of his emotional distance from his material. For a writer of Phillips's temperament, the insertion of these curiosities as hazards of the job, or "negotiations of the Third World," gives only half the picture. If Phillips's account included a rigorous explanation of the genesis of the metropolitan advantage he possessed over his interlocutors, he might be able to achieve a political attitude that would place him beyond the call of essentialist camps. This would involve not only telling the story of growing up black in north England, but also admitting his indebtedness to the black American literary and political cultures: *Native Son* at the beach, and the improvements in civil rights gained through institutional multiculturalism. These stories are nowhere told in *The Atlantic Sound,* despite the extensive personal witnessing that structures the different trips. The subsumption of the author's real relationship to his subjects in scattered pieces of highly wrought gems of irony is the third result of the book's generic shape.

The encounters with Mansour precede several others, all of which reveal the distance between the author and his subject(s). Soon after he arrives in Ghana, Phillips has a conversation with Dr. Robert Lee, an African American dentist long settled in the country. They discuss a group headed by Kohain Halevi, another African American, who has been trying to persuade the government of Ghana to turn the castles at Elmina and Cape Coast into historical monuments on the scale of Auschwitz and Pearl Harbor and who, since his formal emigration to Ghana in 1991, has been trying to buy land on which to build a home. The dentist sneers at this effort, but Phillips notes, "Something had to be wrong with [the settlers'] lives in the US to make them leave [and] something had to be right with their new lives in Elmina to make them want to stay" (154). This is one of the most profound moments in this book. The writer displays his awareness of both the necessity and the contingency of a sense of belonging, but also addresses the incommensurability of material and spiritual yearnings. What Lee says of Halevi's group, that much of "their behavior, consciously or subconsciously, is a criticism of the people they've chosen to settle amongst" (153), may indicate a reason for cultural gaps between blacks in the diaspora and those on the continent. But his statement does not address affect, although one can surmise that his argument about native Africans' lack of interest in the castles does indicate repression.

It is also instructive that when Phillips meets with Dr. Ben Abdallah, a former Ghanaian government official and noted Pan-Africanist, Abdallah does not evince the kind of passionate identification with the legacy of slavery that Halevi and his group do. For a Pan-Africanist, this indifference is close to scandalous. Abdallah's suggestion that blacks in the diaspora have a higher stake in maintaining the castles than do Africans is certainly insensitive, and moreover his use of the phrase "You people" (which Phillips finds offensive) compromises the notion of an "African family" that is at the heart of much Pan-Africanist rhetoric. But Lee's dismissal of Halevi's group also falls short, and is as cynical as Abdallah's speechifying. More importantly, these negative attitudes toward the admittedly complex and complicated project of suturing the dismembered history of the continent are successfully proclaimed in this text because the author does not engage his interlocutors seriously enough. For instance, he does not question Abdallah's argument that "those sold into slavery were not always that good, and that in some respects they got what they deserved" (148), preferring just to confess his incredulity, his inability to respond appropriately to the statement. Similarly, his response to Lee's suggestion that Halevi's group is unrealistically romanticizing Africa is to gather his papers and stand up.

A different picture emerges when, for a moment, one places *The Atlantic Sound* against two recent books with similar agendas that are explored through visits to Ghana: Saidiya Hartman's *Lose You Mother* and Ekow Eshun's *Black Gold of the Sun*. The silences in *The Atlantic Sound* become more poignant when compared to Hartman's daring objective of crossing "the boundary that separated kin from stranger" (2007, 17). Eshun's quest is even more poetic; he goes to Ghana, his parents' country, because though born in England, he has "no home" (2006, 2). Indeed, the movement from the national-racial mode (in which the émigrés Wright and Angelou generationally identified with Nkrumah's Ghana), through Phillips, to these more recent engagements with the legacy of slavery and colonialism is roughly parallel to the successive appearance of black nationalism, black Atlantic cosmopolitanism, and the postnational formation that is difficult to name, but that can be grasped conceptually in Hartman's subsequent declarations. She writes, "The dreams that defined [the émigrés'] narrative of liberation had ceased to be a blueprint for the future," for "what had attracted the émigrés to Ghana were this vision of a new life and the promise of rebirth; what attracted me were the ruins of the old one" (2007, 39, 40). Whatever one may think of the argument that the narrative of liberation is no longer relevant to the prospects of the world, there is ample evidence of a generational and demographic shift between the Nkrumahist vision of a United States of Africa and Hartman's intellectual attitude toward a version of that vision, one mediated by theoretical discourses (feminism, new historicism, psychoanalysis, poststructuralism) and the institutional context of what the scholar Hortense Spillers calls "dispersal" (2003, 460).

Phillips has a strange habit of giving the last word to his interlocutors in Ghana. It is as if he is unprepared for most of their comments, and so is unable to follow up potentially productive points, like the question of who has responsibility for monumentalizing the slave castles in Ghana, which Abdallah flippantly assigns to "those in the diaspora" (2000, 148). This habit seems largely due to the fact that, as a traveling writer, Phillips has a set of ideas on which his inquiries rest. He tells Abdallah that "it is his Pan Africanist 'beliefs' that I wish to ask him about" (142). In the letters he wrote to Lee from London, he had declared that "it was his attempt to purchase a slave fort called Abanze Castle that first brought his name to my notice" (152). Although, in a brilliant moment of self-awareness, Phillips remarks that Lee is merely attempting to answer Abdallah's challenge, he does not pursue this point satisfactorily when the occasion arises. And the occasion does arise during his meeting with a third figure, Halevi, who proceeds on a different premise from the two older men. Phillips calls him by his first name throughout this section, harking back to "John" of Liverpool.

Phillips listens as Halevi relates his odyssey. He was born Wayne Boykin in Mount Vernon, New York, and educated in a Hebrew congregation in Brooklyn. In 1986 he tried to travel with a group of twenty-six African Americans to Israel, but failed. The following year, using links established through his niece's marriage to a Ghanaian, Halevi led another group, now of sixteen people, "on a two-week trip to a place they hoped might be 'the promised land'" (203). This marked the beginning of Halevi's resettlement effort. He formed an association with the Fante king of Cape Coast, Nana Osabarimba Kodwo Mbra V, and by the time Phillips arrives in Ghana, Halevi has been able to help the Afrocentric scholar Leonard Jeffries buy a house belonging to a group of white evangelists. Halevi's journey is straightforwardly narrated, very much like Mansour's, which it closely follows. By the end of his interview with this "dapper and handsome man [who] . . . looks considerably younger than his forty-five years" (199), an unconvinced Phillips confesses his skepticism about Halevi's project. He comments that Halevi "sees himself as a man who can help blacks remake themselves in the land of their forefathers" (206) but suggests that the man's description of his group's work is an attempt to convince himself, and that he must be tired.

What is worth drawing out of the deep-seated skepticism which structures Phillips's interlocutions is the fraught status of cosmopolitanism as an intellectual attitude, and its complex affiliations to neoliberal capitalism and postnationality. One could be charitable and argue that, though he has specific objectives, Phillips proceeds, unlike Hartman after him, without a theory, or more accurately, without directly stating it. He is driven by a complex sense of lived history—in the Caribbean, in England, and in the United States—but he does not let this sense override his subjectivity as a writer. Indeed, he appears to believe that the two are independent. As Darryl Pinckney writes in *Out There: Mavericks of Black Literature,* Phillips's attitude toward his encounters in *The Atlantic Sound* "is a form of protection, a guard against being taken in, a way of preserving the integrity of the enterprise. The brief Phillips gives himself is clear: to mystify nothing, not to be seduced into poetic ambivalence. He must decide, based only on what he sees, and he will see only what he sees" (2002, 130). This constitutes a theoretical perspective in itself, and it differs from the motivation for Hartman's quest in that the latter's interest in "the ruins of the old [African world]" of slavery is a way of working through ideas developed from immersion in specific intellectual traditions and ideas, such as psychoanalysis, feminism, new historicism, and poststructuralism. For Phillips, then, the unstated point of departure is the fraught terrain of cultural identification constituted by black American literary history (the epiphanic apotheosis of Bigger Thomas) and the political tasks of the civil rights movement.

Phillips is unwilling to declare this point of departure in *The Atlantic Sound* because of his assumption that the canvas he is painting is broader than this national context, and this assumption is due to the institutional ground of his own writerly subjectivity, one underwritten by the culture of prestige attached to cosmopolitanism. So far, I have drawn on two distinct but overlapping formations of cosmopolitanism. These are political cosmopolitanism, which Robbins, its most consistent proponent, has also described as "cultural internationalism" (1999, 17), and institutional cosmopolitanism, which is identified with Calhoun, who allies this variety with constitutional patriotism (2002, 149). These formations overlap because central to both their projections is a conception of political practice, belonging in the public sphere that Calhoun's reliance on Habermas necessarily privileges. This conception follows the pattern of global politics so closely that a sense of collective action, or of acting through collectivities, is a basic condition of its possibility. This is why Robbins's primary example is drawn from Susan Sontag's quixotic work in Sarajevo during the Bosnia war (Robbins 1999, 11–37 passim). But these formations can also be differentiated by their methodologies.

There is an aesthetic dimension to political cosmopolitanism, owing to Robbins's investment in artists and intellectuals and to his use of texts, like the novels of Bharati Mukherjee and Michael Ondaatje. Furthermore, Robbins specifies the distinctive objectives of internationalism (the term he prefers, because of its political interests) and cosmopolitanism: the first is collective and stands for political engagement, while the second is individual and deeply invested in aesthetic spectatorship (17). Calhoun has discussed the limitations of assigning negative values to "ethnonationalism" with the objective of stressing the validity of certain forms of nationalism in cosmopolitanism. Yet Robbins, who distinguishes cosmopolitanism from internationalism on the basis of political action, if viewed from a different angle, can be seen to slip into a similar position. The two critics' divergent interests in legal-political (Calhoun) and intellectual-academic (Robbins) forms of social relations draw on scholarly practices that look toward Europe and the United States, respectively, in ways that decisively shape their methodologies. Just as a negative description of nationalism draws attention to the immanence of cosmopolitanism as a practice of institutional marginalization, the idea that overt political action is the pivotal marker of internationalism overlooks the potential of aesthetics to be politically constitutive. Phillips's nonfictional writings astutely show this potential.

Political identification is implicit in Phillips's travels. He has an abiding interest in the subjection of blacks and Jews, so his cosmopolitanism is still not quite Sontag's humanitarian model, of which Robbins is critical. Even when he steps out of the frame of blackness or European minoritization to examine

Waring's travails, he does so on the basis of identity, critiquing race as a practice of exclusion. In other words, he is combining this form of political identification with an aesthetic attitude that, following Robbins (1999, 30), can be described as "disinterestedness." Thus, it is an aestheticized mode of political identification, as can be seen in detail in the destabilization of the genre of travel writing. Nonetheless, his attitude toward his subjects is more complicated. The different locations of Phillips's interviewees underline the paradoxical sense of mission that drives their desires, and Phillips is only intermittently sensitive to this. The legacies of slavery, racism, and colonialism, including their impact on the production of contemporary identities, are worldwide and enduring, but dominant critical and political attitudes have always associated them with the Atlantic, primarily, as Gilroy has argued (1993), because of the importance of race in the American tradition of cultural studies. Phillips's interest in the architectural and economic histories of Liverpool and Charleston, as well as in the careers of the historical figures contained in his book, bears witness to the power of these legacies. However, although Phillips displays his anti-essentialist posture in diverse ways, he also tends to assume that criticizing both blacks and whites safeguards him against picking a side. Thus he not only pointedly refuses to visit W. E. B. Du Bois' grave in Accra, he also refuses to see a play about the man's life, *A Nightingale for Dr. Du Bois*, written by the Nigerian dramatist Femi Osofisan, which premiered at the Pan-African Festival in Accra in 1997 (2000, 215). He expresses suspicion about the enthusiasm of the members of the African Hebrew Israelite Community attending the biannual cultural festival in Cape Coast, Ghana, only to show up later at their base in Dimona, Israel, and write poetically about them, without telling his reader why and how this change of heart, for that is what it amounts to, came about.

Out of this irony, which is at once personal and aesthetic, Phillips hopes to construct a model of political identification against which cosmopolitanism, as I discussed it earlier, continues to struggle. He adopts the ironic posture of the writer whose allegiance transcends binary political positioning without denying his interest in the particular legacies of slavery, racism, and colonialism. What emerges, therefore, is an aestheticized political identification: Phillips pursues his interest in these legacies through a heightened writerly self-awareness. In his insistence on his individuality as a writer, he constantly resists being incorporated into claims of racial solidarity (except once, in Accra, when he advertises this solidarity in an ironic tone). In order to manage this paradoxical insistence on individuality in the midst of conflicting affiliations, Phillips tweaks the forms of travel writing and autobiography to accommodate his diverse positions. Despite his skepticism about figures like Halevi and Stephen who identify with home (in Accra or Liverpool), Phillips uses a hybrid style that aligns historical narratives and fictionalized autobiography, expresses facts, and succeeds in saying things behind the author's back. Halevi's mission, for example, is informed by an abiding faith in the spiritual need for home. He is enthusiastic, and strikes the reader as interesting in spite of his interlocutor's best efforts. This is the paradox of the generic no-man's-land which *The Atlantic Sound* occupies.

As I suggested earlier, the shape of *The Atlantic Sound* is a function of certain narrative strategies necessitated by the author's objectives in undertaking the trips, even when these are not always explicitly stated. It is also informed by his authorial sensibilities, which can be gleaned even in his fiction. Writing about Phillips's work after the publication of *The Nature of Blood*, the novelist J. M. Coetzee notes that "Phillips has progressed from straightforward linear narration and uncomplicated realism to the complex shuttling of voices and intercuttings of narrative lines, and even forays into postmodern alienation effects" (2001, 168). Although Coetzee is speaking of *The Nature of Blood*, similar narrative techniques are present even in Phillips's nonfiction, including *The Atlantic Sound*. Framing the author's shuttles between the different sites of the slave trade are the complementary shuttles between narrative approaches as well as the mixing of different genres, whose goal is to explore how the notions of belonging are shaped by certain historical forces of the modern era. Current discussions of genre in postcolonial studies barely attempt this kind of thoroughgoing questioning of genres, torn as they are between conventional notions of the category (Todorov 1990) and the political weight of artistic works by writers in, but not of, Europe (Hitchcock 2003). It is in order to respond to this oversight that I have taken questions of genre to be politically constitutive—that is, the weight of political issues can be so burdensome that an author is constrained to displace them onto multiple ways of narrating. This idea of genre is also a function of the metropolitan context of an artist's position, as Pascale Casanova notes in discussing the transference of political issues to the aesthetic terrain. Thus, a point of view becomes aestheticized, and the absence of the directly political in a narrative need not indicate a lack of political identification. The downside of this aestheticized form of identification, as can be seen here, is its failure to sufficiently specify the author's authority—his privileged position in relation to his subjects and his material sites of engagement.

Yet genre as a typology of kinds does not exist independently of institutions, and this returns me to the argument I proposed at the beginning of this chapter, namely that there is a structural relationship between nonfiction as a literary form and the situation of writers who produce their works in the institutional context of diasporicity, cosmopolitanism, and expatriation. The experience of displaced intellectuals is no longer commonly explored through the concept of exile, which has yielded place to concepts like migrancy, cosmopolitanism, diasporicity, and expatriation. As Edward Said argues, what differentiates contemporary experiences of exile from those of earlier eras is the sheer scale of displacement, the combination of warfare and imperialism and the quasi-theological ambitions of totalitarian rulers in the twentieth century (2000, 174). But when Said, who in turn has been taken to task on this issue by Aijaz Ahmad, discusses the relationships between exile, refuge, and expatriation (all twentieth-century phenomena), he, like Calhoun, invokes the crucial question of choice, which is usually thought to be less available to exiles and refugees than to expatriates. The dynamics between Phillips and his sites, topics, and interlocutors reveal that choice is determined by social positions, the least visible of which is that of the traveling author. In other words, while Phillips is able to choose where to visit (and thus pass judgments on people he encounters), most others are not. The main effect of the generic instability of *The Atlantic Sound* is to conceal how the author gained that power of cultural judgment. However, Phillips's topics—slavery, racism, colonialism—are historically potent, and to focus on them is to expose the links between prosperous literary and intellectual careers such as Phillips's and the continued abjection of those without such opportunities—who are the majority.

An appropriate conclusion to the struggles between personal history and institutional entitlements can be provided by a brief return to two of Phillips's other books, *The European Tribe* and *A New World Order*. First, as he suggests in the afterword to *The European Tribe*, the United States represents an alternative to Europe in the same way that, according to Timothy Brennan, cultural pluralism is the basis of James's "American seduction" (Phillips 1999, 134; Brennan 1997, 219). However, this alternative has also introduced a fascinating paradox into his conception of the politics of race in the United States. At the end of the introduction (fittingly subtitled "The Burden of Race") to the section of *A New World Order* that deals with U.S. writers and artists, Phillips writes,

> More than ever before, the United States needs a William Faulkner or a Ralph Ellison. It needs individuals whose vision is inclusive, culturally based, and who vigorously reject the self-righteous discourse of racial entitlement. Race matters. Sure it does, but not that much. (2002, 17)

Here is a writer who links his decision to follow the literary path to the effect that black American authors like Ellison, Baldwin, and particularly Wright (with *Native Son*) had on him when he was twenty, a writer who establishes a commonality between his experiences in north England and those of Bigger Thomas in Chicago's South Side. Now that he is welcome to the party, he disavows the importance of race in this social setting, and this disavowal can be construed as questioning the political basis of his own arrival. The remark betrays impatience with what Gilroy calls "brittle traveling nationalisms" (1993, 42), although the obvious con-*textual* target of Phillips's critique seems to be Cornel West's *Race Matters*.

Drawing on this chapter's central trope of shuttling, however, it is possible to ground Phillips's struggle with the burden of race in a more productive intellectual terrain. This is a black Atlantic terrain in the sense that it traverses the triangular geography of the academic Anglophone Western Hemisphere, but it also transcends that geography through its coupling of diasporicity and transnationalism, the unsettled but stimulating process toward which Gilroy strives in the final pages of *The Black Atlantic* (1993).

Although his trajectory is somewhat different from James's, since he grew up in postwar England, Phillips's continuing engagement with the prejudices of racism marks him as a black writer for whom race is an issue, even if it is to be disavowed. Between his epiphany on reading *Native Son* from dawn to dusk on a California beach and his statement that "race matters . . . but not that much" lies a long career of self-advancement enabled by both personal dedication and the specifically American context of affirmative action and multicultural politics. Such is the nature of this intellectual journey, whose contours *The Atlantic Sound* follows, that in the year of the book's publication Phillips finds himself living "in Greenwich Village, only a few short blocks from Charles Street where, back in the mid-1940s, the great American writer Richard Wright endured much difficulty and unspeakable humiliation trying to live and write as a free man in the country of his birth" (2001, 27). Even with the financial security gained through the unprecedented success of *Native Son*, Wright could not buy a house in this New York neighborhood. The Europe that both James and Phillips find unsuited to the full expression of personal freedom provided refuge for black writers and artists of Wright's time; notably, of all the figures whom Phillips discusses in the American section of *A New World Order,* only Spielberg has never made a home in a European country. But the political context of the massive flight to Europe is connected to the sustained struggles that resulted in the kind of institutional power that enabled Phillips to make a home in Greenwich Village. Those struggles included the civil rights movement from the mid-1950s, and the labor and feminist movements.

In other words, questions of race have to be coupled with those of other categories, such as class, gender, and sexuality, to serve the ideals of transnational social justice which animated the careers of Phillips's precursors, such as James and Wright. This broadened terrain also reveals the writer's institutional complicity, as is shown in the political writings of Arundhati Roy, the focus of the next chapter.

6 Spirits of Bandung: A Sarcastic Subject Writes to Empire

One of the most fascinating ironies of neoliberal globalization is that the wide-ranging and deep-running transformations of the world that have accompanied this socioeconomic (dis)order have not crippled political actions of the most uncompromisingly radical kind. If anything, those transformations have often freed radical political imaginations. Technological, institutional, and demographic changes such as I have discussed throughout this book—the emergence of "network society," the dominance of postmodernist, pixilated, or fragmented identities, antipodal identifications, the crisis of modern sovereignty in the polyforum—all suggest different ways of being in and engaging with the world that are hardly reducible to (though not necessarily incompatible with) the old antagonism characteristic of classical binarisms. Perhaps Ernesto Laclau and Chantal Mouffe's reminder that unresolved antagonism is the preferred political situation in a social space (2001, xvi) makes this situation less ironic. This renewed antagonism is the spur for the political writings of Arundhati Roy, the Indian (Keralan) writer who is the focus of the present chapter.

The argument in this chapter is that, as a result of the postcolonial asymmetry, writers aligned with corporate globalization who profess the kind of "writerly" political ambivalence characteristic of dominant cosmopolitanism do so at the risk of concealing the reasons for their position in that institutional context. However, if they adopt a critical attitude toward the neoliberal economic system, they acquire the appellation of "activist," with all the challenges that such an identity poses for genre. Roy engages these contradictions in her political writings as a self-described "subject of empire" deploying several literary figures and tropes, but primarily sarcasm. This is a paradoxical rhetorical posture characteristic of certain postcolonial writers and artists, especially those that are passionately invested in global equality but operate in the interface between the postcolonial locality and the less clearly demarcated space of literary style. Here I will discuss the author's nonfictional writings as a kind of political instrument seeking to reimagine the ideas of socialist tricontinentalism evinced in the earlier careers of James and Sembene, focusing on *An Ordinary Person's Guide to Empire* (2004) and relating the critiques of corporate globalization implicit in the text to the equally pervasive manifestations of the "network" age.

Like Caryl Phillips, Roy is a postcolonial writer, one whose current status as a "writer-activist" is inseparable from the branding of postcolonial authorship as a function of the neoliberal commodification of culture. They both had works nominated for the Booker Prize in London; Phillips's *Crossing the River* (published in 1991) was shortlisted in 1992, and Roy's *The God of Small Things* (1998; originally published in 1997) won the prize in 1997. Unlike the author of *The Atlantic Sound,* however, Roy has consistently used commodification against the institution of neoliberalism, in the process complicating or departing from the variant of cosmopolitanism which holds explicit political action suspect. The institutional context of Roy's emergence as a writer (like Phillips, she is a citizen of a former British colony) and her relationship to "the economy of prestige" of multinational publishing and prize-giving[1] present an interesting standpoint from which to examine how global citizenship may be a form of political responsibility. Again, my procedure here is similar to that of the previous chapter: while focusing on *The Ordinary Person's Guide to Empire,* I will read other political essays by Roy, including *Power Politics* (2001), *The Cost of Living* (1999), *War Talk* (2003), *The Checkbook and the Cruise Missile* (2004), and others, both collected and uncollected.

Best known as the author of the best-selling novel *The God of Small Things,* Roy occupies a solid position in the literary and intellectual formation called "Indo-Anglian" writing. "Indo-Anglian" writers are writers of Indian origin or background whose works (usually novels in English) are published primarily in London and New York, increasingly to enormous commercial and critical success. These writers include Anita Desai, Salman Rushdie, Vikram Seth, Vikram Chandra, Kiran Desai, Amitav Ghosh, Manil Suri, Amit Chaudhary, and a score of others. Although their thematic and aesthetic interests are by no means identical, their reception as Indo-Anglian authors nonetheless reflects a global interest in (marketable) postcolonial Indian depictions of neo-Orientalism. In a June 1997 *New Yorker* essay published as part of a special "Indian issue" to coincide with the fiftieth anniversary of Indian independence, Rushdie approvingly categorizes these writers as Indo-Anglian, saying that "the prose writing— both fiction and non-fiction—created [in the half century of independence] by Indian writers working in English is proving to be a more interesting body of work than most of what has been produced in the sixteen 'official languages of India.'" (2002, 146).[2] Apparently, this categorization is very different from the one prevalent in Indian literary circles, as deployed in R. K. Srinivasa Iyengar's *Indian Writing in English,* as "a native eruption, an expression . . . of the creative genius of the Indian people . . . [and also] as a minor tributary of English literature."[3]

A novel about the complex lives of members of a pickle-making family in the southern Indian state of Kerala, *The God of Small Things* was an unusual first book. It became an instant literary event, won the Booker Prize in England in the year of its publication, and by 2010 had sold more than six million copies and been translated into at least forty languages. As always when a literary best seller is authored by a first-time writer, a second book was eagerly awaited, and when, in 1998, Roy wrote two essays about India's enormous hydroelectric projects and the nuclear bomb for two major Indian magazines, they were hastily published in the United States as the nonfiction *The Cost of Living,* whose publication was intended to refine the brand that Roy was expected to become. The irony has been that, in turning to the political essay, a genre which she claims reinforces the artistic vision in her first novel, she has turned neoliberalism's instrument of commodification against it. The coming together of a world-class novelist and the global effects of neoliberalism has had consequences that are neither simple nor simply ambiguous.

To date, Roy has published five books of nonfiction, a pamphlet titled *Public Power in the Age of Empire,* and *The Checkbook and the Cruise Missile,* a book of interviews with the American columnist and radio producer David Barsamian. In these texts, she has been concerned to lay bare the causal relationships between power and powerlessness, writing about "the distance between those who take the decisions and those who must suffer them even more" and the "unformatted battle" that that distance represents (2004b, 20). To do this, she stakes out India as her ground and connects the country to the rest of the world through the imbrication of both in corporate globalization. Her subjects in this shuttle between a locality and the world include dam projects, the nuclear bomb, corporate globalization, the entrenched demon of communal Hindu fascism in India, the U.S.-spearheaded War on Terror, Islamic fundamentalism, and postcolonial nations' squandering of the gains of the Non-Aligned Movement. Nowhere is this imbrication more obvious than in *An Ordinary Person's Guide to Empire,* in which she offers an exemplary analysis of the invasion of Iraq in 2003. Thus, the conceptual principle behind C. L. R. James's position on Pan-Africanism (the focus of my chapter 1) is also behind Roy's argument in *Guide to Empire.* This principle is encapsulated in a telling question put to Roy by a Dutch filmmaker: "What can India teach the world?" (2001, 83). Identifying what the world could learn from Africa, and vice versa, was central to James's argument.

In generic terms, Roy's nonfiction writings are conceived either as public addresses, lectures, interviews, or opinion articles. If Roy had followed the tradition of literary-political nonfiction visible in the work of writers such as Gore Vidal and Mario Vargas Llosa, these essays might have constituted periodic commentaries on issues generically separate from novelistic engagement, but with palpable consequences for her writerly prestige and canonization. But Roy does not seem to have such a monumentalizing impulse, since she assumes a strong connection between her fiction and nonfiction. Her nonfiction is thus useful, first, for the complex ways that it addresses the complementarity of the political self and the social structure. As a writer and a citizen, she is drawn to consider India's particular social structure and the spectacular and ambiguous results that corporate globalization and ethnoreligious fascism have recently had in that country, but her sense of responsibility to do so is inseparable from her awareness of the role of corporate globalization in shaping India's ambiguous reputation.

Secondly, these works evince analysis in their self-conscious display of a writerly temperament through the use of sarcasm, idiosyncratic but rhetorically astute capitalizations, neologisms, and associated strategies. In them, Roy deploys one main rhetorical tool, sarcasm, but also relies on two secondary (satirical) tools—invented language and extended metaphors—to carry her objectives through. She must do so because sarcasm, a figure of speech, has limited rhetorical use in comparison with a full-fledged literary genre like satire. It is Roy's astute grasp of power's devious way with language, a function of her self-assurance as a writer, that enables her to try to match that deviousness with her own rhetoric. Sarcasm is the central trope in this unequal battle, a complex rhetorical tool both indicating an intellectual unwillingness to trust the adversary's "truth" and reflecting, by the very fact of that tongue-in-cheek knowingness characteristic of sarcasm, an intellectual complicity with it. For postcolonial authors, this rhetoric represents a deep distrust of "the West" which cannot be expressed only as anger, but requires also a kind of derision, a sassy, sarcastic enunciation. The sarcastic subject speaking through Roy's nonfictional writings occupies a complex theoretical position. She sits between the anti-colonial revolt of Aimé Césaire and that of Soyinka and Walcott. The ungovernable Caliban as the protagonist of Césaire's *A Tempest* (1985) is the model for the first, which was enthusiastically claimed for the politics of difference in the Americas in Roberto Fernández Retamar's famous essay (1989). The second is a splicing of the Ariel/Prospero/Caliban complex into the creative-destructive-restorative model of Ogun and the "mulatto of style" (Walcott 1998, 9).[4] The subject simultaneously engages incomplete decolonization and unsettled transnationalization, and combines the responsibilities of national liberation and nation-building that motivated earlier discourses with the demands of politicized (socioeconomic, gendered) identities under neoliberal globalization. On a third level, the subject's relationships to these earlier discourses are analogous to the tensions between the careers of black nationalism, black Atlantic cosmopolitanism, and theoretical transnationalism, for which the figures of Richard Wright, Caryl Phillips, and Saidiya Hartman may be respective representatives, as I argued in the previous chapter.

Roy's sarcasm derives from her activist engagement with issues of her time, and it draws equally on Swiftian, Brechtian, and Orwellian types of satire. The essays in *Guide to Empire*, like those in other books, have different histories and seem to address disparate topics. But a consistent thematic and political thread runs through them, proof of her understanding of the mutual dependence of local nationalism and a generalized neoliberal corporate globalization. Whether she is addressing the rise of fundamentalist movements (both cultural and religious) in India as evidenced by organizations like the Hindu Sangh Parivar, the Rashtriya Swayamsevak Sangh, the Bajrang Dal, and their parliamentary front in the Bharatiya Janata Party, or the distortions of public opinion by the global corporatization of the media, Roy is both a generalist and a particularist. Three complementary steps are necessary to show the connections between the political objectives of her essays and the stylistic objectives of the literary figure propelling them. First, I will isolate her specific engagements with India to pinpoint the emergence of a postcolonial type, the "writer-activist," and then I will look more closely at the problematic identity of writer-activist, using *Guide to Empire* and other books in both efforts. Finally, I will look even more closely at one of the essays in *Guide to Empire* to show how it exemplifies the performance of this identity through an internal critique of the anti-globalization movement that coalesces with sarcasm in the historical context of tricontinentalism.

Roy broaches her engagement with India in the two essays in *The Cost of Living*. The book addresses one of the two aspects of India's national status, its self-presentation as a development-oriented postcolonial country in the context of corporate globalization. That one aspect forks into the two essays in the book. First, there is the ruthless dislocation of communities through the dam projects in such Indian states as Gujarat, Madhya Pradesh, and Maharashtra, in which the thirty dams along the Narmada Valley are sited.[5] Second, there is the country's acquisition of a nuclear bomb in 1998, which drew an international outcry, especially since India's rival, Pakistan, quickly followed. The other important aspect of India's national status is the sinister cancer of fascist ethno-nationalism, or Hindutva, and the violent victimization of Muslims. Both feed into the global war on terror, a tool used opportunistically by the government to further its local agenda both against the poor displaced by the dam projects and against Muslims. (Governmental moves against Indian Muslims are of course a part of the country's fractious relationship with Pakistan.)

In the first essay in *The Cost of Living*, "The Greater Common Good," Roy argues that the controversy about the dams raises fundamental questions about the validity of India's claims to have democratic institutions of good governance and the right to manage and exploit the country's natural resources. But she also exposes the interesting irony of the extent of the government's awareness of the implications of its rhetoric of development. A government supposedly following Jawaharlal Nehru's injunctions to use development as a pointer to "the greater common good" has no statistics on the number of people displaced by the dam constructions. Although she corrects that shortcoming by providing an accurate figure (and with a touch of humor), she is obviously interested in something equally fundamental: a progressive country's treating its citizens with such wanton and cynical disregard. This is a classic case of the postcolonial asymmetry, the pursuit of a "national" ideal simultaneously in the name of and at the expense of the people. As I will show in detail later, Roy's interest in calculating the costs of the dam is of a piece with her sense of what being a writer-activist entails—the rationality of numbers cuts through the smug silence that the neoliberal conferment of prestige on postcolonial authors is suspected to deepen.

In the second essay, "The End of Imagination," she is concerned that India's acquisition of the bomb portends grave danger for the country as well as for the rest of the world. Political and principled opposition to nuclear armament has a long history, embracing such figures as Bertrand Russell and Noam Chomsky, and Roy's outrage against the Indian government's attitude recognizes that history but places it within the larger context of the political cynicism leading nations of the world to the militaristic path. An interesting aspect of her opposition to the bomb is its post-humanistic depth, which is underscored by the essay's poetic dedication: "For marmots and voles and everything else on earth that is threatened and terrorized by the human race." Thus, while she shares the standard horror of the consequences of the bomb—recalling Hiroshima and Nagasaki—she combines such a political response with the larger question of the planet's continuing survival. As a citizen of India she takes umbrage at her country's hubristic action, which she uses as a basis for examining issues that pertain at once to that country and the world. This is her philosophical position as a writer-citizen, one which she clarifies when she writes in a subsequent essay, "Though it may appear otherwise, my writing is not really about nations and histories, it's about power" ("Come September," in Roy 2003, 46).

Early in "The End of Imagination," Roy parenthetically tells a comic but disturbing story of members of the right-wing Vishwa Hindu Parishad (World Hindu Organization) proposing to distribute, as *prasad* (sacred food), radioactive sand from the desert where the bomb was tested. She tells the story to demonstrate the level of ignorance about the bomb in India, but the mention of the Vishwa Hindu Parishad in this context raises concerns about the other disturbing development in contemporary Indian society—the rise of fascist movements dedicated to the idea that only authentic Hindu culture and religion are legitimately Indian. This parenthetical anecdote will be supplemented later by an entire essay, "Democracy: Who Is She When She Is at Home?" (2003, 17–44). The most notorious outburst of these movements was the March 2002 violence against Muslims in the state of Gujarat.[6] Roy's choice to discuss these two developments indicates her political orientation, and by characterizing both the dams and the bomb as "weapons of mass destruction" (1999, 80), she underscores their negative consequences for the country and the world. The principles in the essays have been sharpened or developed in the rest of her nonfictional writings. What she attempts in *Guide to Empire* is a case in point.

The six essays in *An Ordinary Person's Guide to Empire* address conceptual issues of corporate globalization, but they do so by starting from specific Indian cases and examples that are generalizable because they express fundamental concerns about the state of the world. The book's thesis is that those who embarked on the Iraq war were motivated by the neoliberal advance of capitalist interests on a world scale, and those interests promote the spread of ultra-nationalist and fundamentalist movements in India, in the United States, and elsewhere in the world. Although this thesis is not stated explicitly, its truth manifests itself in India as a combination of what Roy calls "indiscriminate privatization" (2004b, 110) and violent and fundamentalist Hindutva, which is championed by both the central government and its local religious and cultural satellites. These two developments can be characterized (as they manifest in Indian public opinion) as two complementary strategies. The development strategy uses projects like big dams and nuclear bombs to promote sociopolitical progress in India, while the communalism strategy uses the construction of the Ram Mandir temple in Ayodhya on the site of a destroyed mosque and the 2002 violence in Gujarat to promote Hindutva. This is what Roy calls "the dual orchestra," in which, "while one arm is busy selling off the nation's assets in chunks, the other, to divert attention, is arranging a baying, howling, deranged chorus of cultural nationalism" (2004b, 109).

"The way vultures are drawn to kills"

One of the problems that arise in discussing Roy's political writings is a very obvious one—the supposed conflict between the identities of writer and activist. She is acutely aware of this problem, and devotes extensive attention to it in the different writings and in interviews, proof that she experiences the conflict in a personal, integral way. Having both these identities also imposes secondary challenges: the difficulties of generic categorization; the writer's responsibility to get facts and figures right; and the antinomy of the neoliberal commodity form and the economics of personal prestige. I will discuss each of these challenges at length later, but first I want to look at the emergence of the intellectual type or figure of the writer-activist. This is a postcolonial type, emerging as an engaged political consciousness out of the combination of social issues with the primarily ethical challenges that are at the core of artistic creativity.

The idea of political commitment among artists has a long history, and has been particularly controversial in the twentieth century.[7] But in the latter half of the century and early in the twenty-first, and especially in the postcolonial societies of Africa, Asia, the Middle East, South America, and the Caribbean, commitment is not simply embodied in works of art as "a process of the dramatization of values," whether mimetic or reflective (Hall 1961, 69). Nor is it simply a function of generic differences between fiction and nonfiction, owing to the way that the rhetorical character of the latter positions the reader. In the postcolonial formations of the writer-activist, there is the additional and significant question of political identification and action, the involvement of the writer or artist in a specific political issue or movement. One may think of the fictional character Puran in Mahasweta Devi's "Pterodactyl, Puran Shay, and Pirtha," the journalist and representative of the mainstream who utterly identifies with the tribal peoples of India. Instructively, Devi calls the novella "an abstract of my entire tribal experience" (1995, xx). Examples from recent post-colonial history include Walter Rodney, the Guyanese scholar and activist, and Ken Saro-Wiwa, the novelist and environmentalist in Nigeria. Although these are figures of political vanguardism, what matters is not just that they paid the ultimate price for their positions but also their identification, their conscious adoption of a position in baldly political settings. This is where the two roles of writer and activist are homologous—distinct but complementary roles.

Yet engaging this figure as it emerges in Roy's political writings requires making distinctions in the discursive structure of complementarity. This is be-cause the figure occupies several terrains at once: the writer as a writer, the writer as an activist, and the postcolonial progressive individual interested in questions of ethical and political conduct in a local context (in this case, India). But such is the nature of the questions, and of the writer's own trajectory as a postcolonial intellectual, that they are more productively posed in relation to the locality's reflection of patterns that are observable elsewhere. This second observation is validated by the fact that the postcolonial writer-activist lives in history and inhabits structures, ideological as well as aesthetic, which simul-taneously recognize individuality (the writer's own style) and collectivity (the anti-globalization movement). Thus, it is as difficult to distinguish between the writer and the activist as it is necessary to do so, exactly because they are com-plementary, and because this complementarity is deepened by the intimate re-lationship between the locality and the dispersed neoliberal forces which con-stitute its contentious identity. Roy the novelist produces nonfiction political essays on a variety of related issues: Big Dams, the nuclear bomb, fascistic Hin-dutva, and the neoliberal agenda to privatize collective patrimony (all of these being specific to contemporary India), as well as the U.S.-led War on Terror, Al Qaeda's fundamentalism, and the postcolonial aftermath of the Non-Aligned Movement, which she often investigates through an internal critique of the anti-globalization movement.

Although Roy has insisted on the wholeness, the indivisibility, of her writer-activist personality, I have to separate the writer from the activist for analytical purposes. I distinguish between the individual who takes part in protests and the writer's voice in the essays. The distinction being proffered here is similar to the one drawn by Jeyifo between "the 'authorial' self of [Wole] Soyinka's works and the 'self-presentation' immanent in his radical activism" (Jeyifo 2004, 22). Roy herself is aware of a tension between the two selves, as she reveals in an interview:

Also, there was this other interesting combination of being a writer and—what does a writer do? A writer hones his or her language, makes it as clear and private and individual as possible. And then you are looking around and talking about what's going on with millions of people, and you are in that crowd saying things that millions of people are saying and it's not at all individual. How do you hold those two things down? These are very fundamental questions. (Roy 2008)

The challenge of holding "those two things down" is not easily confronted, but in opting for political action, both in person and in print, Roy has done much more to complicate and (one might say) transcend the analytical sundering of the activist from the writer.

In her essay "The Ladies Have Feelings, So . . . Shall We Leave It to the Experts?" (Roy 2001, 1–33), there is an extended discussion of the role of the writer-artist in society (4–12). The crux of the discussion is the review of the rise of "Indo-Anglian" authors, whose success has encouraged people, in and out of India, to turn writers into celebrity endorsers of products. Then Roy submits, "There is very real danger that this neoteric seduction can shut us up far more effectively than violence and repression ever could" (9). She writes further,

> Now, I've been wondering why it should be that the person who wrote [*The God of Small Things*] is called a writer, and the person who wrote the political essays is called an activist? True, [the novel] is a work of fiction, but it's no less political than any of my essays. True, the essays are works of nonfiction, but since when did writers forgo the right to write nonfiction? (11)

The problematic appellation of "writer-activist" is thus conflated with extremely slippery questions of genre, and Roy does not shy away from their implications. Fiction is what "dances out of [her]," while nonfiction "is wrenched out by the aching, broken world I wake up to every morning" ("Come September," Roy 2003, 45). The "problem" with the appellation is that "it is strategically positioned to diminish both writers and activists . . . [suggesting] that the writer by definition is too effete a being to come up with the clarity, the explicitness . . . to publicly take a political position. And conversely, it suggests that the activist occupies the coarser, cruder end of the intellectual spectrum" ("The Ladies Have Feelings," Roy 2001, 23).

India and the neoliberal machine are also complementary, and here we watch Roy struggle with different issues. In India, she contends with Big Dams, the nuclear bomb, Hindutva and ethnonationalism, and the neoliberal desire to privatize India. She clarifies these problems by addressing them in relation to urgent questions of corporate globalization, such as the War on Terror (largely driven by U.S. president Bush's neoliberal and fundamentalist agenda), Al Qaeda's fundamentalism, and the postcolonial squandering of the gains of the Non-Aligned Movement. These are the issues in Roy's political writings—the content of her activism.

These issues, though distinct, are largely complementary. Indeed, Aijaz Ahmad, who calls the coupling of Hindutva and corporate globalization "saffronization and neoliberalism," has argued that "there is a structural even though not causal connection between the current fascist offensive in India which passes itself off as Hindu nationalism, the new imperialist offensive which passes itself off as 'globalization,' and the immense brutalization of culture and politics that we are witnessing at present on the national as well as global scale" (2002, xix, xxi). Roy argues that although building big dams in India may appear to be a national modernization project appropriate to a late-industrial nation, the problems of displacement and impoverishment that it entails indicate that it is closely tied to the neoliberal agenda of corporate globalization. The waters and lands of Sardar Sarovar, like those of Kevadia Colony, are natural entities being privatized in the process that David Harvey has termed "the commodification of nature" (2006, 44). The result is that people in the affected areas are dispossessed in the short term through physical dislocation, and in the long term through the effacement of their cultural heritage.

The same relation of complementarity applies to the building of a nuclear arsenal in India. These weapons are ostensibly intended to defend the country against external aggression, under the theory of deterrence ("The End of Imagination," Roy 1999, 97–98), whether that aggression emanates from the far West (Europe and North America) or near West (Pakistan). But who can fail to see that this aggressive policy, partly motivated by religious and cultural essentialism (Hindutva), complements the routine violence against Muslims in India, in which the ethnonationalist and fascist Hindu organizations (the Rashtriya Swayamsevak Sangh and the Vishwa Hindu Parishad) are complicit? The three secondary problems occasioned by the appellation—the challenge of generic categorization, the challenge of getting facts and figures right, and the antinomy of the neoliberal commodity form and the economics of personal prestige—are so integral and fraught that they may well be at the core of most writers' unwillingness to shoulder the burden of activism. In the first instance, and as I argued above, Roy conflates the appellation of writer-activist with complex questions of genre, since the writer supposedly does one thing (fiction) and the activist does another (nonfiction). I do not blindly take her word on this, preferring to notice the presence of "reasons [she does] not fully understand" in the process of moving from writer to activist, especially because the unknown reasons resonate with what Devi calls "an obsession"(1995, xvi).

In a pamphlet titled *Public Power in the Age of Empire,* Roy identifies three dangers confronting contemporary resistance movements: "the difficult meeting point between mass movements and mass media, the hazards of the NGO-ization of resistance, and the confrontation between resistance movements and increasingly repressive states" (2004c, 36). Regarding the first of these dangers, she notes that the mass media are interested in resistance movements largely as political theater, since "starvation deaths are more effective advertisements for impoverishment than millions of malnourished people, who don't quite make the cut" (37–38). This is a common dilemma for political causes, and Roy may have been drawing equally on her experience of working with the Narmada Bachao Andolan trying to prevent the damming of the Narmada River in Sardar Sarovar valley, where, after the initial outburst of outrage, "the international camera crews and the radical reporters . . . moved (like the World Bank) to newer pastures" ("The Greater Common Good," Roy 1999, 41–42). Indeed, in the first essay in *Guide to Empire*, she characterizes this phenomenon as "crisis as spectacle" and notes that both resistance movements and official institutions are implicated in it, the difference being in the kind of spectacle each chooses to magnify (Roy 2004b, 8).

However, the media's role in manufacturing the spectacle begets an irony. In *Public Power* she mentions the roles that Ahmed Karzai and Iyad Allawi (former CIA operatives) have played as political leaders in Afghanistan and Iraq. Once these men were enthroned in their respective countries, the international media turned to other matters. The irony lies in the danger of important political issues becoming dated even when they are being turned into spectacles in the media. Crisis is mediated through commodification, formatting, and spectacularization. Problems that are given air time because they are considered newsworthy (that is, sensational) may receive attention too late to be solved. However, the same is true, in reverse, for the pamphlet genre beloved of the activist. Urgent treatments of immediate political issues (for example, details of the early days of the war in Iraq: "Instant-Mix Imperial Democracy," Roy 2004b, 41–68) risk becoming dated because, drawing their analyses from available resources and data, they may not remain challenging after the conditions producing those resources have changed. In this regard, the essay as a literary genre represents a mode of political action. Such is the nature of the materials that Roy assembles in essay after essay (reproducing or recycling statistics, sticking to a few resonant and connectable topics) and the uses she makes of them that, following a model of literary-political nonfiction, she might very well have published a single book from the different pamphlets.[8] Such a periodic coherence tends not to document, as a matter of immediate political response, but to monumentalize, a procedure of writerly prestige she appears to be hinting at in the conclusion to "The Greater Common Good," where she links Big Dams to nuclear bombs as "weapons of mass destruction" (Roy 1999, 80).

The point here is related to the second challenge, the use of facts and figures, and the formal demands that this use makes on the writer. The challenge results from both the nature of the public-policy issues that are at stake in writing in extra-fictional terms about such things as dams, land tenure, and industrialization, and the deliberate complication of the dismissive (and gendered) stereotype of the writer as "a man of letters" who has no aptitude for "scientific" factuality. In all of her writings discussed in this chapter, Roy is heavily invested in specificity—in getting facts, figures, names, and dates right, and in using them to make political points. The reader is constantly offered pertinent statistics: the disproportionate numbers of African Americans in the U.S. army and in prisons (2004b, 60, 75); the number of families in South Africa evicted from their homes or dying from AIDS (72); the number of people, villages, and acres of land displaced by and lost to the dams and irrigation projects in Gujarat and Madhya Pradesh (1999, 17, 36); the Indian rural and urban populations, the percentage of these living without electricity, the amount (as a percentage of the Indian annual rural development budget) that the Maharashtra State Electricity Board would lose to U.S. corporations if it were to buy ninety percent of Enron's output; and what the international dam industry is worth per year (2001, 43, 57, 62). These are not all, of course, but they prove that Roy is fully aware of the demands that her choice of the political essay as a tool of anti-globalization activism imposes on her status as a writer. In other words, she calculates that she is far from the terrain of the fictional, where images "dance out of" her. Though there is a visceral edge to her apprehension of the demands of producing political essays (they are "wrenched out" of her), a sense of proportion remains integral to the duty.

Nonetheless, there is a formal difference between her approach in these writings and that of the scholar and literary theorist Ahmad, and of the scholarship on the Narmada River development projects. In its criticism of "saffronization and neoliberalism" Ahmad's book, *On Communalism and Globalization,* has much in common with Roy's essays on Indian topics. The two authors are similarly critical of fascist Hindutva and corporate globalization and do not mince words in showing how Indian instances of the depredations of global capital and of emergent fascism are connected. But Ahmad's text is a historically and theoretically dense account of the relationship between globalization and the menace of Hindutva. Indeed, the stylistic difference between them may be seen in Roy's use of the evocative image of a "dual orchestra" (2004b, 109) compared to Ahmad's conceptual "saffronization and neoliberalism" (2004, xix).

The third problem is the antinomy of the neoliberal commodity form and the economics of personal prestige. Roy's recourse to the form of the political essay represents an attack on corporate globalization in India and the rest of the world. The success of *The God of Small Things* is much-storied: it received the largest advance ever paid by a UK agent for a first novel, won the Booker Prize, has sold millions of copies in North America and Western Europe (not to mention in India and elsewhere), has been translated into scores of languages, and so on. On the strength of these accomplishments, a second book seemed natural, and preferably another novel. But Roy used her opportunity differently. As she told an interviewer in *Tehelka* magazine in 2008, "I think it was very important that GOST came out in '97, and in '98, there were the nuclear tests and so that whole trajectory coincided with something dark that began here. The two together put me on a path that I didn't entirely control" (Roy 2008). But it is also important to note that her status in the world, her ability to produce those essays and attract the attention that she does, develops partly out of the culture of prestige attached to the phenomenon of international literary celebrity, one in which Indo-Anglian writers are well represented. The novel's success outside India may not be entirely due to the cultural awareness of the Indian diaspora, a demographic formation that is complexly related to Hindutva abroad, but it is hardly unconnected to that cultural awareness.[9] In an interview following the publication in England of her second collection of stories, *Unaccustomed Earth*, in 2008, the Indian-American writer Jhumpa Lahiri says,

> My parents' generation made their presence known, but not quite in the same way. It's my generation that really seeped into the culture, and spread out and spread through it. People of Indian origin, like myself, they're still engineers and doctors and professors, but they are also writers, cooks, dancers, rock musicians, actors. They're not here for the one purpose of having a respectable job. (Tayler 2008)

This demography is distinguished, and points to the greater visibility of the Indian diaspora in the United States than the African one that resulted from the socioeconomic dislocations of the late 1980s. Thus, the prestige of Indo-Anglian writings is attributable to several sociological factors, two of which are the increasing visibility of India's diaspora communities across the world and the cultural and demographic diversity within India. But Roy's place in this formation is quite complex, and may provide insight into her choices as a writer of political essays. Biographical details aside, the complex depiction of gender, class, and caste relations and the critique of communist politics in *The God of Small Things* might have complicated any perception of that novel as tagged "For Export Only" (Kumar 1999, 88).[10] Her unexpected blend of writerly iconoclasm and Indian location make her unique; most of the better-known Indo-Anglian writers live in Western countries or "have addresses at the creative writing programs of American universities," in Kumar's captious phrase (99). Of course, it is in the nature of the commodity form to make the varieties of this uniqueness the basis of branding: Indian residency confers a putative, ambiguous authenticity, while her assumption of an activist role lends weight to her treatments of social issues. For example, Roy has often told the story of the woman who asked her to write an essay on "child abuse" ("Knowledge and Power," 2004a, 37).

This is what the antinomy of the neoliberal commodity form and the economy of personal prestige implies. The award of the Booker Prize to Roy's first novel and her subsequent visibility reinforce the extent to which calculating the cultural value of her work is a global affair, for, as James English argues with regard to the circulation of prizes in a postcolonial context, it is difficult to evade "the social and political freight of a global award at a time when global markets determine more and more the fate of local symbolic economies" (2005, 298). In Roy's case, however, the impact of these global calculations is felt less on the nationally segmented relationships among India-based writers than on the more decentered phenomenon of personal prestige, which is gendered, ambiguously authentic, and politicized. Her place in this economy squares with the problematic category of cosmopolitanism as I have discussed it in this book. As a winner of the Booker Prize, she circulates in the same cultural and intellectual terrains as Ben Okri, Graham Swift, Michael Ondaatje, Caryl Phillips, and Keri Hulme,[11] combining that aestheticized, expatriated postcoloniality with the distinction of political authorship, of which the Scottish writer James Kelman is perhaps the most recent example among Booker Prize winners. Although Roy's political writings constitute an uncompromising critique of the effects of corporate globalization in India and the world, her ability to advance such a critique cannot be separated from her considerable global status as the author of *The God of Small Things* and as a "woman of color." The dimension of gender is underspecified in her writings, but it is critical to her activism.

In the Spirit of Bandung

This leads me to the question: if Roy is implicated in the very process of neoliberal commodification that she debunks, is her political engagement also doomed to be compromised? To address this question productively requires me to shift my focus from the image of corporate globalization as Leviathan, the great whale inside of whom no kind of resistance is possible, and instead to connect Roy's activist role as a postcolonial intellectual to a history of contestations of which the anti-globalization movement is a logical phase. This history includes the political formation of the Non-Aligned Movement, the tricontinental moment of decolonization that has left its mark on the works of figures like James and Sembene. Roy's political writings serve to connect this history to a movement that is simultaneously postcolonial in the frame of tricontinentalism and constituted in the relationships between decolonization and the progressive forces within the old colonizing countries. This connection demonstrates the importance of India's role in the emergence of tricontinentalism, and perhaps explains why Roy is so insistent that India can be an example, on a global stage, of the fight against contemporary imperialism. Thus her criticisms of India are informed by considerations that are more than nationalist. They provide the basis for global postcoloniality, the development of an artistic and political practice (and an emergent academic formation) suited to a world no longer seen in terms of modernist binarisms or Cold War blocs, but rather with attention to the inequalities integral to corporate globalization.

Recent studies of tricontinentalism and Third World agendas contend that the current retrenchment of those processes in critical and political discourses marginalizes the history which gave colonialism and imperialism a real ideological purchase (Prashad 2007; Gikandi 2001). Indeed, the critic Simon Gikandi critiques globalization and postcoloniality largely on the grounds that they stand for the dissipation of the political energies associated with the earlier discourse of anti-imperialism. Anti-imperialism spoke not of postcoloniality but of the "Third World," in opposition to a Eurocentric view of the world, and Gikandi writes that "in their desire to secure the newness of theories of globalization . . . many critics and analysts of the phenomenon no longer seem interested in the 'Third World' itself as a source of the cultural energies—and the tragedies—that have brought the new migrants to the West" (2001, 645). While not disputing this claim, I am persuaded that one can approach the contradictory relationships between and within decolonization and globalization which motivate these critiques not only by redressing the histories or reinserting earlier terminologies but also, and more crucially, by demonstrating the complex relationships between the poetics of decolonization and the aesthetic transformations wrought by globalization.

The demands of the genre of the political pamphlet, which are determined by neoliberal commodification, prevent Roy from attending to the entirety of these relationships. This neoliberal practice did not similarly restrict James, in whose epoch literary works by politically engaged "persons of color" did not seem to merit the kind of commodification that is at work in the careers of Phillips and Roy. However, by developing rhetorical strategies clustered around the figure of sarcasm, and by mounting an internal critique of the anti-globalization movement, Roy points toward emergent anti-globalization aesthetics and their relationship to the aesthetic of tricontinentalism, whose appearance in James's work I have already described. There are historical antecedents for her work in the writings of Régis Debray and the films of Gilo Pontecorvo, Pier Paolo Pasolini, and Lionel Rogosin, but the figure of sarcasm in her writings complicates the different registers of social realism in the works of these artist-intellectuals.

One essay in *Guide to Empire* where the internal critique of the anti-globalization movement tellingly coalesces with sarcasm is "Do Turkeys Enjoy Thanksgiving?," which was originally delivered as a lecture at the World Social Forum in India. There are two threads running through the essay: an analysis of what Roy calls "New Imperialism" and a plea for an internal critique of the anti-globalization movement. The Orwellian tag "New Imperialism" is sarcastic, and the internal critique of the anti-globalization movement represents an attempt to rally like-minded individuals to combat this new thing. Setting the World Social Forum against "The Project for the New American Century," the nonprofit think tank established in 1997 to promote American global leadership, Roy argues that the old bipolar form of global détente, the Cold War, has been replaced by a "single empire with . . . complete, unipolar, economic and military hegemony" (2004b, 84). The strategy of New Imperialism is a thorough revamping of good old *divide et impera*:

> Poor countries that are geopolitically of strategic value to empire, or have a "market" of any size, or infrastructure that can be privatized, or, god forbid, natural resources of value—oil, gold, diamonds, cobalt, coal—must do

as they're told or become military targets. Those with the greatest reserves of natural wealth are most at risk. Unless they surrender their resources willingly to the corporate machine, civil unrest will be fomented, or war will be waged. (84)

She then links these tactics to the supportive role of the corporate media, which is adept at treating crisis as spectacle and which is a fundamental ideological tool of the neoliberal project. India becomes a useful case study of how this formation works, because both corporate globalization and ethnoreligious fascism have made spectacular appearances in the country in recent times. The March 2002 violence in Gujarat occurred as India's economic power was greatly increasing, and the two developments are so fundamental as to be interdependent. Here is a sharp anticipation of Roy's "dual orchestra," or Ahmad's "saffronization and neoliberalism."

The way that corporate media turn this state of affairs into a spectacle reinforces the rule of empire. It also encourages the legatees of a tradition of "non-alignment" to sully that legacy by taking on the fashionable label of "natural ally," which deviously establishes a supposed anti-terrorist alliance between India, Israel, and the United States. This makes it clear that it was not coincidental that the victims of the Gujarat violence were mostly Muslims, nor did India's opportunistic deployment of its Prevention of Terrorism Act (POTA) in 2002 occur in an ideological vacuum. Not only Muslims but also India's poor and the activists opposing Big Dams and other "development" projects were liable to fall victim to this law. Concomitant with New Imperialism is New Racism, and Roy uses the American tradition of a presidential pardon for a turkey on the Thanksgiving holiday as an extended allegory to underline the relationship between these "new" things. Like the naming of New Imperialism, the allegory functions within the rhetorical figure of sarcasm.

Each year the National Turkey Federation presents the president with a turkey which is to be spared (pardoned), unlike the millions of others that will be slaughtered and eaten across American homes on Thanksgiving Day.

After receiving the presidential pardon, the Chosen One is sent to Frying Pan Park in Virginia to live out its natural life . . . ConAgra Foods, the company that has won the Presidential Turkey contract, says it trains the lucky birds to be sociable, to interact with dignitaries, school children, and the press. (Soon they'll even speak English!) (2004b, 87–88)

Roy argues that this gesture, the selection of "a few carefully bred turkeys," is an example of how New Racism works in tandem with corporate globalization. Her list of the pardoned includes investment bankers, a community of wealthy immigrants, the local elites of many countries, and "some writers (like myself)" (88). Roy's extended metaphor of this practice dovetails with the secondary procedure she calls New Genocide, which she says is facilitated by economic sanctions and designed to perpetuate global inequity. In a series of rhetorical questions, she justifies this assertion by showing how New Imperialism manipulates economic factors in all spheres—manufacturing, agriculture, financialization, the debt crisis—on the reshaped template of the old.

One corrective to this reality, of course, is the anti-globalization movement. Roy made this World Social Forum speech in the aftermath of activists' successful confrontation of the World Trade Organization in Cancún, Mexico, in September 2003. The fifth WTO ministerial conference was organized to discuss trade agreements that the activists adjudged unfair to poor countries, and their intervention was crucial in bringing attention to this inequity. It is ironic that the World Social Forum was involved in the WTO conference, since countries of the global south, like India and Mexico, later claimed credit for derailing those unfair tariffs while working locally against movements like the WSF in places such as Sardar Sarovar and Chiapas. The irony is deepened by the fact that figures like Nelson Mandela of South Africa and Luiz Inácio Lula da Silva of Brazil, who made their names as anti-imperialists, often compromise those credentials once they find themselves in power. In her insistence that the movement not be deceived, Roy is drawing a sharp distinction between old and new anti-imperialisms, and between postcolonial governments and social movements. By turning the critical searchlight on people like Lula, she is differentiating between, on one hand, the political vanguardism dominant at the governmental forums in Bandung and the Non-Aligned Movement, and, on the other, the kind of postcolonial critique which is the basis of James's exemplary reading of historical Pan-Africanism and which she herself is performing. As I have noted, James declined his invitation to the Sixth Pan-African Congress in Tanzania because he was unhappy at the movement's being taken over by governmental bureaucracies, the precise institutional forms he considered detrimental to its goals.

If this example gives kudos to the movement, her next move is a knock, albeit offered advisedly. She writes that "if all our energies are diverted into [periodic forums] at the cost of real political action, then the WSF, which has played such a crucial role in the movement for global justice, runs the risk of becoming an asset to our enemies" (91). The injunction here is that anti-globalization activists must resist the temptation of turning dissent into spectacle, a form of political theater that loses relevance as soon as the media exhaust its potential for sensational newsmaking. She fears that the movement's tactics have so far relied on three tropes of crisis-as-spectacle: the anti-war protests of February 15, 2003, took place on a weekend, which may imply a "holiday mentality"; they were eagerly reported by the crisis-driven media; and within this format they precluded the possibility of victory. Roy's proposition is that in order to move away from this approach, the movement needs "to agree on something" (92), and she suggests three possibilities: the prioritization of Iraq as the culmination of anti-imperialism and anti-globalization struggles, the mobilization of war functionaries (soldiers, reservists) to refuse to serve, and a commitment to liquidating companies known to be profiting from the war in Iraq.

The relationships between these two threads of the essay—the analysis of New Imperialism through sarcasm and the internal critique of the anti-globalization movement—are underscored by the author's assumption of a set of ideological connections: between neoliberalism and Hindutva, a local example of fascism; between old and new imperialisms; and between anti-globalization rhetoric and spectacle and their antitheses. As an example of the workings of crisis-as-spectacle (itself a coinage resonant of disconnection from the older Gandhian model of civil disobedience), India represents both the immediate occasion of the speech and the locality that is streamlined against the general critique of corporate globalization. This implication is magnified by the new rhetoric of the Indian government, a historically "nonaligned" country that is now eager not only to abandon that history but more importantly to fling itself to the opposite extreme, by allying with the United States and Israel in the war on terror.[12] The coinage "New Imperialism" is a sublative (re)naming of colonial imperialism, the late nineteenth- to mid-twentieth-century behemoth which tricontinentalism was sanguinely designed to destabilize. It is a naming that resonates with the extended allegory of turkey pardoning, for just as New Imperialism produces other things—New Racism and New Genocide—turkey pardoning also produces new vocabularies—Chosen One, Frying Pan Park, Fortunate Fowls, and Turkey Choosing Committee. These personifications through capitalization are a ploy to drive the rhetorical point of Roy's sarcasms home with the force of Swiftian satire.

Sarcasm is a prominent part of Roy's stock in trade. This figure should be properly understood. It is not simply satire, for satire, either as a genre or a figure, is constitutive, not an appendage; it is all there is to a "satiric" piece of writing. Roy's objective in each of the essays is substantive and cannot be subsumed to a genre, although it draws on a genre's properties. Nor does it always display the earnestness of social realism, the genre of political writing with which it shares an ideological affinity. Sarcasm makes its appearance in the essays as wry, idiosyncratic phrases or neologisms that attain rhetorical or figural identities by being capitalized, like "Instant-Mix Imperial Democracy," "New Imperialism" (2004b, 47, 84), "Promoting Greater Common Good," and "Single Authority" (1999, 50, 73–76). It appears as a pop quiz on where and how to relocate the forty thousand fisherfolk displaced by the dam project in the Narmada valley, and as an "analysis" of government-approved Adivasi "tribal art" (1999, 67, 65). It also appears in parenthetical comments: "U.S. Attorney General John Ashcroft recently declared that U.S. freedoms are 'not the grant of any government or document, but . . . our endowment from God.' (Why bother with the United Nations when God himself is on hand?)" (2004b, 47).

The deployment of sarcasm in these instances is Swiftian for the reason I have discussed—the construction of an elaborate reality as a shadow of the "unreal" one imposed by official discourse. But it is also Orwellian and Brechtian, in the sense that it is meant to critique the cynicism and impersonality of official discourse and debunk them in the process, as Bertolt Brecht claims in his polemic "Writing the Truth: Five Difficulties (1966)." In an age of "Shock and Awe," when the killing of civilians in military operations is clinically and cynically termed "collateral damage," and Indian citizens displaced by development projects are reduced to acronymic tags like PAP ("project-affected persons"), a matching rhetoric is required to expose the workings of bureaucratese. The spectacular arrogance of power, the bombast and obscurantism it accrues when it becomes solicitous on behalf of fascism, calls for the kind of linguistic inventiveness one sees in Roy's manipulation, inflation, and capitalization of phrases. This indicates a very astute grasp of power's way with language, and is a function of her self-assurance as a writer. Attentive readers will have seen this stylistic predilection in her first novel, which is as remarkable for its narrative and characterization as for its well-wrought, frequently ironic language. Her use of the figure of sarcasm is thus a form of postcolonial aesthetic critique, an inversion of the contemporary cosmopolitan posture in which intellectuals collude with power by presuming to eschew "vulgarity." In this respect, her titling of an essay "The Algebra of Infinite Justice" (2001, 105–124), a refraction of "Operation Infinite Justice," the code name of the war on terror, is clearly on the mark.[13]

So far I have focused on the figure of sarcasm as an aesthetic strategy, but there is no hiding from its implications as political critique. This means that sarcasm cannot stand alone, and that, unlike satire, which embodies its own critiques (political and otherwise), sarcasm requires a supplement in the form of an antithesis. In "The Greater Common Good" (1999, 1–90), there is a notable moment of despair and doubt when Roy contemplates the decision of the Narmada Bachao Andolan activists to call off their hunger strike. The twenty-two-day fast had attracted such international attention and outrage ("crisis-as-spectacle") that the World Bank was forced to announce that the Sardar Sarovar dam project would be reviewed. Although she does not trust that this review will be thorough or fair, Roy's sarcastic depiction of the Indian state as the arbiter of the face-off between it and the activists (she speaks of the state "allowing" the movement against the dam "to exist" [40]) reveals the limits of the kind of activism taking place in the valley. Perhaps this is the genesis of the internal critique of the anti-globalization movement, because one immediate result of the suspension of the hunger strike was the migration of international media attention to a different crisis spot. Her despairing account of this event represents a nodal moment in the challenge of political action.

A similar moment reveals itself in the title essay in *Power Politics* (subtitled "The Reincarnation of Rumpelstiltskin," 2001, 35–86). Roy and other activists were marching in protest to the site of the Maheshwar Dam (in Madhya Pradesh). She tells the reader that all of India was represented in the march, and comments,

As we crossed fields and forded streams, I remember thinking, This is my land, this is the dream to which the whole of me belongs, this is worth more to me than anything else in the world. We were not just fighting against a dam. We were fighting for a philosophy. For a world view. (82)

These are emotions more opaque than clear. The personal, natal identification with India is certainly grounded in the marchers' espousal of human values, but the manner of expressing it seems to dispense with the kind of hardnosed baiting of the agents of corporate globalization informing other deployments of sarcasm. Is this a sign of the charged nature of political action, since the reflections occur in a moment of tactile, corporeal confrontation with potential danger in the form of military assault? The protest was stopped and the activists arrested, and Roy concludes the reflection on a different note: whereas the massive protest had called forth a sense of pride, the fact of being arrested and thrown in the back of a truck produced "a hot stab of shame" (82).

Far from suggesting that the literary figure of sarcasm is effective only on the level of aesthetic critique, I am arguing that for it to have that effectiveness it has to be tested in a context outside of the aesthetic, where its production occurred in the first place. As Edward Said reminds us through his notion of worldliness, the aesthetic occurs in "the real historical world from whose circumstances none of us can in fact ever be separated" (2004, 48). The basis of my discussion of cosmopolitanism through its intersections with technological and demographic changes in this book is the expatriation of postcolonial intellectuals. Roy is not expatriated in the conventional sense of living outside of India, and the nature of her activism in the examples just cited would seem to further localize her role. However, her activism is a product of a broad formation of neoliberal commodification that cannot be reduced to place, and it is possible to locate her role in a historical conjuncture to which she is intimately connected. She is an example of the postcolonial intellectual who is increasingly demarginalized and relocated in transnational culture to engage in a critical practice that aims to disempower the institutional machine that empowers it. I suggest that the political critique which supplements the deployment of sarcasm in Roy's writings is part of the arsenal of that critical practice, and its limitations underscore the antinomial quagmire of undermining one's ground of enunciation. A succinct formulation of the conjuncture leading to this form of critical practice is offered by Pheng Cheah in his introductory essay in *Cosmopolitics*: "In an uneven neocolonial world, how can struggles for multicultural recognition in constitutional-democratic states in the North be brought into a global alliance with postcolonial activism in the periphery?" (Cheah 1998a, 37).[14]

In recent times, articulation of the inequalities in the symbolic exchange between what Cheah calls "the North" and "the periphery" has had to rely on different forms of politicized aesthetics. Roy's political writings constitute an example of a literary genre embodying this aesthetics; in cinema, documentary filmmaking has increasingly advanced similar aesthetic concerns. In fact, the increasing blurring of genres in cinematic works, for instance, is an effect of dealing with the complicated issues of conceptual filmmaking and its institutional support through grants and commissions. One important formulation of this link between genre and institutional dynamics in the scholarship on documentary cinema is the nature of discourse in the nonfiction form, which, according to Michael Renov (1993), is fictive, much like that of conventional feature films, mainly because of their goals and rhetoric. These questions have also arisen in discussions of recent "anti-globalization" films like Abderrahmane Sissako's *Bamako* (2006) and Hubert Sauper's *Darwin's Nightmare* (2005); the latter has been criticized as less than committed in its approach.[15] With such huge questions about the status of genre, closing off the aesthetic from the political in postcolonial criticism seems to raise more questions than it answers. These works and many others like them seek to politicize aesthetics, using the standards by which the value of artistic representations is judged to expose relationships between powerlessness and power, including the power to advance such forms of representation.

I want to conclude this discussion by situating Roy's anti-globalization stance and her self-description as a "subject of empire" in relation to Michael Hardt and Antonio Negri's argument on postcolonialism in their book *Empire*. For the first, I am particularly interested in claims by Hardt and Negri that are in turn critiqued by the Marxist theorist Samir Amin, because I find interesting links between Amin's criticisms and Roy's anti-globalization positions. In their critique of colonial modernity, the two authors take the position that European modernity was the cultural guise in which capitalist sovereignty presented itself. Instructively, they view modernity as a crisis, generated out of the conflict between the religious notions of immanence and transcendence. In racy and oftentimes confounding readings of authors as wide-ranging as Hobbes, Rousseau, Adam Smith, and Hegel, they synthesize the different components of the theory of modern sovereignty: it is the form of command "that overdetermines the relationship between individuality and universality as a function of the development of capital" (Hardt and Negri 2000, 87). This is the synthesis of sovereignty and capital, the modular form in which nationalism was generalized in the age of imperialism.

However, within the worldwide project of the nation-state, Hardt and Negri suggest, sovereignty was bound to undergo what they term a passage. They contend that it was through its determined global effort to rise above the ethnocentrism that plagued other societies in the grip of feudalism (for example, China) that European sovereignty became modular, and this made it the handmaiden of capitalist modernity. These authors' concern with passage is a conceptual interest not so much in supersession as in the transformation of traditional "modular" notions of temporality and spatiality. In other words, while they acknowledge that sovereignty's status had changed at the end of colonialism, they are not suggesting that it had seen a definitive break. Instead, they call the new situation "empire," identifying an encompassing reality that produces a generalized entity called the "multitude," the people out of the nation, or the constitutive force of democracy.

A great deal has been written in critique of the substantive argument in *Empire*.[16] Of this work, Samir Amin's critique comes closest to Roy's political writings in offering a different, political reading of the postcolonial as the deterritorialized rule of empire. Arguing that Hardt and Negri's main theses—that empire is immanent, and that the "multitude" is the constitutive force of democracy—account for neither the earlier history of anti-imperialism (constituting Third World decolonization) nor "the 85 percent of humanity who are the victims of the imperialist project" of the United States, Europe, and Japan (2005, 11), Amin suggests that their theses be abandoned because they essentially represent a liberalist adoption of the "Americanization of the world." In their place, Amin suggests the earlier history of socialist attempts to transform democracy, "the great revolutions of modern times (French, Russian, and Chinese)" (8).[17] Clearly, Amin's references resonate with James's idea that the postimperial world has been transformed by the four great revolutions of the twentieth century (Russian, Indian, Chinese, and African). The references also reinforce two of the political impulses in Roy's writings: the conception of the anti-globalization movement as a recapitulation of tricontinentalism, and the positioning of the postcolonial intellectual as the figure who can best articulate such a historic moment.

These critiques of globalization appear to respond to the injunctions, by champions of tricontinentalism such as Gikandi and Prashad, not to jettison earlier discourses of Third World agendas, and, given the intermeshing of the political and the aesthetic through which Roy has framed her critiques of globalization, responses to these injunctions require more than using the old terminologies for mnemonic purposes. The institutional structures through which the critical responses are articulated must be closely investigated. An interesting instance of this focus on institutions is Roy's decision to publish her political pamphlets not with multinational publishers but with a small, progressive imprint (South End Press), a decision that sheds light on the ideological framework within which James worked in the 1940s, which is now tremendously transformed by institutional changes, by changes in the practices of commodification and identity, and by technological and demographic changes. All these changes combine to make a young Indian woman a figure of such prestige as to command global attention.

Conclusion: Being African
in the World

". . . that impulse toward a more advanced stage of existence which sees
material obstacles in terms of how to overcome them."

—C. L. R. James, "The Artist in the Caribbean"

In his foreword to *No Fist Is Big Enough to Hide the Sky,* Basil Davidson's account
of the liberation struggle in Guinea Bissau and Cape Verde, Amílcar Cabral,
the leader and theoretician of the movement, touches on the contradictions of
cultural liberation in this memorable passage:

> You loved the splendor of our forests which shelter our partisan bases, which
> protect our populations and protected you as well from those criminal bomb-
> ings. These forests are now a real strength for our people, for our struggle.
> Before, they were a weakness, because we were afraid of our forests, sacred
> bastions of *irações* and every kind of spirit. Now we are afraid no longer: we
> have conquered and mobilized the spirits of the forests, turned this weakness
> into a strength. That is what struggle means: turning weakness into strength.
> (Davidson 1981, 4)

The point of this passage, the idea of turning weakness into strength, seems to
me an appropriate way of summing up the complex, contradictory relationships
between decolonization and globalization which the texts, ideas, formations,
and figures in this study engage. The purpose of this conclusion is to clarify the
conceptual ground on which the different issues stand as a way of reflecting on
their intellectual and social prospects.

From the perspective of the relationship between the nation-state and socioeconomic processes, what we now generally accept as globalization used to be
viewed negatively as neocolonialism. My central thesis in this book is that in
order to speak usefully to things as they are, such a perspective requires a steady
focus on the complex relationships between the poetics of decolonization and
the aesthetic transformations wrought by globalization. The relationships are
both contradictory and complementary, as we can see in the trajectories of the
artists covered in this book. These trajectories can be understood in a specific
intellectual context. Exemplified in the differences between Sembene, Kelani,
and Bekolo on the one hand, and between James, Phillips, and Roy on the other,

as well as in the similarities between any two of them, this context concerns the relationship of tricontinentalism and cosmopolitanism to cultural production in the era of globalization. Recent studies of tricontinentalism and Third World agendas, such as those of Simon Gikandi and Vijay Prashad, contend that the current retrenchment of those ideas in critical and political discourses marginalizes the history which gave "colonialism" and "imperialism" contemporary resonances (Gikandi 2001; Prashad 2007, 13). Indeed, Gikandi critiques globalization and postcoloniality for their dissipation of the political energies associated with the earlier discourse of decolonization, which spoke not of postcoloniality but of the "Third World," in opposition to a Eurocentric view of the world. It is less productive to dispute these claims than to argue that the asymmetry underlying those postcolonial political projects (though they were not called that at the time) can be usefully critiqued by demonstrating the complex reasons for the blind spots of politically engaged art of the era of decolonization, as they are evidenced in current artistic practices. Such an argument is possible to make when genre is understood as functioning beyond standard rubrics.

Discussions of genre often dwell on conventional notions of the category as explications of literary typologies or on questions of whether "borrowed forms" (the novel, the melodrama, the sonnet) can bear the political weight of representations designed to upend those forms in unanticipated contexts (Todorov 1990; Hitchcock 2003; Jameson 1991). On a fundamental level, the works discussed in this book display an awareness of the imbrications of postcoloniality with corporate globalization—these authors rely on the elements of neoliberalism embodied in technology and literary celebrity and are committed to varieties of cultural or political assertion. These imbrications are characteristic of representation and of postcoloniality as an asymmetrical force. A postcolonial site (for example, Ghana or India) is important because of the social dynamics it embodies, and for this reason it is of interest to the artist or intellectual. But an artist thus interested is not drawn by simple moral considerations. He or she also sees opportunities, for political or artistic purposes, and the continuing engagement with the place makes the old category of exile quite complicated and open to reinterpretation in the context of wide-ranging technological and social changes which characterize the crossroads of capital. The artist-intellectual may live abroad (in Paris in Bekolo's case, New York in Phillips's) and see such a metropolitan location in terms of opportunities for funding, technical support, and publishing. But he is also engaged with the "old home," out of a sense both of personal or political moralism and of realism, because a place of destitution is material—it matters, and it is the material on which to draw for representational purposes. In any case, with the world as the crossroads of capital, the Western or European metropolis is hardly the only site of those opportunities for funding and technical support, in short for economic security, as the recent developments in Southeast Asia and China have shown.

C. L. R. James's work stands as the central inspiration for this intellectual position. The transgeneric quality of this author's work reveals his humanist attributes. With its historical range, the informality of its presentation, and its use of lengthy quotations that are not overly determined by the protocols of specialist writing, the style targets combative cultural politics outside of academia. Observing relevant details of his life we see a figure who, without personal political guarantees, labored with others to provide political guarantees to groups without representation. Roy, who can be said to carry on the torch of activism from James, is also significantly interested in extending the limits predetermined by the ties between the market and textual forms. By turning the neoliberal market's tool of commodification against it, she draws attention to the uses of activism in ways that James could not have done. There are several reasons for this. First, access to information was determined by the state of technologies of communication and community-building in the 1950s (James's epoch). In this age of the iPhone, YouTube, Facebook, Skype, Flickr, and Twitter, Roy is able to access information in unprecedented ways and reach millions of people within minutes, as a result both of these tools and of her standing as a world-famous writer and activist. Second, the degree of commodification which gives her this status is of a more recent vintage, a factor of the neoliberal practice of mega-deals, six-digit book advances, and publishing conglomerates linked to chain stores and selling books as if they are shoes, not bodies of organized knowledge (Miller 2006). This is a far cry from James's milieu of the Facing Reality collective, when writings were targeted at small presses publishing for small groups, and commodified branding was an ideological anathema. Thirdly, the question of gender gives Roy an advantage over "Comrade Johnson" (James's clandestine name in the McCarthy-era United States), because her identity as a colored woman is an important marketing niche in an age when the readership of literary fiction is still predominantly middle-class and female.

Tricontinentalism and the political solidarity it projected have to be invoked with a great deal of circumspection today, given the socioeconomic changes in countries like China and India, and the specificity of African and Latin American experiences of postcoloniality. All of these countries or regions were part of the tricontinental agenda of the 1950s and 1960s, but today, not only is China the leading "imperial" force in Africa, the unprecedented power of the G20 economic group has drastically changed the terms of global relations on the model of anti-imperialism. The very concept of tricontinentalism masks those changes: in China's global status; in the increasingly wide gaps between African, Asian, and Latin American postcolonialities; and in the nature of postcolonial subjectivities vis-à-vis the discourses of decolonization (whether bourgeois liberal or radical socialist).

This does not mean that cosmopolitanism, the institutional alternative to tricontinentalism, should be invoked without circumspection, either. Important as they are, the differences between James and Roy do not invalidate one significant point: that for both writers, writing, through which genre manifests itself, is calculated to be effective toward social transformation. This is why, for them, writing goes beyond fiction and literary nonfiction to include the genre of the pamphlet. In the hands of Caryl Phillips, whose work evinces the more dominant strains of cosmopolitanism, genre is shown to be politically constitutive; it subordinates over the political goals that the author has in view and in such a way that the politics lack a sharp edge. It is to this kind of blind spot that the genre of the pamphlet seeks to draw attention. Aesthetically speaking, it is in the direction of the negotiated coexistence between both that the antagonists of *Aristotle's Plot* move at the end of the film.

Perhaps the most explicit and serviceable of the different strands of the formation analyzed in this book is that put forth by Craig Calhoun (2002), who sees cosmopolitanism in broadly political terms, arguing that the social solidarity which underlines cosmopolitan citizenship rests on choice rather than on necessity, and that culture is learned rather than inherited. The question of choice is particularly relevant because it is the most decisive factor in the different analytical emphases on exile, expatriation, and refuge, those categories which cosmopolitanism has displaced in critical theory (Said 2000, 181). There are two things to stress here. First, choice does not invalidate necessity, and there are cases where it is unavailable. The choices available to Mansour, Phillips's chauffeur in Ghana, are very few; he is, as Pheng Cheah writes, one of "those postcolonials for whom postnationalism through mobility is not an alternative" (Cheah 1998b, 302). What is often celebrated about globalization—the free movement of capital—is not always matched by an equally free movement of people. Indeed, the anti-globalization position that global markets must be better regulated in order to ameliorate global inequality is often attacked by the same groups which consider the restriction of migration from the global South an ideological necessity.[1] Unlike the mass of refugees desperate to enter the developed world, the expatriated postcolonial intellectuals focused on in this book are talented and world-renowned. However, their works are eloquent testimonies to the social and historical conditions which shape the postcolony.

Second, culture can be inherited: not genetically, but in the sense that cultural institutions are continually produced, replenished, repeated, and perpetuated, and thus transformed into symbolic capital. An awareness of the limitations of the more inclusive examples of cosmopolitanism is guaranteed to show that although those who attack globalization for institutionalizing inequality are making a legitimate point, there is one point which they would do well to articulate just as clearly. This is that although the postcolonial market is filled with wonderful examples of human resilience and innovativeness, it is also not without its contradictions. Why is it that, whereas decolonization has not delivered on its promises, socially retrogressive formations—ethnic militias, religious fundamentalism, and ethnonationalism—are on the rise? An intellectually rigorous account of the postcolony has to pay attention to questions of this nature, and to the illicit practices like smuggling, piracy, human trafficking, international scams, and organized crime that thrive both in the shadow and under the full glare of globalization.

In *Primitive Passions,* her study of the reception of Chinese cinema in the West, the scholar Rey Chow observes that the light and transparency permitted by "translation" are "the light and transparency of commodification. This is a profane, rather than pure and sacred, light to which non-Western cultures are subjected if they want a place in the contemporary world" (1995, 201). It is important to specify the world that Chow has in mind, for it is not just the "global arena" but also the possible existence of a localized cultural practice like Nigeria's Nollywood, with all the attendant internal differentiations and contradictions. While the metropolitan writer or filmmaker's sense of the world changes even in artistic works, it does not appear to change nearly as often in the exhortatory conception of human relations characteristic of Nollywood films. We are faced not with a simple question of fatalism; it is a result of the combination of social and economic contexts. Whereas the cosmopolitan writer or filmmaker tries to invent or create an audience by deploying generic forms, the exhortative artist plays to an audience that has been precreated through the circulation of old or tested patterns. Although Kelani matured in this world of exhortatory morality, the real distinctiveness of his work lies in its even-handed technical treatment of the competing demands within his domain, with its own internal differentiations. Thus he is closer to a hybrid than he first appears, and the task of the intellectual confronted with an artistic practice like Nollywood is to be vigilantly ironic and ethical: given the appropriate kind of political or social atmosphere, the respectful depiction of a particular culture evident in the films is a fertile breeding ground for "bad nationalism." The intersection of Kelani's work with Roy's on this precise point offers a premise on which to test the hypotheses put forward by scholars seeking to imagine practical points of contact between neoliberalism and progressive citizenships.[2]

Such points of contact (being African, postcolonial, civically responsible in the contemporary world, and other less determinate identities and positions) are, I imagine, the fundamental objectives of the idea of Pan-Africanism deployed in this book—an idea of a political movement as developing in the context of historical inequality around the world, a transnational movement for social justice far beyond a dominant particularity, whether racial or geographical. The issues to which race once tried to draw attention—the condition and experience of people of African descent in the Western hemisphere—have continued to appear in bold relief through class and its emanations: poverty, disease, the debt trap, and presumably insoluble social problems. If Pan-Africanism is to have any value beyond racial identification—and I think it should—it must not be confined to the black world on the basis of race, because, though fundamental, that was not Pan-Africanism's only objective. Pan-Africanism, as an ideal, ought to impact any part of the world where class has substantial significance, and that is the entire world. This may sound like a moral argument, but I think it suggests a deeper realism.

In May 2009, I received a postcard from a friend, a native of Cape Verde. On the card is a picture of the statue of Amílcar Cabral in Assomada, on the island of Santiago, crowning the aspiration in the final frame of *Nha Fala,* Flora Gomes's 2002 musical comedy, in which a bust of the revolutionary leader eventually rests on a pedestal facing the sea. On the postcard my friend mentioned another statue that had outraged many people. This was a Mao lookalike, a "Cabral-as-Mao," this time erected in Praia (Cabral's childhood home) as the result of a mind-boggling arrangement between the government and some Chinese business interest. Surely this was not how Cape Verdeans intended to acknowledge the support the Maoists provided to PAIGC, the African Party for the Independence of Guinea and Cape Verde, in the 1960s! Yet this is the point: tricontinental solidarity or not, China has made Africa its business. One should expect no less from an African standing in the world.

Notes

Introduction

1. The name "Sembene" is often written with an accent on the second "e": "Sembène." However, as David Murphy discloses in *Sembene: Imagining Alternatives in Film and Fiction* (2000, 1), the man's declared preference was for the name to be written without any accents. I have adopted this spelling throughout this book.

2. Williams uses the notion of technological determinism to critique certain 1960s theories of "the media," particularly those of Harold Laswell and Marshall McLuhan. He calls these theories "explicitly ideological: not only a ratification, indeed a celebration, of the medium as such, but an attempted cancellation of all other questions about it and its uses" (Williams 2003, 129). While McLuhan formalizes technology into a cause, Laswell excludes cause or "intention" from its principle of communication (122, 129–130).

3. The two positions can be seen in the convocation of two conferences of the Organization of African Unity, one by the "conservative" Monrovia bloc and the other by the "progressive" Casablanca bloc, in the early 1960s, before the socialist liberation movements in the Portuguese colonies got underway. Richard Gott's introduction to *The African Dream*, the diary kept by Ernesto "Che" Guevara during his participation as a guerrilla in the Congo war of the mid-1960s, gives a sense of the complexity of the two ideological positions, even within a single country. Although socialist countries such as Egypt and Tanzania supported Guevara and his Cuban comrades, the attitude of African states to foreign intervention was not always determined by such ideological considerations. For similar observations regarding the Lusophone countries, see Chabal, Birmingham, et al. 2002, 60.

4. The literature often speaks of the phenomenon in plural terms, but nonetheless proceeds to the analysis of *a* systemic form. In this chapter, I use the singular form for analytical reasons, but constantly in relation to the marketplace, in order to indicate that this diverse system simultaneously includes both rational and human attributes. This distinction between the rational and the human is comparable to the one Fredric Jameson (1991, 260) makes between /**market**/ and «**market**»: one is the historical form tied to trade and merchandise, and the other the concept theorized by philosophers and ideologues. The opposition of "human" and "rational" goes back to Tonnies and Weber, and the terms of conjunction in these two philosophical cases are drawn from Abiola Irele's analysis of the responses to industrialization in Romanticism and of non-Western societies' responses to modernity. See Irele 2001, 78.

5. For a critique of the two tendencies, see Mamdani 1996, 13. Mamdani does not mention Bohannan and Dalton, but his reference to Goran Hyden's "economy of affection" is reminiscent of the pair's premarket "primitivism." Nonetheless, in my sense of "human" economic choices, there is an implicit recognition of the sociocultural basis of affect intrinsic to Hyden's formulation.

6. Compare this dictum to Marx's critique, in *The German Ideology,* of an exclusive occupation with labor. He proposes the alternative of a communist society, where it is possible "to do one thing today and another tomorrow, to hunt in the morning, fish in the afternoon, rear cattle in the evening, criticize after dinner" (Tucker 1978, 160).

7. Diawara's essay first appeared as a chapter in a volume coedited by Jameson and Miyoshi. It later formed one of the "Statements" chapters of his genre-defying book *In Search of Africa* (1999).

8. This tendency appears, for instance, in Chabal and Daloz 1999.

9. In their work on the relationships between capitalism and the "occult economy," Jean and John Comaroff (2001) have underlined the importance of localized, disjunctive perceptions of colonial modernity and how these are manifested in millennial formations of capitalism. I take this argument up in chapter 3. For a very engaging perspective on informalization, see Kate Meagher's work on informal institutions and development, most recently her *Identity Economics: Social Networks and the Informal Economy in Nigeria* (2010).

10. Guéhenno's elegantly conciliatory but nonetheless ideological position highlights the relationships between the nation-state and neoliberalism, and his analysis is easily contrasted with anti-globalization arguments, such as those of David Harvey.

11. Where Harvey establishes a relationship between the emergence of a political class in Washington and the rise of lobbying as an instrument of special interests (Harvey 2006, 18–19), Guéhenno sees the profession of lobbying in informational terms, the "fortunate refinement of a democracy that is henceforth more fully informed" (Guéhenno 1995, 21). Furthermore, some of Guéhenno's arguments that sovereignty has passed seem highly premature. For example, his claim that "no nation today is capable of mobilizing such gigantic forces [as those seen in the world wars] around an idea" (116) is dubious in the context of the invasion of Iraq by the United States and its coalition forces in 2003, supposedly as part of the global war on terror.

12. In its inaugural issue, *Antipodes,* the journal of the American Association of Australasian Literary Studies, notes that the expression gained "currency in the fourteenth century and later applied to Australia and New Zealand whose inhabitants literally walked with their 'feet opposed' to those on the other side of the globe" (Ross 1987, 2). The inaugural issue of *Antipode: A Radical Journal of Geography,* which appeared in 1969, explicitly attacks the ignorance that ensures the persistence of such notions in political habits.

13. The film is *Dirty Pretty Things* (2002), directed by Stephen Frears.

14. Guéhenno argues that although the territorial basis of taxation remains a problem under transnationalism, taxes can only remain legitimate in the imperial age by becoming "the simple counterweight of the benefits of 'collective wealth' provided by the state, not . . . an expression of the measure of cohesion in the body politic" (1995, 11).

15. Although, in his introduction to the special issue of *PMLA* titled "Globalizing Literary Studies" (2001), Gunn is very attentive to the broad sociocultural context of literary changes, most of the contributors to the volume aim to "globalize" literary studies, thus unwittingly reinforcing the paradigm of economic globalism and not elucidating how problematic this paradigm becomes when unequal exchange is taken into consideration.

16. Moretti has tried to deliver on this promise in his 2005 *Graphs, Maps, Trees: Abstract Models for a Literary History,* which shifts focus to the quantitative approach much

in use in the social sciences. He has also applied the same model to the dissemination of Hollywood films. See Moretti 2001.

17. For a pertinent critique of both Moretti and Casanova, see Beecroft 2008, 88–91.

18. For interesting arguments about the novel genre and postcoloniality, see Hitchcock 2003 and Edwards 2004.

19. The argument is presented in the context of world-system theory, the academic formation identified with Immanuel Wallerstein and his colleagues at SUNY Binghamton, where a symposium took place in 1989 on the relationship between culture and globalization. In the words of Anthony D. King, editor of *Culture, Globalization and the World System,* the volume in which Hall's essays appear, the conference was designed to provide a forum for thinking of the "world as a whole" (King 1997, 5). Hall's two essays were presented as talks two weeks before the symposium.

20. In the works of writers like Amadou Hampate Bâ and Yambo Ouologuem, these figures are sometimes centralized but are still depicted negatively (Jeyifo 1993, 107–109).

21. Examples include Kenneth Harrow's interest in the *totsis* (urban gangsters) in new African cinema, Ato Quayson's interventions in disability studies, and the work of Gaurav Desai, Juliana Nfa-Abbenyi, Chris Dunton, and Chantal Zabus on African queer identities.

22. Paraphrasing Achebe's famous claim about leadership in Nigeria, Maja-Pearce declares that "the trouble with Nigeria is simply and squarely the failure of the Nigerian intelligentsia to meet the demands of their predicament, proof of which is to be found in the books they write" (Maja-Pearce 1992, 3). Maja-Pearce actually uses the works of Achebe and Elechi Amadi as a platform for critiquing second-generation writers like Emecheta and Iyayi, whom he considers progressive in their depiction of contemporary issues of urban squalor and the oppression of women, compared to their predecessors' chauvinism and investment in the past. But he does not consider these novelists of the 1980s exceptional on aesthetic grounds because, again like their predecessors, they made the novel shoulder burdens for which it was historically not designed (32, 79).

23. The exceptions are the 35mm films in the New Directions series produced with the support of the South African television network MNET. Scholars (including me) use the term "videofilm," giving to the films the same kind of analytical attention as is given to celluloid cinema.

24. When asked in a 1975 interview how he chose roles to play in his films, Sembene answered, "No, you see, these are tricks, there are times when actors who've promised to come—because often certain actors aren't paid, they just promise me they will come—but they don't show up. Then I say, 'OK, I can do it. I think I can do it.' . . . I haven't chosen to play a part in my next film, but I have to be ready in case of an absence" (Sembene 2008, 69).

25. Apart from the fact that, beyond his skepticism, Jameson proceeds to discuss "an imaginary text" called *AlienNATION* (1991, 79), questions of textuality become even more indispensable where the different formats of film and television have been deliberately redesigned to produce videofilms which, as they are in Nollywood, are initiated as narrative cinematic texts. This is the sense in which Jameson hardly anticipates the reconfiguration of video technology in other contexts, and it explains why notions of cultural imperialism have to be taken with a grain of salt.

26. I discuss the relationship between exile and other kinds of displacement further in chapter 6, drawing on the work of Edward Said.

27. In a brilliant formulation of the issues of metropolitan location and cultural judgment implicit in the emergence of nonfiction as a genre, Rob Nixon writes, "Manifestly, Naipaul's prestige as a novelist has assisted him in sustaining his high profile as an interpreter of postcolonial societies. However, by diversifying into nonfiction he has achieved a reputation of a quite different order, not merely as a powerful imaginative writer, but as a mandarin and an institution" (1992, 5).

28. Brennan's 1989 article appeared in revised form in his *Salman Rushdie and the Third World* (1989). Both the article and the book appeared in the wake of the *fatwa* imbroglio, so it is perhaps not ironic that in one of his several efforts at self-defense or explanation, Rushdie expresses the belief of metropolitan left intellectuals that art can be the antagonist of neoliberalism in the absence of communism. See Rushdie 1991b, 427. Brennan has recently updated his critique of Rushdie's work in *Wars of Position* (2006), especially in the chapter titled "Nativism." For a different, less sympathetic reading of Rushdie's pre-*fatwa* fiction, see Ahmad 1992, 125–158.

29. Haruna Isola (d. November 1983) was a prominent Nigerian musician of the *apala* genre between the 1940s and 1980s (Waterman 1990, 85) and later owned a record label. He traveled to England in 1981 and celebrated the trip with a song which begins,

> On my way to London,
> Ko s'ewu rara,
> There was no problem
> De'lu oyinbo.

Although the song's target audience is Yoruba-Nigerian, the English lyrics actually make better narrative sense than the ones in Yoruba. This contrast points to a complex practice of cultural translation in which the musician advertises his facility with English grammar without necessarily assuming that *apala* music translates as a cultural form in England.

1. C. L. R. James Sees the World Steadily

1. For a concrete formulation of these questions, see James 1983, 151.

2. Patrick Gomes is right to note the progression or "transition" in James's thoughts, from the examination of the "political personalities" of Cipriani and Toussaint L'Ouverture in his early writings to the focus on the "revolutionary initiative" implicit in populism that is in evidence in his later works, such as *Nkrumah and the Ghana Revolution* (1977a) and *American Civilization* (1993). However, as Gomes himself agrees, there is a dialectical relationship between the leader and the led, and so what applies to Toussaint also applies to Fidel Castro and Nkrumah (Gomes 1978). In the particular case of *American Civilization,* the identification of democracy with mass social roles resonates with Greek drama in ways that I will demonstrate when I discuss Jean-Pierre Bekolo's critique of *The Poetics* in *Aristotle's Plot* in chapter 4. What is at stake in drawing on James's writings here, therefore, is not the occlusions that occur when the model of charismatic leadership falls short of revolutionary expectations (James addresses Nkrumah's own shortcoming, possibly as a corrective to "undialectic comments" he had made in another context [Gomes 1978, 33]). What interests me about this aspect of James's work is the theoretical problem involved in highlighting the political potentials of cultural forms that are shot through with the contradictions of commodification and other economic calculations.

3. See the editor's prefatory notes to "Toward the Seventh" (James 1984b, 236).

4. James claims there that were four congresses during that decade, but since the next one, in 1945, was the fifth, he must be mistaken.

5. See, for instance, his essays "The Old World and the New" and "George Padmore: Black Marxist Revolutionary," as well as "Toward the Seventh" (James 1984a, 208, 255, 241).

6. Wole Soyinka, who was excluded from the meetings together with the Guyanese historian and activist Walter Rodney, wrote that it was in Tanzania that "the original credentials of the Pan-African movement as an all-come, non-governmental forum had been formally buried" (2006, 248).

7. See Prashad's description of this process in the "Brussels" chapter (2007, 16–30), and Ahmad's periodization in his introduction (1992, 30).

8. In his autobiography, the South African–born writer Peter Abrahams gives a useful account of the Non-Aligned Movement's origin in this crisis (2000, 91). The year was also notable for the establishment of the state of Israel, the UN, and apartheid in South Africa. The movement was formally founded in Belgrade in 1961 (Prashad 2007, xvi, 95–97). The standard scholarly account of the Bandung conference remains George McTuran Kahin's edited volume *The Asian-African Conference,* but Richard Wright's *The Color Curtain* is also a useful reference.

9. The inclusion of the Americans Du Bois and Walker in this list suggests an internationalism which includes but goes beyond anti-racism, and further confirms the contention that race is a subcategory of class.

10. Achebe's *The Trouble with Nigeria* (1983) displays a deep-seated dissatisfaction with Nigeria, whereas Rushdie, in the essays concerning India and Pakistan in *Imaginary Homelands* (1991a,b), evinces relatively little of such tough love. That little was dispensed with in "Notes on Writing and the Nation" (Rushdie 2002, 58–61), a later essay full of nuances, where he specifically cites "Achebe's Nigeria" as an example of the kind of political identification he no longer trusts.

11. For relevant and insightful critiques of the different aspects of cosmopolitanism, see Craig Calhoun's "Imagining Solidarity: Cosmopolitanism, Constitutional Patriotism and the Public Sphere" (2002), Bruce Robbins's *Feeling Global: Internationalism in Distress* (1999), Pheng Cheah and Bruce Robbins's edited volume *Cosmopolitics: Thinking and Feeling beyond the Nation* (1998), Timothy Brennan's *At Home in the World: Cosmopolitanism Now* (1997), and David Harvey's "Cosmopolitanism and the Banality of Geographical Evils" (2001). More recently, Kwame Appiah has written about the subject from the perspective of analytical philosophy. See his *Cosmopolitanism: Ethics in a World of Strangers* (2006) and *The Ethics of Identity* (2005), especially the final chapter, "Rooted Cosmopolitanism."

12. In his response, Clifford urges "recognition for a broader range of cosmopolitical formations than those subsumed (teleologically?) under [Cheah's] formula 'nationalism as given culture in neocolonial globalization'" (1998, 365).

13. The founding of the Economic Community of West African States (ECOWAS) in 1975 might seem a fulfillment of James's political expectations, except that the organization was meant to reinforce the structure of the national state.

14. James's critique of the bureaucratic states of the United States and the Soviet Union in *State Capitalism and World Revolution* has a telling resonance, but in the Nigerian example, it is as telling that both countries supported the Federal side, which was determined to keep the country together.

15. The didacticism of the Hollywood gangster films is pedagogically similar to the exhortation of Nigerian videofilms, and both formations could be used to explore why didactic forms are prevalent in certain political contexts. For example, the "notice" in the opening frame of the American film *The Public Enemy* (1931) rationalizing the choices of the bootlegging gangsters is differently registered in the Nigerian film *Owo Blow* (1996), which urges the viewer to "show someone some kindness today [because] it would make a positive difference tomorrow." Such a rhetorical address is frequently used in Hollywood films, including Spike Lee's *Do the Right Thing*, in ways comparable to the Brechtian alienation effect, counterintuitive as such a comparison may seem. James was obviously working in a professional context different from Boal and Brecht, and he also differs from them by stressing that the audience, the idea of reception, is implicit in the creative process. According to Brennan (1997, 241), this stress also explains the difference between James and European critics of Hollywood like Henri Lefebvre and Adorno. For more on Hollywood and European cultural critics, see Mulvey 1996, 19–28; on the comparisons between James and Adorno, see Alleyne 1999.

16. Implicit in this postulation is the idea of populism, the mass's identification of a figure as the embodiment of its yearning in a revolutionary situation (as it did Toussaint L'Ouverture, and would later Castro and Nkrumah). The identification is now integral to everyday processes because, for the mass—the audience, the readership—the different aspects of life fuse in the constitution of a popular form through the equally integral presence of tools of the mass society.

17. Again, this is what Rob Nixon suggests in his description of Naipaul as "the postcolonial mandarin" (1992).

18. Interestingly, Naipaul praised this book of James's as giving "base and solidity to West Indian literary achievement" (quoted in Phillips 2002, 170). Phillips adds that after this review Naipaul would no longer be so generous to either James or the Caribbean, and mentions a James-like character in Naipaul's *A Way in the World*. In his biography of James, Dhondy (2001) devotes an entire chapter ("Who is Lebrun?") to the relationship between James and Naipaul, using the same characterization as evidence.

19. Adorno and Horkheimer developed the term "culture industry" as a replacement for "mass culture" in their initial draft of their book, *Dialectic of Enlightenment*, "to exclude from the outset interpretation agreeable to its advocates: that it is a matter of something like a culture arising spontaneously from the masses themselves, the contemporary form of popular art." Considering the phenomenon later, Adorno insists that to speak of a "culture industry" is even more radical, as the "culture industry fuses the old and the familiar into a new quality" (Adorno 2001, 98). Even in the initial essay, Adorno and Horkheimer's sense of the cultural apparatus appeared to be limited. For example, their comments that radio was incapable of generating feedback did not anticipate the revolutionary use of radio and the telephone in phone-in radio programs.

20. For useful critiques, see Barber 1987a, Etherton 1982, and Fabian 1998.

21. See Anthony Guneratne's introduction to *Rethinking Third Cinema* (Guneratne and Dissanayake 2004).

22. Richard Gott, who was in Cuba during the filming, has some interesting suggestions on why the film might not have appealed to Cubans (2005).

23. For a useful discussion, see D'Lugo 2003.

24. "Times would pass, old empires would fall and new ones take their place, the relations of countries and the relations of classes had to change, before I discovered that

it is not quality of goods and utility which matter, but movement; not where you are or what you have, but where you have come from, where you are going, and the rate at which you are getting there" (James 1983, 113). It makes perfect sense that this statement is the epitaph on James's grave in Trinidad.

25. Note the derisive tone in which socialism was spoken of during Barack Obama's 2008 presidential campaign.

26. On this, see the views expressed by scholars of James's work (for example, McLemee 1996, ix).

2. Fitful Decolonization

1. Scholarship on Sembene is likely to grow even more. Useful references include, in order of appearance, Paulin Soumanou Vieyra's early study, *Ousmane Sembene, Cinéaste* (1973), covering the period between 1962 and 1971; Carrie Moore's *Evolution of an African Artist* (1973); Francoise Pfaff's *The Cinema of Ousmane Sembene: A Pioneer of African Film* (1984); Daniel Serceau's untranslated monograph, *Sembene Ousmane* (1985); *Ousmane Sembene: Dialogues with Critics and Writers,* coedited by Samba Gadjigo, Ralph H. Faulkingham, Thomas Cassirer, and Reinhard Sander (1993); the volume *A Call to Action: The Films of Ousmane Sembene* (1996), edited by Sheila Petty; and David Murphy's study *Sembene: Imagining Alternatives in Film and Literature* (2000). Numerous articles, interviews, and profiles have also appeared, some of which are cited in the text. A few of the articles in the "Critical Perspectives" section of the 1993 collection reappear in Petty's volume. In 2007, soon after the filmmaker's death that June, Samba Gadjigo released *Ousmane Sembene: Une Conscience Africaine*, an authorized biography of Sembene, in Dakar. The phrase "anti-neocolonialism" belongs to Ken Harrow, whose work is discussed at length below.

2. Since the word means a temporary impotence, it is inherently optimistic, and this optimism shows the depth of Sembene's artistic morality.

3. The texts are Aminata Sow Fall, *Beggars' Strike* (Ibadan: Longmans, 1981), and Mariama Bâ, *So Long a Letter* (Ibadan: New Horn Press, 1981).

4. Gabriel discussed only the attitude of "cine-semioticians," although Laura Mulvey later drew extensively on his essay about *Xala* in her own analysis.

5. In his introduction to *Questions of Third Cinema* (Willemen and Pines 1989), Paul Willemen sees Italian neorealism, the Frankfurt School, and Soviet cinema, as well as U.S. independent cinema, as informing some of the practices of the Third Cinema.

6. This is Brent Edwards's reading of *Xala* (the film and the book), in contrast to Jameson's observations in the essay on national allegory (Edwards 2004, 10–11; Jameson 1986). *Sem-enna-worq* is also invested in depth, in contrast to Harrow's "surface" reading.

7. In this regard, see Ukadike 1994, 48–52, 259. The critique of "the ethnographic camera" itself is a response to negative portrayals of Africans on film, as Ukadike makes clear, yet one has to be attentive to other embodiments of ethnography, such as those which enable, in the concluding sequence of Rouch's *Jaguar,* a comparative understanding of the *yere don* (chanted for Besso) and *oriki*. I discuss the connection between the *yere don* and the *oriki* further in the next chapter.

8. Although, in his analysis of this riposte by Sembene, Edwards suggests that it is a case of "discontinuity between modes . . . mobilized for effect" (2004, 12), it is impor-

tant to add that for Sembene the refusal is also a form of political positioning, resonant with his oft-stated identity as an African artist.

9. See Murphy 2000, 110 for additional information on the local context of these scenes.

10. I gratefully acknowledge Adrien Pouille for providing me with both the Wolof transcription and the English translation of the song; I have edited the translation for idiomatic coherence.

11. The Wolof word *serigne* means "mister" or "fellow."

12. Murphy has argued that Sembene tended to emphasize "the technical nature of his training in Moscow, perhaps as a preventive strike against critics who would search for [Mark] Donskoi's influence upon his work" (2000, 69n7).

13. For a rare concrete example of this suggestion, see Jeyifo 1989.

14. Full disclosure: I first read Harrow's book in manuscript form, when its introduction did not include the section on the structure of a Sembene film (pp. 1–9). That section was later added. As an assessor of the manuscript, I took issues with Harrow's assumption in it of a unified discourse of African cinema, and my response here to that assumption is in the spirit of my initial critique.

15. In this connection, one may recall the statement by the Tunisian filmmaker Tahar Cheriaa: "Your cinema shall be a militant cinema, it shall be first and foremost a cultural action with social and political value, or it will be nothing. If it eventually can also become an economic action, that will only be a by-product" (quoted in Ngangura 1996, 61).

16. For an example of such tricontinentalism in Sembene's case, we have the story the filmmaker told about the conflicting interests of the shah of Iran and the Ayatollah Khomeini in *Ceddo* (Murphy 2000, 237). Harrow takes up the same issues of the discourse of identity in African studies through a reading of Spivak's *Critique of Postcolonial Reason* in an article in the *Journal of the African Literature Association* (2007a). In this article, despite his innovative incorporation of the commentaries of the scholar Susan Andrade, which is calculated to be a "relatively unique form of both an original statement and a series of responses to [Andrade's] provocative reading" (180n1), Harrow essentially restates the premise of his 2007 *Postcolonial African Cinema*.

17. For an interesting formulation of this paradox, see the introduction to Lazarus 1999, which deploys Adorno's injunction to "hate tradition properly."

18. However, Murphy's analysis of the status of sexual anxiety in this section and the place of homosexuals in African literature and cinema omits the fact that in Charlie, the gay patron Mory encounters at the beach in *Touki Bouki,* we are presented with a convincing (if brief) treatment of a homosexual underground in contemporary Senegal.

3. Tunde Kelani's Nollywood

1. The terms used to describe the films vary. English-language filmmakers call their works "movies," suggesting a fascination with Hollywood, while Yoruba filmmakers often say "films." At some point in the early 2000s, the term "videofilm" was adopted, mostly by critics and scholars. It points to the hybrid nature of the form: torn between television and film, and shot on video cameras. Technology has certainly outpaced language, and the term "Nollywood films" has turned out to be both useful and controversial. For an engaging and realistic meditation on these issues, see Haynes 2007.

2. Two caveats are necessary here. First, Kelani is known to have objected to being categorized as a "Nollywood director"; during a conference panel in 2008, he joked that he did not make "Nollywood films." This is a tactical attempt to separate his work from the general run of Nollywood films, but as he himself knows, his career as a filmmaker cannot be productively discussed outside this rubric. Secondly, films from Northern Nigeria (called "Kannywood" because they are predominantly produced in the city of Kano) are glaringly omitted from this discussion. I do so as a matter of tactics, in order to focus my analysis, but I will draw on the work of Brian Larkin and Abdalla Adamu in this area.

3. California Newsreel has also released a documentary about Nigerian videofilms, titled *This Is Nollywood* (dir. Franco Saatchi, 2007).

4. Kelani told me, "I have no apology because . . . I'm a Yoruba man, so what then stops me from expressing myself in my mother tongue, language, and culture? I don't care about that."

5. Barber argues that the changing audiences that emerge with new forms of popular culture can be "variably imagined as regional, religious, ethnic or linguistic constituencies, as nations, as the entire continent or just as 'the people'" (1997, 347). These possibilities give a sense of a community both anonymous and specific, and in the Yoruba word *aye* ("life," "earth," "the world," or "the universe") there is an implicit suggestion of a mystery that borders on the confounding or the sinister. In this sense, it is far from accidental that the theater idiom on which Barber focuses is definitively inserted into cinema through the film *Aye* (dir. Ola Balogun, 1979), produced by Hubert Ogunde, in which exhortation and cinematic effects mutually reinforce each other. See note 22 below.

6. For detailed discussions of ways in which the development of the form was driven by economics, see Haynes 1995 and Adesokan 2007, 63.

7. For a detailed discussion of this film, see Haynes and Okome 1997, 37–39.

8. After this groundbreaking work, Nnebue made a number of films, including the English-language *Glamour Girls 1* and *2*, and some of his collaborators, like Okechukwu Ogunjiefor, went on to produce their own films. Early titles include *Nneka the Pretty Serpent*, directed by Zeb Ejiro and produced by Ossy Afason (1994), and the fascinating *Ikuku* (The Hurricane 1 and 2, directed by Nkem Owoh and Zeb Ejiro and produced by Andy Best Productions, 1995). The plot of this film revolves around the search by the community of Abanubi for a priest of Ikuku to restore the god's shrine and stem the terrible hurricane ravaging the town. The suggestion of cultural dislocation at the film's heart can be read as reflecting the condition of the Igbo people in contemporary Nigeria. The stereotype that Igbo in Nigerian cities are aggressively industrious is often the flip side of the general distrust of the Nigerian state since the end of the civil war. The Igbo are said to have no political power, and the film suggests this lack by continually referencing an international space. Hyginus Ekwuazi has argued persuasively that the early Igbo films were geared toward correcting this stereotype, but his vehement rebuttal of a critic's assertion that there was no future for Igbo films is not so convincing (1997, 81). At any rate, there have been very few films, if any, made in Igbo in the past decade and a half. Nnebue himself drew attention to the paucity of competent writers in the Igbo language who could generate scripts (Iwenjora 2001). Instead, there are films in English featuring excellent Igbo actors, like Nkem Owoh (Osuofia), Victor Osuagwu, Rita Nzelu,

Patience Ozokwor, and Larry Koldsweat. Some, like Ngozi Nwosu and Charles Okafor, appear also in Yoruba-language films, because they speak that language as well. Many of these films show an abiding familiarity with the Igbo language, especially in songs and other expressive forms. In films like *Ukwa Achinaka, Ekwedike, Ijeuwa the Boxer,* and *Omasiri,* the title is the most important element of Igbo linguistic culture. While there are few Igbo films as Ekwuazi defines them, the dearth is largely a structural problem, even if there is validity to the argument that film producers are mainly there for the money.

9. E-mail communication, January 6, 2003.

10. The filmmaker Ladi Ladebo has put the average production cost in the 1970s at "between the equivalent of £200,000 and £500,000, depending on the levels of international involvement in terms of cast and crew" (Ladebo 2004).

11. "From an average of four feature films per year in the last decade, production plummeted to one feature film in 1990, raced up to four in 1991 and dropped a notch to three in 1992, when Brendan Shehu's *Kulba na Barna* . . . was released. The record for the year 1993 was nil. And in 1994, Ladi Ladebo shot and released the only celluloid feature film of the year, *Pariah,* sponsored by the UNFPA [United Nations Family Planning Agency]. Not until two years later did another feature film, *Oselu* by Bankole Bello, hit the screen" (Adesanya 1997, 15).

12. E-mail communication, January 6, 2003.

13. The title has a double meaning; "Ayo" is the name of the protagonist's girlfriend, and the word also means "joy."

14. In part 2 of this film, there is a wonderful close-up of a wall inscription which recalls a similar intratextual close-up in Orson Welles's *Touch of Evil* (1958). Naturally it is not so much the inscriptions as the close-ups that are of interest here.

15. Kelani has also filmed the most popular of these, *Efunsetan Aniwura* (Mainframe Productions, 2005). For a detailed discussion of the relationship between Kelani and the actors and producers in the Yoruba subgenre, see Adesokan 2009b.

16. In my most recent interview with Kelani (July 2010), I brought up this point with respect to his new film, *Arugba* (2010). He did not deny it, but argued that engaging with Yoruba culture was for him a kind of education, for there were Yoruba ideas and practices he did not understand until he began to work them into his films.

17. The military government of General Yakubu Gowon (1966–1975) established the National Youth Service Corps in 1973 as a corrective to the disunity that had supposedly resulted in and obviously been deepened by the Biafran war (1967–1970). University graduates are required to spend a year in a state other than their home state, either teaching or performing similar social or educational duties. Members of this service corps are called "corpers."

18. For a list of 106 roadside (mostly) Pentecostal churches between Abeokuta and Ibadan, see Shields and Joslin 1999; also Obadare 2006.

19. For a penetrating profile of Pastor Adeboye and the conglomerate he oversees, see Rice 2009.

20. In the company's television ads, "Mainframe," rendered as "Opomulero," is an astute translation of Kelani's patrilineal *oriki.*

21. The script is inconsistent on this point. Earlier, one of the *babalawo*'s colleagues advises Mama Tutu against presenting Ngozi's husband for the trial because, as he says,

anything can happen! On the other hand, the assurance that the herbalists can protect him could be a deliberate attempt to put Yinka's mind at rest.

22. Ogunde, a pioneer in this tradition, was asked in 1981 why he, who began his career with socially engaged and anti-colonial plays like *Bread and Bullet, Tiger's Empire*, and so on, did not think to write a play on contemporary issues of political relevance (such as the artificial shortage of food). He answered, "I think the shortage of rice is not as universal a problem as the problem I tried to solve in *Aiye* and *Jaiyesimi*. To me, the shortage of rice is a locality" (Jeyifo 1981, 221–222). This response does show the ethical conception of social relations that undergirds the form's sense of its themes and topics.

23. Arguing that the poetic or proverbial genres should be seen in a continent-wide context immediately raises methodological questions about what commonalities really existed in cultures so widely dispersed in precolonial times, as well as in the significantly different ideological structures of colonial and postcolonial bureaucracies. This is a recurrent feature of scholarly work aimed at debunking narratives depicting Africa as a cultural monolith. However, there are solid grounds for teasing out such commonalities across societies. First, there is the stunning similarity of folktales collected in William Bascom's book *African Folktales in the New World* (1992). From the northwest to southern Africa, the central motifs of most of the tales are retained, although in different forms. Second, Jane Guyer has set the fascinating and convincing standard of using the equatorial template in a 1996 essay titled "Traditions of Invention in Equatorial Africa." Leroy Vail and Landeg White's 1991 *Power and the Praise Poem* is a comprehensive account of the genres in southern Africa, including *izibongo*, while Johannes Fabian's *Power and Performance* (1990) draws on the rhetorical forces at work in genres such as *makumbu* and *kasala*, although his main ethnographic interest lies in sociocultural performances like storytelling, proverbs, and games.

24. Compare this to Fabian's view of the rhetoric of proverbs in Zaire: "proverbs and proverbial expressions are not only characterized by certain formal linguistic and literary criteria; they are also always part of a communicative-rhetorical praxis which is wider than one type of instance. A way of speaking cannot achieve generic status in a community unless it is in contrast to other genres. And all genres of speech or discourse are first of all realized as cultural performances" (1990, 37).

25. Barber's work, of course, stands on the shoulders of work by Yoruba scholars like Adeboye Babalola, Olatunde Olatunji, and Bade Ajuwon. See especially her chapter 2, "The Interpretation of *Oriki*" (1991). For a sense of the range of the genre, compare the following extracts, the first from Barber's case studies, the other from a recent study of *izibongo*:

> Violent masquerader that dances like a man in debt
> Greedy blood-sucking insect of a masquerader that bites himself into a frenzy
> Broad flat pelvis-bone that lies above the arse
> Scabied dog lean-flanked as a whip-lash
> One who harbors schemes of revenge in secret, husband of Tinuomi. (Barber 1991, 228)

> The earth's trembling, gentlemen!
> the rivers all roaring;
> the mountains all shaking;

mighty nations are puzzled,
for small nations are writhing,
straining, striving to burst their bonds.
The earth's surely trembling,
the earth's surely trembling. (quoted in Masilela 2008, 160)

26. The distance between this kind of social self-conception and deconstructionist anti-foundationalism may be measured by Derrida's idea of "Western metaphysics" as "an old cloth that must continually, interminably be undone" (1981, 24). When most contemporary African scholars, who are not necessarily hostile to poststructuralist theory, contend that anti-foundationalism smacks of luxury (i.e., deconstructing what has not been fully constructed), it is likely that they are speaking implicitly to this distance between the need to build institutions in postcolonial Africa and the principled, artistic undermining of those institutions in a strain of postmodernist and poststructuralist theories, although it is also likely that they usually mistake the form of poststructuralism for its content. See Yai 1994 for what seems to me to be a fascinating recuperation of Derrida's notion of *différance* in Yoruba art, without a suggestion of historical or theoretical indebtedness.

27. Like *oriki, yere don* are a means of self-conception. In *We Won't Budge* (2003), his memoir of African expatriation in Europe and North America, Diawara gives an extended and illuminating account of *yere don* as manifested in an encounter with a griot during his cousin's wedding in Paris. According to him, the expatriate Malian's sense of *yere don* is that of self-knowledge, a result of the individual's standing within the caste system, but it is given an innovative, though paradoxical, slant by an emphasis on cultural difference within France. Diawara notes that the Malian immigrants in Paris place greater emphasis on this kind of self-conception than do Malians at home, and that this emphasis reinforces a competitive attitude among them. As with the self-aggrandizing Yoruba "big men," the individual self is the primary focus of the practice, even if that individuality is highlighted through a reference to a collective.

28. Likewise, the transition from stage to screen has created a different form of audience interaction. Kelani says that audiences appraise his work in phone calls, at public screenings, and in comments on his company's web site.

29. Peter Ekeh has written that "the Slave Trade engendered a world view and a distinct rationality that suited conditions of instability. The management of discontinuity seemed central to the proper conduct of affairs in the conditions of the Slave Trade in which whole families and villages were threatened with extinction . . . Such circumstances are different from those of stable conditions in which the management of continuous processes may engender the more conventional rationality which we identify with industrial civilization. In circumstances based on the prospects of discontinuity, it may not be rational to save. On the contrary, it may be entirely rational to develop a spirit of work and consumption that is defined in terms of the here-and-now" (1986, 17–18). Although Ekeh's statement is admittedly speculative, it is possible to historicize this speculation by relating it to the decisive political economies of colonial extraction that followed both slavery and colonialism. In particular, small-scale businesses constituted a productive system that was ubiquitous in twentieth-century African states (Berry 7, 11), and a decentralized despotism is characteristic of post-1960 bureaucratic states (Mamdani 1996, 18). For a materialist, mode-of-production view of the same subject, see Coquery-Vidrovitch 1985, 106–107.

30. In a famous interview with *Playboy* magazine, the Colombian novelist Gabriel García Márquez discloses that in an earlier draft of *One Hundred Years of Solitude,* he tried to make Father Montero levitate by drinking Coca-Cola. Determined not to give the American beverage company free publicity, he decided to change the drink to chocolate (García Márquez 2006). By contrast, in the version of part 1 of Kelani's *Ti Oluwa Nile* made for home viewing, an ad for Izal, a sanitizer, features the famous bad guy of television serials Fadeyi Oloro (*Arelu, Yanpoyanrin*) proclaiming that even his own diabolical magic is inferior to the power of Izal!

31. For example, Lagosians sometimes interpret "AIDS" as standing for "American Idea for Discouraging Sex."

32. In the mid-2000s, Nigerian users of mobile telephones began to believe that anyone who answered a call from certain numbers would start vomiting blood. Lagos newspapers and television news programs reported several deaths. In one of these stories, the person who received a call from one of these numbers reportedly heard incantations being recited at the other end.

33. *GSM Wahala* has no plot, but strives for coherence as a series of sketches, situations and encounters, all held together by the presence of the mobile telephone handset and the nondiegetic sound of a popular tune. A playful treatment of the (bad) manners that this democratized technology breeds appears more important to the director than a plausible story.

34. The implications of digital technology for contemporary Africa are explored in the film *Afro@Digital* (dir. Balufu Bakupa-Kanyinda, 2003).

35. At the 2004 Lagos International Forum on the Motion Picture, Cinema, and Video in Africa, the French Ministry of Cooperation promised more money to Nigerian filmmakers than did the Nigerian government itself. In an email to me on March 1, 2005, Francis Onwochei, producer of the film *Claws of the Lion,* wrote that "going to Cotonou [to shoot] is almost an unwritten part of the agreement, I was also expected to hire at least a member of crew who should be French." Nigeria's then-minister of information announced support totaling 100 million naira, which was explicitly meant to encourage filmmakers to produce works that would educate the public about HIV/AIDS.

4. Jean-Pierre Bekolo and the Challenges of Aesthetic Populism

1. These were *Boyo* (1988), *Un Pauvre Blanc* (1989), and *Mohawk People* (1990). Doubtless as a result of his iconoclastic approach to filmmaking and his often controversial pronouncements on cinema, Bekolo has been the subject of several engaging essays and interviews. While the interviews have presented his views, one essay (Haynes 2005) is remarkable for the way it deals with the two films.

2. Also in 1996, Bekolo directed a film titled *Grandmother's Grammar,* about Mambèty's aesthetics. The film's working title was *An African Named Cinema,* which echoes the name of the character in *Aristotle's Plot.*

3. Jane Guyer writes, in "Traditions of Invention in Equatorial Africa," "Have cultures uniformly taken human mental and emotional eccentricity as new material to be molded, or, as the Equatorial sources seem to suggest, may human variation be treated as a valued potential asset to be created and assiduously cultivated, even at the cost of courting a dangerous social frugality . . . ? It was better, people told me in Cameroon, to be good at anything—even theft—than to be a nobody" (1996, 10).

4. The reference to "movies" immediately suggests Hollywood, for even the most apolitical African filmmaker hardly refers to his work as a movie.

5. Like the profanity in *Quartier Mozart,* this is an indication of Bekolo's own fascination with the work of Spike Lee and with African-American expressive culture in general. In *Quartier Mozart* it is inscribed both narratively and stylistically. In *Aristotle's Plot* the voice of Donny Elwood, the Cameroonian musician who produced the soundtrack, is heard countering the expletives: "What's up, what's up, man? Hey, where's 'What's up?' coming from here in our African neighborhood?"

6. "Tragedy, then, is an imitation of an action that is serious, complete, and of a certain magnitude; in language embellished with each kind of artistic ornament, the several kinds being found in separate parts of the play; in the form of action, not of narrative; through pity and fear effecting the proper purgation of these emotions" (Dukore 1974, 36). For an interesting critique of the notion of art as imitation with special reference to this section of *The Poetics,* see Boal 1985, 9–13; also see Brecht 1992.

7. The fact remains that, thematically, there was little difference between the works of the celluloid directors and those working in video formats. The basis of disagreement was technical. The dramatist Hubert Ogunde, as chairman of Nigeria's Censors' Board in the late 1980s, dismissed the first videofilm submitted for vetting not because of its subject matter but because of its technological template. Kelani's argument for getting on the video "bandwagon" (discussed in chapter 3) is instructive in this respect.

8. Details of this incident were, according to Jonathan Haynes, once available on the Internet Movie Database (IMDb), but the "Statement from the Director" (cited by Haynes) has since been taken down. However, a list of funders is available on the Web site of the French Ministry of Foreign and European Affairs, 2010.

9. For a comparable example of "how things work" in this situation, see Araeen 2000. Olu Oguibe (2004) offers an engaging perspective on the complexities of what he terms "the culture game."

10. A caveat is in order here: Sembene's interest in thematics seems to me to represent a profound anticipation of the reflexivity which marks the work of the younger directors. What I wish to suggest is that some of his characters, significantly Douana in *Black Girl* and Barthélémy in *Guelwaar,* should be viewed as possessing the kinds of subjectivity that African directors display as they encounter difference in a metropolitan context.

5. Imaginary Citizenship

1. For a succinct discussion of exile in modern literature, see Said 2000, especially the title essay.

2. This is the title of the concluding chapter of Phillips 2001.

3. It is certainly not out of place to cite the amusing case of Salman Rushdie's famous disavowal of "Commonwealth Literature" (1991a), a disavowal that did not prevent him from allowing his novel *The Ground Beneath Her Feet* to be entered for the 1999 Commonwealth Literature Prize, which was eventually won by J. M. Coetzee's *Disgrace.*

4. For a brilliant discussion of the relationship between the British writers of the post-Edwardian period, such as Evelyn Waugh and Graham Greene, and postcolonial writers, especially V. S. Naipaul, as evidenced in the genre of travel writing, see Nixon 1992.

5. Griffin and Fish 1998 is a good collection of excerpts from these texts, and also shows an awareness of the "national" character of the anthology's objectives.

6. This phrasing is indebted to John Berger's speech upon receiving the Booker Prize. See Berger 2001, 255.

7. Reading against James Clifford, Natalie Melas (2007) takes up this question in terms of the problem that comparison reveals, where "there is a basis for comparison" between two figures sharing a space "but no ground of equivalence" when it comes to the context of their knowledge (31). What I aim to show here is that "knowledge of" Waring and Mansour, that which is produced through their being written about, is equivalent to "their knowledge" (say, Waring's discursive power).

8. An important exception is the American Diversity Visa lottery, which is dependent on nationality and work experience, although the requirement of certain skills also automatically excludes certain categories of workers. A notice once posted at the visa section of the American Embassy in Lagos listed welders and hairdressers as ineligible for diversity visas.

6. Spirits of Bandung

1. James English uses the phrase "economy of prestige" to analyze the relationship between the market and the field of cultural production, "the strictly functional middle space between acts of inspired artistic creation on the one hand and acts of brilliant discerning consumption on the other" (English 2005, 13).

2. For a detailed discussion of the issues clustered around this idea of India as a consumable object, see Huggan 2001, especially chapter 2. The photograph of a group of writers that accompanies the *New Yorker* special issue includes the Sri Lankan writer Romesh Gunesekera, while leaving out writers like Ghosh and (India-based) Upamanyu Chatterjee, and these omissions are due to the specifically exogenous character of the category's name. For insightful discussions of the works of Indian writers, especially those published or based abroad, see Kumar 1999 and Orsini 2004.

3. Iyengar's book has been extensively and disapprovingly discussed by Ajanta Sircar (1992), in ways which throw the irony of Rushdie's opinions into sharp relief.

4. The more controversial theoretical discussions of these artistic differences have turned on the question of Negritude, with all the frayed edges of that complex literary heritage, but the inclusion of Retamar's work suggests a spatial formation that substitutes tricontinental anti-imperialism for the racial lineaments of Negritude. For an interesting preliminary discussion of this question as "the postcolonial impasse," see Garuba 1999.

5. For details, see the maps in *Power Politics*. Roy's analyses in this book and in her essay "The Greater Common Good" in *The Cost of Living* rely on a vast body of literature specifically on the Narmada River development projects.

6. The immediate cause of the violence was an altercation in the city of Godhra between Hindu pilgrims returning from Ayodhya by the Sabarmati express and Muslim vendors on February 27, 2002. Over the next few days thousands of Muslims were brutally attacked, often killed, while their businesses and houses were destroyed. A detailed reconstruction of the riots can be found in Nussbaum 2007, 17–21. Using the destruction of the Babri Masjid in Ayodhya in 1992 as an example, Ahmad (2002) has advanced the persuasive thesis that the Hindu organizations at various political, cultural, educational, and religious levels are a form of classical fascism. See especially the first essay in Ahmad's book, "On the Ruins of Ayodhya."

7. The standard reference in the twentieth century has been the position of progressive European artist-intellectuals who were caught between the ingrained contradictions of bourgeois liberal democracy (which perpetuated racism and economic exploitation in the colonies) and the spectacular horrors of Nazism and Stalinism, a dilemma for which Jean-Paul Sartre's work, especially *What is Literature?*, remains paradigmatic. An excellent gauge of the politics of engaged artists is John Mander's *The Writer and Commitment*, reviewed in the *New Left Review* by Stuart Hall (1961).

8. For example, the American author Gore Vidal publishes a collection of essays every decade, a practice that Rushdie also seems to be developing, with his two volumes of collected nonfiction.

9. For an engaging discussion of Hindutva outside India, see Purnima Bose's article "Hindutva Abroad," in which she writes, "Rather than draw on the global memory of human rights atrocities against religious minorities on the subcontinent or acknowledge the regard that militant Hindu organizations have for earlier forms of fascism, diasporic Hindu culture in the US tends to localize memory by articulating it with religious practices specific to its US context and by projecting these practices as universal and perennial among its faithful" (2008, 18). Bose also provides useful numbers for Indian populations in the United States (14).

10. In subsequent pages (1999, 89–91), Kumar discusses Roy's work, incidentally comparing her description of herself in her essay "The End of the Imagination" as "an independent, mobile republic" to her characterization of Estha in *The God of Small Things*, and questions Roy's "casual identification of political protest with childish innocence" (91). This overexacting reading of that self-description misses the irony in it.

11. See English's analysis of Hulme's specifically New Zealand base (2005, 312–320).

12. In her critique of the three founding figures (Tagore, Gandhi, and Nehru), Martha Nussbaum suggests that their shortcomings paved the way to the present crisis (2007, 120–121). Ahmad also notes that "it was the collapse of a Left-liberal kind of nationalism that provided the major opening for a fascist kind of nationalism, which set out, then, both to exploit the weaknesses of that earlier nationalism and to formulate a different national agenda" (2002, 21).

13. See Roy 2001, 110 for a clarification of the titling. Both the argument of that essay and the sardonic debunking of the inflated rhetoric at the heart of the official code name can be compared to Rushdie's position on the same subject in his essays "October 2001: The Attacks on America," "November 2001: Not About Islam?," and "February 2002: Anti-Americanism" (2002, 336–344). Rushdie revealingly adopts the rhetorical position of an American patriot in these essays, only to add a hand-wringing footnote to the first lamenting his failure "to foresee the eagerness with which Messrs. Ashcroft, Ridge, et al. would set about creating the apparatus of a more authoritarian state" (337).

14. For a contrary but complementary formulation, see the series of questions posed by Ferguson (2006, 107).

15. See Massing 2008. Also see Adesokan 2010 for comments on Sissako's pre-*Bamako* films.

16. In addition to Samir Amin's work, discussed in the text, the winter 2003 issue of *Critical Inquiry* featured a response to Hardt and Negri from Tim Brennan, a rejoinder from them, and a second response from Brennan (Brennan 2003a, 2003b; Hardt and Negri 2003). A year later, some of the contributors to the journal's Symposium, among them Slavoj Žižek, focused on *Empire* as a significant example of the problems of politi-

cal theory (Žižek 2004). An early review by Ernesto Laclau (2001) was especially critical of the text's use of "multitude" and "immanence," the conceptual ground of its unity.

17. It needs to be added that Amin, as the director of the Third World Forum in Dakar, is one of the intellectual figures behind the Bamako Appeal, a document which shares many commonalities with the World Social Forum.

Conclusion

1. For a very persuasive development of this argument, see Harding 2000.

2. See the series of questions posed by Ferguson (2006, 107), and Spivak's discussion of the ethical challenges facing the twenty-first-century activist-feminist (2004, 52).

References

Books and Articles

Abodunrin, Akintayo. 2009. "A Third Eye for Stories." *NEXT*, June 8, 2009. http://www
.234next.com/csp/cms/sites/Next/Home/5420736-146/story.csp (accessed June
22, 2009).

Abrahams, Peter. 2000. *The Black Experience in the 20th Century: An Autobiography and
Meditation*. Bloomington: Indiana University Press.

Achebe, Chinua. 1983. *The Trouble with Nigeria*. Enugu: Fourth Dimension.

Adejunmobi, Moradewun. 2002. "English Language and the Audience of an African Popular Culture: The Case of Nigerian Video Films." *Cultural Critique* 50:74–103.

Adesanya, Afolabi. 1997. "From Film to Video." In *Nigerian Video Films*, ed. Jonathan
Haynes, 13–20. Jos: Nigerian Film Corporation.

Adesokan, Akin. 2004. "Loud in Lagos: Nollywood Videos." *Wasafiri* 43:45–49.

———. 2005. "Worlds That Flourish: Postnational Aesthetics in West African Videofilms, Africa Cinema, and Diasporic Black Writings." PhD dissertation, Cornell University.

———. 2007. "A Revolution from Below: The Aesthetics of West African Video Films."
Nka: Journal of Contemporary African Art, no. 21:60–67.

———. 2008a. "'Alade' Aromire: An Innovator's Legacy." http://www.nigeriansinamerica
.com/articles/3123/1/Alade-Aromire-An-Innovators-Legacy/Page1.html (accessed February 3, 2011).

———. 2008b. "The Challenges of Aesthetic Populism: An Interview with Jean-Pierre
Bekolo." *Postcolonial Text* 4 (1): 1–11.

———. 2009a. "Baldwin, Paris, and the 'Conundrum of Africa.'" *Textual Practice* 23 (1):
73–97.

———. 2009b. "Practicing 'Democracy' in Nigerian Films." *African Affairs* 108 (433):
599–619.

———. 2010. "Abderrahmane Sissako and the Poetics of Engaged Expatriation." *Screen*
51 (2): 143–160.

Adorno, Theodor W. 2001. *The Culture Industry*. New York: Routledge.

Ahmad, Aijaz. 1992. *In Theory: Nations, Classes, Literatures*. London: Verso.

———. 2002. *On Communalism and Globalization: Offensives of the Far Right*. Jaipur:
Rawat Publications.

Akudinobi, Jude G. 1997. "Survival Instincts: Resistance, Accommodation and Contemporary African Cinema." *Social Identities* 3 (1): 91–121.

Alleyne, Brian W. 1999. "Cultural Politics and Globalized Infomedia: C. L. R. James,
Adorno and Mass Culture Criticism." *Interventions* 1 (3): 361–372.

Amin, Ash, ed. 1994. *Post-Fordism: A Reader*. Malden, Mass.: Blackwell.

Amin, Samir. 1990. *Delinking: Toward a Polycentric World*. London: Zed Books.

———. 2005. "*Empire* and *Multitude*." *Monthly Review* 57 (6): 1–12.

Anderson, Benedict. 1998. *The Specter of Comparisons: Nationalism, Southeast Asia, and the World*. London: Verso.

Andrade-Watkins, Claire. 1996. "France's Bureau of Cinema—Financial and Technical Assistance, 1961–1977: Operations and Implications for African Cinema." In *African Experiences of Cinema*, ed. Imruh Bakari and Mbye Cham, 112–127. London: British Film Institute.

Appadurai, Arjun. 1996. *Modernity at Large*. Minneapolis: University of Minnesota Press.

Appiah, Kwame Anthony. 2005. *The Ethics of Identity*. Princeton, N.J.: Princeton University Press.

———. 2006. *Cosmopolitanism: Ethics in a World of Strangers*. New York: Norton.

Apter, Andrew. 2005. *The Pan-African Nation: Oil and the Spectacle of Culture in Nigeria*. Chicago: University of Chicago Press.

Araeen, Rasheed. 2000. "Save the Johannesburg Biennale/Sao Paulo and the Africans." *Artthrob*, November. http://www.artthrob.co.za/00nov/news.html (accessed December 4, 2009).

Armes, Roy. 1988. *On Video*. New York: Routledge.

Arrighi, Giovanni. 2002. "The African Crisis." *New Left Review* 15:5–36.

Azarya, Victor, and Naomi Chazan. "Disengagement from the State in Africa: Reflections on the Experience of Ghana and Guinea." *Comparative Studies in Society and History* 29 (1): 106–131.

Bakari, Imruh, and Mbye Cham, eds. 1996. *African Experiences of Cinema*. London: British Film Institute.

Balibar, Etienne. 1991. "Racism and Nationalism." In *Race, Nation and Class: Ambiguous Identities*, ed. Etienne Balibar and Immanuel Wallerstein, 37–67. London: Verso.

Balogun, Françoise. 2004. "Booming Videoeconomy: The Case of Nigeria." In *Focus on African Film*, ed. Françoise Pfaff, 173–181. Bloomington: Indiana University Press.

Barber, Karin. 1987a. "Popular Arts in Africa." *African Studies Review* 30 (3): 1–78.

———. 1987b. "Response." *African Studies Review* 30 (3): 105–111.

———. 1991. *I Could Speak until Tomorrow: Oriki, Women, and the Past in a Yoruba Town*. Edinburgh: Edinburgh University Press.

———. 1997. "Preliminary Notes on Audiences in Africa." *Africa* 67 (3): 347–362.

———. 2000. *The Generation of Plays: Yoruba Popular Life in Theater*. Bloomington: Indiana University Press.

Barnes, Sandra T. 1986. *Patrons and Power: Creating a Political Community in Metropolitan Lagos*. Bloomington: Indiana University Press.

Bascom, William. 1975. *African Dilemma Tale*. The Hague: Mouton.

———. 1992. *African Folktales in the New World*. Bloomington: Indiana University Press.

Bastian, Misty L. 1993. "'Bloodhounds Who Have No Friends': Witchcraft and Locality in the Nigerian Popular Press." In *Modernity and Its Malcontents: Ritual and Power in Postcolonial Africa*, ed. Jean Comaroff and John Comaroff, 129–166. Chicago: University of Chicago Press.

Bates, Robert H. 1981. *Markets and States in Tropical Africa: The Political Basis of Agricultural Policies*. Berkeley: University of California Press.

Beecroft, Alexander. 2008. "World Literature without a Hyphen." *New Left Review* 54:87–100.

Belasco, Bernard. 1980. *The Entrepreneur as Culture Hero: Preadaptation in Nigerian Economic Development*. New York: Praeger.

Benjamin, Walter. 1978. "The Author as Producer." In *Reflections: Essays, Aphorisms, Autobiographical Writings*, trans. Edmund Jephcott, 220–238. New York: Schocken Books.

Berger, John. 2001. "Speech on Accepting the Booker Prize for Fiction at the Café Royal in London on 23 November 1972." In *Selected Essays*, 253–255. New York: Vintage Books.

Berry, Sara. 1985. *Fathers Work for Their Sons.* Berkeley: University of California Press.

Boal, Augusto. 1985. *Theater of the Oppressed.* Translated by Charles A. McBride and Maria-Odilia Leal McBride. New York: Theater Communications Group.

Bohannan, Paul, and George Dalton. 1962. Introduction to *Markets in Africa.* Evanston, Ill.: Northwestern University Press.

Bond, Horace Mann. 1956. "Reflections, Comparative, on West African Nationalist Movements." *Présence Africaine,* nos. 8–10:133–142.

Bose, Purnima. 2008. "Hindutva Abroad: The California Textbook Controversy." *Global South* 2 (1): 11–34.

Bougues, Anthony. 1997. *Caliban's Freedom: The Early Political Thought of C. L. R. James.* London: Pluto Press.

Brecht, Bertolt. 1966. "Writing the Truth: Five Difficulties." Translated by Richard Winston. In *Galileo,* ed. Eric Bentley, 133–150. New York: Grove Press.

———. 1992. *Brecht on Theater: The Development of an Aesthetic.* Translated by John Willett. New York: Hill & Wang.

Brennan, Timothy. 1989. "Cosmopolitans and Celebrities." *Race & Class* 31 (1): 1–19.

———. 1997. *At Home in the World: Cosmopolitanism Now.* Cambridge, Mass.: Harvard University Press.

———. 2003a. "The Empire's New Clothes." *Critical Inquiry* 29 (2): 337–367.

———. 2003b. "The Magician's Wand: A Rejoinder to Hardt and Negri." *Critical Inquiry* 29 (2): 374–378.

———. 2006. *Wars of Position: The Cultural Politics of Left and Right.* New York: Columbia University Press.

Brouillette, Sarah. 2007. *Postcolonial Writers in the Global Literary Marketplace.* New York: Palgrave.

Brown, Lloyd W. 2002. "Oral Tradition in *Dilemma of a Ghost.*" In *Modern African Drama,* ed. Biodun Jeyifo, 583–584. New York: W. W. Norton.

Buck-Morss, Susan. 2004. "Visual Studies and Global Imagination." *Papers of Surrealism,* no. 2. http://www.surrealismcentre.ac.uk/papersofsurrealism/journal2/acrobat_files/buck_morss_article.pdf (accessed February 12, 2001).

Buhle, Paul. 1994. "The Paradoxical Pan-Africanist." In *Imagining Home: Class, Culture and Nationalism in the African Diaspora,* ed. Sidney Lemelle and Robin D. G. Kelley, 158–166. London: Verso.

Burton, Julianne. 1985. "Marginal Cinemas and Mainstream Critical Theory." *Screen* 26:2–21.

Cabral, Amílcar. 1979. *Unity and Struggle: Speeches and Writings of Amílcar Cabral.* Translated by Michael Wolfers. New York: Monthly Review Press.

Calhoun, Craig. 2002. "Imagining Solidarity: Cosmopolitanism, Constitutional Patriotism and the Public Sphere." *Public Culture* 14 (1): 147–171.

Casanova, Pascale. 2004. *The World Republic of Letters.* Translated by M. B. Debevoise. Cambridge, Mass.: Harvard University Press.

Castells, Manuel. 2000. *The Rise of the Network Society.* Malden, Mass.: Blackwell.

Celli, Carlo. 2005. *Gillo Pontecorvo: From Resistance to Terrorism.* Lanham, Md.: Scarecrow Press.

Césaire, Aimé. 1985. *A Tempest.* Translated by Richard Miller. New York: Ubu Repertory Theater Publications.

Chabal, Patrick. 1996. "The African Crisis: Context and Interpretation." In *Postcolonial Identities in Africa,* ed. Richard Werbner and Terence Ranger, 31–53. London: Zed Books.

Chabal, Patrick, with David Birmingham et al. 2002. *A History of Postcolonial Lusophone Africa.* Bloomington: Indiana University Press.

Chabal, Patrick, and Jean-Pascal Daloz. 1999. *Africa Works: Disorder as Political Instrument.* Oxford: James Currey; Bloomington: Indiana University Press.

Cheah, Pheng. 1998a. "The Cosmopolitical—Today." Second introduction to *Cosmopolitics: Thinking and Feeling beyond the Nation,* ed. Pheng Cheah and Bruce Robbins. Minneapolis: University of Minnesota Press.

———. 1998b. "Given Culture." In *Cosmopolitics: Thinking and Feeling beyond the Nation,* ed. Pheng Cheah and Bruce Robbins, 290–328. Minneapolis: University of Minnesota Press.

Chow, Rey. 1995. *Primitive Passions: Film as Ethnography.* New York: Columbia University Press.

Clifford, James. 1998. "Mixed Feelings." In *Cosmopolitics: Thinking and Feeling beyond the Nation,* ed. Pheng Cheah and Bruce Robbins, 362–370. Minneapolis: University of Minnesota Press.

Coetzee, J. M. 2001. *Stranger Shore: Literary Essays, 1986–2001.* New York: Viking.

Comaroff, Jean, and John Comaroff, ed. 2001. *Millennial Capitalism and the Culture of Neoliberalism.* Durham, N.C.: Duke University Press.

———, ed. 2006. *Law and Order in the Postcolony.* Chicago: Chicago University Press.

Consentino, Donald. 1987. "Omnes Cultura Tres Partes Divisa Est?" *African Studies Review* 30 (3): 85–90.

Cooper, Frederick. 1981. "Africa and the World Economy." *Africa Studies Review* 24 (2–3): 1–86.

Coquery-Vidrovitch, Catherine. 1985. "The Political Economy of the African Peasantry and Modes of Production." In *The Political Economy of Contemporary Africa,* ed. Peter Gutkind and Immanuel Wallerstein, 94–116. Beverly Hills: Sage.

Cudjoe, Selwyn R., and William E. Cain, eds. 1995. *C. L. R. James: His Intellectual Legacies.* Amherst: University of Massachusetts Press.

Damrosch, David. 2003. *What Is World Literature?* Princeton, N.J.: Princeton University Press.

Davidson, Basil. 1981. *No Fist Is Big Enough to Hide the Sky: The Liberation of Guine and Cape Verde; Aspects of an African Revolution.* With a foreword by Amílcar Cabral. London: Zed Books.

———. 1992. *The Black Man's Burden: Africa and the Curse of the Nation-State.* Ibadan: Spectrum Books.

Davies, Ioan. 1998. "Negotiating African Culture: Toward a Decolonization of the Fetish." In *The Cultures of Globalization,* ed. Fredric Jameson and Masao Miyoshi, 125–145. Durham, N.C.: Duke University Press.

Deleuze, Gilles, and Félix Guattari. 1987. *A Thousand Plateaus: Capitalism and Schizophrenia*. Translated by Brian Massumi. Minneapolis: University of Minnesota Press.

Derrida, Jacques. 1981. *Positions*. Translated and annotated by Alan Bass. London: Continuum.

Desai, Anita, Caryl Phillips, and Ilan Stavans. 1994. "The Other Voice: A Dialogue between Anita Desai, Caryl Phillips, and Ilan Stavans." *Transition: An International Review*, no. 64:77–89.

Desai, Gaurav. 1997. "Out in Africa." In *The Cultural Politics of Dissident Sexualities*, ed. Thomas Foster, Carol Siegel, and Ellen F. Berry, 120–128. New York: New York University Press.

Devi, Mahasweta. 1995. *Imaginary Maps: Three Stories by Mahasweta Devi*. Translated and introduced by Gayatri Chakravorty Spivak. New York: Routledge.

Dhondy, Farrukh. 2001. *C. L. R. James: A Life*. New York: Pantheon Books.

Diawara, Manthia. 1992. *African Cinema: Politics and Culture*. Bloomington: Indiana University Press.

———. 1994. "On Tracking World Cinema: African Cinema at Film Festivals." *Public Culture* 6:385–396.

———. 1998. "Toward a Regional Imaginary in Africa." In *The Cultures of Globalization*, ed. Fredric Jameson and Masao Miyoshi, 103–124. Durham, N.C.: Duke University Press.

———. 2003. *We Won't Budge: An African Exile in the World*. New York: Basic Civitas.

———. 2010. *African Film: New Forms of Aesthetics and Politics*. Munich: Prestel.

D'Lugo, Marvin. 2003. "Authorship, Globalization, and the New Identity of Latin American Cinema." In *Rethinking Third Cinema*, ed. Anthony R. Guneratne and Wimal Dissanayake, 103–125. New York: Routledge.

Dovey, Lindiwe. 2009. *African Literature and Film*. New York: Columbia University Press.

Dukore, Bernard F. 1974. *Dramatic Theory and Criticism: Greeks to Grotowski*. New York: Holt, Rinehart and Winston.

Dunton, Chris. 1989. "'Wheyting be dat?' The Treatment of Homosexuality in African Literature." *Research in African Literatures* 20 (3): 422–448.

Edwards, Brent H. 2003. *The Practice of Diaspora: Literature, Translation and the Rise of Black Internationalism*. Cambridge, Mass.: Harvard University Press.

———. 2004. "The Genres of Postcolonialism." Introduction to a special issue of *Social Text*, no. 78:1–15.

Eke, Maureen, et al. 2000. *African Images: Recent Studies and Texts in Cinema*. Trenton, N.J.: Africa World Press.

Ekeh, Peter. 1975. "Colonialism and the Two Publics in Africa: A Theoretical Statement." *Comparative Studies in Society and History* 17 (1): 91–112.

———. 1986. "Development Theory and the African Predicament." *Africa Development* 11 (4): 1–40.

———. 1990. "Social Anthropology and Two Contrasting Uses of Tribalism in Africa." *Comparative Studies in Society and History* 32 (4): 660–700.

Ekwuazi, Hyginus. 1997. "The Igbo Video Film: A Glimpse into the Cult of the Individual." In *Nigerian Video Films*, ed. Jonathan Haynes, 71–82. Jos: Nigerian Film Corporation.

English, James. 2005. *The Economy of Prestige: Prizes, Awards, and the Circulation of Cultural Value*. Cambridge, Mass.: Harvard University Press.

Enwezor, Okwui. 2001. *The Short Century: Independence and Liberation Movements in Africa, 1945–1994*. Munich: Prestel Verlag.

Equiano, Olaudah. 1999. *The Life of Olaudah Equiano, or Gustavus Vassa, the African*. Toronto, Ontario: Dover Publications.

Eshun, Ekow. 2006. *Black Gold of the Sun*. New York: Vintage Books.

Etherton, Michael. 1982. *The Development of African Drama*. London: Hutchinson.

Everett, Anna. 2002. "The Revolution Will Be Digitized: Afrocentricity and the Digital Public Sphere." *Social Text*, no. 20:125–146.

Fabian, Johannes. 1983. *Time and the Other: How Anthropology Makes Its Object*. New York: Columbia University Press.

———. 1990. *Power and Performance*. Madison: University of Wisconsin Press.

———. 1998. *Moments of Freedom*. Charlottesville: University of Virginia Press.

Fanon, Frantz. 1963. *The Wretched of the Earth*. Translated by Constance Farrington. New York: Grove Press.

Farred, Grant, ed. 1996. *Rethinking C. L. R. James*. Cambridge, Mass.: Blackwell.

———. 2003. *What's My Name? Vernacular Black Intellectuals*. Minneapolis: University of Minnesota Press.

FEPACI (Fédération Panafricaine des Cinéastes). 1995. *L'Afrique et le Centenaire du Cinéma/Africa and the Centenary of Cinema*. Paris and Dakar: Présence Africaine.

Ferguson, James. 2006. *Global Shadows: Africa in the Neoliberal World Order*. Durham, N.C.: Duke University Press.

Folsom, Ed. 2007. "Database as Genre: The Epic Transformation of Archives." *PMLA* 122 (5): 1571–1579.

Forrest, Tom. 1994. *The Advance of African Capital*. Charlottesville: University of Virginia Press.

French Ministry of Foreign and European Affairs. 2010. "*Le Complot d'Aristote*, by Jean-Pierre Bekolo." http://www.diplomatie.gouv.fr/en/france-priorities_1/cinema_2/cinematographic-cooperation_9/production-support-funding_10/films-benefiting-from-aid_13/film-list-by-country_15/cameroon_1049/complot-aristote_1080/index.html (accessed December 16, 2010).

Fuentes, Carlos. 2006. "In Praise of the Novel." *Critical Inquiry* 32:610–617.

Gabriel, Teshome H. 1985. "Xala: A Cinema of Wax and Gold." In *Jump Cut: Hollywood, Politics and Counter Cinema*, ed. Peter Steven, 334–343. New York: Praeger.

———. 1986. "Colonialism and 'Law and Order' Criticism." *Screen* 27:140–147.

———. 1989. "Toward a Critical Theory of Third World Films." In *Questions of Third Cinema*, ed. Jim Pines and Paul Willemen. 30–52. London: British Film Institute.

Gadjigo, Samba, Ralph H. Faulkingham, Thomas Cassirer, and Reinhard Sander, eds. 1993. *Ousmane Sembène: Dialogues with Critics and Writers*. Amherst: University of Massachusetts Press.

García Márquez, Gabriel. 2006. "Playboy Interview: Gabriel García Márquez." Interview by Claudia Dreifus. In *Conversations with Gabriel García Márquez*, ed. Gene H. Bell-Villada, 93–132. Jackson: University Press of Mississippi.

Garuba, Harry. N.d. "And after the Ethnographic Novel?" Unpublished manuscript.

———. 1999. "Re-negotiating the Postcolonial Impasse: Wole Soyinka's *The Lion and the Jewel* and Derek Walcott's *Ti-Jean and His Brothers*." *English in Africa* 26 (1): 113–120.

Geschiere, Peter. 1997. *The Modernity of Witchcraft: Politics and the Occult in Postcolonial Africa.* Charlottesville: University of Virginia Press.

Getino, Octavio. 1986. "Notes on the Concept of Third Cinema." In *Argentine Cinema*, ed. Tim Barnard, 100–106. Toronto: Nightwood Editions.

Ghali, Noureddin. 1987. "An Interview with Sembene Ousmane." In *Film and Politics in the Third World*, ed. John D. H. Downing, 41–54. New York: Praeger.

Gikandi, Simon. 2001. "Globalization and the Claims of Postcoloniality." *South Atlantic Quarterly* 100 (3): 627–658.

Gilroy, Paul. 1993. *The Black Atlantic: Modernity and Double Consciousness.* Cambridge, Mass.: Harvard University Press.

———. 2000. *Against Race: Imagining Political Culture beyond the Color Line.* Cambridge, Mass.: Belknap Press.

Gomes, Patrick I. 1978. *The Marxian Populism of C. L. R. James.* St. Augustine, Trinidad and Tobago: Department of Sociology, University of the West Indies.

Gott, Richard. 2000. Introduction to *The African Dream*, by Ernesto "Che" Guevara. New York: Grove Press.

———. 2005. "From Russia with Love." *Guardian*, November 12, 2005. http://www.guardian .co.uk/film/2005/nov/12/cuba?INTCMP=SRCH (accessed August 12, 2010).

Griffin, Farah Jasmin, and Cheryl J. Fish. 1998. *A Stranger in the Village: Two Centuries of African-American Travel Writing.* Boston: Beacon Press.

Grimshaw, Anna. 1991. *Popular Democracy and the Creative Imagination: The Writings of C. L. R. James, 1950–1963.* New York: C. L. R. James Institute.

———. 1996. Introduction to *Special Delivery: The Letters of C. L. R. James to Constance Webb, 1939–1948.* Malden, Mass.: Blackwell.

GSMA. 2011. "History: Brief History of GSM and the GSMA." http://gsmworld.com/ about-us/history.htm, accessed February 15, 2011.

Guéhenno, Jean-Marie. 1995. *The End of the Nation-State.* Translated by Victoria Elliott. Minneapolis: University of Minnesota Press.

Gugler, Josef, and Oumar Cherif Diop. 1998. "Sembene's *Xala*: The Novel, the Film, and Their Audiences." *Research in African Literatures* 29 (2): 147–158.

Guneratne, Anthony R., and Wimal Dissanayake, eds. 2003. *Rethinking Third Cinema.* New York: Routledge.

Gunn, Giles. 2001. "Introduction: Globalizing Literary Studies." Introduction to a special issue, *PMLA* 116 (1): 16–31.

Guyer, Jane I. 1996. "Traditions of Invention in Equatorial Africa." *African Studies Review* 39 (3): 1–28.

Guyer, Jane I., and Karen Tranberg Hansen. 2001. "Markets in Africa in a New Era." Introduction to a special issue, *Africa: Journal of the International African Institute* 71 (2): 197–201.

Hall, Stuart. 1961. "Commitment Dilemma." *New Left Review* I/10:67–69.

———. 1989. "Cultural Identity and Cinematic Representation." *Framework* 36:68–81.

———. 1995. "Negotiating Caribbean Identities." *New Left Review* I/209:3–14.

———. 1996. "A Conversation with C. L .R. James." In *Rethinking C. L. R. James*, ed. Grant Farred, 15–44. Cambridge, Mass.: Blackwell.

———. 1997a. "The Local and the Global: Globalization and Ethnicity." In *Culture, Globalization and the World-System*, ed. Anthony King, 19–39. Minneapolis: University of Minnesota Press.

———. 1997b. "Old and New Identities, Old and New Ethnicities." In *Culture, Globalization and the World-System*, ed. Anthony King, 41–68. Minneapolis: University of Minnesota Press.

Hall, Stuart, et al. 1980. *Culture, Media, Language*. London: Hutchinson.

Hanhardt, John. 1986. Introduction to *Video Culture: A Critical Investigation*. Rochester, N.Y.: Visual Studies Workshop Press.

Hannerz, Ulf. 1987. "The World in Creolization." *Africa* 57 (4): 546–559.

Harding, Jeremy. 2000. *The Uninvited: Refugees at the Rich Man's Gate*. London: Profile Books and the London Review of Books.

Hardt, Michael, and Antonio Negri. 2000. *Empire*. Cambridge, Mass.: Harvard University Press.

———. 2003. "The Rod of the Forest Warden: A Response to Timothy Brennan." *Critical Inquiry* 29 (2): 368–373.

Harrow, Kenneth. 2007a. "Issues of Discourse and Decolonization in Spivak's *Critique of Postcolonialism* (1999)." *Journal of the African Literature Association* 1 (1): 165–186.

———. 2007b. *Postcolonial African Cinema: From Political Engagement to Postmodernism*. Bloomington: Indiana University Press.

Hartman, Saidiya. 2007. *Lose Your Mother: A Journey along the Atlantic Slave Route*. New York: Farrar, Straus & Giroux.

Harvey, David. 1990. *The Condition of Postmodernity*. New York: Blackwell.

———. 2001. "Cosmopolitanism and the Banality of Geographical Evils." In *Millennial Capitalism and the Culture of Neoliberalism*, ed. Jean Comaroff and John Comaroff, 271–309. Durham, N.C.: Duke University Press.

———. 2006. *Spaces of Global Capitalism*. London: Verso.

Haynes, Jonathan. 1995. "Nigerian Cinema: Structural Adjustments." *Research in African Literatures* 4 (3): 97–119.

———. 2005. "African Filmmaking and the Postcolonial Predicament: *Quartier Mozart* and *Aristotle's Plot*." In *Cinema and Social Discourse in Cameroon*, ed. Alexie Tcheuyap, 111–133. Bayreuth: BASS.

———. 2006. "Political Critique in Nigerian Video Films." *African Affairs* 105 (421): 511–533.

———. 2007. "Nollywood: What's in a Name?" *Film International* 5 (4): 106–108.

Haynes, Jonathan, and Onookome Okome. 1997. "Evolving Popular Media: Nigerian Video Films." In *Nigerian Video Films*, ed. Jonathan Haynes, 21–44. Jos: Nigerian Film Corporation.

Heath, Stephen. 1981. *Question of Cinema*. Bloomington: Indiana University Press.

Heavens, Andrew. 2007. "Phone Credit Low? Africans Go for 'Beeping.'" Reuters. September 25, 2007. http://www.reuters.com/article/idUSHEA92325720070926?sp=true (accessed December 10, 2010).

Hibou, Beatrice. 1999. "The 'Social Capital' of the State as an Agent of Deception, Or, The Ruses of Economic Intelligence." In *The Criminalization of the State in Africa*, ed. Jean-Francois Bayart, Beatrice Hibou, and Stephen Ellis, 69–113. Bloomington: Indiana University Press.

Hill-Rubin, Mildred. 1993. "*Présence Africaine:* A Voice in the Wilderness." In *The Surreptitious Speech: "Présence Africaine" and the Politics of Otherness, 1947–1987,* ed. V. Y. Mudimbe, 157–173. Chicago: University of Chicago Press.

Hitchcock, Peter. 2003. "The Genre of Postcoloniality." *New Literary History* 34 (2): 299–330.

Horkheimer, Max, and Theodor Adorno. 1989. "The Culture Industry: Enlightenment as Mass Deception." In *Dialectic of Enlightenment,* trans. John Cumming, 120–167. New York: Continuum.

Huggan, Graham. 2001. *The Postcolonial Exotic.* New York: Routledge.

IFAD (International Fund for Agricultural Development). 2007. "Migrant Workers Worldwide Sent Home More Than US$300 Billion in 2006, New Study Finds." Press release no. IFAD/44/07, October 17, 2007. http://www.ifad.org/media/press/2007/44.htm (accessed October 24, 2007).

Irele, Abiola F. 2001. *The African Imagination: Literature in Africa and the Black Diaspora.* New York: Oxford University Press.

Iwenjora, Fred. 2001. "*Living in Bondage* was a rejected stone—NEK." *Weekend Vanguard,* October 27.

James, C. L. R. 1963. *The Black Jacobins: Toussaint L'Ouverture and the San Domingo Revolution.* New York: Vintage Books.

———. 1977a. *Nkrumah and the Ghana Revolution.* London: Allison & Busby.

———. 1977b. "The Olympia Statues, Picasso's *Guernica* and the Frescoes of Michelangelo in the Capella Paolina." In *The Future in the Present: Selected Writings,* 226–234. London: Allison & Busby.

———. 1977c. "The British Vote for Socialism." In *The Future in the Present: Selected Writings,* 106–118. London: Allison & Busby.

———. 1980. *Notes on Dialectics: Hegel, Marx, Lenin.* London: Allison & Busby.

———. 1983. *Beyond a Boundary.* New York: Pantheon Books.

———. 1984a. *At the Rendezvous of Victory: Selected Writings.* London: Allison & Busby.

———. 1984b. "Toward the Seventh: The Pan-African Congress—Past, Present and Future." In *At the Rendezvous of Victory: Selected Writings,* 236–250. London: Allison & Busby.

———. 1984c. "George Padmore: Black Marxist Revolutionary." In *At the Rendezvous of Victory: Selected Writings,* 251–263. London: Allison & Busby.

———. 1986. *State Capitalism and World Revolution.* In collaboration with Raya Dunayevskaya and Grace Lee. Chicago: Charles H. Kerr.

———. 1992. *The C. L. R. James Reader.* Edited by Anna Grimshaw. Malden, Mass.: Blackwell.

———. 1993. *American Civilization.* Malden, Mass.: Blackwell.

———. 1996a. *C. L. R. James on "The Negro Question."* Edited by Scott McLemee. Jackson: University Press of Mississippi.

———. 1996b. *Special Delivery: The Letters of C. L. R. James to Constance Webb, 1939–1948.* Malden, Mass.: Blackwell.

James, C. L. R., F. Forest, and Ria Stone. 1947. *The Invading Socialist Society.* Detroit: Bewick Editions.

Jameson, Fredric. 1986. "Third-World Literature in the Era of Multinational Capitalism." *Social Text,* no. 15:65–88.

———. 1991. *Postmodernism, or The Cultural Logic of Late Capitalism.* Durham, N.C.: Duke University Press, 1991.

———. 1992. *The Geopolitical Aesthetic: Cinema and Space in the World System.* London: British Film Institute; Bloomington: Indiana University Press.

———. 1998. "Globalization as a Philosophical Issue." In *The Cultures of Globalization,* ed. Fredric Jameson and Masao Miyoshi, 54–77. Durham, N.C.: Duke University Press.

JanMohamed, Abdul R., and David Lloyd. 1990. Introduction to *The Nature and Context of Minority Discourse.* New York: Oxford University Press.

Jeyifo, Biodun, ed. 1981. *The Yoruba Professional Itinerant Theater: Oral Documentation.* Vol. 2. Lagos: Federal Department of Culture.

———. 1984. *By Popular Demand: The Yoruba Traveling Theater of Nigeria.* Lagos: Nigeria Magazine.

———. 1989. "'Race' and the Pitfalls of Ventriloquial Deconstruction: Gayatri Chakravorty Spivak's Regressive Monologue on Africa." Texts from "Feminisms and Cultural Imperialism: The Politics of Difference," a conference held at Cornell University, April 22–23, 1989, transcribed with glossary and notes. Unpublished essay, held in the Africana Library at Cornell University.

———. 1993. "Determinations of Remembering: Postcolonial Fictional Genealogies of Colonialism in Africa." *Stanford Literature Review* 10 (1–2): 99–116.

———. 2004. *Wole Soyinka: Politics, Poetics, and Postcolonialism.* Cambridge: Cambridge University Press.

Jost, Jon. 2005. "Some Notes on 'Political Cinema' Prompted by Seeing Raoul Peck's *Sometimes in April* in Competition at the Berlin Film Festival." http://archive.sensesofcinema.com/contents/05/35/sometimes_in_april.html (accessed August 30, 2009).

July, Robert. 1967. *The Origins of Modern African Thought.* New York: Praeger.

Kahin, George M. 1956. *The Asian-African Conference: Bandung, Indonesia, April 1955.* Ithaca: Cornell University Press.

Karp, Ivan. 1997. "Does Theory Travel? Area Studies and Cultural Studies." *Africa Today* 44 (3): 281–296.

King, Anthony. 1997. Introduction to *Culture, Globalization and the World System.* Minneapolis: University of Minnesota Press.

Kom, Ambroise. 1998. "African Absence, a Literature without a Voice." Translated by Ruthmarie H. Mitsch. *Research in African Literatures* 29 (3): 149–161.

Kumar, Amitava. 1999. "Louder than Bombs." *Transition,* no. 79:80–101.

Laclau, Ernesto. 1977. *Politics and Ideology in Marxist Theory,* London: Verso.

———. 2001. "Can Immanence Explain Social Struggles?" *diacritics* 31 (4): 3–10.

Laclau, Ernesto, and Chantal Mouffe. 2001. *Hegemony and Socialist Strategies.* London: Verso.

Ladebo, Ladi. 2004. "Experience of a Nigerian Filmmaker." *Guardian* (Lagos), December 5. http://www.guardiannewsngr.com/ (accessed December 5, 2004).

Larkin, Brian. 1997. "Hausa Dramas and the Rise of Video Culture in Nigeria." In *Nigerian Video Films,* ed. Jonathan Haynes, 105–125. Jos: Nigerian Film Corporation.

———. 2004. "Degraded Images, Distorted Sounds: Nigerian Videos and the Infrastructure of Piracy." *Public Culture* 16 (2): 289–314.

———. 2008. *Signal and Noise: Media, Infrastructure, and Urban Culture in Nigeria.* Durham, N.C.: Duke University Press.

Lazarus, Neil. 1999. *Nationalism and Cultural Practice in the Postcolonial World*. Cambridge: Cambridge University Press.

Lukacs, Georg. 1971. *The Theory of the Novel*. Cambridge, Mass.: MIT Press.

Lyons, Harriet D. 1984. "The Uses of Ritual in Sembene's *Xala*." *Canadian Journal of African Studies* 18 (2): 319–328.

Maja-Pearce, Adewale. 1992. *A Mask Dancing: Nigerian Novelists of the Eighties*. London: Hans Zell.

———. 2001. "Onitsha Home Movies." *London Review of Books,* May 10.

Mambèty, Djibril Diop. 1993. "Interview: Djibril Mambèty." Interview by Rachel Rawlins. http://itutu.com/djibril/Interview.html (accessed August 30, 2009).

Mamdani, Mahmood. 1996. *Citizen and Subject: Contemporary Africa and the Legacy of Late Colonialism*. Princeton, N.J.: Princeton University Press.

Manuel, Peter. L. 1993. *Cassette Culture: Popular Music and Technology in North India*. Chicago: University of Chicago Press.

Martin, Michael T. 1995. *Cinemas of the Black Diaspora: Diversity, Dependence and Oppositionality*. Detroit: Wayne State University.

———. 2002. "'I am a storyteller, drawing water from the well of my culture': Gaston Kabore, Griot of African Cinema." *Research in African Literatures* 33 (4): 161–179.

———. 2009. "Podium for the Truth? Reading Slavery and the Neocolonial Project in the Historical Film: *Queimada!/Burn!* and *Sankofa* in Counterpoint." *Third Text* 23 (6): 717–731.

Masilela, Ntongela. 2008. Review of *The Dassie and the Hunter: A South African Meeting,* by Jeff Opland. *Research in African Literatures* 39 (2): 159–161.

Massing, Michael. 2008. "Out of Focus: How Indie Dogma Undercuts the Documentary." *Columbia Journalism Review,* March–April, 41–44.

Mbembe, Achille. 2001. *On the Postcolony*. Berkeley: University of California Press.

McCall, John C. 2004. "Juju and Justice at the Movies: Vigilantes in Nigerian Popular Videos." *African Studies Review* 47 (3): 51–67.

McKeon, Michael. 2002. *The Origins of the English Novel, 1600–1740*. Baltimore: Johns Hopkins University Press.

McLemee, Scott. 1996. "The Enigma of Arrival." Introduction to *C. L. R. James on "The Negro Question,"* by C. L. R. James. Jackson: University Press of Mississippi.

Meagher, Kate. 2010. *Identity Economics: Social Networks and the Informal Economy in Nigeria*. Oxford: James Currey.

Melas, Natalie. 2007. *All the Difference in the World: Postcoloniality and the Ends of Comparison*. Stanford: Stanford University Press.

Mermin, Elizabeth. 1995. "A Window on Whose Reality? The Emerging Industry of Senegalese Cinema." *Research in African Literatures* 26 (3): 120–133.

Meyer, Birgit. 2003. "Ghanaian Popular Cinema and the Magic in and of Film." In *Magic and Modernity: Interfaces of Revelation and Concealment,* ed. Birgit Meyer and Peter Pels, 200–222. Stanford: Stanford University Press.

Miller, Laura. 2006. *Reluctant Capitalists: Bookselling and the Culture of Consumption*. Chicago: University of Chicago Press.

Mishra, Pankaj. 2001. "You Can't Go Home Again." *New York Review of Books,* April 26.

Moretti, Franco. 1983. *Signs Taken for Wonders,* London: Verso.

———. 2000. "Conjectures on World Literature." *New Left Review* 1:54–68.

———. 2001. "Planet Hollywood." *New Left Review* 9:90–101.

———. 2005. *Graphs, Maps, Trees: Abstract Models for a Literary History.* London: Verso.

Mowitt, John. 1993. "Sembene Ousmane's *Xala*: Postcoloniality and Foreign Film Languages." *Camera Obscura* 31:71–95.

Mulvey, Laura. 1996. *Fetishism and Curiosity.* Bloomington: Indiana University Press; London: British Film Institute.

———. 1999. "The Carapace That Failed: Ousmane Sembene's *Xala.*" In *Reading the Contemporary: African Art from Theory to the Marketplace,* ed. Olu Oguibe and Okwui Enwezor, 400–420. London: InIVA; Cambridge, Mass.: MIT Press.

Murphy, David. 2000. *Sembene: Imagining Alternatives in Film and Fiction.* Oxford: James Currey; Trenton, N.J.: Africa World Press.

Murphy, David, and Patrick Williams. 2007. *Postcolonial African Cinema: Ten Directors.* Manchester: University of Manchester Press.

Naficy, Hamid. 2001. *An Accented Cinema: Exilic and Diasporic Filmmaking.* Princeton, N.J.: Princeton University Press.

Naremore, James. 2000. *Film Adaptation.* New Brunswick, N.J.: Rutgers University Press.

Nfa-Abbenyi, Juliana M. 1998. "Ecological Postcolonialism in African Women's Literature." In *Literature of Nature: An International Source Book,* ed. Patrick Murphy, 344–349. Chicago: Fitzroy Dearborn Publishers.

Ngangura, Mweze. 1996. "African Cinema: Militancy or Entertainment?" In *African Experiences of Cinema,* ed. Imruh Bakari and Mbye Cham, 60–64. London: British Film Institute.

Ní Chréacháin, Fírinne, and Sembene Ousmane. 1992. "If I Were a Woman, I'd Never Marry an African: Discussion with Sembene Ousmane." *African Affairs* 91 (363): 241–247.

Nixon, Rob. 1992. *London Calling: V. S. Naipaul, Postcolonial Mandarin.* New York: Oxford University Press.

Nussbaum, Martha C. 2007. *The Clash Within: Democracy, Religious Violence, and India's Future.* Cambridge, Mass.: Harvard University Press.

Obadare, Ebenezer. 2006. "Pentecostal Presidency? The Lagos-Ibadan 'Theocratic Class' and the Muslim 'Other.'" *Review of African Political Economy* 33 (110): 665–678.

Oguibe, Olu. 2004. *The Culture Game.* Minneapolis: University of Minnesota Press.

Oha, Obododimma. 1997. "The Rhetoric of Nigerian Christian Videos: The War Paradigm of *Great Mistake.*" In *Nigerian Video Films,* ed. Jonathan Haynes, 93–98. Jos: Nigerian Film Corporation.

Okome, Onookome. 1997. "'Onome': Ethnicity, Class, Gender." In *Nigerian Video Films,* ed. Jonathan Haynes, 83–92. Jos: Nigerian Film Corporation.

———. 2003. "Writing the Anxious City: Images of Lagos in Nigerian Home Video Films." *Black Renaissance/Renaissance Noire* 5 (2): 65–75.

Orsini, Francesca. 2004. "India in the Mirror of World Fiction." In *Debating World Literature,* ed. Christopher Prendergast, 319–333. London: Verso.

Osaghae, Eghosa. 1998. *The Crippled Giant: Nigeria since Independence.* Bloomington: Indiana University Press.

Peel, J. D. Y. 1978. "Olaju: A Yoruba Concept of Development." *Journal of Development Studies* 14 (2): 139–165.

Petty, Sheila. 1996. *A Call to Action: The Films of Ousmane Sembene.* Westport, Conn: Greenwood.

Pfaff, Françoise. 1982. "Three Faces of Africa: Women in *Xala.*" *Jump Cut* 27:27–31.

214   *References*

———. 1984. *The Cinema of Ousmane Sembene: A Pioneer of African Film*. Westport, Conn.: Greenwood.

———. 1988. *Twenty-five Black African Filmmakers*. Westport, Conn.: Greenwood.

Phillips, Caryl. 1991. *Cambridge*. New York: Vintage Books.

———. 1993. *Crossing the River*. New York: Vintage Books.

———. 1995. Interview by Pico Iyer, together with readings from *Crossing the River*. VHS. Directed by Dan Griggs. Lannan Literary Video Series. Los Angeles: Lannan Foundation.

———. 1997. *The Nature of Blood*. New York: Knopf.

———. 1999. *The European Tribe*. New York: Vintage Books.

———. 2000. *The Atlantic Sound*. New York: Vintage Books.

———. 2002. *A New World Order: Essays*. New York: Vintage Books.

Pinckney, Darryl. 2002. *Out There: Mavericks of Black Literature*. New York: Basic Civitas.

Polsgrove, Carol. 2009. *Ending British Rule in Africa: Writers in a Common Cause*. Manchester: Manchester University Press.

Prashad, Vijay. 2007. *The Darker Nations: A People's History of the Third World*. New York: New Press.

Pyramid Research. 2010. *The Impact of Mobile Services in Nigeria: How Mobile Technologies Are Transforming Economic and Social Activities*. March 16. Abuja: Nigerian Communications Commission. http://www.pyramidresearch.com/documents/ IMPACTofMobileServicesInNIGERIA.pdf, accessed February 15, 2011.

Ramazani, Jahan. 2006. "Modernist Bricolage, Postcolonial Hybridity." *Modernism/ Modernity* 13 (3): 445–463.

Ranger, Terence. 1983. "The Invention of Tradition in Colonial Africa." In *The Invention of Tradition*, ed. Terence Ranger and Eric Hobsbawm, 211–262. Cambridge: Cambridge University Press.

Ray, Robert. 2001. *How a Film Theory Got Lost and Other Mysteries in Cultural Studies*. Bloomington: Indiana University Press.

Renov, Michael. 1993. Introduction to *Theorizing Documentary*. New York: Routledge.

Retamar, Roberto Fernández. 1989. "Caliban: Notes toward a Discussion of Culture in Our America." Translated by Lynn Garafola, David Arthur McMurray, and Roberto Márquez. In *Caliban and Other Essays*, translated by Edward Baker, 3–45. Minneapolis: University of Minnesota Press.

Rice, Andrew. 2009. "Mission from Africa." *New York Times*, April 8, 2009. http://www .nytimes.com/2009/04/12/magazine/12churches-t.html?ref=magazine (accessed April 14, 2009).

Robbins, Bruce. 1993. *Secular Vocations: Intellectuals, Professionalism and Culture*. London: Verso.

———. 1999. *Feeling Global: Internationalism in Distress*. New York: New York University Press.

Rosengarten, Frank. 2008. *Urbane Revolutionary: C. L. R. James and the Struggle for a New Society*. Jackson: University Press of Mississippi.

Ross, Robert. 1987. "Editor's Notes." *Antipodes* 1 (1): 2.

Rouch, Jean. 2003. *Ciné-ethnography*. Translated and edited by Steven Feld. Minneapolis: University of Minnesota Press.

Roy, Arundhati. 1998. *The God of Small Things*. New York: Harper Perennial.

———. 1999. *The Cost of Living*. New York: Modern Library.

———. 2001. *Power Politics*. Cambridge, Mass.: South End Press.

———. 2003. *War Talk*. Cambridge, Mass.: South End Press.

———. 2004a. *The Checkbook and the Cruise Missile: Conversations with Arundhati Roy*. Edited by David Barsamian. Cambridge, Mass.: South End Press.

———. 2004b. *An Ordinary Person's Guide to Empire*. Cambridge, Mass.: South End Press.

———. 2004c. *Public Power in the Age of Empire*. New York: Seven Stories Press.

———. 2008. "Success Devastated My Life. It Changed All the Equations." Interview by Simona Chaudhary. *Tehelka* 5 (9). http://www.telheka.com/story_main38.asp?filename=hub080308success_devastated.asp (accessed January 31, 2011).

Rushdie, Salman. 1991a. "Commonwealth Literature Does Not Exist." In *Imaginary Homelands: Essays and Criticism, 1981–1991*, 61–70. London: Granta Books.

———. 1991b. "Is Nothing Sacred?" In *Imaginary Homelands: Essays and Criticism, 1981–1991*, 415–429. London: Granta Books.

———. 2002. *Step Across This Line: Collected Nonfiction, 1992–2002*. New York: Random House.

Said, Edward W. 1983. *The World, the Text, and the Critic*. Cambridge, Mass.: Harvard University Press.

———. 1990. "Third World Intellectuals and Metropolitan Culture." *Raritan* 11 (3): 27–50.

———. 2000. *Reflections on Exile and Other Essays*. Cambridge, Mass.: Harvard University Press.

———. 2004. *Humanism and Democratic Criticism*. New York: Columbia University Press.

Sekoni, Ropo. 1994. "Yoruba Market Dynamics and the Aesthetics of Negotiation in Female Precolonial Narrative Tradition." *Research in African Literatures* 25 (3): 33–45.

Sembene, Ousmane. 1970. *God's Bits of Wood*. Translated by Francis Price. Garden City, NY: Anchor.

———. 1976. *Xala*. Translated by Clive Wake. Westport, Conn.: Lawrence Hill.

———. 2008. "Interview with Ousmane Sembène." By Michael Dembrow and Klaus Troller. In *Ousmane Sembène: Interviews*, ed. Annett Busch and Max Annas, 63–71. Jackson: University Press of Mississippi.

Shields, Aaron, and Chris Joslin. 1999. "Church Signs Found between Ibadan and Abeokuta, Nigeria." http://www.uni.edu/gai/Nigeria/Background/Church_signs.htm (accessed November 6, 2006).

Sim, Stuart. 1986. "Lyotard and the Politics of Antifoundationalism." *Radical Philosophy* 44:8–13.

Sircar, Ajanta. 1992. "Production of Authenticity: The Indo-Anglian Critical Tradition." *Economic and Political Weekly* 27 (36): 1,921–1,926.

Sklair, Leslie. 1991. *A Sociology of the Global System*. Baltimore: Johns Hopkins University Press.

Slaughter, Joseph. 2007. *Human Rights, Inc.* New York: Fordham University Press.

Solanas, Fernando, and Octavio Getino. 1976. "Towards a Third Cinema." In *Movies and Method*, ed. Bill Nichols, 44–64. Los Angeles: University of California Press.

Soyinka, Wole. 1976. *Myth, Literature, and the African World*. Cambridge: Cambridge University Press.

———. 2006. *You Must Set Forth at Dawn: A Memoir*. New York: Random House.

Spillers, Hortense J. 2003. *Black, White, and in Color: Essays in American Literature and Culture.* Chicago: University of Chicago Press.

Spivak, Gayatri Chakravorty. 1990. *The Postcolonial Critic: Dialogues, Strategies, Interviews.* Edited by Sara Harasym. New York: Routledge.

———. 2004. *Death of a Discipline.* New York: Columbia University Press.

Stam, Robert. 2004. "Beyond Third Cinema." In *Rethinking Third Cinema,* ed. Anthony Guneratne and Wimal Dissanayake, 31–48. New York: Routledge.

Stoneman, Rod. 1996. "South/South Axis: For a Cinema Built by, with and for Africans." In *African Experiences of Cinema,* ed. Imruh Bakari and Mbye Cham, 175–180. London: British Film Institute.

Tarbuck, Kenneth, ed. 1972. *"The Accumulation of Capital—An Anti-critique,"* by Rosa Luxemburg; *"Imperialism and the Accumulation of Capital,"* by Nikolai Bukharin. New York: Monthly Review Press.

Tayler, Christopher. 2008. "Change and Loss." *Guardian,* June 21, 2008. http://books .guardian.co.uk/review/story/0,,2286727,00.html (accessed June 27, 2008).

Taylor, Lucien. 1998. "Créolité Bites: A Conversation with Patrick Chamoiseau, Raphaël Confiant, and Jean Bernabé." *Transition: An International Review,* no. 74:124–160.

Todorov, Tzvetan. 1990. *Genres in Discourse.* Translated by Catherine Porter. Cambridge: Cambridge University Press.

Tryon, Chuck. 2009. *Reinventing Cinema.* New Brunswick, N.J.: Rutgers University Press.

Tucker, Robert C. 1978. *The Marx-Engels Reader.* New York: W. W. Norton.

Turvey, Gerry. 1985. *"Xala* and the Curse of Neocolonialism: Reflections on a Realist Project." *Screen* 26:75–87.

Ukadike, Nwachukwu Frank. 1994. *Black African Cinema.* London: University of California Press.

———. 2002. *Questioning African Cinema: Interviews with Filmmakers.* Minneapolis: University of Minnesota Press.

———. 2004. "Video Booms in Anglophone Africa." In *Rethinking Third Cinema,* ed. Anthony Guneratne and Wimal Dissanayake, 126–143. New York: Routledge.

UNESCO Institute for Statistics. 2010. "Nollywood Rivals Bollywood in Film/Video Production." Analysis of the UIS International Survey on Feature Film Statistics. http://www.uis.unesco.org/ev.php?ID=7651_201&ID2=DO_TOPIC (accessed August 13, 2010).

Vail, Leroy, and Landeg White. 1991. *Power and the Praise Poem.* Charlottesville: University Press of Virginia; London: James Curry.

Vieyra, Paulin Soumanou. 1987. "Five Major Films by Sembene Ousmane." In *Film and Politics in the Third World,* ed. John H. Downing, 31–39. New York: Praeger.

Walcott, Derek. 1998. *What the Twilight Says: Essays.* New York: Farrar, Straus & Giroux.

Wallerstein, Immanuel. 2003. *The Decline of American Power.* New York: New Press.

Waterman, Christopher. 1990. *Juju: A Social History and Ethnography of an African Popular Music.* Chicago: University of Chicago Press.

Willemen, Paul, and Jim Pines, eds. 1989. *Questions of Third Cinema.* London: British Film Institute.

Williams, Raymond. 2003. *Television: Technology and Cultural Form.* London: Routledge.

Wiredu, Kwasi. 2000. "Our Problem of Knowledge: Brief Reflections on Knowledge and Development in Africa." In *African Philosophy as Cultural Inquiry,* ed. Ivan Karp and D. A. Masolo, 181–186. Bloomington: Indiana University Press.

Wright, Richard. 1956. *The Color Curtain: A Report on the Bandung Conference.* Cleveland: World Publishing.

Yai, Olabiyi Babalola. 1994. "In Praise of Metonymy: The Concepts of 'Tradition' and 'Creativity' in the Transmission of Yoruba Artistry over Time and Space." In *The Yoruba Artist: New Theoretical Perspectives on African Art,* ed. Rowland Abiodun, Henry J. Drewal, and John Pemberton, 107–115. Washington, D.C.: Smithsonian Institution Press.

Young, Robert. 2000. *Postcolonialism: A Historical Introduction.* Malden, Mass.: Blackwell.

Zabus, Chantal. 2008. "Of Female Husbands and Boarding School Girls: Gender Bending in Unomah Azuah's Fiction." *Research in African Literatures* 39 (2): 93–107.

Žižek, Slavoj. 2004. "The Ongoing "Soft Revolution." *Critical Inquiry* 30 (2): 292–323.

Filmography (by director)

Adepoju, Kareem. 2002. *Ekun Oko Oke* [The Indomitable Tiger]. In Yoruba. Yem-Kem Ventures. Nigeria. VCD. Approx. 120 mins. Color.

Animashaun, Debbie. 1998. *Majemu Ikoko* [Secret Covenant]. In Yoruba with English subtitles. His Glory Drama Ministries. Nigeria. PAL. 92 mins. Color.

Aromire, Muyideen. 1986. *Ekun* [Tiger]. Alade Productions. Nigeria. VHS. 86 mins. Color.

Bakupa-Kanyinda, Balufu. 2003. *Afro@Digital*. In English, French, Jula, and Yoruba with English subtitles. California Newsreel and Akangbe Productions. Congo and France. VHS and DVD. 53 mins. Color.

Bekolo, Jean-Pierre. 1992. *Quartier Mozart*. In French. Kola Case Productions. Cameroon. VHS with English subtitles and 16mm. 80 mins. Color.

———. 1996. *Le Complot d'Aristote* [Aristotle's Plot]. JBA Production and British Film Institute. France and Zimbabwe. 35mm. 70 mins. Color.

———. 2005. *Les Saignantes* [The Bloodettes]. Quartier Mozart Films and é4 Television. France and Cameroon. Digital betacam. 92 mins. Color.

Boughedir, Férid. 1983. *Camera d'Afrique*. In French with English subtitles and some narration in English. Idera Films. Canada and Tunisia. 35mm. 99 mins. Color.

Cissé, Souleymane. 1987. *Yeelen*. In Bambara with English subtitles. Atriascop Paris and Les Filmes Cissé. Mali. 35mm. 105 mins. Color.

Egoyan, Atom. 1994. *Exotica*. Miramax Home Entertainment. 35mm. 104 mins. Color.

Frears, Stephen. 2003. *Dirty Pretty Things*. Miramax Home Entertainment. 35mm. 97 mins. Color.

Gomes, Flora. 1988. *Mortu Nega* [Those Whom Death Refused]. In Portuguese Criolo with English subtitles. Fado Films. Guinea-Bissau. 35mm and VHS. 93 mins. Color.

———. 1992. *Udju Azul di Yonta* [The Blue Eyes of Yonta]. In Portuguese Criolo with English subtitles. Fado Films and Arco Iris. Guinea-Bissau. VHS and 35mm. 90 mins. Color.

———. 2002. *Nha Fala* [My Voice]. Creole dialogue, with optional French, English, Spanish, Italian, or Portuguese subtitles. Les Filmes de Mai and Samsa Films. DVD. 89 mins. Color.

Kalatozov, Mikhail. 1996. *I Am Cuba*. Dialogue in Spanish, Russian, and English with subtitles in English. Mosfilms, ICAC, and Milestones Film and Video. VHS and 35mm. 141 mins. B/w.

Kelani, Tunde. 1993–1995. *Ti Oluwa Nile* [The Earth Belongs to the Lord]. 3 parts. In Yoruba with English subtitles. Mainframe Productions. Nigeria. VHS and VCD. Color.

———. 1994. *Ayo Ni Mo Fe* [Ayo Is My Choice]. 2 parts. In Yoruba with English subtitles. Mainframe Productions. Nigeria. VHS and VCD. Approx. 180 mins. Color.

———. 1995. *Koseegbe* [The Reformer's Dilemma]. In Yoruba with English subtitles. Mainframe Productions. Nigeria. VHS and VCD. 96 mins. Color.

———. 1997. *O Le Ku* [Fearful Incidents]. 2 parts. In Yoruba with English subtitles. Mainframe Productions. Nigeria. VHS and VCD. Approx. 180 mins. Color.

———. 1999. *Saworoide* [Brass Bells]. In Yoruba with English subtitles. Mainframe Productions. Nigeria. VHS and VCD. 95 mins. Color.

———. 2001. *Thunderbolt: Magun.* In English, Yoruba, and Igbo with occasional subtitles. California Newsreel. Nigeria and the United States. VHS. 110 mins. Color.

———. 2002. *Agogo Eewo* [The Sacred Gong]. In Yoruba with English subtitles. Mainframe Productions. Nigeria. VHS. 100 mins. Color.

———. 2004. *Campus Queen.* In English. Mainframe Productions. Nigeria. VHS and VCD. 96 mins. Color.

Lee, Spike. 1989. *Do the Right Thing.* In English. 40 Acres and a Mule Filmworks. United States. 35mm. 120 mins. Color.

Mambèty, Djibril Diop. 1973. *Touki Bouki.* In French with English subtitles. Cinegrit and Studio Kankourama. Senegal. 35mm. 85 mins. Color.

Nacro, Fanta Régina. 2004. *La Nuit de la Vérité* [The Night of Truth]. In French, Moré, and Dioula with English subtitles. Global Film Initiative. France and Burkina Faso. DVD and 35mm. 100 mins. Color.

Ngangura, Mweze, and Benoît Lamy. 1987. *La Vie Est Belle* [Life Is Rosy]. Congo and Belgium. 85 mins. 35mm. Color.

Nnebue, Kenneth. 1992. *Living in Bondage.* 2 parts. In English and Igbo with English subtitles. NEK Video Link. Nigeria. VHS. Approx. 4 hrs. Color.

Ogidan, Tade. 1996. *Owo Blow.* 2 parts. In Yoruba with English subtitles. First Call Production & Support. Nigeria. PAL. Approx. 4 hrs. Color.

Okereke, Afam. 2003. *GSM Wahala.* In English and Pidgin. Sunny Collins Production. Nigeria. PAL. Approx. 110 mins. Color.

Owoh, Nkem, and Zeb Ejiro. 1995. *Ikuku* [The Hurricane]. 2 parts. In Igbo with English subtitles. Andy Best Productions. Nigeria. VCD. Approx. 4 hrs. Color.

Paul, Wemimo Olu. 2002. *Kodun, Kopo, Kope* [K.K.K.]. 2 parts. In Yoruba with English subtitles. Wemimo Films and Bonag Industries. Nigeria. VCD. Approx. 3 hrs. Color.

Peck, Raoul. 2005. *Sometimes in April.* In English and Kinyarwanda with French or Spanish subtitles. HBO Films and Velvet Film Productions, in association with Yolo Films. United States. DVD. 140 mins. Color.

Ramaka, Jo Gaï. 2002. *Karmen Gei.* In Wolof and French with English subtitles. California Newsreel, Arté France Cinéma, and Euripide Productions. Senegal and France. 35mm and DVD. 83 mins. Color.

———. 2005. *And What if Latif Were Right?/Et si Latif Avait Raison?* In French and English, with English and French subtitles. L'Observatoire Audiovisuel sur les Libertés. Senegal. 35mm and DVD. 120 mins. Color.

Rouch, Jean. 1957. *Jaguar.* In French with English subtitles. Films de la Pléiade. France. 16mm. 92 mins. Color.

Saleh-Haroun, Mahamet. 1999. *Bye-Bye Africa.* In French and Arabic with English subtitles. California Newsreel, Productions de la Lanterne, and Télé-Tchad. Chad and France. VHS. 86 mins. Color.

Sauper, Hubert. 2005. *Darwin's Nightmare*. In English. Mille et Une Productions and Coop 99. Tanzania, Austria, and France. 35mm. 107 mins. Color.

Sembene, Ousmane. 1963. *Borom Sarret* [The Wagoner]. In French and Wolof with English subtitles. Films Doomireew and New Yorker Films. Senegal. 35mm and VHS. 20 mins. B/w.

———. 1965. *La Noir de . . .* [Black Girl]. In Wolof and French with English subtitles. Films Doomireew and New Yorker Films. Senegal. 35mm and VHS. 80 mins. B/w.

———. 1971. *Emitaï* [The Thunder God]. In Dioula and French with English subtitles. Films Doomireew and New Yorker Films. Senegal. 35mm and VHS. 96 mins. Color.

———. 1975. *Xala*. In French and Wolof with English subtitles. Films Doomireew and New Yorker Home Video. Senegal. 35mm and DVD. 123 mins. Color.

———. 1977. *Ceddo*. In Wolof and French with English subtitles. Films Doomireew and New Yorker Films. Senegal. 35mm and VHS. 112 mins. Color.

———. 1988. *Camp de Thiaroye*. In French with English subtitles. Films Doomireew, SATPEC, and New Yorker Films. Senegal, Tunisia, and Algeria. 35mm and VHS. 152 mins. Color.

———. 1993. *Guelwaar*. In Wolof and French with English subtitles. Films Doomireew, Channel IV, and New Yorker Films. Senegal. 35mm. 115 mins. Color.

———. 2000. *Faat Kine*. In Wolof and French with English subtitles. Films Doomireew and New Yorker Films. Senegal. 35mm. 110 mins. Color.

———. 2004. *Mooladé*. In Moré with English subtitles. Ciné-Sud Promotion, Films Doomireew, and Les Filmes Terre Africaine. Burkina Faso. 35mm. 124 mins. Color.

Sissako, Abderrahmane. 1999. *La Vie sur Terre*. In French with English subtitles. Haute et Court and La Sept Arte. Mauritania, Mali, and France. 35mm. 61 mins. Color.

———. 2006. *Bamako*. French and Bambara with optional English subtitles. Louverture Films, ARTE France, and New Yorker Video. Senegal and France. 35mm and DVD. 117 mins. Color.

Wellman, William A. 1931. *The Public Enemy*. Turner Entertainment and UA Home Video. United States. VHS. 83 mins. B/w.

Index

Abani, Chris, 18
Abeokuta, 101, 194n18
Abrahams, Peter, 189n8
Achebe, Chinua, 17, 18, 19, 44, 187n22
Adeboye, Pastor Enoch, 92, 194n19
Adejumo, Moses Olaiya (Baba Sala), 85
Adepoju, Alhaji Kareem, 8, 87
Adesanya, Chief Abraham, 8
Adorno, Theodor W., 51, 104, 190n19, 192n17
Aeschylus, 49
Africa, 30, 32, 108, 129, 149, 158, 183; absence of nations in precolonial, 60; anti-colonial consciousness in, 36; anti-colonial struggle in, 45; armed struggle in postwar, 54; capital flow available to, 43; China as "imperial" force in, 180; C. L. R. James's encounter with, 32; as a cultural monolith, 195n23; decolonizing societies of, 53; European colonies in, 26; exhibition of foreign films in, 116; films from, 59; folklorists in contemporary, 60; implications of digital technology in, 197n34; implications of modernity in postcolonial, 75; institutions in postcolonial, 196n26; migration to the West from, 133; nationless map of, 60, 70; "natural," 124; notion of cultural inferiority which colonialism attached to, 55; place of, in the artistic heritage of the world, 130; political and governmental leaders from, 42; politics of film financing in, 61; postcolonial societies of, 162; postcolonial sovereignties in, 105; publishing climate in, 68; role of Christianity in the colonization of, 142; V. S. Naipaul's fiction about, 26; yearnings of broad population in, 58
African cinema, xii, xiv, 11, 21, 58, 76, 108, 111–112, 114, 121, 126–128, 131; accessibility of, 122; anti-colonial history of, 74; category of, 111, 120, 131; charters associated with the emergence of, 122; criticism of, 73, 74, 75, 122; critics of, 73; disalienated, 119; diversity of, 122; early, 131; film-

making styles in, 120; first two generations of, 129; Francophone, 107; historical basis for, 73; as an institutional form, 115; institutionalization of, 131; new, 187n21; perspective of the "I" in, 112; political traditions in, 110; preoccupations of, 109; revolutionary objectives of, 51; scholars of, 57; as system of cultural difference, 122; technologically savvy, 105; travails of, 110; unified discourses in, 75, 120, 192n14
Afro@Digital (Bakupa-Kanyinda), 197n34
Agogo Eewo (Kelani), 106, 107
Ahmad, Aijaz, 25, 154, 164, 167, 199n6, 200n12
AIDS (Acquired Immune Deficiency Syndrome), 103–104, 167, 197nn31,34; global discourse of, 82, 90
Ajuwon, Bade, 195n25
Akudinobi, Jude G., 124
Alabi-Hundeyin, Tunde, 81
Althusser, Louis, 74
American Civilization (James), 31, 34, 44, 48, 50, 134, 144, 188; idea of integration in, 31; jazz musician and audience in, 55; nature of art and representation in, 54; "simplicity" of, 31
Amin, Samir, 176, 177
Anderson, Benedict, 110
Andrade, Susan, 192n16
Andrade-Watkins, Claire, 61
Anikulapo-Kuti, Fela, 17
Appiah, Kwame A., 46, 189n11
Aristotelianism, 116, 129
Aristotle, 114
Aristotle's Plot (Bekolo), 2, 27, 29, 108–123, 125; aesthetic thesis in, 110; African cinema as a category in, 120; argument of, 126; characters of, 113; as a commissioned work, 111, 122, 125; complexities of metropolitan location in, 123; conceptual ground of, 120; on conceptual middle ground, 29; critique of *The Poetics* in, 188n2; deployment of mimesis in, 49; ge-

neric character of, 126; issues of conceptual filmmaking decisive in, 130; name of character in, 197n2; narrative strands in, 112; negotiated coexistence of antagonists in, 181; release of, 128; themes in, 128; urban gangsters and self-absorbed cineaste in, 14; voice of Donny Elwood in, 197n5; voice-over narration in, 22, 132. *See also* Bekolo, Jean-Pierre

Armes, Roy, 21

Arrighi, Giovanni, 43

Atlantic Sound, The (Phillips), 3, 24, 29, 134, 136, 137, 148, 149–150, 155, 157; compared with "national-racial mode," 138, 151; generic instability in, 133, 138–139, 153–154. *See also* Phillips, Caryl

Aye (Hubert Ogunde), 193n5

Ayo Ni Mo Fe (Kelani), 86

Azikiwe, Nnamdi, 38

babalawo, 83, 86, 87, 90, 92–94, 96, 97

Babalola, Adeboye, 195n25

Baldwin, James, 135, 137

Balibar, Etienne, 145

Bamako (Sissako), 110, 130, 175

Bamako Appeal, the, 201n17

Bandung, 42, 52, 172, 189n8

Barber, Karin, 100–101, 106, 107, 193n5, 195n25

Barnes, Sandra, 8, 104

Bascom, William, 195n23

Bates, Robert, 6

Bekolo, Jean-Pierre, xiii, 2, 11, 22, 24, 27, 29, 108–123, 125–132, 178, 197nn1,2; as actor in *Aristotle's Plot,* 112; aesthetic populism of, in *Quartier Mozart,* 113; awareness of "Hollywood formula," 116, 128, 129; characterization of Sembene, 74; and conceptual filmmaking, 119, 129–132; conceptual frame of mind of, 110; corrective to oppositional filmmaking and apolitical cinema, 115, 120; critique of *The Poetics* in *Aristotle's Plot* by, 188n2; deployment of mimesis in *Aristotle's Plot,* 49; distinct diction of, 112; fascination with work of Spike Lee, 198n5; idea of filmmaking, 128; limitations of aesthetic choices, 121; Paris location of, 132, 179; parodies in *Aristotle's Plot,* 130; polemicism of, 126; postmodernist bluff of, 113; questioning of mimesis by, 115–116, 120; reflexive style

of, 2, 74; relationship with BFI, 125–126; success with *Quartier Mozart,* 126; use of indigenous culture by, 127; work as documentary, 121, 122

Benjamin, Walter, 28, 51

Berger, John, 199n6

Bertolucci, Bernardo, 111

Beyala, Calixthe, 19, 50

Beyond a Boundary (James), 34, 37, 40, 50; generic openness in, 50; hero and the crowd in, 55; nature of art and representation in, 54

BFI (British Film Institute), 122, 124–126

Bhabha, Homi K., 44, 123,

Black Girl (Sembene), 198n10

Black Jacobins, The (James), 36, 37, 39

Black Man's Burden, The (Basil Davidson), 8

Blair, Tony, 16

Boal, Augusto, 49, 190n15

Boggs, Grace Lee, 40

Bohannan, Paul, 6, 7, 185n5

Bollywood, 81

Bond, Horace Mann, 43

Borom Sarret (Sembene), 63

Bose, Purnima, 200n9

Boughedir, Férid, 60, 61

Bougues, Anthony, 37

Brecht, Bertolt, 49, 51, 174, 190n15

Brennan, Timothy, 26, 31, 34, 44–45, 50, 154, 188n28, 189n11, 190n15, 200n16

Brouillette, Sarah, 25–26

Buhle, Paul, 32

Burton, Julianne, 59–60, 73

Bush, George, 16

Bye-Bye Africa (Mahamet Saleh-Haroun), 130

Cabral, Amílcar, 18, 32, 71, 75, 178, 183

Calhoun, Craig, 145–146, 151, 154, 181, 189n11

Cambridge (Phillips), 141–142

Camera d'Afrique (Férid Boughedir), 60

Camp du Thiaroye (Sembene), 76, 125, 129–130

Campus Queen (Kelani), 111

Casanova, Pascale, 13, 25, 26, 153, 187n17

Castro, Fidel, 42, 188n1, 190n16

ceddo, 74, 77

Ceddo (Sembene), 60, 61, 131, 192n16

celluloid, film format, xxiv, 2, 21–22, 83–85, 119, 187n23, 194n11, 198n7

Césaire, Aimé, xiv, 34, 56, 74, 130, 159

Chamoiseau, Patrick, 19

Chandra, Vikram, 157

Chaplin, Charlie, 50, 53, 71
Chatterjee, Upamanyu, 199n2
Chaudhary, Amit, 157
Cheah, Pheng, 44, 146, 175, 181
Checkbook and the Cruise Missile, The (Roy), 157, 158
Cheney-Coker, Syl, 19, 50
Chériaa, Tahar, 192n15
Chomsky, Noam, 11, 161
Chow, Rey, 182
Cissé, Souleymane, 52, 60
Clark, Arthur, 33, 48
clientelism, 9, 94, 101, 103
Clifford, James, 44, 146, 189n12, 199n7
C. L. R. James on the "Negro Question" (James), 31
Coetzee, J. M., 135, 153, 198n3
Color Curtain, The (Richard Wright), 189n8
commodification, xiv, 4, 14, 15, 19, 25–28, 51, 109, 157, 177, 182, 188n2; international media and, 166; as neoliberal's instrument, 157–158, 169, 170, 175, 180; VHS tapes as, 131; *Xala* and, 65–66
conceptual filmmaking, 126, 129–132, 176
cosmopolitanism, xiv, 18, 25, 30, 41, 44–46, 50–51, 106, 133, 134, 145–146, 153, 156, 159, 169, 175, 180–181, 189n11; affiliations to neoliberalism, 150–152, 157; relationship to cultural production, 179; "Third World," 26
Cost of Living, The (Roy), 157, 158, 160–161, 199n5
Crossing the River (Phillips), 139, 141, 142; Booker prize shortlist of, 157

Dakar, 33, 191n1, 201n17
Dar es Salaam, 33
Darwin's Nightmare (Hubert Sauper), 176
Davidson, Basil, 8, 178
Davies, Ioan, 32
de Tocqueville, Alexis, 34, 48
decolonization, xi, xii, 2, 3–6, 9, 11, 14, 25, 26, 28, 38, 43, 76, 159, 179–180, 181; aesthetics of, 14, 17–19, 109, 129, 131, 169–170, 178; as anti-imperialism, 177; Bandung Conference and, 42; C. L. R. James and, 55; filmmaking practices and, 52; Sembene and, 76–77; *Xala* and, 57–58
Deleuze, Gilles, 12
Derrida, Jacques, 196n26
Desai, Anita, 136, 157
Desai, Gaurav, 187n21

Desai, Kiran, 157
Devi, Mahasweta, 42, 162, 165
Dhondy, Farrukh, 32, 55, 190n18
Diawara, Manthia, 7, 8, 20, 99, 186n7; analysis of *yere don* by, 101–102, 196n27
Diop, Cherif Oumar, 68
Dirty Pretty Things (Stephen Frears), 186n13
Disgrace (J. M. Coetzee), 198n3
Dissanayake, Wimal, 190n21
Do The Right Thing (Spike Lee), 190n15
Dostoyevsky, Fyodor, 34
Du Bois, W. E. B., xiv, 35, 36, 38, 42, 137, 152, 189n9
Dunayevskaya, Raya, 40

Edwards, Brent Hayes, 191nn6,8
Efunsetan Aniwura (Kelani), 194n15
Egoyan, Atom, 27
Ejiro, Zeb, 81, 193n8
Ekeh, Peter, 196n29
Ekun (Muyideen Aromire), 84
Ekun Oko Oke (Kareem Adepoju), 7–8, 87
Ekwuazi, Hyginus, 193–194n8
El Saadawi, Nawal, 17, 26
Ellison, Ralph, 137, 154
Elwood, Donny, 112, 113, 198n5
Emecheta, Buchi, 19, 187n22
Emigrants, The (Lamming), 140
Emitaï (Sembene), 60, 77, 131
Empire (Michael Hardt and Antonio Negri), 176–177, 200n16
English: education, 36; language, 12, 28, 82, 112, 117, 157, 188n29; and literary studies, 13, 17; Nollywood and, 82–83, 86–87, 107, 193n8
English, James, 24, 26, 168, 199n1, 200n11
Englishness, 16, 140
Equiano, Olaudah, 142
Eshun, Kodwo, 149
ethnonationalism, 11, 146, 151, 181; Hindutva as, 160, 164
European Tribe, The (Phillips), 133, 134, 135–136, 137, 154
exile, 19, 24, 26, 50, 55, 133, 135, 187n26, 198n1; as displaced by cosmopolitanism, 181; in relation to expatriation, 153–154, 179
Exotica (Atom Egoyan), 27
expatriation, xiv, 4, 14, 15, 19, 24–28, 50–51, 55–56, 153, 175, 181; African, 196n27; in relation to exile, 153–154

Faat Kine (Sembene), 76, 98, 129
Fabian, Johannes, 101, 102, 195nn23,24
Facing Reality collective, 180
Faleti, Adebayo, 83
Fanon, Frantz, 11, 32, 45, 47, 57, 74
Farred, Grant, 45
FEPACI (Fédération Panafricaine des Ciné-
astes), 51, 122
Ferguson, James, 5, 200n14, 201n2
FESPACO (Festival Panafricain du Cinéma et
de la Télévision de Ouagadougou), 113,
116, 131
Folsom, Ed, xiv
Frears, Stephen, 111
French, language, 66, 70, 112, 117
French Bureau of Cinema, 59, 61
French Ministry of Foreign and European Af-
fairs, 198n8
Frenchness, 64
Fuentes, Carlos, 134
Future in the Present, The (James), 31

Gabriel, Teshome, 59, 60, 72, 73, 191n4
Gadjigo, Samba, 191n1
García Márquez, Gabriel, 197n30
Garuba, Harry, 18
Gerima, Haile, 129
gewel, 63
Ghosh, Amitav, 157, 199n2
Gikandi, Simon, 4–5, 169–170, 177, 179
Gilroy, Paul, 135, 152, 154, 155
globalization, xii, 3, 11, 28, 41, 43, 45, 51, 75,
99, 102, 109, 129, 156, 158–160, 167, 169,
178, 182; aesthetic changes and, xii, xiii, 4,
12, 13–16, 52, 170, 178, 187n19; contents
of, 9, 179; decolonization and, xi–xii, 3, 11,
25, 170, 178; discourses of, 4–6, 12, 173,
176–177; ethnonationalism and, 167, 171;
market and, 6–9, 179; postcoloniality and,
4, 9, 45, 169, 179; technology and, 22–24
God of Small Things, The (Roy), 11, 157, 167,
168, 169, 200n10
Godard, Jean-Luc, 59, 111, 122
God's Bits of Wood (Sembene), 52
Gomes, Flora, 52, 129, 130, 183
Gomes, Patrick I., 188n2
Gomis, Alan, 109
Gott, Richard, 185n3, 190n22
Gowon, General Yakubu, 194n17
Grimshaw, Anna, 31, 32, 54–55
griot, 63, 72, 100, 101, 196n27

Ground Beneath Her Feet, The (Rushdie),
198n3
GSM Wahala (Afam Okereke), 105, 197n33
Guattari, Félix, 12
Guéhenno, Jean-Marie, 9–10, 186nn10,11,14
Guelwaar (Sembene), 68, 76, 77, 198n10
Guevara, Ernesto "Che," 185n3
Gugler, Josef, 68
Guneratne, Anthony, 190n21
Gunesekera, Romesh, 199n2
Gunn, Giles, 186n15
Guyer, Jane, 6–7, 195n23, 197n3

Habermas, Jürgen, 145–146, 151
Hall, Stuart, 15–16, 18, 35, 55, 56, 187n19,
200n7
Hanhardt, John, 21
Hardt, Michael, 176–177, 200n16
Harrow, Kenneth W., xiii, 61, 73–76, 77,
187n21, 191nn1,6, 192nn14,16
Hartman, Saidiya, 149, 150, 159
Harvey, David, 5, 164, 186nn10,11, 189n11
Haynes, Jonathan, 125, 192n1, 198n8
Heath, Stephen, 73
Hindutva, 160, 162, 163, 164–165, 167, 168,
173, 200n9
Hitchcock, Peter, 17
Hollywood, 21, 37, 45, 49, 59, 81, 113, 127,
187n6, 192n1, 198n4; as formula, 115–116,
117, 121, 122, 123, 126; political values of,
144, 190n15
Home in the World, At (Brennan), 26, 34,
189n11
Hondo, Med, 74, 124, 129
Horkheimer, Max, 190n19
Huggan, Graham, 25, 199n2
Hyden, Goran, 185n5

Ifa, divination system, 85, 91, 106
Igbo: actors, 87, 193n8; identity, 89, 94, 95, 96,
97, 193n8; language, 97, 193n8, 194n8
Igwe, Amaka, 81
Ikuku (The Hurricane I & II, dirs. Nkem Owoh
& Zeb Ejiro), 193n8
In-Between Life of Vikram Lall, The (M. G.
Vassanji), 25
India, 43, 158, 159–162, 170, 173, 174–175,
179, 180, 189n10, 199n2; authors from,
157, 164, 167–168; diaspora of, 168, 200n9;
fascism in, 164, 165, 171; films from, 81;
V. S. Naipaul's nonfiction about, 26; neo-

liberalism and, 159, 163, 164, 165, 167, 169, 172; nuclear bomb in, 158, 164, 165
Irele, Abiola, 185n4
Isola, Akinwumi, 86–87, 90
Isola, Haruna, 28, 188n29
Iyayi, Festus, 19, 50, 187n22
Iyengar, Srinivasa R. K., 157, 199n3
izibongo, 7, 99, 100, 195nn23,25

Jaguar (dir. Jean Rouch), 102, 191n7
Jamaica, 33, 106
James, C. L. R., xiii, 2, 4, 11, 14, 26, 28, 30; aesthetic/artistic interests of, 41, 44, 45, 48–50, 190n15; books by, 31, 40–41; break with Trotskyite Marxism, 36–37, 40, 47; on class and gender, 48, 58; compared with Phillips, 29, 44, 134, 144, 154, 155; compared with Roy, 158, 170, 172, 180; compared with Sembene, 28; cosmopolitanism in, 44–46, 50–51; critique of "bourgeois intellectualism," 33–34; critique of pan-Africanism by, 34–36, 38, 41, 46–50, 57, 189nn4,13; critique of state capitalism, 189n14; cultural background of, 55–56, decolonization and, 28, 29, 169; empiricism in, 32; genre in, 51, 170, 177, 180–181; idea of tricontinentalism in, 5, 41–44, 50–53, 156, 177; integration in, 30, 31, 33, 55; literary characterization of, 190n18; method in, 32, 53–55; personal "philosophy" of, 191n14; professional ambition as author, 44–45, 178; review of Marxist theory of revolution by, 39–40; on revolutionary leadership, 188n2, 190n16; role in party factions, 37; role in Sixth pan-African congress, 38–39, 172; scholarship on, 31–32, 191n26; style in, 34–35, 180; view on Pan African Congress (1945), 36, 38, 41
Jameson, Fredric, 22–24, 109, 185n4, 186n7, 187n25, 191n6
JanMohamed, Abdul, 10
Jeyifo, Biodun, 17–18, 51, 163

Kaboré, Gaston, 108
Kahin, George M., 189n8
Kalatozov, Mikhail, 52
Kelani, Tunde, xiii, 2, 4, 11, 29, 81, 82–83, 96, 182, 194n15; on "alternative technology," 85, 198n7; attitude toward Nollywood, 83, 84, 86, 87, 94, 97, 106, 107, 193n2; attitude toward Yoruba culture, 85, 86–87, 91, 92, 193n4, 194n16; collaboration with (Akinwumi) Isola, 86–87; commercialization in, 197n30; compared with Bekolo, 111, 120, 178; compared with Roy, 182; compared with Sembene, 58, 63, 89, 178; cultural agenda of, 87, 90, 93, 103; exhortation in, 104; features of work by, 83, 96, 106; manifestation of *oriki* in, 102, 194n20; pre-Nollywood work, 85; relationship with audience, 196n28; relationship with Yoruba actors and producers, 87, 194n15; style of soap opera used by, 85; work by, 86, 87
Kelman, James, 169
Kenya, 25, 38, 102
Kenyatta, Jomo, 38
Khomeini, Ayatollah, 192n16
King, Anthony, 187n19
K. K. K. (*Kodun, Kopo, Kope,* dir. Wemimo Olu Paul), 104
Koldsweat, Larry, 194n8
Kom, Ambroise, 19, 50
Koseegbe (Kelani), 86
Kumar, Amitava, 168, 200n10

La Vie Est Belle (prod. Mweze Ngangura), 108, 116
La Vie sur Terre (Abderrahmane Sissako), 130
Laclau, Ernesto, 156, 201n16
Ladebo, Ladi, 85, 194n10
Lagos, xi, 12, 84, 92, 101, 104, 197n32, 199n8
Lagosian, 103
Lahiri, Jhumpa, 168
Lamming, George, 48, 51, 135
Larkin, Brian, 23, 91, 102, 193n2
Laswell, Harold, 185n2
Lenin, Vladimir, 34, 40
Les Saignantes (Bekolo), 111, 119, 127, 130, 132
Lloyd, David, 10
Lonely Londoners (Selvon), 140
Lukacs, Georg, 14, 17
Lyons, Harriet, 60, 72

magun, 58, 63, 83, 87–91, 97, 103, 104; discourse of, 93–94; as an icon, 97
Maja-Pearce, Adewale, 19, 187n22
Majemu Ikoko (Debbie Animashaun), 92
makumbu, 7, 99, 100, 195n23
Malian immigrants, 102, 196n27
Mambèty, Djibril Diop, 60, 74, 108, 112, 121, 129, 132

Index   227

Mamdani, Mahmood, 185n5
marabout, 57, 62, 65, 77
market, 6–10, 20, 22, 27, 79, 82, 84, 94, 97,
    107, 116, 185n4; as marketplace, 6, 7, 99–
    103, 181; neoliberal, 83, 131, 180, 199n1
Martin, Michael T., 108, 120
Marx, 40, 60, 64
Marxism, 15, 32, 35, 45, 54, 73, 75; traditional,
    37; Trotskyist, 36, 37
Marxist theory of revolution, 38, 39, 54
McKeon, Michael, 14, 17
McLemee, Scott, 37, 53
McLuhan, Marshall, 185n2
Meagher, Kate, 186n9
mégotage, 1, 20, 22, 52. *See also* Sembene,
    Ousmane
Melas, Natalie, 14, 199n7
melodrama, 64, 82, 179
Melville, Herman, 48, 49, 53
Meyer, Birgit, 91
Miller, George, 111
mimesis, 2, 49, 109, 112, 113, 119, 126;
    Bekolo's interrogation of, 115–116, 120
mobile communication, 105
Mooladé (Sembene), 76, 77, 129
Moretti, Franco, 13, 17, 186n16, 187n17
Morrison, Toni, 137
Mortu Nega (Flora Gomes), 52
Mouffe, Chantal, 156
Moussa Sene, Absa, 24, 109, 129
Mowitt, John, 59, 60, 70, 71
Mukherjee, Bharati, 151
Mulvey, Laura, 60, 64, 67, 69–70, 72, 73,
    190n15, 191n4
Murphy, David, xiii, 79, 185n1, 192n12
Murray, Albert, 137

Naficy, Hamid, xiv, 27, 122–123
Naipaul, V. S., 26, 51, 135, 139, 190nn17,18,
    198n4
nationalism, 5–6, 11, 18, 24, 27, 44, 45, 76,
    138, 143, 145–146, 151, 159, 165, 176;
    anti-colonial, 17, 18, 26, 35, 75; black, 32,
    39, 149, 159; bourgeois, 17, 18, 75; cul-
    tural, 19
Nature of Blood (Phillips), 139, 152
N'Dour, Youssou, 131
Negri, Antonio, 176–177, 200n16
Négritude, 199n4
neoliberalism, 5, 8, 11, 29, 75, 137, 158, 179,
    186n10, 188n28; Ahmad's critique of, 167;

cultures of, 32; paradox of, 110, 131, 182;
    Roy's critique of, 2, 28, 157–158, 173
Neslé, Robert, 20
network society, xii, 5, 9–10, 156
New World Order, A (Phillips), 133, 135, 144,
    154, 155
Nfa-Abbenyi, Juliana, 187n21
Ngangura, Mweze, 108, 116
Nha Fala (Flora Gomes), 183
Nigeria, xi, 20, 21, 43, 46, 50, 60, 83, 88, 92,
    100, 103, 105, 111, 144, 146, 163, 187n22,
    189n10; cinema and video production in,
    23, 29, 81, 82, 84, 118, 182, 193n2, 197n35;
    ethnic relations in, 103, 193n8; structural
    adjustment in, xi, 83. *See also* Nollywood
Nixon, Rob, 188n27, 190n17
Nkrumah, Kwame, 5, 38, 40, 43, 47, 55, 149,
    188n2, 190n16
Nkrumah and the Ghana Revolution (James),
    31, 34, 38, 41, 45, 53, 55, 188n2
Nnebue, Kenneth, 81, 84, 193n8
Nollywood, 20, 21–24, 29, 81–83, 84, 85, 90,
    92, 94, 96, 98, 101–102, 106–107, 132, 182,
    187n25, 193n2
Notes on Dialectics (James), 31, 40, 53
Nwosu, Ngozi, 194n8
Nyerere, Julius, 34, 39, 43
Nzelu, Rita, 193n8

O Le Ku (Kelani), 86, 90
Obakan (prod. Monsuratu Omidina), 106
Obama, Barack, 191n25
Ogidan, Tade, 81
Oguibe, Olu, 198n9
Ogunde, Hubert, 84, 193n5, 195n22, 198n7
Okafor, Charles, 194n8
Okri, Ben, 19, 50, 51, 169
Olatunji, Olatunde, 195n25
Ondaatje, Michael, 151, 169
One Hundred Years of Solitude (García
    Márquez), 197n30
Onwochei, Francis, 197n35
Ordinary Person's Guide to Empire, An (Roy),
    2, 28, 156, 158, 161
oriki, 7, 99–102, 105, 106, 191n7, 194n20,
    196n27
Osofisan, Femi, 152
Osuagwu, Victor, 193n8
Owo Blow (Ogidan), 190n15
Owoh, Nkem, 193n8
Ozokwor, Patience, 194n8

Padmore, George, 34, 36, 38, 41, 43, 45, 56
Pan-Africanism, xiv, xv, 30, 31, 32–34, 37, 39, 46
Parker, Charlie, 130
Peck, Raoul, 108
Pentecostalism, 91–93
Phillips, Caryl, xiii, 2, 4, 19, 24, 51, 132, 133–135, 144, 145, 159, 169; attitude toward nationalism by, 136–137, 149; belonging in *The Atlantic Sound*, 148–149, 151, 154, 156; belonging in work by, 135, 147; compared with James, 11, 29, 44, 144, 178; compared with Roy, 29, 50, 156–157, 170, 178; compared with Sembene, 3; cosmopolitanism in, 150–151, 180; critique of England by, 135–136; critique of Naipaul by, 190n18; critique of race by, 138, 152, 154; genre in, 139–140, 143, 152–153; style in, 141–143, 147, 150, 152
Pinckney, Darryl, 150
Polsgrove, Carol, 38
polyforum, 12, 106, 133, 156
postcolonial asymmetry, 9, 19, 29, 57, 100, 101, 105, 156, 160
postcoloniality, xi, xiv, 2, 25, 59, 91, 136, 169–170, 179, 180; elements of, 4, 109; genre and, 50, 187n18; globalization and, 9, 45, 169, 179
Pouille, Adrien, 192n10
Power Politics (Roy), 157, 174, 199n5
Prashad, Vijay, 177, 179, 189n7
Public Enemy (William Wellman), 190n15

Quartier Mozart (Bekolo), 111, 118, 126, 127, 130, 132, 198n5

Reed, Ishmael, 137
Renov, Michael, 176
Retamar, Roberto Fernández, 159, 199
Robbins, Bruce, 44, 151, 152, 189n11
Rodney, Walter, 32, 42, 163, 189n6
Rosengarten, Frank, 31
Rouch, Jean, 102, 191n7
Roy, Arundhati, xiii, xv, 2, 11, 19, 25, 43, 155, 156, 199n5, 200n13; anti-globalization aesthetics in, 29, 170; as "brand," 28, 158, 167–169; compared with Bekolo, 132; compared with James, 2, 158, 170, 178, 180; compared with Kelani, 182; compared with Phillips, 29, 50, 156–157, 170, 178; critique of anti-globalization move-

ment by, 35, 172–173; critique of Hindutva by, 161, 162, 171; critique of neoliberalism by, 160, 169, 170–172, 176; genre in, 156, 158, 173; India by, 160–162, 167, 169; style in, 159, 171, 174–177; work by, 157, 158, 200n10; as "writer-activist," 162–167, 169
Rushdie, Salman, 27, 44, 157, 188n28, 189n10, 198n3, 199n3, 200nn8,13

Said, Edward W., 25, 26, 31, 153, 175, 187n26, 198n1
Saleh-Haroun, Mahamet, 24, 109
sarcasm, 156, 159–160, 170–173, 174–175. *See also* Roy, Arundhati
Saro-Wiwa, Ken, 163
satellite television, 16
Saworoide (Kelani), 87, 106
Sembene, Ousmane, xiii, 1, 2, 4, 18, 60, 79, 81, 122, 124, 184n1, 191n8; compared with Bekolo, 108, 120, 121, 178; compared with James, 28, 156; compared with Kelani, 2, 29, 89, 98, 178; compared with Phillips, 3; compared with Roy, 169; critique of fetishism by, 64–66, 72, 76; decolonization in, 11, 20, 61, 77, 131; dialectical camera of, 76–77, 198n10; funding of films by, 125; Harrow's critique of, 74–76, 192n14; *mégotage* in, 20, 22, 27–28, 52, 68, 112, 187n24; quest for artistic freedom by, 61–62, 191n2, 192n8; scholarship on, 191n1; social realism in, 52, 58; style in, 60, 63, 66–67, 71, 129–130; technical training of, 52, 192n12; tricontinental politics of, 192n16; work by, 57, 60, 76, 129
Senegal, 2, 11, 33, 60, 65; film production in, 79, 125; homosexual underground in, 192n18; reception of *Xala* in, 61, 75; Sembene's depiction of, 58–59, 65, 78
Senghor, Léopold Sédar, 59, 61, 67
Seth, Vikram, 157
Shagari, Alhaji Shehu, xi
Sklair, Leslie, 83
Sometimes in April (Peck), 131
Soy Cuba (Kalatozov), 52
Soyinka, Wole, 17, 18, 127, 135, 159, 189n6
Spillers, Hortense, 149
Spivak, Gayatri Chakravorty, 192n16, 201n2
State Capitalism and World Revolution (James, with Dunayevskaya and Lee Boggs), 40, 53, 189n14
Stavans, Ilan, 136

Stoneman, Rod, 123–124, 125–126
structural adjustment programs (SAP), 7, 20, 22, 83, 110
Suri, Manil, 157
Swift, Graham, 169

television, xi, 21, 84; cameraman, 83; commercials, 103, 194n20; miniseries, 33; network, 27, 122, 123, 131, 187n23; producer, 110; production company, 81, 87; programs, 101, 187n25, 197n32; sets, 78; soap operas, 84, 85, 86, 87, 91, 92, 192n1, 197n30
Third Cinema, 51–52, 59, 76
Thunderbolt: Magun (Kelani), 2, 58, 83, 89, 91; compared with *Aristotle's Plot,* 108; compared with *Xala,* 63; context of, 29, 81–82, 87, 96; didacticism in, 106; enchantment in, 92–94; image in, 87; mode of arbitration in, 101, 102; strategic opportunism in, 103–104; stylistic aspects of, 87, 92; thematic interests of, 82. *See also* Kelani, Tunde
Ti Oluwa Nile (Kelani), 85, 86, 87, 104, 106, 197n30
Todorov, Tzvetan, 14, 17
Touch of Evil (Welles), 194n14
Touki Bouki (Mambèty), 60, 78, 192n18
Touré, Samory, 61, 71
"Toward the Seventh" (James), 28, 30, 32–34, 39, 46–48, 189nn3,5
Toynbee, Arnold, 33
tricontinentalism, xiv, 5, 18, 41–44, 50, 73, 160, 169, 177, 180, 192n16; aesthetics of, 50–52, 76, 170; cosmopolitanism and, 50, 51, 179, 180; socialist, 30, 57, 156, 173
Tryon, Chuck, xiv
Turvey, Gerry, 70

Udju Azul di Yonta (Flora Gomes), 130
Ukadike, Nwachukwu Frank, 121, 128, 191n7
UNESCO (The United Nations Educational and Scientific Organization), 83, 109
uneven geographical development, xii, 7, 9, 11, 17, 19–20, 22, 24, 28, 103, 146–147; as a theoretical notion, xiii, 5, 10, 16

Vail, Leroy, 195n23
Vassanji, M. G., 25
video, 2, 9, 21, 83, 192n1; aesthetics of, 23; drama, 21, 104, 119, 198n7; film and, 123;

instructional, 90; production, 29; technology of, 21, 22, 84, 187n25
Vieyra, Paulin Soumanou, 191n1

Walcott, Derek, 45, 159
War Talk (Roy), 157
Washington Consensus, the, xi, 43, 83
Weep Not, Child (Ngũgĩ), 25
Welles, Orson, 194n14
Wells, H. G., 33, 35, 46, 48
Whitman, Walt, 34, 48
Williams, Opa, 81
Williams, Patrick, xiii
Williams, Raymond, 70, 146, 185n2
Williams, Sylvester, 35
Windrush generation, 139
Wolof, 60, 62, 63, 66, 70, 71, 192n10
World Social Form (WSF), 170, 172, 201n17
Wright, Bukky, 94
Wright, Richard, 137, 155, 159

xala, 57, 58, 62, 65, 67, 70, 72; as cultural practice comparable to *magun,* 58, 71, 75, 77, 89; intramural discussion of, 66; proletarianization as the social root of, 68, 76; Sembene's skepticism about, 63, 77, 78
Xala (Sembene), 1, 2, 14, 28, 52, 59, 75, 109, 191n6; censoring of, 61; commercial success of, 75; compared with *Aristotle's Plot,* 108; critique of African elite in, 3, 57; as novel, 1, 2, 68, 191n6; plot of, 62; production context of, 29, 79; scholarship on, 57, 60, 73, 191n4; thematic aspects of, 29, 58, 72, 76

Yai, Olabiyi Babalola, 196n26
Yeelen (Cissé), 60
yere don, 7, 99, 100, 101–102, 191n7, 196n27
Yoruba: as expressive culture, 83, 86–87, 194n16, 196n26; filmmakers, 87, 192n1, 194n15; identity, 95, 195n25, 196n27; Kelani's identity as filmmaker, 82–83, 86; language, 83, 84, 86, 90, 106, 188n29, 193n5
Young, Robert, 42–43

Zabus, Chantal, 187n21
Zaire, 101, 195n24
Zimbabwe, 76, 111, 125
Žižek, Slavoj, 200n16

AKIN ADESOKAN is Assistant Professor of Comparative Literature at Indiana University Bloomington and author of the novel *Roots in the Sky*. His writings have appeared in *Screen, Textual Practice, Chimurenga,* and *Research in African Literatures.*